The Strength of Grace

A tribute to those who wear the Miss America crown

Their Tears - Their Triumphs

Kate Kitchen

Eastman
Press

Eastman Press, 4619 Country Woods Lane, Greensboro, NC 27410 www.eastmanpress.com

Printed in the United States of America by PSG: Printing Services of Greensboro, Inc.

First Printing: August 2004
10 9 8 7 6 5 4 3 2 1

ISBN: 0-9759189-0-7

Art direction and graphic design by Robin Mykytyn
Initial preparation of photographs by Chuck Toulouse.

"...being confident of this, that he who began a good work in you will carry it on to completion until the day of Christ Jesus."
(Philippians 1:6)

Introduction

Each Miss America profiled in *The Strength of Grace* represents a portrait of a special woman who not only dared to dream, but found the inner strength to make her dreams come true. However, winning the title of Miss America and the coveted crown that represents the culmination of that dream does not protect her from the reality of life. And such is the myth we want to dispel in this book.

The Miss America crown has never insulated the wearer from sorrows, disappointments, nor the psychological devastation that tragedy can bring. Being Miss America does not guarantee a fairy tale life. Many of us have been through hell—and back. And many have had happy, satisfying lives, enjoying solid marriages, wonderful families and successful careers. But most importantly, each of us has forged our own path to happiness.

At her crowning, Miss America can never possibly know the impact this single moment will have on her life, nor the lifetime expectations of others. She must be gracious and always wear a smile! And if she slips, as all of us do from time to time, she may find a disappointed public. As regal as she may seem at that one special moment, she is still an ordinary woman with convictions of her own, obstacles to overcome and a full life to live.

The doors that are opened to us because of winning the crown carry many blessings—beginning with the academic scholarships that help us mold our professional careers. Miss America travels hundreds of thousands of miles each year, representing our beloved United States of America. She meets scores of special people who, in their own way, are inspirations to all of us.

The Strength of Grace offers an in-depth, real-life look at the young girls we were, the women we have become; and how earning the right to wear the crown has shaped our lives. In reading our stories, you will learn that we all share one constant anchor—a personal relationship with God.

Grace is felt through our openness to receiving God in our daily lives. That grace has a sustaining power that helps us face our challenges with compassion and integrity in order to become the women God wants us to be. We have all drawn upon that sustenance to carry us from the outward appearance of the grace the public accepts as elegance or beauty to the grace within that comes from knowing God's unending love.

The remarkable women you will meet in this book are all unique, and yet their stories could be your story or the story of a woman you know. After meeting these women through their own personal lives so generously shared with the author, I hope you will be inspired to triumph in your own life. I hope that you, too, will have the courage to overcome life's difficulties, that you will share the conviction to follow through, the compassion to touch another's soul with generosity and love, and the ultimate wisdom to come to know your own strength of grace.

—Jacquelyn Mayer, Miss America 1963

Our thanks to the following Miss Americas
who graciously shared their stories.

1938	Marilyn Meseke	1969	Judith Ford
1939	Patricia Donnelly	1976	Tawny Godin
1942	Jo-Carroll Dennison	1977	Dorothy Benham
1943	Jean Bartel	1978	Susan Perkins
1945	Bess Myerson	1979	Kylene Barker
1947	Barbara Walker	1981	Susan Powell
1948	BeBe Shopp	1985	Sharlene Wells
1953	Neva Langley	1987	Kellye Cash
1954	Evelyn Ay	1988	Kaye Lani Rae Rafko
1955	Lee Meriwether	1989	Gretchen Carlson
1958	Marilyn Van Derbur	1990	Debbye Turner
1960	Lynda Mead	1995	Heather Whitestone
1961	Nancy Fleming	1996	Shawntel Smith
1962	Maria Fletcher	1997	Tara Holland
1963	Jacquelyn Mayer	1998	Kate Shindle
1964	Donna Axum	1999	Nicole Johnson
1965	Vonda Van Dyke	2001	Angela Perez Baraquio
1967	Jane Jayroe	2002	Katie Harman
1968	Debra Barnes	2004	Ericka Dunlap

Acknowledgments

The thirty-eight Miss Americas featured in this book have been so generous with their time. They're all extremely busy women and I appreciate so much their sharing sometimes painful stories throughout hours and hours of interviews, collecting personal photographs, and taking the time to approve the written word. Thank you.

The Miss America Organization has offered its unfailing, full support and cooperation from the beginning. Our special thanks to President and Chief Executive Officer Art McMaster for giving me the administrative support, especially the required permissions to reproduce photographs from the archives. Nearly all the pageant night shots of crowns and gowns remain the property of the Miss America Organization. Thank you.

The staff of The Miss America Organization have been spectacular in their efforts to assist me in coordination of so many efforts: helping me contact Miss Americas, scanning photographs, gathering information. There are two exceptional people that I must single out. They are: Princesa J. Santos, public relations coordinator and Ric Ferentz, historian and community hall moderator. Their consummate professionalism, their willing spirits and enthusiasm for this project bolstered me when I thought my shoulders would sag under the weight of it. I never interrupted even their busiest of days with a question or a plea for

assistance without receiving a bright, positive "Can Do—Will Do" attitude from both of them and I owe them a great debt of gratitude. Thank you.

My art director and graphic designer Robin Mykytyn was a godsend to me during the design development and production of *The Strength of Grace*. Her skills and talent, her discipline, her willingness to go above and beyond did not go unnoticed. Without her calm, gentle spirit and ability to plod along with me until we got it right, I could not have completed this book. Thank you.

What would I have done without my Vente decaf-iced-skim lattes with sugar-free hazelnut? A special thanks to Starbucks Manager Matt Swider for not charging me rent during the tedious proofreading process; and for hosting the Greensboro launch and in-store book signing to benefit children's literacy.

And to my family and friends. My son Christian and his lovely wife Jane who put up with months and months of, "I can't play. I have to work." (I promise to make it up to you both.) Their emotional support and Christian's expertise as a computer programmer were welcomed in the development of *www.thestrengthofgrace.com*. And Judy, now we can go antiquing—and Mandy, get out the Scrabble board! Thanks to all of you for being so patient with me.

–Kate Kitchen

Foreword

Kate Kitchen has done a masterful job at capturing the true essence of the Miss America experience. And she did it in a most compelling and powerful way, through the winners' own words.

Though its roots lie in the simple and unapologetic beauty pageants of the 1920s, any resemblance to our bathing beauty predecessors is strictly cosmetic. The competition that television viewers watch each September is just the tiny tip of the iceberg of a rock-solid program of educational opportunity for intelligent, resourceful and hard-working young women.

The Miss America story is a complex and moving narrative, a chronicle of the human spirit. It is a tale of ambition, victory, glamour, achievement and resolve. As these pages reveal, it is a story not without tragedy, pain, loss and defeat. Kate presents the whole, unembellished and honest, behind-the-scenes story. *The Strength of Grace* is a document of human triumph, in and out of the limelight.

The young women who choose to pursue a place in this unique and historic American icon are driven, determined and destined to succeed. Few set out to become "Miss America." Most were drawn to the program to further their goals to better themselves through higher education, to prepare themselves for a lifetime of accomplishment—and to make a difference in the world.

Photo courtesy of the Miss America Organization.

They are true winners—positive role models in a world that needs role models now more than ever. They are the kind of people who know how to succeed, prosper and overcome adversity. And adversity has visited many of them, perhaps none as dramatically as Kate's inspiration for this book, Jacquelyn Mayer, Miss America 1963.

Jackie suffered a debilitating stroke at the young age of 28. Yet displaying true Miss America grit and determination, Jackie has since fought her way back to nearly full physical ability—and turned her misfortune into a lifelong opportunity to inspire and encourage others all over the world.

Her story, like many of her Miss America colleagues, is one of victory in the face of long odds. It is a testament to what can happen when a young woman says to herself "I can do that."

Each in her own way, our Miss America representatives have contributed something very special to the people whose lives they have touched through their beauty, charm, talent, faith in God and boundless devotion to making a positive difference. We could not be more proud of them. Now, thanks to Kate, Jackie and the others are able to share that sense of pride with the world.

On behalf of the entire Miss America Organization, we thank all those who generously gave of their time to participate in this book.

—Art McMaster, President and CEO
The Miss America Organization

Miss America 1938

Marilyn Meseke

State - Ohio
Age - 21

Talent: Marilyn performed a routine of tap, ballet and musical comedy to the tune *In a Blue Room*

Photo courtesy of the Miss America Organization.

"Sometimes there would be cattle in the streets so we couldn't get to our event on time. We would have to wait patiently for them to move."

—Marilyn Meseke

Marilyn Meseke

Marilyn Meseke had a rough start in life. It was certainly not the idyllic beginning one would think appropriate for a future Miss America. She was two months old when her father died. He was only twenty. Her teenage mother was suddenly faced with raising two children alone and working full-time to support them. There was no choice but to divide up the family. Marilyn's grandmother adopted the baby and the little girl grew up in Marion, Ohio.

At the age of four, Marilyn was introduced to dance lessons and for years, she took ballet, toe and tap. She began teaching dance at the tender age of thirteen and her exposure to the arts didn't stop there. Marilyn's grandmother made sure the child learned to play piano and violin, trying to make up for the losses the child had experienced early on.

"We would go every weekend to Columbus where my grandmother would enter me in bathing beauty contests," she said.

The years of disciplined rehearsals and recitals culminated in Marilyn's winning one pageant after another. She earned several titles from 1933 on: Miss Columbus, Miss Marion, then Miss Ohio. The national title became hers in 1938. After competing at Cedar Point in Sandusky, then in Cleveland at the Masonic convention hall, she wore a broomstick skirt "because it didn't wrinkle" on the *Beauty Train* from Camden, New Jersey to Atlantic City where she finally captured the crown.

The rule at the time was that Miss Americas under the age of twenty-one had to be chaperoned during their travels. Marilyn won the title just one week before her twenty-second birthday. Her grandmother wouldn't permit her to travel alone so the protective guardian lied to officials about Marilyn's age, saying she was younger, so the woman could accompany her.

It proved to be a fascinating year for a young woman from a small town in Ohio. Marilyn went to New York to celebrate the opening of The Hollywood, a nightclub where for the rest of her life Marilyn would cherish the memory of meeting the incredible Ethel Merman.

The club was to be publicized by temporarily changing a street name from Broadway to Hollywood Boulevard. Each movie studio sent a woman to unveil the street name for publici-

Marilyn at five as Miss Columbia in a parade in 1921.

Three Miss Americas

ty purposes. Harriet Hilliard, Sonja Henie and Ethel Merman each vied for the honor. Not wanting to play favorites among the movie stars of the day, however, the nightclub owners permitted Marilyn to do the unveiling.

Next on the ladies' agenda was Knoxville, Tennessee and the dedication of the Smokey Mountain National Park where the local preliminaries were held in preparation for the next year's national pageant.

And on they went to Kentucky where the Sandy Valley Grocery Company contracted with Miss America for a year to promote its grocery warehouses in five states. Marilyn's duties included speaking on the importance of good nutrition as it related to health and beauty. She signed autographs, attended conventions, and appeared in one town after another, reading the scripts they wrote for her. During that tour she met Milton Berle who was headlining at The Chez Paree, a Chicago nightclub. He introduced Marilyn and they performed a short skit together.

Among all the small towns, minor problems threatened to hinder her appearances but she always found a way to overcome them.

"Sometimes there would be cattle in the streets and we couldn't get to our event on time. We had to wait patiently for the cows to move," she laughed.

On they traveled, through the rural areas of Tennessee and Kentucky, where family feuds often spanned generations. They would be driving down a street on the way to an appearance and someone would point to a corner and say matter-of-factly, "That's where five people were killed last month."

Marilyn's reign ended too soon as far as she was concerned, and she had to return to Ohio. She had, after all, left her dancing school to become Miss America. It was time to get back to making a living. A Hollywood director saw great potential in this beautiful, talented young woman and invited her to California for a screen test, but despite all the years of grooming for this moment, she was unable to accept. Marilyn's grandmother wouldn't permit it.

"I almost rebelled once when I was in New York," she confessed. "I was asked to become a model for John Robert Powers, but my grandmother quickly vetoed that opportunity." It was an era when good girls never questioned authority.

Marilyn explained, "My grandmother had total control over me. I

Marilyn and friend Dr. J.B. Hall
in 1994

didn't grow up with any feeling of independence at all. If I disobeyed or talked back when I was little, she would make me go into the yard and get a switch. I'd come back to her and let her switch me. That was just the way it was in those days."

Her post-pageant life in Marion, however, was by no means dull. Marilyn still made appearances and was able to travel, to judge pageants and to do some public speaking.

And then along came a love interest. His name was Stanley Hume and he was from Spokane. He had been a commercial pilot for Eastern Airlines and allowed to go on leave from Eastern to join the Air Force. It was wartime. As luck would have it, Stanley met Doc, Marilyn's brother-in-law in Holyoke, Massachusetts and the two men were sent overseas together where they became roommates. Once Stanley saw the picture of Doc's wife (Marilyn's sister) he quickly pestered his friend to tell him, "Does she have a sister?"

Can you imagine his surprise at finding out that the woman he was searching for happened to be a Miss America? Stanley wrote Marilyn, sending her a photograph, and she quickly replied. They wrote for a year, with the help of Marilyn's grandmother who insisted on helping Marilyn doctor her letters so they would sound more interesting. A year later, Stanley Hume returned to the states, stopping off in Ohio to meet his love. Every bit the gentleman, and of course under the watchful eye of Marilyn's grandmother, the serviceman stayed at a hotel. Three days later, he asked Marilyn to marry him and she said yes.

Stanley returned to Spokane to visit with his own family. Missing his fiancee', he asked Marilyn to come to Spokane to marry him. Marilyn's grandmother refused to permit the young woman to make the trip, so the poor fellow, having traveled practically around the world rode back to Ohio on the train, married her properly in her home, then took his lovely bride back to Spokane on the train. This trip would symbolize how they would spend their lives together, a lifetime of travel.

Stanley was transferred from one city to another. They lived in Santa Monica, Nashville, Memphis, then Wilmington, Delaware as he flew overseas to Paris and India and Casablanca, transporting tires and other supplies for the military for his employer, Crescent Airlines.

Marilyn worked sometimes as a secretary, sometimes as a teller in various banks as they relocated. During a time, when she lived in New York working for the Great Neck Trust Company on Long Island, he would fly into Wilmington, after being gone weeks at a time, and her employer would permit her to take the train to go visit him. Their nomadic adventures continued throughout the war years as they moved from New York to Miami, to New Orleans, Houston and finally Stockton, California. But they never tired of uprooting themselves, for even after the war, they continued to move around as he resumed flying with Eastern.

Five miscarriages marked their life as husband and wife and Marilyn was so grateful to finally be blessed with a healthy son. She was thirty-one when Michael was born. (Michael followed in his father's 'flight path' with a career in aerospace engineering.) Stanley died of kidney disease at the age of forty-six, when Michael was seventeen. He had been ill a long time. Marilyn said, "He was a good pilot. He flew for Eastern for twenty-three years."

Friends and fate soon took a hand in Marilyn's life. She and Michael were living in Miami when friends of the family introduced her to another pilot. He had lost his wife at the age of forty-six as well. Marilyn and Benjamin Franklin Rogers married in 1966. "We had a good marriage for twenty-four years," Marilyn said, "then Ben suffered a massive stroke. He died in 1990.

In a Toni commercial 1972

Ben's son Frank was the same age as Michael. More than six feet tall, he was strikingly handsome and everyone who met him liked him.

Unfortunately, Frank had suffered a stroke as well, which affected his sight. People grew to love him, to look forward to seeing Frank with his guide dog. His disposition never changed.

"You'd never know anything was wrong. He was always nice and pleasant, so easy to get along with," Marilyn said.

On August 24, 1992, Frank was in the hospital recovering from complications from epilepsy when Hurricane Andrew ripped out the heart of Florida. As if he hadn't had enough trouble with his failing health, the forty-nine-year-old lost his apartment. It was demolished by 140 mph winds. Immediately after he was discharged from the hospital, he went back to assess the damage and ran into a man at his apartment complex. It proved to be a fatal meeting. The man was a convicted felon who had violated parole from Attica. He abducted Frank in his car, at knifepoint.

Frank's guide dog had either been taken, too, or had somehow managed to follow his master and the stranger's car. Three weeks later, after a frantic, community-wide search, Frank's lifeless body was found ten miles south of Miami, having been thrown on top of a trash heap, trash from Hurricane Andrew. For three weeks, his body had lain undiscovered until one day people in a restaurant looked out the window to see a large scrawny guide dog trudging down the highway, his head down. He was desperately foraging for food. The restaurant patrons immediately recognized the dog from the flyers that had been posted all over the city, flyers showing a smiling Frank with his faithful companion. The police were called immediately and the mystery was solved. The dog had stayed with his master's body for three weeks.

Asked how she could possibly have dealt with this depth of grief, Marilyn responded slowly. "One day at a time," she sighed, her voice shaking with the horrifying memory.

It was difficult for Marilyn to try to justify why this happened, but she said there was nothing to do except try to heal the pain. She was always thankful for her church and her support system of friends she made over the years.

This was Marilyn's final interview: She died Sept. 12, 2001 at the age of eighty-four.

Miss America 1939

Patricia Mary Donnelly

Fashion Model and Big Band Singer
State - Michigan
Age - 19   Height - 5' 7''

Talent: Pat sang two songs: *To You* and *Old Man Mose*.
She "slapped" the stand-up bass during the last chorus.

Photo courtesy of the Miss America Organization

Pat underwent a laryngectomy, her second surgery for throat cancer, in 1986. She was unable
to speak for a year. Asked how she found the courage to overcome that challenge, she said,
"What are you going to do, curl up and die? Going on—that's the whole point, isn't it?"
——Patricia Donnelly Harris

Patricia Donnelly

Patricia Donnelly was the last Miss America to be crowned in the Marine Ballroom of Atlantic City's Steel Pier. Shortly thereafter, the pier was destroyed. But no one could destroy the memories.

It was the era of the big bands and Pat, still a teen and already a big band singer, recalls fondly the bandleaders of the time.

"There was Rudy Vallee, Buddy Rogers—who was married to Mary Pickford—and all the great names." This was the decade of Jimmy and Tommy Dorsey, Benny Goodman and all the other swing bands who had brought a generation of young people happily to their feet.

Pat had started singing with Dixieland bands in Detroit, her hometown, then graduated to the big band sound in high school. She was thrilled when Woody Herman's manager offered her a job after hearing her sing. However, she was a little disappointed when she finally met Herman himself. He was quite short and he took one look at the statuesque beauty and shook his head. "We'd have to sing together, and you'd make me look like a shrimp," he confessed.

The year prior to the pageant, Pat, now eighteen, worked as a fashion model at J.L. Hudson, a well-known department store. She had the glamour look of her day and an indomitable spirit that reminded one of Katharine Hepburn. But she never took herself nor her glamorous reputation seriously.

As for the standard USO tour that Miss Americas undertake, the year of her reign was one year that pageant officials did not choose to take advantage of air travel. War had bro-

ken out all over Europe. According to Pat, the government would have permitted her to leave the country, but there was a catch.

They told us, "We'll get you there, but we can't guarantee to get you back!" So this Miss America was quite content to tour the continental United States and did so with previous winners. The pageant was not very sophisticated at that time and Pat recalls the story about a former Miss America, a very brief Miss America.

"I recall when Betty Cooper, Miss America 1937, won the title—then ran away without stopping to accept the crown!" she laughed.

Pat was not a typical Miss America, even for

Hollywood glamour shot

A family photo—Pat and Robin with Steve (lt) and Amanda

the late 1930s. She decided one day to fly upside down in a two-seater plane. She would have been a great talent for a Nike commercial—she just did it!

She was in St. Louis appearing at the local circus when she realized the event wasn't going very well. So she decided to help them with their promotion by flying upside down in a plane as a publicity stunt.

Did it help? "No."

Was she scared? "Not much." She added, "I was far too interested in seeing what everything was all about."

As her glamour shots reveal, Patricia Donnelly has always been an extraordinarily beautiful woman. And yet, she has always been a no fuss, no frills, no-nonsense kind of person. She has always preferred trousers to dresses, even at a time when trousers were not yet fashionable. "I never have liked dresses. I didn't particularly care what anyone thought about it. I was much more comfortable in trousers. I always had a boyish figure."

After the pageant, she worked for a year with Rita Hayworth in the movie *Cover Girl*. World War II had begun in earnest. Pat lived in Los Angeles in the early '40s, frequently going to the Hollywood canteen. "I'd dance with the kids, and make sure they had a bite to eat," she said. In those days, according to Pat, people weren't terribly interested in the Miss America Pageant. "When I went to Hollywood, I didn't even tell anyone who I was," she confessed.

Even meeting Jack Warner on the famous Super Chief en route to Chicago had not dissuaded her. The famous movie mogul had looked at her and said, "You look like Ann Sheridan." Later, he sent her a contract from Warner Brothers.

"But I didn't sign it." She shrugged off the incident as if it were nothing. She had no pretense about herself, having sung on stage for years. A movie career simply didn't appeal to

her. "I didn't even like being recognized when I walked down the street. I didn't like wearing makeup. I just wanted to be comfortable," she said.

Then at age twenty-eight, Pat fell head-over-heels in love. She had met her husband-to-be on a blind date. "A girlfriend fixed us up," she related fondly. "I married Robin Harris in April of 1948. He was a newspaperman with the New York Daily News." They had met while he was working as a screenwriter for 20th Century Fox.

Returning to New York, Pat worked in several Broadway shows as a showgirl and modeled for John Robert Powers. She worked as a model in the garment district and a showgirl in the casinos at Saratoga. She still takes it in stride that she sang at the famous Stork Club as well as at La Rue, an elegant supper club on New York's East Side. The glitter and glamour of show business never seemed a big deal to her.

Pat soon relinquished her career to stay home and become a "house mom." Pat frequently waves off questions about her career except for one special title she earned. "I was once asked to go down to Virginia from New York to be their Peanut Queen," she said. Her grown son Steve teases her to this day, extolling the virtues of his mother's celebrity by exclaiming fondly, "My mother was Queen of the Nuts."

For forty-six years, Robin and Pat Harris

were partners in life. And for their last twenty years together, they were professional partners as well, sharing a double byline as travel editors for the Hearst newspapers: Robin and Patricia Harris.

They traveled the world several times, not even permitting major illness to curtail their wanderings.

In 1980, Robin suffered a stroke but seemed to rally, and the travel editors continued their journey. The same year, Pat had been diagnosed with throat cancer and had undergone a partial laryngectomy. Physicians were as worried for her as they were for Robin, wondering if she, temporarily unable to speak, would be able to manage his illness. In 1986, they were dealt an even more serious blow that threatened once again to stop them from doing what they loved most.

Pat had begun to lose weight and had been hoarse for some time. Her symptoms continued to worsen until she found she could no longer swallow. A trip to the doctor and a surgical biopsy confirmed her suspicions. She was diagnosed with throat cancer.

She wasn't surprised to hear the diagnosis, but being the trouper she has always been, her main concern was to continue her immediate travel assignment. She and her husband had been planning a trip to Nova Scotia to write an article and she didn't want to ruin their trip.

Her doctor agreed to wait for two weeks to perform the surgery to remove her larynx. After their trip, Pat returned for her surgical appointment and the result saved her life but left her mute.

"I couldn't speak, but I could write. And that's what I did. We continued to travel. We went to India and all over the world."

She did not have to undergo radiation treatments or chemotherapy, for which she was grateful, because the severity of those treatments would have made it impossible to travel. To complicate matters, however, Robin suffered a second stroke during the year she was unable to speak. This made it even more difficult to care for her husband. Together they managed, but by the end of the year she was terribly frustrated about being unable to speak. She asked her doctor if he could offer some options.

He referred her to a hospital in Indianapolis

Pat with grandsons Matthew (lt) and Jack

where two young men, Eric Blom, speech therapist and Dr. Marc Singer, a surgeon, had learned from their research with animals to use a particular prosthesis and puncture method.

This method was said to be effective in permitting people who had undergone laryngectomies to regain their ability to speak.

Pat immediately went to Indianapolis, had the necessary surgery, and the very next day was thrilled to learn she could speak once again. Ironically, her own physician was later diagnosed with cancer and died shortly thereafter.

The couple traveled as long as they could, but finally moved to Atlanta in 1993, leaving their beloved New York City apartment, which had been home base for thirty years. "I knew it was time to really slow down," Pat recalled. "Robin was now wheelchair-bound. When he got too sick to travel, I was heartsick. We'd had such a good time together. But he had already suffered two strokes. He was eighty-six."

One afternoon in Atlanta, the finality of death ended their partnership.

"He was watching the news in the living room," explained Pat. "I was reading in another room when I heard him call out to me. He had reached for the remote control and lost his balance. When he fell, he broke his hip."

Pat was grateful that she had had time to call their children who flew down from New York and Boston. The family had the opportunity to say goodbye.

She remembers the feeling she had at the moment of his death. "I awoke at five a.m. that Tuesday morning at home, with the strangest sense of urgency. I knew I should get to the hospital quickly. A few minutes later, the doctor called to let me know that Robin had died."

Somehow she had known the very moment their forty-six years together had ended.

The marriage produced two children. Their son Steve Harris, following in the family's journalistic footsteps, is a sportswriter for The Boston Herald. Two active grandchildren, John "Jack" Robin Harris (born in 1994) and Matthew Lynch Harris (born in 1996) round out Steve's family.

Pat's daughter Amanda is a reporter for Newsday. Her husband, Drew Fetherston, formerly a writer with Newsday, recently launched a book, *The Chunnel*, about the underwater tunnel that connects England and France via the English Channel.

One particular activity that delights Pat is to attend the Miss America reunions in the fall. "There's such camaraderie, such fun! The best time I've had in years!" exclaims Pat every year

Still stylish, Pat is asked to model even today.

that she returns. Her dear friend of more than fifty years, Addie Pason, attended with her until her death in the late '90s.

Pat was particularly pleased at the 1997 reunion when Kellye Cash (Miss America 1987) started singing *Amazing Grace* in the hospitality suite and everyone joined in. "There was such harmony, musical and otherwise. We all share stories. We all care about each other, and it shows."

Twelve years ago, Pat lost her natural voice to cancer. She is convinced her disease was caused by cigarette smoking. It is quite difficult for her to speak for a long time without tremendous effort, but it doesn't detract from her indomitable spirit.

In 2001, Pat felt she needed a warmer climate and moved from the northeast to Naples, Florida where she resides today. She is active in her community and periodically does a bit of fashion modeling for charity when she appears on the runway for the Children's Hospital fundraisers. She is also an advocate of St. Jude's Hospital in Memphis and with animal welfare charities.

Yet even the elegance she still possesses cannot be compared to the certain, quiet beauty she expresses from within. Patricia Donnelly Harris is one gracious lady.

Miss America 1942

Jo-Carroll Dennison

Student: Federal Institute Business School
State - Texas
Age - 18   Height - 5' 6"

Talent: Costumed as a cowgirl, she sang *Deep in the Heart of Texas*.

Photo courtesy of the Miss America Organization

"To me, fear is the devil. I really learned that those things I didn't do out of fear hurt *me,* and those things I did from a source of strength and out of love always turned out to be wonderful."

—— Jo-Carroll Dennison.

Jo-Carroll Dennison

It was wartime. Born and raised in her father's small medicine show, Jo-Carroll performed onstage from the age of two until she was ten years old. She received top billing as "Baby Jo-Carroll Dee and Her Ma and Pa," singing and dancing her way through childhood. But when she was ten, the child's world fell apart at the death of her father. To keep the family going, she and her mother joined a larger medicine show, which became their life for the next seven years. Jo-Carroll decided to leave the show at seventeen, after graduating from high school.

"I wanted more out of life than performing in a medicine show," she said. So she went to Tyler, Texas to live with an aunt while attending Federal Institute Business School.

"I was tired of being in the public eye." But the public eye, at least *the eye of Texas* was upon her, and the public evidently had not yet seen enough of Jo-Carroll Dennison.

One day she was walking by the Citizens National Bank. A bank officer approached her and offered her a free bathing suit if she would agree to be a contestant in the Miss Tyler competition. Today, a young woman may have cause to be concerned at both the circumstance and proposition. This was a small Texas town in a different time, a different place.

She had never heard of the Miss America Pageant. "I didn't have a bathing suit, so I entered the pageant," she laughed. Her sponsor's money was well spent. She won the title of Miss Tyler—and the bathing suit!

She thought her fifteen minutes of fame was over. "Then someone from the Junior Chamber of Commerce called and said that if I would go to Dallas for the Miss East Texas competition, they'd buy me a set of luggage." She came home with new luggage after winning the competition in Dallas.

The pageant had not yet grown in sophistication, and there were no scholarships awarded at the time. The prizes were small, donated informally by sponsors. In Austin, she was invited to stay at the Governor's mansion as she competed for the Miss Texas Pageant. She agreed to enter because she was offered a complete wardrobe for that competition. She still says today that she won the Miss America title only because of greed. This is merely a tongue-in-cheek remark, disproved by a lifetime of service.

It was only after she won the title of Miss Texas that Jo-Carroll discovered she was obligated to go to Atlantic City to compete for the national competition. Her show business background had already prepared her for performing in public, and she was fearless. The media soon picked up on her energy and her feistiness, for they immediately dubbed her "The Texas Tornado!"

The evening gown she had chosen could have been worn for high school graduation. For her second evening gown competition for the top ten, her sponsor begged her to wear something more elegant, but cost was a factor. With World War II in full force, Jo-Carroll was barely making a living as a secretary and struggling to pay for business school. But she acquiesced and the sponsor took her to a thrift shop where they found a blue velvet gown. "It was frightfully expensive," she said laughing. The gown cost her all of eleven dollars!

After the pageant, she toured as Miss America, traveling from city to city, performing in theatres and nightclubs. With no official pageant chaperone assigned to her, Jo-Carroll asked her mother to accompany her. She did promotions for sponsors, but her primary duty that year was to sell war bonds. "It was more than a duty," she said. "It was a privilege." However, being Miss America was more of a disruption for Jo-Carroll than anything else.

"I loved my life in Tyler," she said. "I was dating for the first time in my life. We'd go dancing to all the big bands. All the great names came to Tyler—Benny Goodman, Tommy Dorsey, all of them." And she had had to leave her job, working for U.S. Senator Earl B. Mayfield.

The prize for winning Miss East Texas had been an introduction to a talent scout from MGM. He offered her a contract, but she politely declined. She had had enough of performing.

After she won the Miss America title, another Hollywood agent who had seen the pageant took her to the 20th Century Fox office in New York, and she was offered another contract, but her mind was elsewhere. "I wanted to go to college and had finally made enough money for tuition."

During the year of her reign, while touring nightclubs and theatres at night, she was going to defense plants and military bases by day. "I'd never had an idea what our country really meant to people. I was astonished at the way defense plant women and servicemen treated me, as a symbol of the flag. To them, I wasn't just a bathing beauty, I was a symbol of what they were working and fighting for. It made a vast impression on me. I didn't feel I deserved it. After all, I wasn't the Statue of Liberty! I

Photo courtesy of the Miss America Organization.

was extremely impressed at their depth of emotion. The men were ready to die for our country and the women had come out of the kitchens and gone into the defense plants. It was so moving."

During her tour, Jo-Carroll began to mature. She began to feel a genuine gratitude for the opportunity that had been handed her. "When I was invited to dine with the generals at the bases, I would tell them I wanted to eat with the servicemen. Those were the people whose attitudes changed my life," she said quietly. "You know, you can't get a feeling of patriotism from a medicine show," she laughed. "The Miss America experience became a pivotal point in my life."

Jo-Carroll began questioning the constant adulation. "I thought, *I certainly don't deserve this. I'm going to do something with my life to be worthy of it.*" Now the desire was planted. She just didn't know what her purpose was, and wouldn't find it for years to come.

After the tour and after turning down two Hollywood contracts, Jo-Carroll was forced to re-examine her decisions. "Mother had quit the medicine show to tour with me, and after the year of my reign, I didn't want her to have to go back and work so hard in concessions, so I decided I'd go be a movie star." Just like that!

She knew she could do it and she had already had offers. It was that easy. Once she made up her mind, Jo-Carroll called Darrel Zanuck and asked him flat out, "Still want me?"

Zanuck wasted no time saying yes, so off she went to Hollywood where there were certainly major changes in store for her. While under contract with 20th Century Fox, she met comedian Phil Silvers, also a contract player. The Brooklyn native was born Fishel Silver and changed his name to enhance his image in Hollywood. The two hit it off and after two years of dating, they were married.

In this case, art certainly imitated life. People will remember him as Sergeant Bilko, a charismatic G.I. with a penchant for gambling, in the black and white TV series named for his character.

"He was a gambler and that was his focus. He wasn't cut out to be a husband," she said. Jo-Carroll still speaks of him fondly, saying, "He was wonderfully funny and knew everyone in the business. He introduced me to people who helped me learn about music and art. But I couldn't compete with his gambling, and I wanted stability." Their five-year marriage ended in divorce. They remained friends until his death from a heart attack on November 1, 1985.

Jo-Carroll worked in Hollywood for a while and made her mark in the war movies that were so popular at the time. One movie of note was *Winged Victory* with Jeanne Crain and Judy Holliday. And she worked in television in the 1950s when shows were on the air live— and if you made mistakes, the whole nation knew it.

After her divorce, Jo-Carroll toured Europe for a while. "I was still paid well for promoting products, so I could afford to travel. Then I decided I wanted to do something else, something to improve my character, still looking for that purpose."

Upon her return to the States, she went to The Big Apple. Her celebrity opened the door for her and she landed a secretarial job with none other than Rodgers and Hammerstein. She laughed while explaining, "I was very bad at my job, but they liked me."

Jo-Carroll attended night school and later became a production assistant on the LUX Video Theatre in Los Angeles. Again, it was live TV and a lot of pressure, but LUX had movie stars on their show constantly and Jo-Carroll was thrilled to work with all the major celebrities. It never seemed to turn her head. "It was just a lot of fun," she said.

And then she met Russell Stoneham, a television producer. Russell offered her the stability she was looking for and they were happily married—for twenty-five years. Due to their respective business responsibilities, the couple lived on both coasts during their marriage, some years in New York, other years in Los Angeles.

Jo-Carroll changed her focus when she became a mother to two boys and decided to stay home to raise her sons. "I always felt my purpose at that time was to stay home with my kids and to learn to be a good cook," she said.

Jo-Carroll became an activist in volunteering, even to the point that she was heavily involved in peace marches, women's rights and civil rights. "The Miss America experience had enlightened me to the need for volunteering and I was committed to so many worthy causes," she said. For several years, as a mom and a housewife, she was also an advocate for animal rights, helping the ASPCA. And when they lived in New York, she volunteered to teach Spanish children to speak English.

After twenty-five years of marriage and once her sons were grown, Jo-Carroll discovered that she and her husband had grown so far apart, they needed to end their marriage. She knew she had some serious thinking to do, and Jo-Carroll accepted an invitation to use a friend's house in San Miguel Allende, Mexico.

"I stayed two years, just thinking and working on a book," she sid. Her introspection was deep and the results were a renewed philosophy about women and their place in the home and in society.

"I always felt I had great purpose in staying home and caring for my husband and my children," she explained. "But I had become less interesting to myself as a person because I wasn't exposed to the activity you're exposed to when you're working outside the home. Even my volunteer activity, although valuable, didn't give me the depth of interests I needed to continue to build my life. It seemed I no longer knew who I was, or more importantly, whom I could still become."

After realizing how small her world had become, and how much vitality she had lost, she decided to work to regain her identity. "One of the things I did to help myself, after the divorce, was to take back my maiden name. After a quarter century as a Mrs., I knew now I had to get out there to find myself, to strengthen myself. I strongly believe that we women need to continue to grow, not merely to subordinate ourselves to our husbands, if we want to remain a viable, vibrant person, and many of us lose that focus after a time."

Jo-Carroll took to journaling to help her sort out her direction. But her self-imposed therapy of writing her memoir stopped after the pageant experience and she decided she was healed and didn't need to use that medium anymore. "I had already thought everything through, felt better about my life and was again looking for purpose. I had learned a great deal by taking time to think, to write, to remember who I was and what I was about. Any hang-ups I had had as a kid, I'd worked out. The experience of writing just that much had served its purpose."

The process had been difficult but fascinating. "I couldn't get it published," she explained, "because publishers wanted me to continue the book and I was done with that experience.

"It was a powerful process," she said, "but there was another pivotal time. I was on a spiritual quest. My mom died in the '60s, and although I was terrified to watch her die, I did. She left with such peace and without fear."

Jo-Carroll then found a place that seemed to answer her spiritual quest. She had been to a place called Idyllwild, located about two hours from Los Angeles. It's six thousand feet above sea level. "I had been there with friends. I immediately knew I belonged there and bought a house. Now I know I was divinely guided."

For a year she roamed the hills, staying away from social engagements, still thinking, still exploring her mind, her spirituality. "Then I realized that the best place for you is to open your heart and give of yourself. I was ready to participate again. So I began volunteering at a school for girls. I was finally becoming happy again, happy and at peace—with dog, with cat, with self," she laughed warmly.

After deciding she needed to volunteer on a more intense level, she took classes at Hemet Hospice, down the mountain from her home, and became a patient support volunteer, working with the terminally ill. And suddenly the quest she had begun as Miss America so long ago, that need to be worthy, clicked into place.

"I was so happy and at peace. I did that for a year. Then a woman resigned and I was given the position as community-relations coordinator. At first I didn't want the job because it would require me to drive an hour down the mountain to get there, but I felt it had been sent to me. And I guess an added benefit to the patients was that they got a kick out of speaking to a former Miss America."

Jo-Carroll shares a poignant story that brings her life full circle from pageant times. "One day a woman called me. Her dad had met me in 1943 during his induction into the Navy. He was terribly depressed, having lost his wife. He remembered that he had cut out my photographs in *Stars & Stripes*, the military newspaper. He told me how important it had been to the guys, the Miss America title. Still, that symbol of the flag—overseas."

Several years ago, at the 75th anniversary of the pageant, Jo-Carroll and that veteran were reunited during the pre-show and he talked about how important Miss America had been to him, to all the servicemen.

Jo-Carroll worked for hospice for eleven years. She retired in the fall of 1998. "I feel my purpose has been fulfilled. What you do for the people, the accomplishment of giving, is enormous. My job was so fulfilling. We now have two hundred fifty volunteers in Hemet."

And when she called upon her sisterhood to help with a fundraiser for the hospice program, six former Miss Americas appeared on her telethon.

She talks about her first experience. "Learning to work with hospice and being with that first patient was difficult. I was fearful, but he was so darling. I learned from the experience that those people who weren't afraid to live weren't afraid to die. Those afraid to get out there and take chances were afraid to die because they obviously had felt they hadn't lived their lives!

"To me, fear is the devil. I really learned that those things I didn't do out of fear hurt *me*, and those things I did from a source of strength and out of love always turned out to be wonderful."

Ever the philosopher, Jo-Carroll now enjoys the time she can spend on her mountaintop, surrounded by peace and quiet, her books, her music—and her thoughts. A special person and a very special journey.

Jo-Carroll's two sons live in Dallas and Colorado Springs. They are both in the computer industry.

Miss America 1943

Jean Bartel

Student - University of California - Los Angeles
State - California
Height - 5' 8"

Talent: Jean sang Cole Porter's *Night and Day*.

Photo courtesy of the Miss America Organization

"I never made a million dollars. But the friendships and travel have meant much
more to me than a million dollars! I'm so grateful for the Miss America experience."
—Jean Bartel

Jean Bartel

Jean Bartel was able to claim a lot of *firsts*, but may well be the only Miss America with *this* particular distinction: She has lived in the same house for more than fifty years!

Raised in West Los Angeles by "wonderful, spiritually-minded" parents, she remembers well the night before the pageant.

"My darling mother read a biblical passage to me: I Chronicles 29: 11-12. It's the passage in which King David praises God, acknowledging that He is supreme ruler of all."

This special passage seems to have kept everything in its proper perspective for Jean all throughout her life. She still recites it by heart.

She had an early start as a performer and has not stopped working since her early teens. At fourteen, she sang with the Civic Light Opera in Los Angeles, having already earned an Actors Equity card. She was privately tutored three hours a day during the season, which included a two-week performance in San Francisco. During the regular school year, when she was able to attend school in person, Jean was a student at University High School and even with all her extracurricular activities, became student body president.

People who remember the first Crest commercial on television will remember Jean Bartel, yet another entry on her list of firsts. She was the first college girl to win the title and the first to refuse to wear a swimsuit after she was crowned. Jean was also the first Miss America to perform a lead role on Broadway. *Of Thee I Sing* was the musical.

Perhaps one of her greatest achievements that year was that she sold more Series E $25 War Bonds than anyone else in 1943. Jean

received a special citation from the Secretary of the Treasury for her efforts that netted more than two and a half million dollars.

Jean Bartel is every bit as energetic today as she must have been during her reign.

She works five days a week at a travel agency in the Los Angeles area, still acts on television, travels as much as she can, laughs a lot and absolutely loves life.

She regales with laughter when she tells her Miss America stories, recalling the tale of one particularly hardened female reporter who sat down in front of her in Bridgeport, Connecticut, propped up her feet and said, with a cigarette dangling from her mouth, "Okay, Chippie, what's *your* story?"

Jean recalls that at first, the Denver Post wouldn't send anyone to interview her. "There just wasn't any interest in what they assumed to be a 'cheesecake' promotion," she said. "Then when they were told that this Miss America was a wholesome and typical American college girl with talent, they wrote the most beautiful articles."

One of the most important roles Jean undertook during her year as Miss America was to help develop the scholarship platform with Lenora Slaughter, former pageant official.

"Lenora had an in with college girls due to my Kappa Kappa Gamma sorority membership, and as we barnstormed the country and she talked to college girls about the pageant, I made a suggestion," Jean said. "I thought it would be wonderful if we could offer women college scholarships."

Thus, after two years of lobbying the board of directors to approve the idea, Lenora Slaughter finally got the scholarship program approved and the rest is history. The Miss America Organization is the largest scholarship provider for women in the world today.

Jean was also the first Miss America to go on tour.

"At that time," Jean explained, "Miss America only toured four months—from September

through December. It's quite different now, with the ladies touring all year long."

One day, shortly after the end of her brief reign, Jean Bartel found herself locked out of her room at the Waldorf. She had been in such a hurry to make an appearance that she had forgotten her key. As fate would have it, along came the president of the Radio Federation of Brazil. Recognizing her as Miss America, he invited her to sing for him. She did. That strange encounter led her to be hired for six weeks, all expenses paid—in *Brazil*!

"It was war time," she recalled. "You could only fly sunrise to sunset. But off I went to Brazil."

When she arrived at the Copacabana Palace, she found her suite filled with orchids. "Actually, I just sat around for two weeks and was introduced to Brazil's high society. I didn't have to go right to work. It was the strangest experience."

Jean's award for winning the Miss America title was three thousand dollars. She performed throughout Europe, in the Middle East

Singing with Big Bands was a favorite pastime.

and in South America. It was an unusual life for a single woman in the '40s. She loved traveling so much, she created a travel business.

She didn't meet her future husband until more than twenty years later. "In October of 1969, I was in Japan working for NHK-TV and also in my travel business. I was shopping for a sewing box and looked up—and there was a man shopping for stationery." That man was Bill Hogue, an American businessman who had come to Japan as a consultant with Mitsubishi.

Jean and Bill connected immediately and he asked her for a date. For a reason she still cannot explain, Jean got the days mixed up and failed to show up. But fate refused to take no for an answer. Bill Hogue was not to be ignored and they soon reconnected.

When he returned to the states, he went to visit her in Los Angeles. Jean had just lost both her parents. They died two years apart, and it seemed as if this kind, wonderful man had been sent to her. They married a year later in Kyoto, Japan. Their marriage remained strong for thirty-one years until his death in 2001. Bill had undergone heart surgery and was hospitalized for four months when his heart gave out on Easter morning.

She was still acting in minor roles, even appearing in a *Rockford Files* episode with James Garner in 2000. It was called *L.A. Burns.* She also appeared with Michael Caine in *The Debtors.*

"I'm still grateful for the experience of being Miss America," she said. "I wouldn't have competed for the world except I thought it would give me an opportunity to get to Broadway, which it certainly did. But the result is that even today, I have friends all over the world. And the friendships have meant more to me than a million dollars." Jean enjoys returning for pageants when she can find the time in her busy schedule. She was the first Miss America to be invited back to judge the pageant (in 1946).

Jean with her beloved companion, Teddy.

One memory is particularly poignant. A few years ago, Jean and several former Miss Americas were participating in an annual fundraising event for the Boys and Girls Clubs in Huntington, West Virginia when a gentleman told her he remembered her from her Miss America days. She had toured the Great Lakes Naval Hospital in Chicago and met him while he was a patient there.

In May 2004, she was invited to attend the ceremony celebrating the new World War II Memorial being built in Washington, D.C. "It really takes me back to pageant days and all the war bonds I sold," she said. "I remember touring the General Electric plant at two a.m. and watching the women work on the assembly line, making some kind of miniature light bulbs."

Although Jean still loves to travel, her activities are curtailed a bit now. A year prior to his death, Bill brought home a yellow labrador they named Teddy and her new love keeps Jean a little closer to home.

Miss America 1945

Bess Myerson

Graduate - Hunter College
State - New York
Age - 21   Height - 5' 10"

Talent: Bess played classical piano and flute

Photo courtesy of the Miss America Organization

"What I have acquired is a splendid talent for living.
It's the best. Life is my lover."
—Bess Myerson

Bess Myerson

Her story reads like a *Who's Who* of *Who's Who*. How one woman can have packed so much substance and philanthropy into one lifetime seems nearly incredible. But Bess Myerson has, she continues to do so, and according to her, she has a whole lot of living to do. A survivor of polio, ovarian cancer, a stroke suffered in 1980, and a mugging in a Russian airport in 1991 that resulted in a fractured leg all did nothing more than to slow her down for a moment or two along the way.

Perhaps even more incredible is that so much self-direction and so much accomplishment would come to this poor Jewish girl who, as a child, shared a one-bedroom apartment in the Bronx with her parents and two sisters. Louis, her father, arrived in the United States from Russia at the age of eighteen, her mother Bella from Russia at ten. Her father had told the horrifying story of hiding as a boy with a cousin, both jammed into a hole underneath the floorboards of a little shack. Bess' father survived. The other child did not. Life had not been easy for Jews in Russia. Surely life in America would be easier.

Louis took great pride in providing for his family by painting apartments for a living. He was highly respected for the care he took with his craft. Bella's job was to nitpick and she did it well. Perhaps Bess' mother had good reason to turn her back on happiness. She had lost her second child, their only son, when he was three years of age. How does a mother recover from such a loss? If her life was shaped by that tragedy, so were the lives of her children, Sylvia, Bess and Helen. The girls were well educated, were given music lessons, coerced into practicing

and practicing—and practicing. They studied and learned and practiced some more, struggling to overcome their humble beginnings to become the best they could be. All three girls became concert musicians.

Bess was born in 1924. She grew up during the depression in a housing cooperative, Sholom Aleicheim. The Myersons were one of two hundred fifty families living at the development. She was just a tall, scrawny, gangly, awkward kid who was, according to her, "built like a boy." The time she spent at the piano became her sanctuary. Their little apartment that housed a family of five, somehow found the space for a used grand piano. Louis had sewn together bits of

Bess calls this her schoolmarm "Lilith" look.

carpet, placing them under the base so the neighbors downstairs wouldn't hear the incessant music. Someone was always complaining. Helen started violin lessons at eleven, Bess was introduced to the piano at seven, and Sylvia began learning piano at nine.

Bella Myerson insisted that her girls *become* someone and thought that in the United States as in Russia, becoming a musician would surely help them find their way out of the poor neighborhood. Bess had expressed the desire to become a doctor only to be told by her mother, "Girls are not doctors! Boys are doctors! Study music and later if you want to be a doctor, you'll be a doctor who plays the piano!" It was settled.

The future Miss America certainly had no pageant aspirations growing up. While other girls were cast in school plays as fairy tale characters, Bess was cast as a cartoon character—Olive Oyl, Popeye's girlfriend. Later she would laugh when people told her how lucky she was to have always been so beautiful.

Bess' sole concern while growing up was the same as her parents'—survival. Times were hard. They would often walk home from school to see a neighbor's furniture on the street. Someone had been evicted. Hearts in their throats, they would hope they wouldn't see their belongings there.

But someone would find it in her heart to take the outcast family in, or temporarily store for them a bureau, a chair, a bed—perhaps a mother sleeping with one family, a child with another. These people lived communally and learned from the beginning to face their hardships together.

The last thing on Bess Myerson's mind while growing up was physical beauty or fashion. "I had two blouses and a hand-me-down skirt to take me through the school year," she said. "But we had values. We had family. We had social conscience. We had everything that was important."

New York Mayor Fiorello LaGuardia had a vision for a public school that focused on the arts and through that vision, in 1936, the High School of Music and Art was born. Only artistically gifted students were invited to attend. Bess was accepted in 1937 and attended the school until her graduation in 1941.

The students who played piano had to choose a second instrument. Bess chose the flute and played in the orchestra. It was this experience that inspired her to want to become a conductor. The praise she earned during those school years plus the loving compliments she was awarded by her piano teacher served to remove some of the unhappiness she suffered from the constant, bitter words from her mother. Nothing she ever did was quite good enough. Even when Bess knew she had performed exceptionally well, her mother would find just the right thing to say to bring Bess back down to earth.

Suddenly Bess came of age and the image in the mirror changed almost overnight. She had developed into a beauty. Her brilliant smile and air of elegance made people take notice, especially boys. The ugly duckling was gone, at least on the outside. But it would take a long time to build her self-esteem.

Sheltered among 'her people' at the housing cooperative, she had learned a great deal about her heritage and was proud to be part of an ethnic group that had struggled to overcome so much prejudice and hardship for so many centuries. The present only served to be a continuation of struggle, a struggle for survival itself as the war raged on in Europe. Many of the parents in the housing cooperative didn't speak English, so Bess and the other children learned to read, write and speak Yiddish so they could more fully communicate. "The whole world to me was Jewish," Bess said. "I was so steeped in that tradition, so proud of my people."

She began to realize that her mother was right. Her music might just be the key to getting her out of the project and into a bigger, better world.

She was thrilled when Antonio Brico, a professional conductor and close friend of Albert Schweitzer, came to lecture at the school. He said, "When it comes to music, there is no difference in ability between men and women." She wanted desperately to become a serious orchestra conductor. "It wasn't enough for me to be good," she explained. "I had to excel, to be the very best. And I knew what I wanted."

After high school, she attended Hunter College, a free-tuition city college that would offer her a bachelor's degree in music. She worked as a department store clerk, she taught piano at fifty cents an hour, she babysat, she did everything she could do to support herself while going to college.

"I needed car fare and the most basic of things—and I needed most of all to be able to continue to take private lessons." She was grateful for the tuition-free school. All in all, those four years at Hunter College cost her fifty-seven dollars!

In the summertime, she was hired as a counselor at a camp for girls. "It was a very strange, surreal time to be a young woman," she said in her book, *Miss America 1945*. As she said goodbye to the fellows in the boys' camp next door, she knew they would be going off to war in Europe to fight the Germans and the Japanese.

During the war years, from 1941 until her graduation in the spring of 1945, Bess was insulated from the horrifying atrocities that were taking place in the concentration camps in Europe, the atrocities against her people.

In her daily life, she continued to become a skilled and accomplished musician, and she grew more beautiful as months went on. She took no time to admire her reflection, however. Her mind was still on her humble beginnings. She was keenly aware of the poor people in her housing cooperative and how difficult it was, post-depression and right in the middle of a war, trying to put food on the table, pay the rent and provide shelter and clothing for the children.

In the summer of 1945, Bess Myerson found herself once again a camp counselor. She now had her degree, was highly successful as a flutist and pianist and was constantly being told how beautiful she was. She longed for what most women longed for in the '40s, a husband. At five feet ten, there weren't many boys tall enough to compete for her hand however, and others were too intimidated to ask her out because she was so lovely and so incredibly accomplished.

In her third year at Hunter, she was discovered by a photographer who paid her five dollars an hour to sit for photographs. She was turned down by the two top modeling agencies in New York, but still acquired a nice collection of photographs and her earnings went for—what else? More piano lessons.

Her sister Sylvia and John Pape, the photographer, entered Bess in the Miss New York City Pageant. They chose not to reveal this fact to Bess until she was advised she was chosen from a field of twelve hundred contestants to a final selection of sixty. Still totally unaware of her beauty, still suffering from a "too tall and too thin!" lack of self-esteem from too many years of listening to her mother's constant criticism, Bess at first refused to go. Her sister insisted and arranged for her to take time off from camp.

Finally, tired of arguing, Bess borrowed a bathing suit and went off to the big city. It was in a borrowed suit she won the bathing suit competition. For her talent, she created a piano arrangement of her own from a Grieg Concerto, and also played a Gershwin piece on the flute. She and fourteen other young women made the finals but no winner was to be announced until the judges had reviewed them all. Bess returned to camp, feeling a little better about herself.

A week later she was told to return to New York for the finals and walked away with the title of Miss New York City.

Having taken note of her as she won that title was a top New York designer who created three lovely gowns for Bess to compete in during her next pageant. She was thrilled. She took the gowns and two of her own skirts, one bright blue and one lime green. With blouses to match, and a bit of creativity, she could alternate the tops and have not *two* but *four* outfits!

The war was finally over and the pageant was trying to make up for the years of conflict by creating the best pageant ever. Lenora Slaughter, executive director, had worked tirelessly to develop the pageant's first scholarship fund and sponsors now had a check for five thousand dollars pledged and waiting in the wings for the new Miss America. Whoever the lucky woman was, she would receive those monies at the completion of her tour, upon entering a college or university. This was Bess' chance to get a master's degree in music.

Forty women competed that year. Here was Bess, a poor Jewish girl from the Bronx who had never even stayed in a hotel before. She was representing the sophisticated women of New York.

There was little time to spare between the state and national pageants, and Bess immediately ran into a conflict that made her think about this issue ever since. Slaughter and Philadelphia businessman and a pageant sponsor, Jack Kelly, stopped Bess backstage and suggested she change her name—possibly to Beth Merrick. It was true that Hollywood stars, even hopefuls, had done so thinking it would be easier to get good contracts and heavier roles if they had names that were more publicly appealing—perhaps less ethnic. But why, Bess wondered, was she asked to change her name when none of the other contestants were approached. It didn't take a rocket scientist to figure that out. Bess thought about her father and knew it would break his heart. She stood firm.

This was the first time she had been forced to take a political stand and Bess Myerson was beginning to realize exactly who she was. With that realization came an awesome responsibility, one she has never since turned away from. "I never regretted that decision," she said. "If I were to win, I decided it would have to be as Bess Myerson, the Jewish girl from the Bronx."

That night, Bess Myerson stood onstage straight, tall and proud of her heritage as she received the crown that told her she was now representing every young woman in America. Never before had a Jew won the crown and title. Some people wondered how this could have happened. Legislators and their constituents were famous for excluding Jews in elected positions. Academic institutions, especially medical schools, were careful to exclude Jews from their rosters to leave room for the young men from 'pure bred' American families. Even as judges were leaving their hotels that night to go to the pageant, it was reported that several of them received mysterious phone calls threatening that if they voted for Bess, they wouldn't be asked to judge again.

The stalkers, the phone calls to her family's apartment, the derogatory and threatening notes and letters started almost immediately. But the day Bella Myerson opened a letter to find a condom inside was the day she became so irritated with it all, she decided to throw them away. Hundreds upon hundreds remained unanswered, unread.

The first contract Bess was given after winning was to perform in Vaudeville. She toured with the other contestants, the top five. Somehow the picture of her in her long, flowing elegant gown, seated at a Steinway on a Vaudeville stage just didn't seem to fit in with all those years of accomplishment as a classical pianist. The audiences didn't think so either, as men in the audience would yell catcalls to her, asking to see her in her bathing suit. The ladies were required to appear on stage in their bathing suits, and it wasn't Bess' favorite part of the show. She certainly didn't want it to be the highlight of the performance.

At the end of that commitment things went from bad to worse. After months of Lenora's unsuccessfully trying to get Bess hired by sponsors, Bess was finally invited to Wilmington, North Carolina to a special event. It was to be held at a country club. During her trips to the South, as Miss America, she had become painfully aware of prejudice. She would see signs for public bathrooms and over one door would read WHITE—over another, COLORED. And it wasn't limited to African-Americans. There were signs in the North, too. Just one offensive sign of note was in Jackson Heights at an apartment house. It read "No Catholics, Jews or dogs allowed."

Her sense of the lack of equity among people was beginning to stir her up and she wasn't sure yet what, if anything, she could do about it. But at this moment, she had an opportunity to be the guest at a lovely country club where she would sell war bonds, perhaps play the piano, and where things might just turn around for her.

She was taken to an elegant antebellum mansion to change into her spectacular gown. She took her time getting ready. This was to be a special evening. Once dressed, she nearly waltzed down the circular staircase, ready to be driven to the club. Bess stopped short on the stairs as she overheard her hostess' voice. The woman was obviously embarrassed and tried to explain the horrible mistake. The country club was *restricted*, Bess heard the woman say. It didn't matter that the guest of honor had a college degree, rare for that era. Neither did it matter that she was an accomplished concert pianist, nor even that she represented all the young women in our land as Miss America. She was a Jew.

As Bess stood on that staircase, she felt the breath nearly sucked from her lungs. The pain in her heart was sharp enough to make her think a knife had stabbed her in the chest. And where others might have dealt with this blow with less grace, the tall slender beauty in the ballgown turned, quietly walked back up the stairs to the bedroom, changed her clothes and asked to be driven to the train station. Only when she was alone did she permit herself to absorb the shock of what had just happened. *How—where—*she wondered, *did people learn to hate—and why?*

Bess Myerson's purpose was born that night. And that night, without knowing it, Bess became an advocate for anyone persecuted for their race, color, creed—even for their economic status. She wanted desperately to count for something more than a beauty queen. She wanted to do something about this prejudice that disguised itself in some sort of socially acceptable civility. *How does hate start*, she wondered. *And what can I do to stop it?*

Bess continued to visit wounded veterans in hospitals. She sat with them by the hour, playing the piano or flute, talking to them, listening to them.

One day a physician asked her to stop by to see a mortally wounded man. As Bess approached the hospital room, the soldier's mother stood in the doorway barring her entrance. The poor distraught woman made it clear to Bess that it was because of the Jews that our country had gone to war in the first place, that if it hadn't been for Bess' people, her son would still be whole.

Bess never blamed the woman for her outburst. The woman's cost had been too dear, her grief too strong and overpowering. *No one should have to suffer the loss of a child*, Bess thought, remembering the grief her own mother had experienced at the loss of her son.

And to prove lessons still weren't learned, bigotry suddenly sprang up all over our country, stronger than ever. Black and white high school students were pitted against each other. Synagogues were desecrated. Parents continued to teach their children how to hate. And now, Bess knew if we as a people were going to learn tolerance, it would have to begin with education and education would have to begin with the children.

Bess refused to be part of the problem. She decided to become part of the solution and became involved with the Anti-Defamation League of B'nai B'rith. In 1945, the ADL, the NAACP and the Urban League teamed up to bring ethnic groups together. Halfway through her reign, Bess Myerson had answered the call by developing a social platform. This overt act, finally, gave her a way to use her title to benefit others, a title she would hold for a lifetime, a title she could bring dignity to and always be proud of—and she would use this accomplishment to become a voice for the downtrodden.

She would do what she could to lift them up. This all happened many years before Miss Americas were required to develop such a platform. To say that she was ahead of her time is an understatement.

Bess began to receive offers to appear everywhere, at schools, in civic groups, on behalf of fraternal organizations, even the Red Cross. Now she could speak for the common good and try to heal some gaping wounds that had been left open since the war.

For the remainder of her reign, she spoke out against intolerance, urged people to see beyond the color of someone's skin, begged them to overlook how people prayed or to whom, but rather to celebrate their cultural differences.

Her theme was *You Can't Be Beautiful and Hate*. She was scheduled initially to appear in fifteen cities. Racial troubles had been breaking out in schools in urban areas, especially Chicago.

It was there that the Mayor's Commission on Human Rights sponsored Bess. That year there was so much racial violence in schools, twenty-five hundred white students went on strike demanding that school administrators remove the Negroes from school. A friend and wounded war veteran, Harold Russell, had joined Bess on tour. He had lost his hands in the war. He would hold up the steel hooks where his hands had been and shake them in the air, shouting, "Did I lose my hands so you can keep some Negro kid off the Student Council? Or some Jewish kids out of your lily-white neighborhoods?"

Russell had starred in a movie called: *Best Years of Our Lives*, as a wounded war veteran and it was easy to get the students' attention. And as he spoke, the students began to listen

Bess took her speaking tour from Milwaukee to the northeast, finding that children were crowding around her to look first at the Miss America persona, but always staying to listen. Students came up to her frequently after a talk, promising to change their behavior. While visiting Buffalo, she made nine appearances in two days. It was from her efforts in this domestic war that her future professional career began. The producer of *The Big Payoff* saw her speak and hired her years later for the television show.

The year 1945 had been a year of pain, a year of pleasure and most of all, a year of tremendous professional growth. She had enhanced her strength of character and been offered the springboard from which she would launch her career to serve humanity. By now, the pageant had evolved into a socially conscious vehicle for women who wanted to develop their careers. It had become a viable, valuable resource for young women who wanted to achieve merit on their own rather than holding the philosophy that marriage was the one instrument that would totally define a woman.

In 1946, nearing the end of her tour, Bess was invited to play as soloist with the New York Philharmonic at Carnegie Hall. She prepared the Rachmaninoff *Second Piano Concerto*. This was a fitting tribute to a lady who well deserved it. She had begun her reign in Vaudeville on shaky ground. She had not been hired by sponsors as she had expected to be. She had been banned from restricted clubs and despite it all, perhaps because of it all, had found herself and her purpose. Now she would play at Carnegie Hall as a featured soloist.

After her performance at Carnegie Hall, her beloved piano teacher praised her to her mother. Never one to relish compliments nor to give them, Bella responded gruffly, "I don't know why she was so good. She never practiced!"

Would Bess go home after her reign? Possibly the only thing worse than being a minority at that time was being a spinster. Certainly there was another option.

A handsome army captain who was returning from the war quickly filled that bill. Allan Wayne had recently completed his four-year tour of duty in the Pacific. The alternative to marriage would have been for Bess to return to the family apartment in the Bronx. Nice young women did not live independently at that time. The couple married and because there was a housing shortage after the war, they moved in with his parents.

A year later, their lovely daughter Barra was born. Bess began giving piano lessons again, but was feeling unsettled. She didn't really know why until a young student looked up at her one day and asked her why she wasn't doing more with her life. "Weren't you Miss America?" he asked. Something clicked inside her and in no time at all, Bess was appearing on television.

The Big Payoff was a big payoff indeed for Bess. She was hired in 1951 and stayed with the program for eight years. She appeared on all the big name shows of the '50s, the *Dave Garraway Show*, the *Jackie Gleason Show*, *I've Got a Secret* and others. Their marriage proved to be unsuccessful early on, but her precious daughter and busy career fulfilled her.

She worked tirelessly for ADL and hundreds of other philanthropic organizations, museums and the like. She was commentator of the televised Miss America Pageant from 1954 - 1968. She moved into the political arena, serving under Mayor John Lindsay as Commissioner of Consumer Affairs of New York City and under Mayor Ed Koch as Commissioner of Cultural Affairs. She was a contributing editor of Redbook Magazine for several years. She was appointed by three presidents to various commissions and has served on more committees and boards than there is room to print on one page. Bess Myerson even ran for the U.S. Senate and was awarded four honorary doctorate degrees.

And to think it all started when her sister sent her picture to the local sponsors of the Miss

America preliminaries!

"My sister wanted me to win the Miss America title so we could buy a new piano with the five thousand dollar award," Bess said. "I was skinny as a broom. I didn't think I had a chance."

More than twenty-five years ago, Bess was encouraged to run for public office, although that may have been a positive professional move, it was too late. She had to refuse, having just been given the debilitating news that she had ovarian cancer.

She fought that disease with the same spirit by which she has undertaken all challenges. After surgery, Bess underwent extensive chemotherapy. And still she remained undaunted, serving such prestigious organizations as the National ADL Commission and various arts councils.

Every adversity gave her yet another cause and her newest cause became ovarian cancer. She may have done more to enlighten women about this disease in the past two decades than anyone. She became the largest single financial contributor to the cause, and the Bess Myerson Ovarian Cancer Program was named in her honor.

In 1980, Bess suffered a stroke. But it couldn't keep her down because it was 1991 and there was the Chernobyl incident—Russia's children needed her. While in an airport in Russia, after going over to help coordinate the efforts of getting children to health-care facilities for cancer treatment, Bess was mugged and her leg broken. But that didn't stop her either.

Bess Myerson worked diligently as a co-founder to create a Living Memorial to the Holocaust at the Museum of Jewish Heritage. She donated more than a million dollars to develop a film library at the museum. She is fond

Bess with daughter Barra.
Photo by Ed Keneger

of saying, "Writing out that check cleared my sinuses and my mind!"

With a generous hundred thousand dollar donation, she funded the Annual Bess Myerson Campus Journalism Award, open to newspapers and college journalists who write with a positive sensitivity about cultural differences and intergroup harmony

But perhaps her greatest achievement is daughter Barra Grant, a successful Los Angeles screenwriter. One has to wonder what incredible gifts this young woman has realized from a mother so strong, so accomplished and so dedicated to service. Bess Myerson doesn't mince words, she never has. She's just as feisty and outspoken today as she was in 1945 and is still as dedicated to wiping out hatred as she was then. What a role model for our youth. And what a Miss America! She sums up her life today with these philosophical thoughts: "What I have acquired," she said, "is a splendid talent for living. It's the best. Life is my lover."

Books by Bess Myerson:

• *Miss America 1945 and the Year That Changed Our Lives* - Audiobook - 1999 - Jewish Contemporary Classics

• *Miss America 1945 and the Year That Changed Our Lives* - with Susan Dworkin 1987 - Newmarket Press

• *The I Love New York Diet* - 1982, Wm. Morrow & Co. (17 weeks on N.Y.Times Best Seller List).

• *The Complete Consumer* - 1979 - Simon & Schuster

Miss America 1947
Barbara Jo Walker

Student - Memphis State College
Age - 21   Height - 5' 7"

Talent: Barbara, a lyric soprano, accompanied herself
at the piano as she sang *One Kiss*.

Photo courtesy of the Miss America Organization

"All the Miss Americas are special. They all have a very special something."
—Barbara Walker Hummel

28

Barbara Jo Walker

Barbara Walker was a Sunday School teacher when she won the Miss Memphis title.

"They were looking for the girl-next-door type. Jean Bartel, Miss America 1943, and I were college girls, not show girls."

Yes, things were different then. The country had just gone through World War II. Johnny had come marching home and the Miss America Pageant reflected the family values the war had brought to mind. Since there was no rule against marriage during her reign, Miss America became Mrs. John Hummel. The pageant even encouraged the marriage. Everglaze, one of the pageant sponsors, made the wedding dress and eight bridesmaids' dresses for Barbara's wedding. "I got married in June and finished my Miss America reign in September."

It was almost as an afterthought that Barbara Walker, a twenty-one-year-old student at Memphis State College (now University of Memphis) entered the Miss America preliminaries. The Jaycees operated the pageant in Memphis and college seniors were encouraged to enter.

"A local promoter, an advertising man, urged me to compete. I was engaged to be married and just didn't see any point to it. But he said, 'Do it! You can get a free trip to New York!'"

"Okay," was the half-hearted response. But time literally flew. It took only three weeks from winning Miss Memphis to winning the Miss America Pageant.

Not all states were represented in the mid-forties. And rather than competition taking place one year and being named Miss America for the following year, Barbara actually won in 1947. She explained, "They started post-dating the pageant titles in 1951. This was also the first time they had had the Miss Memphis Pageant." The city must have been good to her. She made her home in Memphis.

Her scholarship award for winning the Miss America crown was five thousand dollars, an enormous amount of money at the time. "I bought a piano and finished my degree," she said. Her major was in French and English and

Barbara and John all decked out for a '50s party-1984.

Barbara with Andy, Patti, Drew, and Cady—a Louisiana Thanksgiving -1993.

in addition to her degree, she earned a teaching certificate. Since she didn't need all the money for her own education, pageant officials generously permitted her to use it for rent. She had married Dr. John Hummel, an intern in Obstetrics and Gynecology at Johns Hopkins University. She had missed his graduation from medical school because she was in Mexico, traveling for the pageant. (Dr. Hummel later delivered another Miss America—Kellye Cash!)

She remembers her pageant history well. "I traveled for the pageant after I completed my degree. It was a big transition at the time. All through the war, the Miss Americas had sold war bonds. In 1945, Bess Myerson was Miss America and the war was suddenly over. They didn't know what to do with the new Miss America so they booked her into Vaudeville. Bess was such an accomplished pianist and naturally didn't fit in with Vaudeville."

During Barbara's year, the pageant started working diligently for sponsors to inspire scholarship programs for the women. Everglaze manufactured a glazed cotton fabric. Barbara explained. "The material was more suited for curtain material and we had to wear their clothes, but," she said graciously, "they were wonderful people."

Barbara also recalled the Catalina company who sponsored the pageant until they stopped crowning Miss America in swim suits. "Then they pulled out," she said.

"The pageant talked even then about totally getting rid of the swim suit, but of course they never did." However, that year was a landmark year for the swimsuit, as it was the only year, until recently, that a two-piece suit was worn in the pageant. Barbara was the last Miss America to be crowned in a swimsuit. After the pageant, Barbara worked in television

for seven years. "It was during the '50s," she said. "I did a show called *Lady of the House* during which I interviewed guests. At that time the networks started broadcasting at seven p.m. so we had a lot of local daytime shows."

Barbara returned to Atlantic City several times. She judged the pageant in 1948 and when she returned to judge the 1956 pageant, she captured a very special memory.

"I was six weeks pregnant with my third child. I was nauseated during the entire nine months and only gained nine pounds the whole time. But I may have been the only woman who hosted the pageant *pregnant*." She returned to judge the pageant the next year as well.

Barbara and Dr. John Hummel eventually celebrated their golden anniversary. Their marriage produced three children and five grandchildren.

According to Barbara, they have a brilliant son in Texas, with Lockheed-Martin, a son in Memphis, who is a "computer whiz" with the city, and a daughter who is a registered nurse and who works in Memphis in the home health field. "They're all healthy and happy," Barbara said proudly.

Several years ago, John had a heart attack and Barbara found herself married to a shopoholic. "He had to stay home for two months to recuperate so he spent his days shopping through catalogs. Every day, we'd get another box of something he had ordered, in the mail."

It was imperative to Barbara that she get him back on his feet and back to work, so he would stop shopping!

"As a busy physician, he had never been around the house much, and I just continued doing my volunteer work and the things I did with civic organizations. I think you need to get away from each other. I wasn't the clinging type. It wouldn't have worked if I had been. He was always so busy, I wouldn't have had anyone to cling to!" she laughed.

Regardless of the stress of dealing with a loved one's illness, Barbara Hummel seemed to always keep her head.

"You face your mortality when somebody in your family is really sick. You just never know which way it's going to go." She recalled a night when John had been ill all night but they had thought it might be ulcer related. Finally, at six-thirty in the morning, they decided to go to the hospital. The emergency room staff asked, "How did you get here? Where's the ambulance?"

"We drove," was the response. Within two and a half hours, John was in surgery having a triple bypass.

"People go through these things," said Barbara, matter-of-factly. "They adjust the best way they can."

Asked how she adjusted to the transition from his working so many hours as an Ob/Gyn and then fully retiring, she said, "I worked in his office during his last ten years of practicing, so we got used to being together. Although," she laughed a little, "when he retired completely, we had to get used to being together all over again."

Barbara served as president of the local opera board of directors and the local art guild.

She never forgot the pageant experience. "I went back in 1995 for the 75th anniversary. Thirty-five of us returned. It was wonderful. And eight of us still get together once a year, the same group, every year. All the Miss Americas are so special. They all have a very special something."

Miss America 1947 certainly did.

We lost Barbara in 2000. She died several months after losing her husband John.

Miss America 1948
BeBe Shopp
State - Minnesota
Age - 18   Height - 5' 9''

Talent: BeBe performed Kreisler's *Caprice Viennese* on the Vibraharp

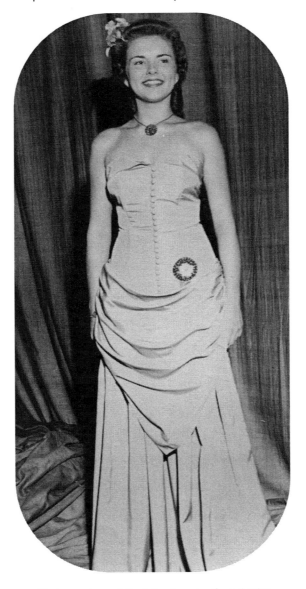

Photo courtesy of the Miss America Organization

"Being Miss America isn't easy. It's difficult for some people to accept you without visualizing a crown on your head. But I'm who I am. I go for bread without makeup. I wear blue jeans. I'm not Donna Reed!"
—BeBe Shopp

32

BeBe Shopp

Beatrice Bella Shopp's first title, albeit unofficial, was the Cream of Wheat baby!

"My father Edward worked for the company and because I had to eat it all the time, I really grew to dislike it," she laughed.

Thus was the child, nicknamed BeBe, marked for fame. The child that eighteen years later would earn another title: Miss America—and fifty years after that, the title of Grand Marshall of the Miss America Parade.

BeBe grew up an only child in Hopkins, Minnesota where church and a strong belief in God became her mainstay.

All her faith bases were covered. "My dad was a Baptist, Mom was a Lutheran. I went to a Christian Science Sunday school and a Congregational Church. In high school, I often attended a little mission church out in the country where I was exposed to a missionary from Africa who rounded out the ecumenical experience," she explained.

At seventeen, she knew she was too young to be considered for the Miss America crown but she competed in the Miss

Minnesota Pageant, determined to gain experience for the next year. And her practice run paid off, for the next year she won it all—the scholarship of five thousand dollars, the convertible coupe worth three thousand dollars, and the title! Fifteen thousand people watched her crowning in Convention Hall in Atlantic City.

"I really wanted the scholarship. And because of it, I was able to attend the Manhattan School of Music in New York. I can't imagine how my life would have been had I not become Miss America. If I had remained in Minnesota, I wouldn't have met my husband nor had my four daughters. The pageant direct-

BeBe with the four runners-up and emcee Bob Russell. She was the first Miss America crowned in a gown rather than a swimsuit.

After the parade in 1998-BeBe and Bayard with their daughters, Myalisa, Laurie, Wendy and Kimberly.

ed my whole life from that one event," she said.

BeBe and her husband-to-be met under the clock at the Biltmore in New York City.

"That's where all the college kids met," BeBe said. "Bayard was on the Harvard lacrosse team. He actually was with someone else at the time. I didn't even know what lacrosse was," she laughed. A group of students had gone to New Jersey where the team was playing and every time Bayard could make his way to the stands, he would talk to her.

They began dating in the spring of 1951. Shortly thereafter, her beau joined the Air Force, halting communications for eight months.

BeBe had been on the road, playing vibraharp in a trio, and came home from a trip one day to answer to her father's concern. Thinking she might be missing something spe-

cial, he suggested, "Why don't you write that nice young man I met?"

And so she did. The gentleman received her letter on the day he was to ship out to Korea. But he did not forget that special send-off. As soon as he returned to the States, he came for a visit and sparks were quickly rekindled. After returning to his home in Massachusetts, he called her one evening.

"I'm sitting in my mother's bedroom. She wants to know why I didn't ask you to marry me—so here I am."

BeBe didn't hesitate. She said yes. She was twenty-four when they were married in 1954. Four beautiful daughters later, they have now been together for nearly fifty years.

In Minneapolis, she had been hosting a television show five days a week. But after Bayard's military service was completed, BeBe decided to put her career aside. The happy couple settled in Massachusetts. Their roots remain strong in the Northeast and even today, all four girls live nearby with

BeBe (lt) with other Miss Americas at a reunion. Jean Bartel, Evelyn Ay, Lee Meriwether, Marion McKnight, Barbara Walker.

BeBe and Bayard at The Great Wall.

their families. To date, BeBe and Bayard have been blessed with ten grandchildren ranging in ages from five to twenty-two.

Nearly fifteen years ago, children grown and gone, BeBe found that she needed some professional challenge in her life. She made a two-year commitment to the VISTA organization and moved, by herself, to Little Rock, Arkansas. Her mission: to work on the Drug-Free Youth program, taking messages of prevention to elementary school children. Her husband remained in the Northeast and BeBe returned home for visits as her work permitted.

"It was refreshing," BeBe said. "After all those years primarily in a care-giving role as a wife and mother, it was a great learning experience for me and I began to become more confident. "Somewhere along in life, after you've raised your family, you just sometimes need to do something entirely different!"

She has been involved in community theatre with the Lynnfield Spotlighters for twenty-five years. Bayard and BeBe both enjoy community theatre. In earlier days, the couple would alternate their involvement so a parent would always be home with the children.

BeBe's favorite pastime is to travel with friends. She has traveled to Ireland and to Paris, France with a group of former Miss Americas. On another trip, she climbed the China Wall, sadly creating the irritating necessity for a knee replacement. She gets together with her Miss America friends whenever possible. And she frequently returns to the pageant.

"I was always involved with the Miss A Pageant, from emceeing to judging the state pageants, which I do currently. I still have that identity. Returning to the pageant stokes my fires!"

"Once I married and left Minnesota, I never went back to a professional music career, but I continue to this day to perform, and especially to use those gifts for others," she said. Several years ago, BeBe joined a local musical group that performs in the area. It's called "Share the Music." Performances keep her on her toes, as

The Historical Society displays the gown she wore.

the singers are required to memorize the music. Currently, her added responsibility is to be in charge of props for their events. "It's a vocal variety event based on Broadway musicals and composers of the American songbook," she said.

BeBe still plays the piano daily and uses her talent to comfort and entertain residents at the local nursing home. Volunteers hold frequent prayer services. Occasionally, BeBe offers the entire service, where she shares a sermonette and plays old hymns for the residents. "The music really means something to them, even when they may not be completely lucid. There's still something very sweet and special there," she said.

This giving soul truly understands the art of offering others your spiritual gifts. "It makes me sad to go there, but God gave us these gifts to share with others, and it makes me feel wonderful that it means something to them," she said. "I think we need to be thankful for what God has given us. I know I am."

BeBe and Bayard certainly did well in the parenting department. All four daughters are college educated. "Two are in education, one's in the restaurant business and one is currently dancing on Broadway in *The Producers*. Her husband is performing in *Mama Mia*," BeBe said proudly.

BeBe is heavily involved as a licensed lay reader in the Episcopal Church, and takes communion to shut-ins and to nursing homes. Her husband co-manages the Amelia Peabody Foundation in Massachusetts.

"He's very involved in strengthening inner city school activities for children, with the YMCA and the Child Development Program, also known as Pathways for Children."

And as if she didn't do enough community service, Bebe volunteers at the local high school, taking care of babies so new moms can continue their education. "I get to feed them

Still a loving couple.

and hold them," she said warmly. "It's something my mother had always expressed an interest in doing, helping these young mothers. So I guess I'm fulfilling my mother's dream."

Asked if she had any words of wisdom, BeBe mentioned a philosophy shared by several of the women interviewed for this book. "So many of the girls marry right after the pageant. It's just too fast. I would say to them that perhaps they need to hold off for a while. I'd say, Go find out who you are and in what direction you're going before you make a lifetime commitment to another person."

She added, "So often throughout your life, you change direction. I think both men and women need to be allowed to be free for a while to change direction until they grow into whom they really are, whom they really want to be."

She continued, "During the times I reflect on my life coming from the Miss America perspective, I think of the people who caused such change in my life and offered support throughout my life. I'll always appreciate Rudy Shogren, the Miss Minnesota director at the time, and Ross and Agnes Daniels, encouraging family friends as well as my pageant family. And of course my parents who gave me so much love, advice and devotion. Without all of these people and a husband who has always supported my adventures," she smiled warmly, "I would probably never have had such an incredibly satisfying life."

She thought for a moment, then added, "The years Lenora Slaughter directed the pageant were tremendous years of change. She had a vision and I happened to have fallen into that vision of change.

As a result I became an advocate, believer and staunch supporter of the scholarship program. Without Lenora's insight and vision, there are thousands upon thousands of women who would have never had so many incredible personal and professional opportunities. The Miss America experience afforded me not only a college education, but took me well into the business world and beyond. It enabled me to become a better wife, mother and humanitarian."

BeBe's spiritual

The grandchildren

focus has sharpened over the years and she generously shares her thoughts about the road now traveled. "There were times when I took the wrong fork in the road, especially before my marriage. There are circumstances from the outside that influence you, as well as things on the inside. I made mistakes in my life which I regret, but I learned from them all. Mistakes only serve to reflect our human frailties and Miss Americas have those frailties, just like anybody else. But He forgives you for sins, for mistakes. And in the long run, I'm so glad that I made the choices I did, both personally and professionally. Especially when I went off to Little Rock with VISTA. I found myself worrying about the little children and things outside of my world that made me refocus my priorities and recover my spirit."

BeBe is enthusiastically grateful to the special and ongoing support she has received from her husband through the years and equally as appreciative of his work with the foundation.

"He does so much more than gathering insti-

tutional money to fund a program," she said. "They do incredible work to strengthen the children's character and enrich their lives. I'm so proud of him," she said.

Overall, this Miss America not only bubbles over with personality plus, but is inwardly just as joyful. "I feel I've been very blessed because I haven't had a lot of tragedy. And when I was faced with challenges, I've come out of them all right because of my faith in God and the constant love from my husband and family."

BeBe has a personal prayer list by her bed where she lifts up those who need her prayers. And just reflecting on that list helps her realize how blessed she continues to be.

"You know, God didn't promise us a rose garden. He expects us to keep our part of the bargain," she said wisely. "I know bad things often happen to good people, but God doesn't do that. He gives us what we have. He gives us our bodies—our temples—our gifts, and gives us the rules for life. We're expected to follow them and take care of what we have. But sometimes just as Jesus found Himself calling out in the wilderness, we do the same. We have our own wilderness. Thankfully, He's always there to answer."

Miss America 1953
Neva Langley

Student - Wesleyan Conservatory and School of Fine Arts
State - Georgia
Age - 19   Height - 5' 6½''

Talent: Neva, a classical pianist, played *Khachaturian Toccata*.

Photo courtesy of the Miss America Organization

"Whatever the goal is, it takes a lot of work, a lot of discipline! I've always
thought it required ninety percent work and ten percent talent."
—Neva Langley Fickling

Neva Langley

Originally from Lakeland, Florida, Neva Langley began playing the piano at an early age. Her strong spiritual foundation was developed early, mostly as a result of her being raised in a Christian family. At thirteen, she became the pianist for her church. "I learned responsibility very young," Neva said. "I had to be there twice a week, every week." Schedule permitting, Neva performed that role for seven years.

At seventeen, she started college, attending Florida Southern for her freshman year because her mother thought she was too young to go away to school. Her beauty and personality earned her the title of campus queen. In addition to her talent as a budding classical pianist, Neva quickly began to develop other professional skills by serving on staff of the college newspaper and the business staff for her college yearbook.

The next year, she was permitted to try her wings away from home and further develop her musical talents. Neva was accepted at the Wesleyan Conservatory and School of Fine Arts in Macon, Georgia. If her mother had only known that this year would catapult her daughter from little hometown girl to international celebrity, perhaps the outcome would have been different. At the end of Neva's sophomore year, she chose to put school aside as she was named Miss Georgia and went on to win the crown of Miss America 1953.

There had been so much focus, so much discipline required that second semester. First the local pageant, then the state pageant, rehearsal and more rehearsal—all the while working on college studies, going to classes, somehow fitting everything in. But after Neva had won the Miss Georgia title, the momentum accelerated and the Miss America Pageant seemed to take on a life of its own, culminating in a regal walk down that long runway in Atlantic City.

The morning after Neva was crowned, the reality of who she was suddenly took hold. She recalls that according to tradition, she gave her first press conference, clad in a swimsuit on the beach in Atlantic City. She would never again be required to pose in a swimsuit. For that she was grateful. She was suddenly faced with an incredible schedule that would take her to places she had never been. Starting close to the pageant venue, she was immediately whisked away to the Pennsylvania State Fair. Her reign had begun!

It was the year that Ike, the country's favorite war hero, was elected President. The country was celebrating its first Republican President in a long time. Neva was invited to ride in the inaugural parade and during the year, she attended congressional luncheons and other events in Washington. Asked if she was nervous meeting all the dignitaries, she reflected for a moment before answering. "I don't recall being nervous," she said, "although I do believe that being Miss America created a wonderful introduction into the realm of public relations. Diplomacy played such a major role during that year." She explained, "Not everyone loves Miss America immediately, although I must admit that I was there at the prime time. The title was more respected then than it is now."

But even Miss Americas are not infallible, and with a frantic schedule of appearances looming before her, Neva was forced to return home to recuperate from pneumonia. She had become ill during the inaugural activities.

There were several policy changes for Miss America that year, and Neva's illness signaled the necessity for one of them. The schedule was grueling. Historically, Miss As had been available to the public from dawn until dusk, sometimes far beyond. Pageant officials had begun to realize that the schedule of breakfasts, lunches, dinners and evening events was just too much for one person. They began to make concessions about the number of hours Miss America could be required to appear, now offering her a badly needed rest period during the day.

Photo courtesy of the Miss America Organization

Travel was much more difficult in the early '50s. There were no coast-to-coast, non-stop flights. And with each layover, there would be a photo opportunity scheduled for Miss America. The cities all began to look the same. There were no first-class accommodations, and services on board were minimal. Tourist class in the airplane only indicated that people were willing to fly at night. (That later became known as the red-eye.) Traveling day after day after day, meeting tight deadlines, making sure clothes were pressed and ready, carting bags from here to there—these were difficult maneuvers for anyone, let alone someone who was required to smile and always, always behave with grace and dignity.

Some of the trips were difficult for Neva because she usually traveled alone. There was no official guardian to assist her with the constant demands from photographers and the press. There was no one to protect her from over-zealous media or fans. There was no buffer, no one to introduce her to dignitaries, to handle last minute schedule changes, to brief her on events, and to offer the public relations support that today's chaperones do. Sometimes, however, her mother, sister or pageant sponsor was able to travel with her. This always made the trip much easier. But there weren't such dangers then as there are today for celebrities.

"I do remember one scary incident," Neva recalled. "I was in some town by myself, and a young man kept trying to see me. He kept calling and insisting that he come up to my room. One day, I was in my hotel when I heard a persistent knocking at my door. I immediately called security and they took care of it."

Once during an auto show in New York City, Neva found herself in the middle of a heavy throng of fans, all crowded into a space much too small for that number of people. Luckily, her chaperone helped her get out, but to this day, she still remembers the feeling she had, jammed into that small space. "I felt claustrophobic during that experience. It was truly frightening."

In August, nearly at the end of her year as Miss America, Neva received a call in Lansing, Michigan from the pageant officials. They informed her that there would be a guardian from that point on. They were sending a companion for her. Another policy was changed, obviously for the better.

During most of her appearances, Neva performed for her audience. The only problem was, although well trained from her years of practice, she still required practice time in order for her to perform up to her standards. Her solution was to go on a "piano hunt" at each hotel where she stayed. Somehow, she managed to build rehearsal times into her heavy schedule. Sometimes, she did not. Regardless of whether she was well rehearsed or not, she performed. "But sometimes," she recalls laughing, "it was on a yucky piano."

Neva crowns Evelyn Ay
Photo courtesy of the Miss America Organization.

Miss Americas weren't required to have a platform developed to address social issues at the time, but Neva felt compelled to share her Christian values and to set an example for young people. "I wasn't a forceful person," Neva explains, "but I was fully aware of the opportunities I had to share my beliefs. I didn't have a platform, per se, but I was always focused on two things: my Christian values and the piano."

At the completion of her tour, Neva Langley was invited to perform as guest artist with the Miss America Symphony. It was a special treat for the audience that year as just moments prior to relinquishing her crown, they watched Miss America play *Hungarian Rhapsodie.*

It had been a wonderful year. She had met President Dwight D. Eisenhower several times. She had met a "very young" Richard Nixon. She had performed and appeared throughout the nation and had seen and done incredible things she had never before considered. "You definitely come away from that experience with a broader education that you wouldn't get in just four years of college," Neva said. "My life has been so much more enriched because of that opportunity."

Neva's strong Christian values had given her a grace that warmed her to people. The discipline that had taken her through years of music had been enhanced by the demands on her time, talent and energies. And her five thousand dollar scholarship in hand, she would return to the Wesleyan Conservatory to complete her studies and her musical education. And she would return to a very handsome young man whom she had met a year before, just two months before she had left for Atlantic City.

Would they continue dating where they left off? They did. What had she liked about him, she was asked. "Oh, gosh, everything!" she exclaimed without hesitation. "His looks, his brains, his personality, his background." William Arthur Fickling, Jr., born in Macon, was from a strong southern family. And although they had met prior to the Miss

America Pageant, Neva had seen fit to keep her perspective and not become sidetracked. "I had watched girls run off and get married, and not be able to fulfill their dreams," she explained. Neva credits her level head to being a product of the depression. She remembers well the older girls, during World War II, the girls who would run off on a whim and marry soldiers. It was a romantic time. But Neva had kept her focus. "I always wanted to be able to sign my own marriage license," she said. (The age of consent in Florida was twenty-one.)

And just as she had kept her priorities straight throughout college and the Miss America experience, she kept her promise to herself. She became Mrs. William Arthur Fickling, Jr. halfway through her senior year of college.

Asked what words of advice she might offer those who are struggling to fulfill their own dreams, Neva Langley Fickling is adamant about what it takes. "Whatever the goal is," explained Neva, "it takes a lot of work! You have to have discipline and work hard. I've always thought it was ninety percent work and ten percent talent."

Her philosophy is that "you have to be prepared to give up things, at least temporarily. I gave up playing and performing for twenty-five years to raise my family." Any regrets? "No." There is no martyrdom here, only a life being fulfilled. "Being the youngest of three girls, I had the opportunity to see mistakes made and the pain caused by those mistakes. I learned, inherently, values that I wouldn't have known otherwise."

And therein lies the lesson. She had given up college temporarily and the wonderful man she had just met to reach one goal. The Miss America opportunity provided her with an exceptional future, and there would be time for other things, other dreams to come true. And because she was willing to focus on the pageant, she was able to return to the conservatory with a scholarship that would allow her to complete her bachelor's degree in Music.

Her future husband was still very much in the picture, also taking care of business, his studies. A few years later, after they had had four children together, Neva recognized her priorities once again and this time put the performance on hold until the time was right. The family would need to come first, at least for a few years.

Was it a perfect marriage from the start? Was he prince charming? Was he supportive of her having a career when they were young? Neva laughed at the questions. "No, he wasn't so supportive at the time. We were both very young. He wasn't *dis*couraging, just not *en*couraging. He was the only son in a traditional Southern family." That culture, as she explained, especially in the '50s, preferred women to have more traditional roles.

Is he supportive now? She responds warmly, "So much so that he was instrumental in my returning to piano."

Some time ago, Neva's husband Bill insisted on giving his wife a nine-foot Steinway grand piano. Neva, although a bit wary about performing again, decided quickly that she didn't

Photo courtesy of the Miss America Organization

want anyone else playing that beautiful piano better than she could! So she returned to her first love, classical piano, received some coaching and began to play again.

She is fond of sharing this anecdote. "Now, Bill's more nervous about my playing than I am. When I'm ready to perform, I have to remind him to stop nervously jangling the coins in his pocket, because I can hear them."

In early years, she performed with the former Macon Wesleyan Orchestra, the Atlanta Pops Orchestra and the Miss America Symphony. During the past two summers, Neva has played in concert tours in Italy, preferring at this time in her life to share the stage in a two-piano duet. She believes that duets create a safer environment, and with less pressure than having a performance rest solely on one's shoulders.

Neva believes she has had the best of both worlds, being blessed with musical talent and the opportunity to use it. At the same time, she was able to enjoy raising her family by keeping her priorities in order.

But real life happens to people of celebrity just as much as it does to those who don't have that moment of fame. There have been difficult times in Neva's life, too…times when she relied heavily on her strong spiritual faith.

In 1987, her daughter Jane, then a bride of six months, had to undergo a life-saving liver transplant. That kind of surgical procedure wasn't done frequently at the time. The family went to Pittsburgh to see her through it, renting an apartment so they could be as close to her as possible. After surviving chronic liver failure and a transplant, Jane had to remain either in the hospital or clinic for three months. It was a test of strength and faith for the whole family.

Neva still highly praises the Starzl Transplantation Research Center in Pittsburgh, along with attributing her family's Christian faith for getting them all through it. The bride is now a mother herself, healthy and happy.

Tragedy struck again in 1994 when Neva lost Ouida, an older sister, to Alzheimer's. She recalled the pain of watching her sister's illness for three years before her death. The disease is normally diagnosed in a later stage, and denial may have prohibited the family from pinpointing it earlier.

Neva explained, "I got the feeling that there was something terribly wrong at times, and yet when we brought it up to her husband, we wouldn't get a confirmation, so we'd let it go." The first time Neva noticed that something was not right about her sister's memory was when her first grandson was born, and true to Southern form, had become "William Arthur Fickling IV." While on the phone with Oida, shortly after the boy was born, her sister asked, "Now, *what* did you name the little boy?"

There were other times the warning was there but ignored until finally, the doctor put a name to it. According to Neva, "she didn't seem to have it terribly long from the diagnosis until her death." The family believes that Ouida's condition may have been accelerated from two major traumas: her heart bypass and the loss of her husband. "He protected her and would never confirm there was anything

wrong," Neva explained. No one else in the family has experienced this disease, so they all have the best hopes for healthy futures. Asked if she's afraid of contracting this disorder, Neva responded honestly, "It scares the living daylights out of me!"

Neva's children are now grown. Their professions run the gamut from veterinary science to real estate. Her husband is responsible for founding Charter Medical, the largest psychiatric corporation in the world. He is now chief executive officer of a health management organization, an entity he also created.

An active volunteer for many years, she has served on the Georgia Council of the Arts and the Board of Directors of the Atlanta Symphony Orchestra plus several other community service organizations. Neva was honored in the mid-'80s with an honorary doctorate in Fine Arts at Wesleyan College.

She performs as guest soloist with the Macon Symphony Orchestra. Neva has recently performed with the Utah Symphony Orchestra and the Symphony Orchestra in Benevento Italy.

Yes, there has been a great deal of achievement and success in Neva Langley Fickling's life. The reign of Miss America may be brief, but it's a lasting reminder to Neva and to others that there are opportunities out there for people who are focused toward achievement. That the five thousand dollar scholarship was just the first step in the Miss America process that helped her form the rest of her life.

It was a means to an end for the little girl who played the piano for her church in Lakeland, Florida, a little girl who had the discipline to work hard, set her sights high, and never give up. A little girl who went on to become an accomplished performer, a respected member of her community, even a Miss America, but perhaps most important of all, a loved and loving wife and mother.

Miss America 1954

Evelyn Ay

Student - University of Pennsylvania
State - Pennsylvania
Age - 20   Height - 5' 8''

Talent: Evelyn performed a poetry recitation: "Leaves from My Grass House"
from the book *Vagabond House* by Don Blanding

Photo courtesy of the Miss America Organization

"As for handling grief and the like, I think where else can you go when you
find a hole in your heart, but to ask for the blessing of God to fill it?"
—Evelyn Ay Sempier

Evelyn Ay

When Evelyn Ay won the title as Miss America 1954, her proud father said, "This could happen only in America!" This night was truly the culmination of his American dream, for Evelyn was the daughter of German immigrants Richard and Paula Ay, who had chosen America as their homeland more than twenty years before.

In 1932, while working as chief engineer on tankers for Atlantic Refinery, Richard dreamed about becoming an American citizen. He made multiple crossings from his hometown of Hambourg to Philadelphia, always falling short of realizing his dream. For located just a city block away from the docks was the Office of Naturalization. Unfortunately, as a foreigner employed on an American ship, the eager young man was prohibited by law to leave the ship.

Committed to complying with the law but focused on realizing his dream, one day Richard approached the captain and said, "I want to become an American and I can't leave the ship. If I work for nothing and am no longer employed, can I get off?" All he wanted was to visit the Office of Naturalization to obtain the necessary papers to start the citizenship process.

His captain responded, "If you work for free, they'll accuse me of using slave labor." Impressed by the young man's sincerity, the captain said, "I'll give you a penny for the voyage. That way, you won't be a slave or an employee."

At the next docking in Philadelphia, Richard Friederick Ay lost no time in securing the required documentation and was well on his way to realizing his dream. He had fallen in love with a woman from his hometown; and he and Paula decided to be married in Hamburg before Richard's ship turned around to come back to America. How ironic that on a cold day in November, they rushed excitedly to the American consulate for their wedding only to be stopped at the door by an ominous sign that proved to thwart their efforts:

CLOSED - AMERICAN HOLIDAY
THANKSGIVING.

One day later, the determined couple

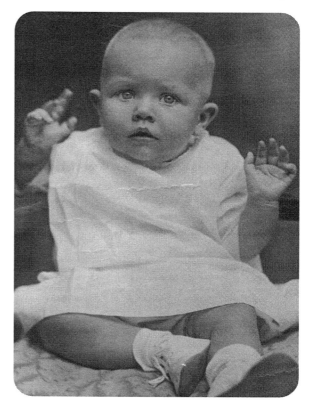

retraced their steps to the consulate and made wish number one come true. Shortly thereafter, Richard headed for America and Paula followed behind, as soon as she was able to leave Germany. Theirs was a union that would last a lifetime. "Mom died in 1966 at the age of fifty-four, and my father died in 1972," Evelyn said.

Family life was so important to Evelyn's parents that they made every effort to provide a solid foundation. They initially settled in Philadelphia. Richard continued his employment on tanker ships; he was out to sea for months at a time.

Evelyn was born in 1933. When she was three years old, Richard asked to be transferred to the Keystone Pipeline, Atlantic's ground division, which would allow him to be home more often. In true German precision, Richard studied a map of the area for which he would be responsible and pinpointed the halfway mark between Philadelphia and the Blue Mountain region of Pennsylvania. The target would be home and home it became, not only to Evelyn's family, but they had arrived smack-dab in the middle of Pennsylvania Dutch country where they were immediately welcomed, surrounded by the Amish and Mennonite communities. The town was Ephrata (pronounced Ef'-ruh-tuh) and this strange-sounding place provided them with an idyllic home life.

This was a wonderful era for collecting lovely childhood memories. Evelyn and her younger brother, named Richard for their father, enjoyed small town life as the two roller-skated on sidewalks, sledded down hills after snowstorms, walked to school and even came home for lunch, an event that is rarely practiced today. "We walked to the movie theatre when movies were still twelve cents," Evelyn laughed. It was a time of safety and security and family values were so solid, it wasn't even necessary to discuss them.

"I graduated from high school in a class of seventy-two students, having attended first grade on with the same people," Evelyn said. "It was a time where we all felt safe. We walked to the corner grocery store—we walked everywhere. We would sit on the front porch and visit with each other and have a wonderful evening. Sometimes we'd listen to baseball games on the radio." It was a time that created great feelings of nostalgia.

Miss America-to-be at the age of three.

Evelyn's foundation included a commitment to her church as well. She sang in church choir every Sunday morning at St. Luke Lutheran and was later married in the same church.

Upon high school graduation, Evelyn enrolled at the University of Pennsylvania where she majored in Medical Technology. "It was mostly a boy-boy school," she laughed, adding, "They only enrolled women at the time because someone said, 'You have to have a few.'" Housing for women was sparse at best, and she found herself in a dormitory converted from a three-story row house on Locust Street across from the fraternity house of Sigma Chi.

"You have to realize that there was no campus, then," she said. "The university was built right in and around the city." Evelyn and her roommate noticed that among the very cute Sigma Chi boys lived a Great Dane. What an icebreaker!

"We grinned as we said to each other, 'That dog needs to be walked.'"

"So we'd pop on over to Sigma Chi, knock on the door and volunteer to walk Rip (nickname for Euripides)." Evelyn and her roommate walked the dog quite often but had not yet met its master because Carl Sempier, the dog owner and fraternity boy, was busy playing football in the winter and running track in the spring. It wasn't until March that Evelyn finally met her furry friend's owner and when she did, she carefully cut out his photograph from the football program and took it home to show her mother. "I remember Mother and I were standing in the kitchen at the sink and I said, 'Mother, if I should ever marry, I will marry him.'"

The two didn't start dating right away because Carl was preoccupied with sports, but they managed to share an occasional sandwich and coffee, and on Thursdays, when young ladies were *allowed* to swim in the university pool, they would go swimming together. "There was no big fancy dating then," she said. "We just got to know each other by talking."

In 1953, Carl was about to graduate and Evelyn was completing her sophomore year. The Korean conflict had started and the young men learned that they were all to be drafted upon graduation. Carl told Evelyn, "I don't do army," and immediately applied to get into the Royal Air Force, who in turn replied, "We don't do Americans." So Carl quickly applied to Officers Candidate School, OCS, with the United States Navy at Newport, Rhode Island and he was accepted without question.

With nothing to do that summer, before the start of fall semester, Evelyn did a favor for her father that literally changed the course of her life. "Ben Herr, the president of the local Junior Chamber of Commerce had signed a franchise for the Miss America local preliminaries and my father felt he was such a good friend that we should support him. I had never entered a pageant of any kind, but we decided to do it as a favor. Favor notwithstanding, Evelyn Ay, in short order, became Miss Ephrata.

"Then my brother and I read where the state pageant was awarding a television set to the winner, and Richard said he wanted me to win so he could get the television, so I went forward, never imagining that would come true. And my little brother got his TV."

There was also a scholarship of several hundred dollars tied to this title, approximately half the cost of a semester's tuition at the University of Pennsylvania. Coupled with the scholarship Evelyn had earned from her father's work, Atlantic Refinery, this was an added incentive.

And win she did! This small town girl was now representing thousands upon thousands of young women she had never met as she carried the new title of Miss Pennsylvania. And now on to nationals for this lady who, just weeks before, had known practically nothing of the pageant world.

Evelyn and Carl had spoken of marriage during this whirlwind as Carl began to pursue his OCS training at Newport. Not giving nationals a second thought, they decided that during his break in November, they would be married. "On the Saturday before I left for Atlantic City, Carl drove down from Newport with a beautifully written letter asking my parents for my hand in marriage. My mother kept the letter until she died and I still have it," Evelyn said.

Evelyn went to the Miss America Pageant sporting a sparkling new diamond on her hand and several of the girls asked if she thought that was appropriate. "Do you really think you ought to wear that?" they asked. To which Evelyn replied, "This thing is one week; the ring is my whole life."

This pageant, in the fall of 1953, was the last pageant held that was not carried to the world via television. Carl and his buddies at OCS huddled around the radio to pick up intermittent break-ins to find out who the finalists were.

"Carl called me long distance from Newport. You didn't make expensive long distance calls idly, at that time," Evelyn said. "He kept asking me if I thought I was *in* the top ten, did I think I had *made* the top ten, and all I could say repeatedly, during that very expensive phone call was 'I don't know.'"

The radio announcer broke in to list the top ten finalists. Later, he broke in again to announce the top five finalists, then finally came back on to announce the runners up.

"Four, three, two...and then they announced my name," Evelyn said. Carl's buddies turned to him and said, "You'll never see her again. If she's any kind of person, she'll send your ring back in a paper bag."

Evelyn is philosophical about having won the prestigious title. "I think the reason I was fortunate enough to win might have been my attitude overall. I felt carefree and I was open to enjoying every minute of the process.

Evelyn and Carl on their wedding day.

Everything that came my way was a new experience, but my life didn't depend on winning that crown."

Although their marriage had to be postponed for a year, winning the pageant was in hindsight probably best all around for the committed couple, as Carl completed OCS and then flight training, on his way to becoming a fighter pilot. "We saw each other four times during that year when I was scheduled at events fairly close to him. He came to see me in Mobile, Alabama and Pensacola, Florida," Evelyn said. During the year, she became known as "Who? from Where?" Evelyn explains, "I was introduced as Evelyn Ay from Ephrata and people didn't know where that was." She never took herself so seriously that these things upset her.

Her tour was naturally memorable, but one special day has stood out forever in Evelyn's mind. Thousands of executives were drawn to a Community Chest charity event in Detroit and the Honorable Reverend Billy Graham gave the keynote address. Evelyn had always made a practice of speaking extemporaneously

and when Mary, her chaperone frantically asked her what she was going to say after hearing Reverend Graham's wonderful words, she just shook her head. She was sure these high-powered executives hadn't come to hear her.

As she stood at the podium and looked around at the impressive audience, she began to speak from her heart, moving them so deeply that when she completed her inspirational talk, they rose as one and honored her with a standing ovation. The Detroit Times heralded her success the next day and to this day, Evelyn doesn't remember what she said. The press was even upstaged however, by the next thing that happened. Someone called from Billy Graham's troop and asked Evelyn to join their tour. Obviously, she had to graciously decline.

Evelyn kept a level head during the pageant year and although she enjoyed her travels and meeting special people, she handled her duties without fanfare and in September of 1954, after crowning her successor, Lee Meriwether, she stepped aside to take the walk down the aisle in November that had been postponed a year before.

The newlyweds went off to Brownsville, Texas where Carl earned his wings, then transferred to Virginia Beach to a navy squadron where he flew FJ-3s, Cougars and Crusaders. "We stayed there until Carl was out of the service. After he returned from his nine-month cruise on an aircraft carrier, he decided that was enough for him, and came home for good," she said. During their tour in Virginia, Evelyn and Carl were blessed with a baby girl, Carlyn, born in 1956 at Portsmouth Naval Hospital. Her name is a poetic combination of her parents' names. Evelyn still remembers the high cost of delivery. "She cost $7.37," Evelyn laughed. Their second daughter, Stacy, came along in 1959, and the family was complete.

They had moved to New City, New York where Carl had joined the world of technology and computers as he went to work for IBM. After twelve years, they moved back to the area of Berwyn, Pennsylvania where they've remained to this day.

Through the years, Evelyn spoke a great deal to women's groups. "They would bring the wives of executives to seminars and ask me to offer the keynote to the women at the lun-

Evelyn with her first dane, Rip.
Photo by Perry Breon, Norfolk Virginian Pilot

body!'"

The only negative about the breed is their short lifespan and to handle the losses more easily, having survived six great Danes, Evelyn and Carl decided early on to adopt one, then another a couple of years later.

So Euripedes' space eventually gave away to Baron's, then another, then another. All dogs were male and all fawns. "We had Rommel and we lived on Roselawn, so his papers read *Rommel, the Fox of Roselawn* as a tribute to German General Erwin Rommel, the Desert Fox. Currently, we have Bismarck," she said. Bismarck handles his prestigious position in the household as do most Great Danes, by sitting on his master's lap or backing up to the couch to carefully place his hiney on the sofa while his front paws rest comfortably on the floor.

"There's something about having a dog in a family, a feeling of responsibility; and you feel

cheons," she said. Evelyn developed several topics but one special address was, "The Care and Feeding of Management." She wanted to share the Christian woman's point of view: How do you juggle hearth and home when you live with a high-powered executive? "That's what Carl was," she said proudly.

Regardless of how politically correct or incorrect it may have been, she almost always started out with the same salutation: "I am Evelyn Sempier and I am a Christian."

Although she has spoken to hundreds and hundreds of groups throughout the years, she always declined invitations that caused a hardship or threatened to become a burden to her or her family. She tempered her life with balance and was fulfilled at home and as a professional woman. "I have tried to avoid all shades of gray," she said. "That's when you flounder. I try to keep things as black and white as possible."

Their continuing penchant for Great Danes has resulted in a lifetime of sharing their home with the gentle giants. "Euripides came with us when we married and moved with us in the Navy. He was guardian of our first child and he loved that baby," Evelyn said. "It was as if he were telling people, 'nosey people can come in and look at that baby but it will be over my

Love still blooms. Evelyn and Carl at the pre-pageant gala - Sept. 2003.

that unconditional love and companionship. They fill an empty house," Evelyn said.

Evelyn and Carl have not had to deal with a tumultuous life; they remained constant with each other and their faith. "We have had to experience the death of parents," she said. "Carl's mom lived with us for twenty-four years. But as for handling grief and the like, I think where else can you go when you find a hole in your heart but to ask for the blessing of God to fill it?" She said, "Some days you think you can do it on your own, and you realize you can't."

Yet her strength comes from a measure of integrity and personal commitment as well. Regarding marriage, she noted that she and Carl have had ups and downs just like anyone else. "But it's a one-day-at-a-time proposition," she said. "You just have it in your mind that you've made this commitment and you'll live up to it. There's a give and a take."

Coming from a simpler time, a time of Betty Crocker recipes and Donna Reed TV shows, Evelyn says that she is pleased so many doors have opened for women, but adds that many women have slammed doors on their life. "It's become so important to be successful, to be somebody, to have *things*. And now, you can even have all that and children too, but I think children may be too often shuffled off, and oh—what they're missing! I don't think forty-five minutes of TV a night with your children or a couple of pages read from a book are a substitute for real quality time."

Evelyn made a choice when she and Carl were raising their daughters to not permit work to interfere with their home time. And she believes strongly that each woman is free to make her own choice.

"When I gave occasional speeches, I would

Evelyn celebrates the 2003 reunion with her Miss America pals, Lee Meriwether (lt) and Pat Donnelly (rt).
Photo by Kate Kitchen

do that in the evening when I was certain Carl would be at home with the children, or speak during the day when my little ones were in school and I would be there when they got home from school," she said adding, "I was satisfied and they were satisfied. I don't think female and male egos were as prominent then as they are now." Nevertheless, Evelyn remains pro-active with the pageant and is an advocate for women being personally and professionally fulfilled.

"The reason I've stayed affiliated with the pageant is because of the scholarship program, but I think it's important for young women to realize that even at the grass-roots level, they get recognition. They don't have to make it all the way to Atlantic City."

She underscored that statement by adding, "This last fall, at the 2003 Pageant, they announced that more than forty million dollars was awarded from local through the national level to women all over the country. So the ground roots pageants offer a wealth of scholarship and wealth of experience. It shouldn't be just about winning the big crown."

Evelyn and Carl still reside in Pennsylvania where they are the proud grandparents of Charlotte, age ten and Drew, age seven. And yes, the proud parents of Bismarck, age one and a half.

Asked what makes her happy, Evelyn laughed heartily, then responded, "I thank God every morning when I wake up on the right side of the grass!"

Miss America 1955

Lee Meriwether

Student - the City College of San Francisco

Age -19

Height - 5' 8½''

Talent: Lee presented the dramatic reading - *Riders to the Sea*.

Photo courtesy of the Miss America Organization

What if I forget the lines? she thought. *I can't ad lib Shakespeare!*
——Lee Meriwether

Lee Meriwether

A West Coast girl, Lee Meriwether was born in Los Angeles. She moved to Phoenix with her folks at the age of three. When she was twelve, her father got a job as an accountant for a chemical compound company in San Francisco and the family relocated to the Bay area. And that's why she was in the right place at the right time to become Miss America 1955.

Like a couple of other Miss America sisters, she missed one meeting and was drafted to participate in the pageant. She never knew she was a candidate until the day of her audition. She discovered it totally by accident.

For years, local pageants were run by entrepreneurs. Lenora Slaughter, who was at the helm of the national organization, was committed to upgrading the local pageants by having the Junior Chambers of Commerce (later—Jaycees) take them over. The Chamber in San Francisco had done just that, sending letters to the colleges' social fraternities. They were each asked to select a participant for the local pageant.

All candidates were required to maintain an excellent grade average. They had to have talent in order to compete, and had to demonstrate an outgoing personality. The letter

requesting that the fraternities select a candidate was read at the meeting. Lee, however, was busy working on her Radio course finals. A broadcast major, she had to accumulate a lot of time at the studio, selecting music from City College's music library and doing general production work.

Carrying the hours to earn her degree in a double major of Radio-TV and English, with Theatre "thrown in," Lee was shouldering an enormous workload of more than twenty-one credit hours. She hadn't given the Miss America preliminaries a thought. But this co-ed's whole life was about to change course dramatically, just because she missed a meeting.

What makes this story even more delightful to share is that the people who had selected her

Lee with her mother Ethel and brother Don.

had *forgotten to tell her!* Scurrying from one class to another, Lee ran into an old friend from high school.

"How's it going?" he asked.

"Fine," she said. "I've got all my 78s lined up."

"Are you going to do a record pantomime?"

"What?"

"For the Miss San Francisco thing."

"What Miss San Francisco thing?" Lee asked, wide-eyed.

The conversation must have sounded much like a play by Ionesco. Finally, her friend was able to break through the fog. He said, "You're one of five gals representing City College. Auditions are today!"

Her shocked response was, "I *have* to do this?!"

The Chamber's recruitment had been so successful that nearly two hundred and fifty young women had applied. Auditions were spread over a three-day period.

"This was at noon," Lee explained. "I called my mother. Mommie called my father. Daddy called an executive at the Fairmont Hotel to see if the pageant were indeed on the up and up. Then on I went, to my next class."

Just two hours later, Lee was on her way downtown. She decided en route to do a pantomime she had done in high school for USO shows. It was a pantomime about a high school girl who sits on her gum at a dance. After she arrived, checking to see if her name was truly on the roster, she sat outside the ballroom to wait. Suddenly, she realized she was hearing a sophisticated aria from Madame Butterfly, followed by an exceptional pianist playing Moonlight Serenade. Finally, she peeked through the door to see a lovely ballerina dancing to the music of Swan Lake.

Scrambling to come up with something more worthy than a silly pantomime, Lee suddenly recalled a Romeo and Juliet monologue she had memorized for a class. She toyed with that idea, then insecurity grabbed her and she thought, *What if I forget the lines? I can't ad lib Shakespeare!*

Just at that moment, they called her name. In the four or five seconds it took to walk across the ballroom to greet the judges, something flashed through her head. "I remembered the soliloquy in *Riders to the Sea.*" What

Lee as Losira in *Star Trek.*

she didn't recall, she hoped she could ad lib if she needed to.

"And I did. Afterwards, I prayed that my Irish accent had been acceptable. I thought at least I had tried."

Lee forgot all about the audition for the next two weeks. She received a letter saying she was one of sixteen semi-finalists. "I've come to learn that when you audition for something, don't worry about it afterwards. I've found that if you don't linger on it, then you're seldom disappointed when it doesn't happen."

She didn't have to be disappointed this time. She went out immediately and bought a copy of the play and re-memorized it, working with Mrs. Dickson, her former drama teacher at George Washington High School, until she had the monologue down pat. "She even let me use the costume I'd used in high school. I wore that costume and my dad's black socks."

Lee was happy to be in the preliminaries as a contender, but had already selected the young woman she thought would win. "She was a writer and had already written a book and a

As Cat Woman

play. And… "Lee said, still recalling the admiration she had for her colleague, "she read one of her original poems."

But the title of Miss San Francisco would go to Lee Meriwether and no one was more surprised. The Miss California Pageant was held in Santa Cruz and Lee took that title as well.

To prepare for the Miss America Pageant, Lee went to Los Angeles.

"There were people there who wanted to meet me–Warner Brothers wanted to give me a screen test and two of the judges, Al Tresconi, the casting director at MGM and Bud Westmore, the famous makeup artist had both wanted to help me. I couldn't let those opportunities pass me by."

While in Los Angeles, Lee suffered a severe emotional blow. "I was staying with a friend and his mom. He had been in drama class with me at college." (Years later, he became Lee's personal makeup artist. Scott Hamilton is now a makeup artist for the Frazier show).

Scott's mom, Gina, received a call from Lee's mother in San Francisco. It fell upon Scott to deliver the bad news. Lee's father had suffered a cerebral hemorrhage and died. He was only forty-eight. Numb with grief and shock, Lee was given a book from Gina's book shelf. It was *Angel Unaware*, the book Dale Evans Rogers had written about the little girl she and Roy had lost at the age of two. Lee felt comforted by that book and flew home, knowing she would never see her father again.

It was so difficult for her to think of preparing for a pageant after such a loss. How could she prepare for a talent presentation, put her heart and soul into smiling and being upbeat when her heart was breaking? Lee told officials she was dropping out. They quickly reminded her that her scholarship award money won as Miss San Francisco and Miss California would have to be returned as well as the scholarship money she would receive for competing in Atlantic City. After discussing the dilemma with her mom, she decided that her father would have wanted her to go on. At least her college would be paid for, and he certainly would have wanted that for her.

Lee's mother finally capped the decision when she said, "He was looking forward to Atlantic City. He'll be watching."

"And sure enough," Lee says, "when I won in Atlantic City, I thought maybe Daddy *was* there! I just couldn't believe it. Because when I got to know the ladies there, I thought they were so beautiful, so fantastic. I think I just won by accumulating so many points as everyone's second-place winner." Lee's humility was sincere.

Asked about the year of her reign, she chides herself. "I rue the day that I didn't keep a journal. I tell every new Miss America to please keep a journal. I know they think they'll remember all this the rest of their lives, but it goes so fast and we're so busy, it's just impossible. They should write something every night."

She does remember one very special meeting, however. She met Juan Peron before he was ousted from Argentina. This was quite an experience, according to Lee.

Lee's stunning career in the limelight began during her reign. She had two appearances on the Philco Television Playhouse that year. She was asked to be on the *TODAY* Show as their first woman on-air editor.

"I did that for a year and two months, then started doing appearances on episodic TV," she explains. "I used the scholarships to study theatre with Lee Strasburg in New York."

Lee's television career took off immediately. At twenty-three, she married Frank Aletter, an actor whom she had met in a dance class. They had dated for six months, were engaged for a year and were married for fifteen years. They had two lovely daughters, now grown. Lesley Aletter is a stunt woman and her work can be seen in the most recent Alien movie. She did the stunts for Sigourney Weaver. Kyle Oldham is currently busy being a wife to Rory and "Mommie" to daughter Ryan. She is an

In a performance of *Lion in Winter*.

actress as well. Both daughters live in the Los Angeles area and remain close to Lee, working together whenever possible.

Asked about her first marriage, Lee responded, "It was a good marriage while it lasted. After fifteen years, we just grew apart. We had moved to L.A. after we married. He got a series, *Bringing up Buddy*, which was on for a year (television was still black and white at that time)."

After her divorce, Lee was alone for fourteen years, busy with her kids and her career. During that time, she did a lot of television. "I did the *Barnaby Jones* series for eight years. My mom lived with the girls and me. I don't know that I would have had the career I had without her help." Lee recently lost her mother at ninety-four.

After so many years alone, Lee was quite content and wasn't looking for anything. But that's just when love seems to come along.

"I was getting ready to do the play, *Angel Street*. It's the original of *Gas Light*. I had asked the producer, a friend of mine, if I could be involved in the casting. I wanted Kyle, my daughter, then twenty, to play the maid. And I had asked for certain other actors. The producer agreed, but wanted a fellow by the name of Marshall Borden to play the inspector.

During the first rehearsal, in our read-through, he read well and seemed quite pleasant. Then he started really working on the character, each day coming in trying a different attitude, different stage business, twirling his hat, using a different accent, all very inventive and exciting to watch."

Lee found herself going out to dinner with Marshall a couple of times, just as fellow actors. As her admiration for him began to grow, she discovered that both of them had been married the same length of time and divorced the same amount of time.

The play ran for four weeks at Earl Holliman's Fiesta Dinner Theatre in San Antonio, Texas. Marshall then went on to the Wichita Opera Company for a singing role and Lee said to him, "I'd love to see you do that."

He responded, "You're welcome to come and watch."

Suddenly she found herself following him to Toronto, then to Alaska to do another role. Now, she laughs, "I suddenly realized I was chasing him all over the country and wondered, *Why am I doing this?* Duh! I guess I just kept chasing him until he caught me!" They were married in 1987.

According to Lee, "it was such a nice, slow, wonderful relationship that grew and continues to grow, which is just

Get a grip, Lee! At the end of the 2003 pageant, Lee poses with the grips preparing to strike the set. Everybody loves Lee!
Photo by Kate Kitchen

Lee with daughters Kyle and Lesley

lovely."

The magic is still very much in evidence. During our initial interview, Marshall teased her from the kitchen as she tried thoughtfully to answer questions. He was definitely trying to upstage her, and nearly did, for in addition to his tongue-in-cheek responses, he was preparing a gourmet Sunday brunch consisting of an omelet and Spanish potatoes with capers and dill. Throughout the interview, they bantered back and forth as if they were still courting.

While in New York, close to current theatrical obligations, Lee's recurring role of Ruth Martin on the ABC soap *All My Children* and Marshall's playwriting, the happy couple live in his "old, small" bachelor pad, with a "small" living room, a "smaller" kitchen, and a Murphy bed that comes out of the wall. "It's VERY small!" she laughs, adding, "We really work at our marriage. Plus, you have to get along when you share such a small space with only one closet!"

She attributes part of their happiness to the fact that they share so many interests: "the business, life, love—so far so good. We're having fun!"

Marshall's *The Count of Monte Cristo* adaptation was sold to the National Theatre of Canada and was pre-

sented at the Stratford Festival for the 2004 season.

They now spend most of their time in Los Angeles when they're not working.

They have done musicals together and have been performing in *Plaza Suite* "all over the place." Marshall performed in *Pirates of Penzance* for the Chatauqua Opera Company and they both appeared there in Stephen Sondheim's *A Little Night Music.*

For those who haven't seen Lee on the soap, they might remember her as Cat Woman in the original Batman movie. Adam West was her leading man. Then she did *Time Tunnel* for a year with Robert Colbert and James Darren. Many will remember her in the role of Losira in a Star Trek episode (Lee now has a sci-fi cult following)...and of course her eight-year run on *Barnaby Jones* co-starring with Buddy Ebsen. As if she weren't busy enough, she added a new aspect to her career, that of the character voices in John Saul's audio version of

Lee and Marshall with granddaughter Ryan

56

his best-selling Gothic thrillers. In 2003-2004, Lee performed in a 21-city tour in the 20th anniversary all-star company of *Nunsense*.

Asked how she remains so grounded though a celebrity most of her life, Lee thought for a minute before responding. "My parents offered us the family values we needed. They always let us choose, as soon as we were old enough. They didn't force their beliefs on us. My brother and I were given the opportunity to go to church—or not. We weren't forced, we really wanted to go." (Lee's brother Don lives in the Bay area and has four daughters of his own.)

There seems to be a remarkable absence of trauma and tragedy in Lee's life. When asked about that, Lee responded, "I've been so lucky. Our family has been healthy. Mommie lived a long life, I've just been so fortunate."

Lee and Ryan

But Marshall's special brunch is ready and he is preparing to serve his leading lady. And Lee Meriwether is excused from a very pleasant interview to share a lovely meal with her gourmet-cook-of-an-actor-husband in their "very, very small" apartment in Manhattan.

Lee Meriwether certainly is a lucky lady. And it seems she's led a charmed life. But make no mistake about it, her successes should be attributed to the fact that from the onset, she has always worked hard, remained grounded and maintained a positive outlook. Lee Meriwether was and is, for all her talent and beauty, for all her celebrity, still just a truly humble woman, a woman of unquestioned grace.

Miss America 1958

Marilyn Van Derbur

Student - University of Colorado
State - Colorado
Age - 19   Height - 5' 8½''

Talent: Marilyn performed an organ recital of *Tea for Two* and *Tenderly.*

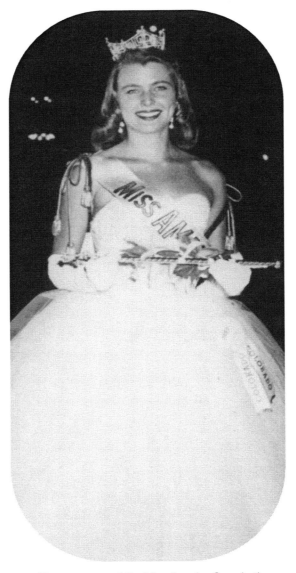

Photo courtesy of the Miss America Organization

"A list of my accomplishments times one hundred pales before the most
significant accomplishment of my life—I survived incest."
—Spoken on the night Marilyn Van Derbur Atler broke her silence.

Marilyn Van Derbur

We all know that the person who leaves the room during a meeting is the one elected. This is exactly how Marilyn Van Derbur took the first step to become America's sweetheart. During her sophomore year at the University of Colorado - Boulder, Marilyn left a meeting to respond to a long distance telephone call from boyfriend Larry Atler. It was a moment that would change her life forever and possibly the catalyst that saved her life.

The meeting was with her sorority sisters of Pi Beta Phi. When she returned to the meeting, she was told they had drafted her as their choice to represent them in the Miss America preliminaries. She had only two words to say, and she said them firmly. "I decline."

"You can't decline!" was the excited response. "We've already nominated you and we'll be fined if you don't follow through. Be a good sport, Marilyn!"

Her pleas fell on deaf ears. Marilyn would be a good sport, a role she was used to. She would play the Hammond organ beautifully in the talent competition. She would glide across the stage—beautifully. She would respond to questions from the judges—beautifully. Marilyn would be the perfect representative for Pi Beta Phi and the state of Colorado, and she would strive to do it all—beautifully. This was how she had been taught to perform throughout her entire childhood. After all, hers was the perfect life. She was a perfect child from a perfect family, with a perfectly successful, handsome and prominent father as the head of the family.

Marilyn was encouraged throughout her idyllic childhood to take music lessons and she excelled at playing the piano. She was encouraged to participate fully in life and to take lessons in everything that might remotely interest her, so she would become an accomplished, well-rounded young lady. A lady of quality. She had learned not only to ride horses, but to train them as well. She was very good at that. She learned to behave with decorum, to dress well, to speak quietly—to be daddy's perfect little girl.

All her training would now serve her well, for she would suddenly become Miss Colorado and two months later, in September—Miss America. Yet no one was more surprised than

Marilyn at three.

59

Marilyn with her sisters

Marilyn.

"My goal was never to become Miss America. My only goal was to not fall off the runway!" she admitted with candor. "But—" she added thoughtfully, "my year as Miss America set the stage for the rest of my life. That one year made my current mission possible."

To this day, Marilyn attests to the startling fact that in a way, the worst possible thing that could have happened to her was to become Miss America. For the *perfect* young woman had suppressed a deep, dark secret. On the night of the crowning, something just didn't feel right. She knew she wasn't worthy of this great honor, but she couldn't explain why, not even to herself.

This beautiful young woman with sparkling green eyes and an engaging smile stood for a moment at the end of the runway, scepter in hand, her gown billowing around her as if she were standing on a cloud. Her brilliant crown sparkled in communion with the tears in her eyes as she accepted the cheers of twenty-two thousand onlookers in Convention Hall.

But inside the heart and mind of that beautifully composed woman, the woman who was at that very moment the focus of every little girl's dream, was hidden a severely traumatized little girl—a little girl who had been sexually molested by her successful, handsome, dynamic father from the time she was five years old until the age of eighteen. Marilyn was now twenty and consciously knew nothing of those horrific nights buried in her past, her recent past. And still, even this night—especially this night, something felt terribly, terribly wrong inside.

The worst possible thing that can happen to an incest survivor, according to Marilyn, is to be made yet another model for perfection, a representation of what people think is right and pure and good about our young American women. The only reason Marilyn could stand on that stage, seemingly serene, perfectly poised and patently in control was because Marilyn had *absolutely no memory* of what she had endured from her father. Years of night visits in her room did not exist in her conscious mind. Her brain would not permit her to recall the physical pain, the emotional tor-

The Van Derbur sisters going for a spin.

Marilyn with her family the night she was crowned.

ture, the sense of worthlessness, of shame and disgrace.

As with many children who suffer severe emotional trauma, her brain had completely removed her consciously from that horrific experience. She had suffered a dissociative disorder and successfully split her mind into *two* children—children whom she learned much later to identify as *the day child* and *the night child*.

The day child excelled at every single thing she could possibly accomplish in order to counterbalance the unspeakable horror the night child had to endure at the hands of someone who was supposed to be her knight in shining armor, her sole protector.

How else could a five-year-old child possibly handle the mental chaos, the emotional terror of being subjected to this kind of treatment over and over again by someone she relied on to provide for her well-being, someone whose job it was to love her and keep her safe from harm?

The year of her reign was a blur. Marilyn explains, "I never took myself that seriously, but I took the job of being Miss America seriously. I made myself be the very best Miss America I could possibly be, just as I had struggled to do everything well in my childhood."

Several former Miss Americas who were interviewed for this book remarked at what an "excellent speaker, an exceptional presenter, a wonderful talent, a generous spirit" Marilyn Van Derbur is, calling her a role model for all Miss Americas. Little did they know that during her reign, she had had lots of practice in trying to be perfect in every way. She strived constantly to overcome her shame, a shame that she didn't even consciously recognize.

She recalls that during her tour, she had panic attacks every single day. Before engagements, she would spend hours preparing for her appearances, and in between dizzy spells and feelings of actually wanting to vomit, she would walk out onto a stage or up to a podium and calmly, quietly, look around at her audience and smile, the perfect picture of poise. But her insides were churning and she didn't know why. She remembers the intensity, even today, more than forty years later.

"I lived and breathed being the best Miss America I could be. I did the best I could do. I had walked through the fires to get there. Every time I spoke, I thought I was going to die!"

She remembers the first time she was able to put a name to her condition: *panic attack*.

"I saw a talk show about someone who described the raw terror of it, the total feeling of despair. Now at least I could define it. I just didn't know why I had those symptoms."

These attacks didn't just occur during the year of her reign. Marilyn suffered severe panic attacks throughout her adult life, throughout her career as a public speaker, throughout her marriage, throughout the decades until her fifties, when she finally admitted publicly that she was an incest survivor.

"Once my memory was finally triggered, by a kind and generous youth minister I had known since my childhood, I was released. I had always felt that if people knew who I really was, they wouldn't even let me in the room.

Marilyn with her father.

Now they welcome me with open arms. As soon as I *named* it, it *freed* me. And now there's *no more shame!*"

It took years for Marilyn to recognize what had happened to her, to name it, to confront the realization of the experience, to confront her attacker—her very own father. She needed to finally share her realization with those closest to her in order to begin the healing process and her struggle became a long, arduous process. And by her side, from the moment she named it, stood her *real* protector, a man who had loved her since they were adolescents, a man who had waited patiently by until she found herself.

Marilyn's youth minister, Reverend D.D. Harvey of the Montview Presbyterian Church in Denver, finally uncovered the mystery of Marilyn Van Derbur. A good friend for years, he found himself feeling rather disturbed at occasional comments she would let slip in his presence. He had tried to figure it out for a long time—what could possibly be behind this gentle and graceful demeanor, this perfectly composed face? What could this lovely young woman be hiding that was obviously so terribly upsetting?

One day while lunching with Marilyn, now in her early twenties, at the Beverly Hills Hotel, D.D. put together two cathartic words in the same sentence—*father* and *bedroom*. In recalling the moment, Marilyn believes he may even have asked her if her father had come into her bedroom at night. To this day, Marilyn doesn't quite recall the exact words that broke the dam, only their impact.

What she does remember, however, is that she felt his words cut through the core of memory her brain had so carefully protected for so many years. Sitting in the middle of a posh Beverly Hills restaurant, she suddenly remembered—remembered it all. Marilyn crumpled into convulsive sobs, sobs that went on and on until she thought they would never stop.

Suddenly she remembered. Yes—her father had come into her bedroom at night and now three people knew it, her rich and powerful *loving* father, her special friend and confidante, Reverend D. D. Harvey, and finally—Marilyn herself.

She had already begun a self-destructive pattern, a pattern incest survivors are prone to, subconsciously feeling that they are both shamed and worthless. She had married a quasi-celebrity, a professional football player. Three months later, she divorced him. Had she not uncovered her deep dark secret, Marilyn feels today that she would have continued on such self-destructive behavior until her unknown torment might have forced her to take her life.

"D.D. saved my life that day, and stopped me from continuing down the path of self-destruction because he reached out to a wounded little girl who had become a desperately wounded young woman."

For nine years, since their first meeting at a Student Council event at East High School in Denver at the age of fifteen, Larry Atler had waited patiently for Marilyn to respond to his love.

"When we met," she said warmly, "I just felt my *soul* wrap around him. I never permitted boys to kiss me, but somehow, on our first date, as we were dancing, I looked into Larry's

Marilyn and Larry at home

eyes and he kissed me. I remember it as if it were yesterday."

They had dated on and off for years, but every time their relationship began to take a serious turn, Marilyn would push him aside and run away. For nine years, Larry had been pushed around and he was tired of the games. He had finally given up. And yet, his was the first name she mentioned when D.D. brought her back to reality. Between sobs, she had begged him, "You mustn't tell anyone!"

Most people would have promised immediately not to tell a soul. But this had gone too far. Her friend and pastor wisely responded, "Who mustn't I tell?"

"You must never, ever tell Larry," she whispered quietly, her shame overwhelming. She knew Larry would never want her now and she couldn't blame him.

D. D. stood up. "Then Larry's the only one we *have* to tell!" Firmly taking her arm, he walked her directly to the pay telephone in the lobby. They placed the telephone call that would change her life once again.

As fate would have it, they were able to reach Larry. He was living in Denver at the time. Marilyn had been living in New York since the end of her tour. He answered the telephone and she responded, exhausted from emotion, "I need to talk to you. Will you fly to Los Angeles?"

She should have expected the terse reply, but was too vulnerable to have prepared for it. "No. I've come running for nine years. I can't do it anymore."

Marilyn began to sob. Picking up the cue, D.D. took the phone from her, telling Larry, "If you *ever* loved her, Larry, you have to come."

The next afternoon found the three sitting quietly in a church office in Los Angeles—a minister and trusted friend, a young woman who was more vulnerable on this day than she

had ever been in her life, and Larry Atler, a young attorney who had long ago given up on ever winning the heart of the love of his life.

Ever the serious young man, he briskly took out a yellow legal pad, prepared to take notes. He had no idea why he had been called. He never could have imagined the depths of emotion the following words would bring, to him or to Marilyn.

D.D. was the first to speak. "Marilyn has something to tell you."

Larry waited patiently, quietly, tersely.

"I can't." Marilyn began to sob. She couldn't bring herself to say the word *incest*. Afraid to look him in the eyes, afraid of the disdain and rejection she knew she would see on his face, she paused, sobbing, still unable to speak.

"You have to, Marilyn," D.D. encouraged her.

"As I told him," Marilyn recalls quietly, "I had put myself in the *shame* position, head bowed, shoulders hunched over. When I finally looked up, I saw *total love* on his face and I knew then that *he understood all!*" Even today, Marilyn cannot tell that story without tearing up, without reliving the wonder of that incredible moment.

This was the man who stood by her side, day after day, year after year—the man who gave her all the time required to deal with the trauma done to that abused little girl inside her, the child who had been emotionally beaten into submission and shame for so many years. He

63

Marilyn and Jennifer

stood by and helped the damaged little child grow into a woman, a whole person, a person who would eventually become a freely loving and trusting wife and mother.

Larry Atler is a name that belongs to a hero. He was Marilyn's hero many years ago, has remained Marilyn's hero through the years, and will always be Marilyn's hero. After a marriage of forty years, his reward is to be so totally cherished and respected that his wife cannot even speak about him without emotion.

Their marriage has been sorely tested through the years. Her admission, her awful recognition of what happened in her childhood was just the first small step in a long, painful journey that will never end.

Marilyn suffered a complete emotional breakdown when their daughter was five, the same age she had been when the abuse started. After intense and ongoing psychiatric therapy, she finally said one day, "I don't want to live in this body anymore." More had to be done and Marilyn didn't know how to save herself or her family.

Part of the healing process was in finding the strength to tell their daughter. Jennifer was only thirteen. Marilyn sat before her one afternoon, scarcely able to breathe. "I truly feared that she wouldn't want me to be her mother anymore," she confessed quietly. But instead, it was Jennifer who sat weeping with her, saying over and over, "Mom, you didn't do anything wrong! You didn't do *anything* wrong!"

At the time, Marilyn was working with underprivileged street kids. Here she was, wife of a prominent Denver attorney, a former Miss America, a wife and mother from the right side of the tracks. And it was Jennifer who kept encouraging her to tell her story.

"Mom, the kids will relate to you better. You've got to start telling people."

But Marilyn still held back, thinking that if

people knew who she really was, they wouldn't even let her approach them, let alone talk with them.

One of the problems was her father's cavalier attitude during their one and only confrontation. Marilyn finally gathered the courage one day to approach her father. She talked to him about how he had destroyed her childhood, and literally destroyed her emotionally.

His response was pathetic and vile for someone guilty of such a charge.

"If I'd known it would hurt you, I wouldn't have done it," he said simply. Case closed.

They never spoke of it again. When he died, the local newspapers extolled his virtues for what monumentally philanthropic acts he had performed for the community.

But what about Marilyn's mother? How incredibly sad and inexplicable it was that she defended her husband to the very day she died. Along with a sister who also spoke out, Marilyn calculates that among the girls, there was sexual abuse going on in their *lovely, perfect home* for eighteen years. How can a pedophile live such an existence for so long and his wife turn the other cheek? It's a question she has continued to wrestle with throughout the years.

The support Marilyn continued to receive from Larry's parents helped to make up for the loss, both physical and emotional. "God gave me an incredible mother-in-law," Marilyn said gratefully, her voice thick with emotion. "Nan is so nurturing and loving and caring. She doesn't realize what she does. She doesn't get it."

"What do I do, darling?" she'll ask.

And Marilyn states simply, "For one thing, she'd lay down her life for me!" Marilyn praises her mother-in-law for empowering their family, saying that in her own family, while growing up, she was taught that women had no

Marilyn at a speaking engagement

power.

"My father-in-law loved me, too," Marilyn explained. "I felt his love to the depths of my being. He'd look at me when I'd come into the room and his eyes would just twinkle! He died some time ago. I tell incest survivors now that your family doesn't have to be blood, you can find other family. I'm so incredibly blessed."

This woman who still has never slept one night without medication, whose life was nearly destroyed from year after year after year of sexual abuse at the hands of her own father, this woman who has given of herself over the years, talking, listening, crying with those who need her support still considers herself blessed. Finally she can be at peace, having wrestled through a lifetime with the demons that tortured her existence.

The demons stopped just a few years ago as Marilyn, at the age of fifty-three, stood before an audience in Denver, Colorado at a center for abused children. She told the story—with her mother present—of her nights of terror. She looked around the room to see if her worthlessness were reflected on the faces before her. There was only love and understanding on those faces. And thus began the walk toward a

peaceful, productive life for Marilyn Van Derbur Atler.

For years, she appeared as a keynote speaker for major corporations and civic groups, offering inspiration wherever she went. Today she's on a mission. Those who listen to her find an acceptance, an unconditional love and support, from one who understands the human condition so well. Then they are able to find the courage to tell their own story—and tell it and tell it until finally, somebody listens!

Men and women stand in line for hours, needing to touch her, to receive a hug, to share her tears. Sometimes they just want to thank her for sharing her. And when she comes home exhausted from so many tears, there he is, standing quietly in the doorway—a gentle smile on his face, waiting for the woman he has loved since he was fifteen. Larry Atler, attorney, husband, father and still—above all else—Marilyn's hero.

Marilyn's book, *Miss America By Day*, was published in the summer of 2003 and at this writing, was on the Best Seller List in Colorado for fourteen weeks.

To book Marilyn as a speaker or to acquire her book, visit www.MissAmericaByDay.com

Miss America 1960

Lynda L. Mead

Student - University of Mississippi
State -Mississippi
Age - 20   Height - 5' 7''

Talent: Lynda presented a dramatic reading.

Photo courtesy of the Miss America Organization

"As Miss America, you're speaking every day, traveling constantly, meeting one schedule after another. It was exhausting, but the education I got far exceeded anything I could have received in a classroom."
—Lynda Mead Shea

Lynda Mead

Lynda Mead caught the brass ring the first time she rode the carousel. She was a nineteen-year-old sophomore at the University of Mississippi when her Chi Omega sisters called in a favor. She had made a promise the year before, a promise she was now obligated to keep—one that would change her entire life. Lynda had never entered a competition of any kind. She had never given pageants a thought. Her sorority sisters had literally ganged up on her one night during her freshman year and pleaded with her to enter the Miss University Pageant.

Her response was succinct. "No, no, absolutely not!"

They argued until one girl finally said, "I'll tell you what. If you don't do it this year, will you promise to do it next year?"

As Lynda tells it, "When you're eighteen, next year will never come." It seemed a long time off. But in 1959, her sisters kept her to her word and Lynda found herself in the backyard at home, on school breaks, letting her brother direct her talent presentation. It was a comedic sketch entitled *Schizophrenia*. It was about a teenage girl changing her personality. It's still a surprise to her that she won. She still declares today that she won in spite of her talent presentation, not because of it.

The strange thing was that Lynda didn't even realize at the time that the university pageant was the preliminary to the state pageant, which led to the national pageant. Before she had time to worry whether she may have gotten in over her head, she had become Miss University, Miss Mississippi, and in short order, Miss America!

Her reign brought with it the usual rewards, and for a girl from Natchez, Mississippi, this was bigger and better than a trip to Disneyland. There was a fashion tour in Europe that took place in London, Rome and Geneva. Joseph Bancroft Company (Banlon and Everglaze fabrics) was one of the pageant sponsors and that year underwrote the fashion extravaganza. Lynda stayed at the Dorchester in London and felt every bit a movie star.

The impact on her life was monumental and taught her to reach for the stars. "That year

Lynda in 1980
Photo by Tom Mitchell, Jr

67

Photo by Poland Photographers Memphis TN

inspired in me a desire to see so much more of the world. It jump-started me and made me realize that you can do anything if you decide you want to do it. I knew then that I wanted to travel and to know the world."

A charmed life so far? Not so, for Lynda Mead, throughout her young life had held a sorrow and a secret that had colored her entire life as a child. She was already determined it would not affect her life as a woman. Her family had moved from New Orleans to Natchez, Mississippi when Lynda was six. Her mother worked at home as a housewife. Her father had bought a Ford dealership and started his new career. Lynda and her brother did not seem to be affected by the move. It's easy to make friends when you're young. But their mom had not adjusted so easily, having left her folks behind.

Lynda's family had a solid church background, but it didn't offer all the support she needed. Her mother became an alcoholic and was, for most of Lynda's childhood, a recluse. The young girl couldn't bring friends home and had to quickly adapt to becoming the adult in the family.

"I never remember learning anything from her," Lynda said gently, and her voice reflected that she was speaking from a heart of understanding rather than judgment. "Mom was one of twelve kids in a big, Irish Catholic family. Maybe she lost her support group when they moved away from New Orleans, who knows?"

All Lynda does remember is a series of confrontations and crying scenes with her mother calling out, "Nobody needs me! Nobody cares about me!" And from time to time, her mother would be in the hospital, then she would come home.

"There wasn't the support and professional help for alcoholics that there is now," Lynda explained. "There wasn't an awareness."

And what could a young girl be expected to do about it? She merely maintained, attended school, studied, played with friends (but not at home) and became *joined at the hip* with her brother. "We were so close," Lynda recalled. "I remember in the mid-'50s when Herb, my brother, became King of the Pilgrimage." This is a tourist attraction in Natchez that takes several months to prepare for, culminating in a month-long celebration. "During those nine months of preparation, Mother never took a drink." She paused, then continued quietly, "The night his reign was over, she went on a binge. You could never count on her."

Lynda was shopping for dresses for the Miss America Pageant. She had so little time, certainly no time to waste even a precious second. Remembering how well her mother had behaved during Herb's celebration, she drove her mom to Jackson, Mississippi. She was on a quest for a beautiful wardrobe and thought that if she were to share this experience, it might be a turning point for her mother.

"But you couldn't let your guard down for a minute. Mom was so sick and so nervous during the trip, it just wasn't worth the effort of taking her with me, worrying about her every second."

She was so exhausted and disheartened that on the trip home, she could hardly speak. What had happened in their lives that required a young woman to switch roles with her mother?

When asked how her mother had handled

companion, woke her to tell her the news and they caught a morning flight to New Orleans. Even Miss Americas aren't impervious to grief and loss. Lynda had lost her mother twice, but although she still had no answers, this time there would be closure. Trouper that she was, she resumed her duties the next week.

Immediately upon completing her tour, Lynda went straight back to school. She had missed her classmates and sorority sisters. And she desperately wanted to graduate with her class, even after being gone for a year. "It wasn't difficult to go back," she explained, "just different." She signed up for twenty-two hours over two semesters, then fourteen hours during the summer, and somehow kept her grades up while she used her weekends and breaks to continue her appearances as a former Miss America.

Upon graduation Lynda moved to New York to attend Parsons School of Design.

"I had grown up in a beautiful town with beautiful architecture. And my scholarship permitted me to study in New York at a wonderful school where I could learn interior design."

A friend introduced her to someone very special. "His name was John Shea and he was a surgeon," she explained, her voice softening. "That was in 1963."

Lynda was quite smitten with the up-and-coming doctor who had graced the cover of Life Magazine the year before. He had been featured in a story of one hundred young

the media, Lynda responded, "She was so reclusive, the press wouldn't have been able to get to her. Besides, people back then tended to ignore the disease. They just swept it under the rug."

Knowing the woman had controlled her drinking during her brother's special celebration caused Lynda to wonder if her mother could have controlled herself better afterwards and didn't. Perhaps it was a choice. No one will ever know, because her mother's health deteriorated so completely that she died at the age of forty-eight.

Lynda was on tour as Miss America when the persistent ringing of the telephone shattered her peaceful dreams in the middle of the night. Peggy O'Neill Lloyd, her traveling

The Sheas in 1997—Paul, John, Susanna, Lynda and Peter with Dearie and Bo

Americans who were said to be pioneers in their fields.

John had been divorced for eight years and was raising two children, eleven and thirteen, alone. In December 1964, they were married, and Lynda was blessed with an instant family.

Lynda and John eventually honored the family name with the birth of three more children, now grown. Paul followed in his father's footsteps and is a practicing physician, Susanna is an attorney and Peter is completing his MBA at Vanderbilt.

Coming from a home of secrets, Lynda always was especially close to Herb, her brother. Lynda had lost her father in 1976 and ten years ago, lost Herb to colon cancer. He was only fifty-two. "Herb had had a bout with colon cancer ten years before and had received a clean bill of health," Lynda said. "Suddenly, ten years later, it just came back, it recurred everywhere. He died six weeks after his diagnosis." If there was good to come out of this, perhaps it was in the fact that Herb had recently moved to Memphis and for six months, he and his sister Lynda had been reunited. "This was the greatest loss," Lynda said quietly.

She's not a quitter. She's not a victim. And growing up, she didn't have things handed to her on a silver platter. She worked for everything she has attained. Lynda Mead Shea today owns an interior design business and an antique shop - French Country Imports - in Memphis. She is as much in love with her husband as she was the day they married in 1964. And as for the impact that being Miss America had on her life, Lynda said, "It's a lot of hard work, but I learned the value of that early on. And the education I got far exceeded anything I could have received in a classroom."

Miss America 1961

Nancy Fleming

State - Michigan
Age - 18   Height - 5'6''

Talent: Nancy modeled dresses she designed. Bert Parks
referred to her talent as a "reverse strip tease."

Photo courtesy of the Miss America Organization

"I learned that you need to be able to accept your imperfections and do the
best you can. I didn't have the ability to get up and sing a song and be done
with it. I had no background in public speaking. It was terrifying!"
—Nancy Fleming Lange

Nancy Fleming

Montague, Michigan was a safe, sleepy little town with a population of two thousand. And one of those two thousand residents was about to put the little town on the map. Nancy Fleming, a recent high school graduate, had enrolled at Michigan State. Her full academic scholarships included Betty Crocker and Rotary Club awards. But she still needed money for living expenses.

A high school Drama instructor had told her that he was a member of the Jaycees, a proactive civic organization in the community. Jaycees have historically sponsored pageants in small towns all over the country. He asked her to enter the pageant so he could find out what it was all about. Then, he said, after a year of college, she might be poised enough to return

Nancy with her mom.

the next year. He suggested that she *might* then be able to win the two hundred fifty dollar local scholarship.

"Actually," she laughed, "he had five girls signed up and needed six contestants in order to rent the hall." Her matter-of-fact response was immediate. "I don't have a talent."

That didn't seem to concern him. "Oh, read a poem or something."

So Nancy Fleming entered the local pageant two weeks after high school graduation and to her surprise, won Miss White Lake. The local title automatically entered her into the state competition and in short succession, she became Miss Michigan. Now the scholarship money was growing and her stress about college was easing. She would enter Michigan State in the fall and be able to concentrate on her studies without worrying about where her next meal was coming from.

The national pageant was at the time held the week after Labor Day, and there was still time to return to school. But the normally conscientious, thoroughly prepared and well-rehearsed straight-A student had forgotten to ask one important question: *What happens if you win?*

She didn't read a poem, but she won the talent portion of the national competition. No one from Montague or anyplace else, for that matter, would have believed it could be done. She didn't sing, she didn't act and she didn't dance. She had one very specially crafted talent and had to figure out how to use it. A creative and gifted seamstress, she had designed and created her wardrobe for the pageant. She

Nancy in High School

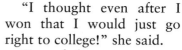

wasn't trying to impress the judges with that. It was simply cost–effective, and therein lay her talent.

"Bert Parks teased me about doing a reverse striptease," she said about her performance. Nancy developed her own skit, taking the audience through a day with a girl at the office who is changing her basic professional outfit into evening wear. It was simple, it was delightful and it was pure talent. The audience loved it and the judges obviously appreciated it because the initial promise of a year's wait for a two hundred fifty dollar reward on the local level was forgotten as she was named Miss America 1961. She had earned a scholarship award of ten thousand dollars!

That night at the Governor's Ball, while dancing with the Governor of Michigan, the impact of becoming Miss America suddenly dawned on her and she found herself wondering—*Can I get through this?* The next day, pageant officials talked with Nancy and her parents, who discovered *for the first time* that

the young woman was committed to an entire year, beginning at that moment! Nancy had absolutely no idea her whirlwind tour of the country was to begin the next day. It was just one of those things that sponsors sometimes fail to communicate to contestants. She had intended to enter the university immediately after the pageant. She was stunned.

"I thought even after I won that I would just go right to college!" she said.

One of the sponsors was Joseph Bancroft, and after watching her creative talent program, the company wasted no time using Nancy's fashion design expertise in doing fashion shows for McCall's patterns.

By this time in pageant history, each woman had a chaperone who would act as mother, sister, nursemaid, travel coordinator, public relations person and whatever else was needed. Her chaperone was Peggy O'Neill Lloyd and by necessity, they soon learned to play good cop - bad cop.

"Peggy's energy level was amazing. We'd come into a community, our time purchased by a sponsor, but every other organization in town wanted a piece of Miss America, five minutes here, five minutes there."

Nancy would always respond graciously and let Peggy take over as bad cop to get her out of the situation so she wouldn't be late for the next event.

"I learned so much on that tour," she said. "I learned to be able to accept your imperfections and do the best you can. I didn't have the ability to get up and sing a song and be done with it. I had no background in public speaking. It was terrifying!"

At the time, the Miss America Pageant did not require the women to develop a platform or discuss social issues. The basic question she was asked was, "What is it like to be Miss America?"

Nancy, a perfect student, did not like being so unprepared and she had to learn to speak on her feet. "As the year went on, I gained experiences I could use, but early on, what could I say? I didn't just want to be a beauty queen."

Oddly enough, Nancy's perception of self was that she was the smart girl, not the pretty one. The experience became surreal as she tried to adapt to what was required of her. She is quick to point out, even now, that she wasn't a 4.0 student. "Oh, I was, in high school," she admited modestly, "but in college, I had a 3.98." (Her one shameful, terrible C was in tennis.)

After her year as Miss America, even though she would have been accepted at any school in the country, she returned to Michigan State in East Lansing. "I still had a full academic scholarship waiting for me." But from the start, that college experience was not a wonderful one.

"It was a big school, and although it is a first-rate university, many students were rather provincial at the time in their response to having a Miss America on campus," she explained. "People weren't at all cool about who I was. Jerks would get drunk and call up our room at all hours. They would point and shout at me on the street. It wasn't pleasant."

Refusing to permit the negatives to outweigh her purpose, she found solace in the basement of the dormitory. "I discovered an old raggedy chair down there and it became my library. I just sat there and studied. It was too horrible to be on campus. Then on the weekends, I'd put on my gown and crown and make appearances as a spokesperson. I finished two full years there in one year, hiding in the basement studying. I went through as fast as I could." What a sad commentary. The experience should have been such a positive one.

But she didn't 'hide' in the basement forever. At the end of the year, she came out of her

Steig (lt) and Ingrid playing in the river.

Nancy with the kids, all grown up

sanctuary long enough to meet a young Political Science student whom she married the following spring. They decided to go to the University of California at Berkeley and she switched her major from Journalism to Humanities. It was the summer of 1963. What a year to be at Berkeley, with the political awakening, the free speech movement, the beginning of the Vietnam War protest.

"Just being at Berkeley at that time offered a social environment that was so enriching," Nancy said.

Being in entertainment was evidently in the cards for Nancy. She was given the opportunity to host the television broadcast of the Miss California Pageant. Her senior year was the formative stage for her career.

"At that point, I needed to decide what to do with my education. I decided to earn teaching credentials, then halfway through, received an invitation from ABC television to do *AM San Francisco*—without an audition. They already knew who I was. That door had already been opened for me."

Nancy with parents at an ABC-TV reception.

She became busier than ever. "I was doing an early morning broadcast, doing student teaching, going to school and was pregnant with my first child."

Her husband had a job with a judge in the U.S. Federal District Court. They moved to Sacramento, but she had indeed left her heart in San Francisco. They remained in Sacramento for two years.

"My daughter was born there. I taught school and my son was born on the very day we were moving back to San Francisco. I packed up, ready to move back, had the baby then moved directly from the hospital to San Francisco. I couldn't wait to get back!" she laughed.

With two babies less than two years of age, Nancy and her husband bought what she still refers to as "an old ramshackle house in the Haight-Ashbury." The area became depressed for a few years, then turned around and became 'the' place to live. Nancy was doing some freelance work and substitute teaching. Their nine-year marriage was not to continue, however, and Nancy felt guilty.

"I looked at my parents' marriage and all the struggles they had gone through and I felt weak." The young woman who had a habit of excelling had finally failed at something very big and it hurt tremendously.

Looking back at the early years, she believes now that they married young, perhaps to escape. This was the young woman who had been plucked out of a tiny Michigan town to wear a national crown then was forced to spend her time studying alone in a basement. During her college years, she should have been dating normally, going to ball games and parties and making lots of close friendships. Coming from that history, is it any wonder she would make a decision to marry someone and try to create a safe haven for both of them? Whatever the reasons, she felt she had failed so many people. "I did feel it was a black mark against me as a Miss America."

Thinking for a moment, she continued, reflectively. "I think many Miss Americas marry very quickly after the pageant. I married the 'big man on campus,' a guy who was very much at ease socially. And even after all my travels, I still wasn't. At that point in my life, I wanted to be the quiet one and have the man take over that responsibility."

She suddenly remembered her pageant experience and shuddered. "I was the oldest of six children. Our mom worked out of necessity. I think I probably cut her heart out when I answered the pageant interview question. I said women should stay home while their children are young. That's such a young age to be asked such complex questions. We're so naïve and full of untried ideals."

And now it was a totally different era. The feminist movement had started and Nancy and her husband, through circumstance, were becoming more and more distant. "Neither of us put the energy into our marriage that you must consistently demonstrate to have a successful partnership. I had so much responsibility. Women were supposed to be able to do this, that, and the other—and be supportive as well. I'd helped him through law school and gotten through school myself, was raising the children and working—there was just too much upheaval."

So at the age of thirty, Nancy Fleming was divorced and after substitute teaching for several years, needed to find a full-time profession.

"There was a glut of teachers in California. A friend asked me to become involved in a program he was directing for television, about women and minorities. I would have the opportunity to work in all stages of production, even technical. So I audited his program and got a job working as a writer and researcher for a health related program through UCSF Medical School."

Nancy went on to become the segment producer and eventually the reporter. For perhaps the first time, in a long time, she felt she was really on track.

"It was interesting because I had gotten my first television job only because I had been Miss America. Now—I was more grounded, I had learned the business, earned each progressive step along the way and I finally realized that it was me doing this and not Miss America."

Her efforts and willingness to start at the bottom quickly led to a morning program she hosted in the Bay area for nine years.

A busy and productive professional and a happy, fulfilled mom, Nancy was now in her element. Although she dated occasionally, she didn't think she would ever marry again, and she was quite content with her life. That seems to be the time when people meet the one they're meant to be with.

Jim Lange had been hired to co-host a morning show with Nancy. He was well known for doing the *Dating Game*. After working with Nancy for a few months, Jim left the program

to do radio. But he would call her from time to time. Nancy explains, "We were just working partners, then just friendly, then friends. We met in 1975 and were married in the fall of 1978."

Asked how she knew this time that he was the right guy for her, she answered easily, "He's a grown up! He's just a real trustworthy guy, easy going, much more than I. It's a good balance," she said. "Even though we didn't work together for very long, just knowing how secure he is scored points with me. Very few men work well with a woman on the air, and there was just no competition with him. He doesn't play that game. He knows who he is."

It all must have worked because Jim and Nancy recently celebrated twenty-five years of marriage. They returned to Hawaii, where they had their first romantic get-away, to honor their silver anniversary.

Nancy has worked on various television projects, including a PBS special in cooperation with Vogue patterns and a sewing machine

Nancy during her PBS special

manufacturer. She interviewed such design notables as Bill Blass and Victor Costa, among others.

And today, she is "comfortable and happy in my marriage, and the kids have done great."

Nancy's daughter Ingrid graduated from University of California—Berkeley, with a degree in Psychology. She has a master's in Marriage and Family Therapy and a law degree from Hastings College of Law. She practices family law with her father. Nancy's son Steig is also a U.C. Berkeley graduate and has a PhD from the University of Texas - Austin in Physical Anthropology. He is currently working in Madagascar with the Institute for the Conservation of Tropical Environments. His wife, Avri Beard, is a PhD candidate at UC - Berkeley.

"I also feel blessed to have Jim's three children, their partners and two grandsons in my life," she said. "Our children are our greatest accomplishments and we often share holidays as one big extended family."

Nancy has expanded her homespun talents to include gardening. In 1992, she completed a Master Gardener's training program and became chair of the Steering Committee. The program was developed under the auspices of the University of California.

She still considers her divorce as the most traumatic issue of her adult life. "Trying to parent as partners when you're no longer married to the person is so difficult. You need to expend a lot of energy for that. But we were successful. Our children are great and we often all spend holidays together."

A life lesson well learned was tragically a result of her father's death ten years ago. "We had had a troubled relationship," she explains. "Sometimes it's more difficult when someone's dying. I was with him at the time of his death. If you had a loving relationship, and you've done everything you could do for each other, then everything's resolved. I've gained more

wisdom about it in later years, and maybe this will help someone."

She thought for a moment, then continued. "He had a rough life. He was a difficult man to be with, being bipolar and an alcoholic. As a young man, he had overcome tremendous odds and had wanted so desperately to be a 'big deal.' He was a successful B-24 pilot. He had had his moment of glory in WWII while stationed in Hawaii. He was doing weather reconnaissance. He was home on leave when his father died and his crew was shot down while he was away. He never overcame the guilt. And he never realized that sense of importance in his life, never again."

Nancy learned a great deal from her dad's life story. "I had become Miss America at a young age, and needed to remain grounded and not let that happen to me." Nancy is firm in her conviction that one's sense of self cannot rest on one moment of glory.

Her mother still lives in Michigan and Nancy and her husband visit frequently. "We have fun. This is a good time of life. He loves to play golf and I do gardening and volunteering. We love to travel. We both love art museums."

She's learned a lot of lessons in her twenty-five year marriage and in sharing them, hopes that others might benefit. "Our primary interests are independent and we both let each other be free. But I'm looking forward to his retiring. We both enjoy traveling for extended periods, and you can't do that working full time."

Her future dreams include exploring other cultures and getting to know people from foreign lands more closely. She is currently studying Italian with that goal in mind and thinking about perhaps house trading with someone in Italy for a while.

As to words for our youth, Nancy has thought long and hard about her own experiences and praises the decision in 1989 of pageant officials to require social platforms from the contestants.

"It makes them research and learn and think about issues that are important," she said. "The platform offers these young women a solid focus to talk about rather than just being Miss America."

Nancy also thinks high schools should require community service. "Besides the win-win situation of teaching students about their community and different cultures, it helps the organization—and," she smiled, "it keeps the young kids busy and out of trouble."

All this wisdom from a little girl who excelled in home economics and got straight As in high school, just a small town girl from Montague, Michigan—population two thousand.

Miss America 1962

Maria Beale Fletcher

Rockette: Radio City Music Hall
State - North Carolina
Age - 19   Height - 5' 6''

Talent: Maria danced and sang *Somebody Loves Me*
to her voice she had recorded in three-part harmony.

Photo courtesy of the Miss America Organization

"Honor with your life the loving, exploding passion—follow through.
Once you recognize the drumming—dance the dream that's true for you."
—Maria Beale Fletcher
(Excerpt from a poem "Walter" - in honor of her brother
who lost his life in an airplane accident.)

Maria Beale Fletcher

Born in Fletcher, North Carolina, Maria Beale Fletcher grew up dancing. Her parents, both professional dancers, pulled their little house trailer throughout the United States and Canada, performing their Vaudeville act in ballrooms and nightclubs. "My grandmother traveled with us and practically raised me in that little trailer," Maria said lovingly.

When Maria turned six, the family decided it was time to settle down, and the couple opened a dance studio. Born into a performing family, Maria was dancing and singing in Mountain Youth Jamborees and dance recitals as far back as she can remember.

She especially loved to tap dance, having watched her father and mother with the same kind of esteem others had for Fred Astaire and Ginger Rogers.

She went on vacation with her family one particular summer and what she saw impacted her life forever. Her folks took her to see the Rockettes at Radio City Music Hall in New York City. Maria was enthralled.

Realizing at that moment she didn't want to waste time in high school, Maria promptly shared her dream with her principal, telling him that she intended to go through high school in three years instead of four. His reply was equally as prompt. "No young woman is going through my high school in three years just to become a *Rockette*!"

So she spoke with another principal at Reynolds High School, demonstrating the moxie that is purely Maria. One principal said, "I'd be honored to have someone in my school who aspires to that goal."

Of course that's where she went, taking sum- mer courses to complete her requirements in order to graduate in three years.

Maria and her dad called the director of the Rockettes to request an audition. The response wasn't positive. The director explained that he had just finished a series of auditions and was all set for the next two years, but agreed to speak with her upon her arrival, as a professional courtesy to her family.

Just before Maria was to leave for New York, however, the local Jaycees asked her to compete in the Miss Asheville Pageant. They

Already a cover girl at 14

explained that if they could get twenty-five girls to compete, the Jaycees would win a prize and there would be a two hundred fifty dollar prize for Miss Asheville.

Maria agreed to compete, but her dad had told them, "Don't count on her being around for the year if she should win, because she's going to New York."

They agreed on the condition that Maria would return in July to compete in the Miss North Carolina Pageant. So she gave her word. The next thing she knew, Maria had won the local pageant.

Almost immediately,

A Rockette at 18 - Christmas 1960. Photo by Delmar.

she boarded a train for New York and rented a room for thirty-five dollars a week at the Tudor City Hotel across from the United Nations. With her dad's weekly gift of seventy dollars, half of her money went for room and half for food and incidentals. Her two hundred fifty dollars in prize money from the pageant paid for dancing lessons.

After she had been in the Big Apple for six weeks, Maria received a call from the Rockettes. A dancer had become very ill and had to be replaced. Did she still want to try out? Did she! After an hour-and-a-half audition, the director explained he could hire her, but only on probation. Her kicks needed to be two inches over her head. As good as she was, she just couldn't kick high enough.

Maria wouldn't let

him off the hook. Not only did she urgently promise to develop her high kick the way he wanted, but she also told him she had to ask for a leave of absence for the following July because she had given her word she would return to compete in the Miss North Carolina Pageant.

He was so bowled over by the integrity of her request and her spunk that he hired her, threatening in the same breath to fire her if she was unable to make the grade. She had six weeks to improve her kick.

"For weeks, during our breaks," she recalled, "a fellow Rockette, Lorraine Holscher, would sit on my left leg while another, Rosalie Bower would stretch my right leg, then they'd reverse positions." They did that three times a day for several weeks. At the time, they were performing the Christmas routine, *Parade of the Wooden Soldiers* (and wooden soldiers don't

Maria at 19 with her family during an Asheville homecoming.

kick).

"The schedule was incredibly grueling," said Maria. "I danced five shows a day, seven days a week for five weeks straight before getting four days off." Then she would learn a new show in three days before starting the schedule all over again.

She re-auditioned in six weeks only to hear the director say, "You're in like Flynn, only—" he paused.

She felt a lump in her throat. "Only what?" she asked, her heart racing with the fear of rejection.

"Only—your kick is an inch too high," he smiled, putting his arms around her and giving her a well-deserved hug.

So Maria Beale Fletcher became "Dancer Thirty-six," the seventh woman from stage right. She worked so hard that she damaged her feet. By February, she had broken the metatarsal arches in both feet. She was in agony. She had abused her joints so badly that her hip socket would pop loud enough for the audience to hear.

Yet her only concern was that she would have to stop dancing. "This is what our lives are about," she explained. "We're here to do the work we're able to do. That," she said reflectively, "and to love one another. Both were finally possible with the Rockettes. I had found my dream job and yet from those women, I found such wonderful, true lifelong friendships."

Although she was forced to take a few weeks off for her feet to heal, she returned to work in March, wearing heavy pancake makeup over the white bandages that covered her feet. She was in so much pain, tears would stream down her face during the routines. The doctors wanted to operate but told her if they did, she would never dance again. "I told them I couldn't have an operation. That I was Miss Asheville and had to compete in the North Carolina Pageant."

Before long, however, it was time to return to North Carolina. A friend reminded her of the mathematical odds against winning Miss North Carolina and she just shook off his comments, repeating, "I made a commitment to the Jaycees. I have to honor it."

Totally supportive, the Rockettes had gotten together to plan her going-away party and had borrowed a cape from the costume department. They created a makeshift scepter and presented her with roses and a crown made of aluminum foil. Her banner didn't read Miss North Carolina, however. It read *Miss America*! And so Maria Beale Fletcher was crowned Miss America in a dressing room backstage in Radio City Music Hall a full four months before she was crowned in Atlantic City.

After winning the Miss North Carolina Pageant, she went on to the Miss America Pageant and danced her heart out on that stage, tapping to the song, "Somebody Loves Me," a song she had recorded in three-part harmony with a band, using her own voice. The crown was hers.

She still attributes a great deal of her successful reign to her idol, Marilyn Van Derbur. "The morning after I won the title, I attended the breakfast at which Marilyn spoke. She has always been a gifted speaker. I was so nervous and feeling inadequately prepared, I expressed my anxiety to her. I said, 'I'm not brilliant. I'm not a debutante. I haven't been to college—I'm a Rockette. What do I know about public speaking—about being Miss America?'"

Maria will never forget the response. Marilyn took her hands and looked into her eyes, her words soft and gentle. "Maria, you can just be the best 'Maria-Miss America' that you can be!"

Maria took that message to heart as she started her pilgrimage of hundreds of thousands of miles she would travel that year, representing the image of who Americans had for years welcomed into their towns and cities as their sweetheart.

"The lesson began with Miss America. I wanted to honor women, then grew to love speaking. I felt I really had something to say. But the lessons throughout life, over and over have been that if I can't be Maria, then I'm not being true to my purpose, to who I am and who I'm meant to be. If we're true to the gifts God gives to us, we must be true to ourselves."

As soon as the press learned that the new Miss America was in a chorus line, rather than in college, they became intrigued. And the news was not well received by pageant officials. According to Maria, Lenora Slaughter, who ran the pageant, was very specific in her instructions.

"You are to *play down* the Rockettes. You are not to go around the country talking about your involvement with them."

Maria with Jackie Mayer, Miss America 1963. Maria crowned Jackie in September 1962.

What she had worked so hard for now seemed to be for nothing. Maria was proud of her association with the Rockettes and they were equally proud of her. The girls had requested that she return to New York for a homecoming so they could honor her with a party. They had sent her telegrams, letters, flowers. But Slaughter refused to permit Maria to return their phone calls, saying, "If you do go back and play this to the hilt, I will see to it that the crown is removed from your head."

Maria really struggled. *What had she done that was so shameful?* Yet she was reticent to challenge the system. "In the South, you're raised to be totally respectful of authority. A good girl does what she's told. I wanted to be the best Miss America I could possibly be!"

She was devastated that she couldn't go back to share her success with the girls she had worked so hard with, the girls who had completely supported her through her rookie year.

She remembered Marilyn Van Derbur coming to visit her. She said, "When I became Miss America, I felt I had earned the title. Then during the whole year, I felt I was having to earn it again, every day."

Maria was no less proud of earning her sixty-seven dollars and fifty cents a week, take-home pay from the Rockettes that year than she was of earning seventy thousand dollars in appearances as Miss America.

That conflict remained internalized for years. She admits, "I admired Lenora Slaughter so much, but she gave me so much pain over that."

She has since come to a place of forgiveness, gaining a greater understanding of her unwillingness to stand up for herself. It was, after all, another time.

"The scepter is a double-edged sword," she

Maria with Vanessa Williams outside a stage door in 1994. Vanessa was performing in *Kiss of the Spiderwoman*.

explained. "I was no more *wonderful* at nineteen than I was at eighteen, when I had won my audition as a Rockette. What I learned in later years," she said pensively, "is that it's none of my business what others think of me. It's what I think of me that matters. I must always honor my inner self."

"I took the *job* very seriously, but I was careful to not take *myself* too seriously."

And what did she learn? "I was the first one in a long time to visit our troops in England, Germany and France; the Berlin wall was constructed a month before I was crowned. How fortunate we were, I thought, to be able to pray to our God and have the freedom of expression that we are allowed as Americans. I really felt privileged, especially to be traveling with a former history teacher who made everything come alive for me. But another thing I loved most about being Miss America was having the ability to be in the presence of ordinary people—just like me."

She remembers speaking with an eighty-five-year-old woman who had asked for an autograph because Maria reminded her of her own daughter by the same name, a girl who had been killed at Maria's age. "And then to be in the presence of a five-year-old who asked to wear my crown. That's what being Miss

America is all about."

Upon further reflection about the pageant experience, she has conflicting philosophies, recognizing all the good it does, with scholarships and offering women the experiences of a lifetime.

Maria's advice is molded from years of introspection and self-examination. "She's a nobody one day, then the next day she has a crown, so she'd better not take herself too seriously."

Maria is reminded of the Vanessa Williams incident. "This is why I can turn around, years later, and empathize completely with Vanessa Williams. When they jerked away her crown because they discovered that three years prior to the pageant, she had made a mistake in behavior, no one was able to destroy the woman. Her inner core was not taken from her. I think the experience made her a stronger woman."

She continued, "I told her once that she was so much bigger than the Miss America Pageant. That it would be a wonderful thing *for her* to forgive them in her heart. Not for them, but for her. Maybe she needed to know that there are lots of us who don't condemn her or judge her. I hope so."

The conflict with the Rockettes background gave Maria such inner turmoil that for months, she felt she had no control over her life. But determined to be a good Miss America, she suppressed the conflict and went about her duties. The conflict manifested itself only in one small way and she laughs about it today.

"Whenever I flew," she explained, "I never wore my seat belt. I'd put my coat on my lap, flowers, whatever...anything to cover up the fact that I wasn't wearing my seat belt. It was the only thing I felt I had any control over, and it didn't hurt anyone. No one knew."

Her tour over, Maria toyed with several career offers. Joan Crawford had judged the pageant that year, and told her that she foresaw a career for Maria in Hollywood. The superstar asked the young beauty to stay in touch.

Maria had always planned to go to college. Her ten thousand dollar scholarship would give her the best of both worlds and for that she was grateful. She applied to only one school, Vanderbilt in Nashville. In the meantime, David Merrick promised her a small role in a show, and Monument Records offered her a recording contract based on her pageant perfor-

Maria with her son and daughter in 1989.

mance. She recorded two songs on a 45-rpm record during spring break, then told the executive in charge she couldn't do more because of her school commitments. She simply didn't have the time to go to school, produce recordings and promote her own records.

Although Vanderbilt accepted her, they weren't quite ready for a Miss America. The powers-that-be asked her to live off campus for the first semester, thinking her presence might be a distraction to the students. So school began with Miss America declaring a major in French, living off campus, and happily settling down to academic life.

When she was a freshman, something happened that again refocused her direction. A male friend confided in her that the fraternities had *targeted* her, offering points to the upper classman who could declare her a *trophy*. As naive as she was at the time, Maria was devastated to hear that. Now even her Miss America title was standing in the way of her being accepted just for herself.

Once again, she wasn't to be acknowledged for her work, her discipline, her successes, but for something completely meaningless and

superficial. Unable to be a normal co-ed at a prominent university, Maria was determined, once again, to make the best of the cards she had been dealt. She decided to date only freshmen, as they wouldn't be involved in the fraternity trophy competition. At the tender age of twenty, Maria began to date a freshman who was to become her husband three years later.

Maria spent her sophomore year in study abroad. She lived in Aix-en-Provence in the south of France. Maria loved the experience. "I wasn't Miss America, I was just Maria, studying French and philosophy. And I especially loved philosophy!"

After graduation, her celebrity status continued and she worked summers hosting state pageants and appearing at events as a former Miss America, earning enough money to help her husband realize his dream—medical school.

A year after she graduated from Vanderbilt, while still in Nashville, she began co-hosting a daily television show and produced her own radio show.

After her children were born, Maria produced two inspirational albums, one of which was called *Cradled in His Love*. She composed the title song, wrote all the lyrics and sang, using several of the musicians who had worked with Burl Ives and Dolly Parton. "It got some air play," she said. "As I traveled to speaking engagements, I often sang to the tapes of the music I recorded," she said.

The marriage to her college sweetheart lasted twenty-five years and produced two incredible children, according to Maria. Her daughter Robyn graduated from the Academy of Dramatic Arts in Pasadena, having been asked back for the by-invitation-only prestigious second year; then proceeded to graduate from Belmont University in Nashville with a double major in Psychology and Drama.

At this writing, she is directing the stage play *To Kill a Mockingbird* at the Tennessee Performing Arts Center in Nashville. Maria's son Jim is currently working on a Ph.D. in Church History at Catholic University in Washington, D.C. He has two master's degrees from Franciscan University and he and his wife Molly have recently presented Maria with her first granddaughter.

Through painful life experiences, divorce and loss, Maria has kept her passion for learning.

But no experience, no matter how painful, could match the trauma and tragedy that befell her family in 1988.

"For six months, I had been having dreams—horrible dreams—of an airplane crashing, flying into the west at dusk and exploding. I had the same terrifying dream eight times." The dream frightened her so much because both Maria's dad and brother Walter were private pilots and absolutely loved to fly. "It was their passion—dance and flying, both of them," she said.

Walter and his wife Linda, who lived in Asheville, had come to Nashville to take care of the children while Maria and her husband were off on a ski trip in Banff, Canada. It was April 1, 1988.

"When we returned home to Tennessee, I found myself feeling increasingly anxious as I prepared breakfast for everyone the next morning. Walter and Linda were leaving for North Carolina. As Walter got into the car, I kept run-

Digging out from underneath a Lake Tahoe snowstorm.

ning around trying to find the camera that was still packed somewhere in my suitcase. I desperately wanted to take a picture of my brother. Walter said they needed to be on their way and that I could take a picture the next time I saw him."

As her brother and his wife waved good-bye and sped on down the street, Maria stood in the driveway and began to cry hysterically. Her husband asked her what was wrong and she sobbed, "I've just seen my brother alive for the last time, and I wanted a picture of him."

Maria and her daughter Robyn have always shared an intense spiritual connection, and two months later, on June 22, now in Incline Village, Nevada in their new vacation condo, they found themselves walking around the house and looking at each other as if they were about to receive some horrible news. Walter and Linda were scheduled to visit them in the next few days in Lake Tahoe. Maria didn't have to say a word to Robyn. She didn't have to. They both knew something was terribly wrong.

Early that evening, back in Asheville, North Carolina, Walter got into his little antique Luscombe, a small plane, and flew out to look at an irrigation system in a pastureland. He invited his dad to go with him, but his father had a dance lesson to teach and was unable to join him.

Walter flew into the west, into the glare of the sun. It was dusk, around seven o'clock. He was flying low. He didn't see the power lines. The plane exploded.

"Just like in my dream," Maria whispered, reliving that awful memory.

When Maria's phone rang, it was a phone call that would forever be imprinted in her memory. She was devastated at the news. There would be no more pictures, no more visits, no more animated telephone conversations, no more hugs from this man who loved her unconditionally, a man who had lived his passions.

And as with most tragedies, for those of us left behind, we pick up the pieces of our lives with lessons learned. Maria's lesson allowed her, forced her—to grow spiritually.

"Perhaps no one says it better than Solomon in Ecclesiates, when he talks about seasons. For some reason, this was the time for Walter to leave us." Later, the passage says: *a time to mourn and a time to dance,* (Ecclesiastes 3:4). I

1995 in Atlantic City reunion (lt to rt) Miss Americas Sharon Kay Ritchie, Maria, their chaperone Peggy O'Neill Lloyd, Donna Axum and Nancy Fleming.

knew I would *dance* again and be able to think of Walter in a way that would celebrate his life rather than mourn his loss."

Two years later, Maria was taking an acting class in Pasadena. The students had been instructed to meditate. Quieting herself, she suddenly felt Walter's presence and in her heart she heard his voice, "You can do what you have to do."

Shortly before his death, Walter had been one of the few people Maria had confided in. She was trying to find the inner strength to go through with a divorce that was excruciatingly painful. She had been wrestling with the decision for more than two years. And somehow, now she knew she could.

Three years later, Maria was once again a single woman, reinventing herself and trying to figure out her place in the world.

In 1994, her dad died suddenly and at his memorial service, she decided she would carry on his business. With her mother ill with cancer, Maria knew she was needed in the Asheville area. Luckily, her dad had left enough clues on his computer, and Maria studied everything she could from his notes. She ran the business for the next three and a half years. Her work included coordinating dance contests over the tri-state area. This involved several hundred dance students representing as many as fifty dance teachers performing in several competitions each spring.

Maria followed her father's mission statement. She, too, was "dedicated to inspiring young people to a greater effort in all phases of the performing arts—to dance, to sing, to speak, to act, to make music and touch the heart of a kindred soul."

In 1995, Maria started building her dream home in Lake Tahoe. Six months of the year, she developed the dance contests and ran the business and for six months, she would go to Tahoe and work on the house. Realizing she couldn't continue the status quo, and with her mother becoming increasingly ill, Maria knew something needed to change. She had to close down the business in the summer of 1997.

She moved her mother to Nevada for the next several months where she could take care of her and have people there who could provide around-the-clock care. Peggy Fletcher died in April of 1998 with her three daughters at her bedside.

Maria made a giant leap of faith in the year 2000 that began to heal a lot of old wounds. The process began with a seemingly innocuous brochure she had received in the mail. Now divorced for nine years, Maria was living in her dream house; a house she had built on Crystal Bay in North Tahoe, having fallen in love with the Switzerland-like image of mountains and crystal lakes.

"I love to ski—I love the physiology of it. I was in a beautiful area where I could watch the moon rise over the lake from my house, and I did—every night for three and a half years. I was living in nature and enjoying a very spiritual life, but there was something missing," she said. Maria's family was all on the east coast and here she was in paradise—alone.

"The brochure lay on the desk in my house for six weeks, taunting me," she laughed. "It was an invitation to a Tony Robbins seminar and I don't know why, but I couldn't make the decision to go. And I guess I didn't want to make the decision not to go."

Maria kept thinking if she waited long enough to call, the seminar would be filled and she wouldn't be able to attend, so the decision would be made for her. And yet the brochure continued to taunt her. Interestingly, the seminar was entitled *Unleash the Power Within.*

Every day she tried to ignore that piece of paper. She couldn't throw it away. She couldn't respond.

Finally, one day, just two weeks before the Denver-based seminar was scheduled to start, Maria summoned the courage to call the 800 number on the brochure, knowing the seminar would be filled. It wasn't, and within days, Maria found herself on the airplane bound for Denver reading the fine print in the brochure:

"Please bring comfortable clothes with jeans you can roll up so they don't get burned during the *fire walk.*"

Maria, what in the world have you gotten yourself into?!

Maria credits Tony Robbins for creating a paradigm shift in her life. The influence he and his seminars (she attended several, all over the world) would have on her would only serve to remind her of a time gone by.

"My Scottish grandmother had the same kind of influence on my life," she said. "She never had doubts and was able to instill that attribute in others. She used to say that in order to move forward in your life and to make the best decisions, you cannot walk in fear. You must be totally integrated and of one mind. You have to visualize yourself actually doing it, and then give thanks for it as being done."

Maria didn't know Tony taught that premise, but she soon learned, and she knew she needed reminding once more. Her grandmother's teachings were now coming full circle. Maria was now reminded of those nights when she was little and her parents were dancing all over the country, when she was being cared for in that little trailer by her grandmother. Her words of wisdom were never forgotten.

"When you're stuck, you not only waste physical and mental energy, you waste precious resources. And then you squander your spiritual energy. It's a self-destructive path."

Maria has accomplished the fire walk twice. She has attended Robbins' progressive seminars worldwide—including events in Colorado, Nevada, Hawaii, Fiji, Australia, England, and on a cruise in the Mediterranean.

And among her travels, she wandered through one spiritual awakening after another, enabling her to leave her home in Tahoe and establish new roots in North Carolina, closer to her family. The seminars have taught her well, but it is the seed planted earlier by her grandmother that was germinated to give her a new life.

"From the time I was three, my grandmother imbued me with the fact that I was never alone; that God lived in me, so I never felt alone. I could walk in nature, I could be with animals, I could extend myself to others—we all sometimes forget we have that source we can tap into. Tony's seminars reminded me of the faith and the positive energy my grandmother brought to my life and now I'm living life more fully—creatively and emotionally."

As it is with most of us, the process takes us a while to learn but today, after years of soul-searching, of struggling to find out just exactly who she is, she has learned to take control of her life.

Maria is generous in giving the pageant its due, saying, "We all make choices, right and wrong, suffer consequences and learn life lessons. Without becoming Miss America, without that incredible opportunity, I wouldn't have been able to acquire the wonderful education I did from a great university, or to travel and come to know so many kinds of people—and myself. And now I know who I am and can accept that. I have a lot to be grateful for, and the Miss America experience surely counts as a wonderful blessing. But if you think about it, this world is just a giant classroom. And I expect to keep on learning. And what I've learned is best summed up in the poem I wrote about my beloved brother who died at the age of thirty-five."

Walter
by Maria Beale Fletcher

Walter burns to fly
In Luscombe wings and power lines
Evening sunlight-blinding vision
Ending now his dance sublime

Fairy tales of heroes conscious
Soaring through the centuries
Cry to us of passions craving
Wings to speed their histories

Walter listened-heard the singing
Answered with his love for lore
Danced the passion-climbed the mountains
Raced the sunlight to the shore

Western Carolina sunset
Highlights wreckage of the plane
Illuminates within destruction
Gifts of love for those ordained

Symbolized by Walter's hearing
A single piece of flesh unburned
There we find the understanding
And his lessons we might learn

Honor with your life the loving
Exploding passion-follow through
Once you recognize the drumming
Dance the dream that's true for you

Miss America 1963

Jacquelyn Jeanne Mayer

Student - Northwestern University
State - Ohio
Age - 20   Height - 5' 5''

Talent: Jackie delivered a medley of song and dance, concluding
with a dramatic interpretation of *The White Cliffs of Dover*.

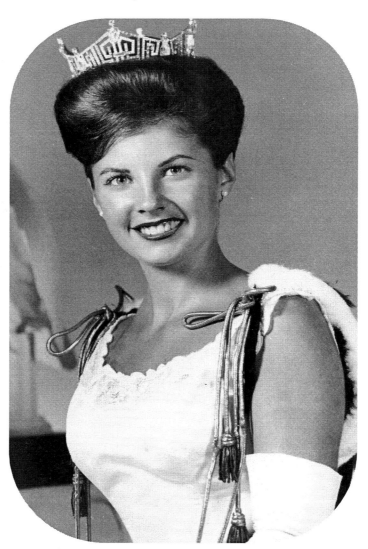

Photo courtesy of the Miss America Organization.

"I lay in my hospital bed in ICU, afraid to fall asleep for fear I would die.
I couldn't tell the doctor I was frightened, because I was unable to speak."
—Jacquelyn Mayer, after suffering a stroke at 28.

Jacquelyn Jeanne Mayer

In a few short months, the petite brunette with the dazzling smile had charmed not only the state of Ohio, but the entire nation. As she stood at the end of the long runway in Atlantic City, waving to twenty-thousand appreciative fans in Convention Hall, her lovely radiance was beamed electronically by CBS to sixty million Americans. What a challenge it had been to get this far! But it was nothing compared to what life had in store for this new Miss America.

Neither Jackie nor her audience could possibly have known the terrible tragedy that was stalking her, waiting silently in the wings.

Jacquelyn Jeanne Mayer spent her youth as a self-proclaimed tomboy in her hometown of Sandusky, Ohio. Lazy summer days would find her playing such non-girly roles as the singing cowboy Roy Rogers. "I always had to be Roy," she laughed, "and my friend Tom had to be Dale Evans." The strong, healthy limbs of the big apple tree would become Trigger at a moment's notice.

Her family was not unlike many other families of the 1940s and '50s with multiple generations living in the same house. Jackie's family lived in a five-bedroom home with one bathroom shared by her parents, Jackie and her two brothers and a sister, "Aunt Dindie" and "Bama," her grandmother.

Jackie and her sister Beth shared a bedroom. They even shared clothing, although Jackie admits she couldn't wear many of Beth's clothes. "I was a pudgeball," she offered candidly.

When she became a freshman in high school, Jackie decided that if she wanted to date, she alone would have to assume the responsibility for losing weight. It was a struggle, but she did it—a difficult challenge for a teenager.

Jackie sang in her mother's church choir with Beth and her brothers, Lynn and Jim. Her musical studies included piano, clarinet and bassoon plus a thirteen-year regime of tap, ballet and exhibition ballroom dancing. Lynn was only to eager to become involved in the latter and it didn't take Jackie long to figure out why.

"Lynn was such a tease, I think the only rea-

son he agreed to take ballroom dancing with me was so he could throw me around!"

During her senior year, she was accepted as an exchange student for the American Field Service program, established in 1945. Kapfenberg, Austria was a world away from Sandusky, but Jackie was eager to explore another culture. For a semester, she lived with an Austrian family. "Papa" was head physician of a hospital and the family lived on the third floor of the hospital. "Mutti" made sure her two daughters Irma and Helga and her 'adopted' daughter from the States were all introduced to the opera, which they frequently attended in Graz and Vienna.

The competition to become one of six young women to represent the U.S. that year in Austria prepared Jackie for her later role—ambassador to the world as Miss America. "I learned early on that if you dream big dreams and work very hard, you can make those dreams come true!"

After graduating from high school, Jackie became a drama student at Northwestern University. She was given the opportunity to audition for Fred Waring and the Pennsylvanians. Once selected, Jackie took a hiatus from college and toured throughout the country for a year with the thirty-seven-member cast.

During the tour, she renewed her acquaintance with an old family friend, John Townsend. John was an MBA student at Stanford. One morning, between West Coast performances, John and Jackie met for breakfast. The meeting sparked the beginning of a relationship that would lead to marriage.

Jackie had expressed to her tour roommate, Jean Elverum-Miss Minnesota 1960, her concern for finding the money for tuition to return to school. Jean suggested that Jackie could earn scholarship money by entering the Miss America preliminaries. She was informed that scholarships were awarded from the local level on up through the national level.

The year of performing on stage had served her well, and the poised young woman walked away from her first local competition with the title Miss Vacationland, the steppingstone that led her to become Miss Ohio.

Her friend and mentor Fred Waring not only approved, but offered professional advice.

Jackie Mayer, on her first attempt at the crown and coveted title, walked away with the scepter and enough scholarship money to finish school. She was now and forever—Miss America 1963.

Unfortunately, in her desire to be absolutely candid, she had unwittingly baited the media at her first press conference. In sharing her frustrations at being overweight as a teen, Jackie had hoped she might be an inspiration to others struggling with the same battle. Instead, national wire services spit out the headlines, "Former 150-pound Butterball Becomes Miss America!"

Rather than let it get her down, she decided to focus on collecting happy memories instead. One of those special memories was at an Oldsmobile-sponsored event. An executive had introduced Jackie to his daughter, explaining that his child had been so inspired by Jackie's example that she had decided to lose weight. After nearly a year, the girl had lost fifty pounds of excess weight and was delighted to find herself standing before a Miss America. She shook Jackie's hand and the moment became a special one for both of them.

When asked to pinpoint the one thing that had the greatest impact on her life during he year of her reign, Jackie responded without hesitation: "The people—how absolutely wonderful they were."

Each Miss America is given a homecoming. Sandusky, proud of its American beauty, took Jackie by motorcade past one grade school after another, where children waved excitedly to their own Miss America from the front steps of each school. She was hosted at events at the junior and senior high schools and there were several formal dances, even a parade in her honor. She was moved to find out how much time and effort had gone into the planning of so many orchestrated events, how everything came together in such a loving tribute.

One event turned out to be very special, indeed. As several hundred people prepared to dine in the gymnasium that had been artfully turned into a dining hall, Jackie looked up to see a familiar face. The smiling man walking toward her, arms outstretched—was none other than Fred Waring! The warmth of this special relationship would last through the years, until his death.

Post-pageant life seemed idyllic. Jackie resumed her studies at Northwestern with the help of her ten thousand dollar scholarship. She married John, now a law student at the University of Pittsburgh, and they settled in Washington, Pennsylvania.

Jackie continued with her studies at Washington and Jefferson College for Men. The only woman at the all-male school for more than two years, she had to transfer to the University of Pittsburgh because the charter of "W and J" would not permit a woman to graduate from that school. In 1968, she earned a Bachelor of Science in Humanities.

Just two short years later, Jackie would discover that the fates had a different path planned for her. She was to be given a mission—and, as are many of life's lessons, this one at first seemed terribly cruel.

It was November 1970. Jackie, now twenty-eight, had been rushing around all week preparing for Thanksgiving dinner for twenty. John's parents and extended family were coming. There were children to care for, groceries to buy, a house to clean and meals to prepare. With the grace that always seemed to be a part of Jackie's demeanor, she did it all and did it well. She had a lot to be thankful for.

The day did not turn out the way Jackie had expected. She had been plagued with an excruciating headache throughout the day. It had gotten worse as the day wore on. The family, realizing she was not feeling well, had pitched in to help with dinner.

Finally with the day behind her and everyone gone, she was eager to put the little ones to bed. John helped her tuck Billy, five, and Kelly, nine months old, into their beds and the family settled in for the night. The day had been too

Billy and Kelly just prior to Jackie's stroke.

much for Jackie. All she wanted to do was to lay her head down on the pillow and fall asleep.

Jackie slept deeply, too deeply for her to be aware of what was happening inside her brain. At three in the morning, Kelly's hungry cries could be heard throughout the house. Thinking Jackie was too exhausted to get up, John gave little Kelly her bottle and went back to sleep.

As Jackie finally awoke at six a.m. to Kelly's renewed cries, she thought, *I have to feed her.* But as she tried to move, nothing happened. Frightened, at first she thought her leg might be asleep, and tried again. This time she struggled to move her right hand.

Thinking she must be in the middle of a nightmare, she lifted her right hand with her left one. It dropped lifelessly to the bed. As Kelly's cries became more frantic, so did Jackie. *What's wrong? Why can't I move?* Terrified, Jackie reached for her husband, desperate to tell John that something was wrong, but no words would come. She could not utter a sound! Silent tears streamed from her eyes.

By this time, John had awakened. He realized instantly that something was terribly wrong. He immediately called the doctor and was told to just keep her comfortable, that she would come out of it. Several phone calls and panic-stricken hours later, John disregarded the doctor's advice and insisted on taking Jackie to the hospital.

Even today, Jackie considers it a spiritual gift that a fine neurologist, Dr. Lowell Lubic from Montefiore Hospital happened to be the visiting doctor in the emergency room on that traumatic day. After examining Jackie and administering a spinal tap, Lubic began giving orders and suddenly there was action all around her. Jackie was lifted into an ambulance and with sirens wailing, she was quickly transported to Pittsburgh's Montefiore Hospital, thirty miles away.

The ambulance ride seemed to take an eternity. She had questions, so many questions. *Why can't I walk? Why can't I talk?* These and a dozen others born of sheer panic, flooded her mind. She remembers the look of fear and compassion on the face of the nurse sitting beside her. As the miles sped by, Jackie pleaded silently, over and over, *Please, God, don't let me die!*

And now she faced a different kind of runway—a long, white hospital corridor. And this time she wasn't walking it, she was being rushed through sterile white halls on a cold, steel-hard gurney, looking up at bright, white ceiling lights that frightened her in their starkness as she was wheeled through the hallways. *Jackie*, she thought, *something's terribly wrong*!

The all-American dream had, in one terrible tragic instant, turned into a horrific nightmare. There would be something far more valuable than a crown and a scepter to fight for at the end of this corridor—she would need to fight for her life!

After several more hours filled with silent fear, additional tests and a long night in the Intensive Care Unit where she was afraid to fall asleep for fear she would never wake up, the diagnosis was confirmed. An artery on the left side of Jackie's brain had become damaged, cutting off life-giving oxygen and destroying cells that controlled the right side of her body and her speech.

Finally, sitting on the bed beside her, Dr. Lubic took her hand and said quietly, "Jackie, you've had a stroke. It's completed now and you are going to live."

Nearly three weeks later, Jacquelyn Mayer Townsend, still unable to speak, the right side of her face, her right hand and foot still paralyzed, went home to her husband and her little ones. Home to a very different kind of life.

She had so many questions and the fears remained. *How can my family cope? How long will it take me to get better? How can I possibly take care of a five year old and a tiny baby? And where do I start?*

At the time, there were no known rehabilitation facilities available to stroke survivors, no wide acceptance of psychological counseling for stroke survivors and their families. She had only one option. Jackie and her family would have to handle her therapy themselves. The task was daunting, nearly overwhelming.

Her husband was often heard to say that he raised *three* children.

Billy, their son became a wonderful teacher. He taught his mom to button her blouse, to tie her shoes and to tell time. She learned to say the ABCs with Kelly, their daughter. They sat for hours, putting numbers and letters on magnetic boards and playing games that taught them all how to sort colors and to count money.

But it wasn't fun and games. Jackie became so frustrated that her dear friend Fred Waring devised a special challenge for her. Calling her long distance every day for more than a year, he would ask her what she was wearing, cooking or doing. Then he would give her three one-syllable words to say and she would have to practice them until their next phone conversation.

The game continued without fail—two syllable words, then three syllable words. He would call and ask, "Where are you? What are you doing?"

"Litchen," she would respond, "cricking dog hots." *NOOOOOO!* She would scream silently to herself. *That's not what I wanted to say*! Then Jackie would slow her words down, think very hard, and finally the words would come out the right way, "I-am-in-the-kitchen-cooking-hot-dogs."

One afternoon, she answered the phone and immediately wished she hadn't. "The word for today," Fred said charmingly, "is juxtaposition." It took Jackie two years, practicing every single day, before she could repeat clearly back to him - "juxtaposition."

She knew then that she would once again be able to enjoy a good quality of life, even a fulfilling professional life. If she could say juxtaposition, she could certainly begin to speak to stroke survivors in order to help them learn how to cope. *Is it possible? Can I help others from my experience?*

But Jackie had a long, long way to go. The next step was to learn to string words and tasks

94

Sroke survivors and advocates Jackie and actress Patricia Neal receiving the Award of Hope and Courage.

together. Often Jackie would forget in the midst of a sentence what she was talking or thinking about, or forget what she was doing, right in the middle of a task. She would try mentally to spell words, but even with words as simple as 'brown,' all she could print was 'brn.' A sense of humor was her saving grace as Jackie struggled to say words correctly. Billy would laugh at her attempts to say anything with the letter 'R' in it and together, they would laugh hysterically.

It took five solid years of work—every waking hour, every single day. Jackie was fiercely determined. She refused to be beaten, even when she was exhausted from trying, even when she fell subject to tears as stroke survivors often do. She fought every step of the way until she was almost whole again.

Jackie with Kylene (lt) and Pat Donnelly (rt)

According to Jackie, stroke survivors have only one thought, one goal, one focus—to survive.

"Nothing else is important. When you come that close to dying, all you think about is how much you want to live. I was a prisoner in my own body. I couldn't walk, I couldn't talk, I couldn't remember, but *I could think*! And my husband, children and friends were my support for many years."

And life went on at Rising Wind Farm where Jackie and John worked hard to breed, raise and sell standardbred horses. The right side of Jackie's face was still numb. She was working with a yearling one day and was kicked in the face. "Thank God, it was on the numb side," she said.

Eventually she found herself, twenty years later, thinking that she needed to find a mission other than mucking out stalls and foaling mares and running a horse business.

From the moment Jackie recovered enough to speak publicly, she became an advocate for stroke survivors. She began to speak to medical associations, to members of the medical profession—speaking from a patient's point of view. She spoke at hospital functions, in board rooms, lobbied Congress for funds for stroke research, and honed her skills at sharing her story and educating others so they in turn might be inspired to enlighten and comfort their own patients and families.

And in every city she went into, she visited the stroke units at the local hospitals, walking into patient's rooms and telling them she understood—that she truly knew what they were going through.

"I have walked in your shoes," she would say, holding their hand or embracing them and letting them weep on her shoulder.

You can almost watch the healing process

Jackie in Occupational Therapy at a Colorado hospital with a stroke survivor-1990.
Photo by Kate Kitchen

begin when, in those quiet moments, Jackie sits with a patient, touching his hand, looking into his eyes and saying, "I know it's hard, and I know how you feel." She sits with them, listens, talks when they can't, and gives them hope where before they had none.

In 1982, Jackie and her family were asked to participate in an educational film for the American Heart Association. The film told her story as a stroke survivor and was entitled: *A Different Kind of Beauty.* She became AHA's lay spokesperson on stroke. She served as an original board member of the National Stroke Association for sixteen years. For her efforts as a stroke survivor, Jackie was honored with the Award of Hope and Courage and The Unsung Heroine Award.

In 1990, Jackie was thrilled to be invited to become a member of the Advisory Council of the National Institute of Neurological Disorders and Stroke, an affiliate of the National Institutes of Health (NIH). The

March 1990 - Jackie came to speak to the medical staff at the Colorado Neurological Institute in Englewood, Colorado. Jackie and Kate were meeting for the first time.
Photo by Kate Kitchen

majority of members are medical specialists and Jackie was excited that she could use her status as Miss America combined with her recovery and educational work in stroke to contribute to an organization so prestigious.

"It was through this advisory council that TPA, preventive carotid artery surgery and other pioneering medical developments have been accomplished, and I felt such an incredible value and purpose in serving on this panel," she said. She traveled to Washington, D.C. several times a year to meet with this group and always returned home hungry to learn more, to do more.

As Jackie found herself increasingly involved in hospital work, she realized that her life on the horse farm was never going to meet her needs nor honor her gifts. She and her husband had been drifting apart for years, both going in opposite directions. But a lifetime spent in a value system that didn't believe in divorce kept her tied to a marriage that was no longer fulfilling either of their needs. She was at an impasse. The children were grown and married and well on their way to creating their own lives. She felt a calling elsewhere, and was paralyzed with fear at striking out on her own.

"I wanted to devote whatever time I had left to service, to giving people hope and encouragement. The more work I did with patients, the more I realized how much more there was to do and how small my life had become on the farm. And I needed to feel once again that life

Bill's college graduation.

was important; I needed to be of value—to myself and to others."

Oddly, her sense of humor helped her finally put things into perspective and find the strength to break the bond. She was at home on the horse farm when she received a call from a salesman.

She laughs when she thinks of that special star-studded moment at the end of the runway in 1962 in 'juxtaposition' with that phone call. The man was trying to sell her something. Evidently frustrated because he wasn't getting anywhere, he shouted, "What do you know? You're only an uneducated farmer's wife." Jackie realized in that instant that she was still, at the very least, limiting her potential, short-changing herself and others.

"I knew I had something more to give to the world, that God had given me back my life and the strength of character to get well so I could help others. And now I knew that a decision I'd been wrestling with for several years was made."

In the fall of 1997, Providence Hospital in Sandusky, Ohio had decided to honor Jackie's own inspiring recovery and her tireless efforts with stroke survivors by naming a medical unit The Jackie Mayer Rehabilitation and Skilled Nursing Center. In the span of one weekend, Jackie was presented with the Woman of Excellence Award and had a rehabilitation center named in her honor. She felt that God was blessing her again through His grace, and trying to tell her something.

"I had been traveling back and forth from the farm to the hospital where my dad, now eighty-six, was struggling with heart failure. It was a seven-hour round trip which I made weekly, while still trying to keep the farm together." By this time, John was also focused on other things and it was difficult just to get the work done that needed to be done.

Jackie has a delightful sense of humor, which obviously was shared by her father. After peripheral vascular surgery, her father Jack had to undergo painful rehab and was fond of saying, "When I die, I'm either going to Heaven or to Rehab!"

On April 17, 1998, Jackie's dad died in the very center named for his daughter.

She had come to know the chief executive officer of the hospital, Sister Nancy Linenkugel, who had seen something very special in Jackie, and the wheels began turning. In the summer of 1998, the board of directors offered Jackie a part-time position working at the hospital and assisting the staff with stroke patients, being a presence there where so many knew her

Celebrating her parents' 50th anniversary. (Back) Lynn, Dad, Jim and (front) Beth, Mom and Jackie. *Photo courtesy of Alden Photographers.*

Grandchildren Daryn (lt) and Alayna (Kelly's girls)

name and where she could be of great value to patients and families.

And now she had a dilemma. "This was a big decision for me," she said. "I knew it would literally be the end of my marriage. It was a real turning point. But I knew I was meant at this time in my life to give more than I could give mucking out stalls and foaling mares, in a marriage that had already dissolved. I needed a mission in my life and I knew it had to be something that would require more of me, that would require me to be of greater service to others."

Weighing traditional values against the potential of being fulfilled professionally and spiritually, Jackie wrestled with that decision. As she signed her employment contract, she knew she was signing a document that would end a thirty-four-year marriage.

"It was a very sad time," she said. "I could never forget how John stood by me during my stroke and my recovery. He had to be the breadwinner, take care of the business, the house, Billy and Kelly, and help me cope until I got better. I'll never forget it. Yet somehow, during the past twenty years or more, we both lost something that I knew now we would never be able to recover. It was just time to move on.

"I still had responsibilities at the farm for a long time," she said. "Once I came back to Ohio and started working, I would drive home every two weeks to clean the house and

One happy grandmother - Jackie with Bill's boys Colton and new baby Pierce.

work the farm, selling horses, preparing the house for sale, and tying up loose ends. That went on for nearly three years, and I was exhausted trying to live in both worlds."

Jackie found early on that she had become so devoted to the hospital and the patients, that no matter how long it took, she needed to break the ties that bound her to her farm so she could focus on the people who really needed her.

Eventually, the horse farm was sold and Jackie was able to move to Sandusky and focus on her work at the hospital.

Now she was on her way to fulfilling her dream. And she was happy. "I was growing again, spiritually, emotionally, mentally," she said. "I felt at times that I almost lived there. Even though it was a part-time job, I'd sometimes find myself going to the hospital morning, noon and night. It was liberating to be doing what I had found a passion to do."

Jackie knew from experience how lonely a hospital feels at night to patients who are frightened, often afraid to go to sleep for fear they might not wake up. "I remember one patient in particular. I just sat with her and rubbed her back until she fell asleep. Another special moment was late one night when I was sitting at the bedside of a patient who had suffered a stroke. I looked up to see another stroke survivor in the hall. Somehow we just started softly singing together, *Amazing Grace*. It was such a special moment of love, hope and peace."

The ladies autographing a book for a fan—Jackie, Maria, Lee and Eveyln.

Jackie served Providence Hospital in that capacity for three years until the hospital was sold. Under new management, she stayed another year and a half, but felt once again her growth was becoming stunted. It was time to look for something with more potential.

During the summer of 2003, the first summer Jackie had taken off for probably her entire adult life, she decided to hone her therapeutic skills and signed up for a Life Course through Stein Hospice. She soon became certified as a hospice volunteer. Then she took a course in Reiki and became a certified Reiki practitioner. To continue her growth, she followed up her renewed appetite for learning with a course in Stephen Ministry and was commissioned in May 2004. And among all her studies and classes, she allowed herself to stop long enough to be installed into the Ohio Women's Hall of Fame. As if that weren't exciting enough, Ohio Governor Robert Taft finally approved an award that was initiated nearly forty years before. The Erie County portion of Highway 2 is now named The Jackie Mayer Miss America Highway.

Recently, Jackie spent some time with Ericka Dunlap, Miss America 2004, during Ericka's

Jackie celebrating the new highway sign.

tour, and they posed for pictures beside the highway sign. Ericka immediately pulled her cell phone out, called her mother and said, "I want a highway named after me, too!"

Jackie agreed, laughing. "It's quite an honor!"

Jackie remains busy professionally as she continues to honor speaking engagements for healthcare institutions, colleges and corporate sponsors. In 2001, she spoke for commencement ceremonies at Lourdes College in Ohio, where she accepted an honorary doctorate, the first one bestowed from that college. She followed that event by offering the inaugural keynote at Chatfield College in Cincinnati in honor of Sister Nancy who was recently named president of that institution.

Jackie's appearances on network television included *The Phil Donahue Show, Good Morning America* and *Miss America...Beyond the Crown.* Her inspirational story has appeared in newspapers and magazines throughout the country.

"Everything that I have ever wanted and worked hard to achieve is coming true in my life," she said.

To this day, Jackie considers herself about ninety percent recovered, and she is still, she said, "a work in progress."

She never asked, "Why me?" The answer was obvious to her.

"There is a master plan for me. One day, I was on top of the world and in one moment I was literally thrown into the 'valley of the shadow of death.' I think sometimes you have to be in the valley in order to climb out, to discover what is truly important in your life. The years after my stroke were tremendously difficult for my family and me, but I feel truly blessed for having gone through those years. I thank God for my faith, for my family, for my friends. Their support and love gave me the courage to overcome. Through this experience I found a new commitment, a new purpose in my life."

"No matter what you attain in life," Jackie said, "there's always an experience coming just around the corner that will help you keep things in perspective."

She laughed suddenly, filled with a sense of wonder for what life has yet in store. "I'm just so grateful to be here and to be of service. Isn't life fantastic?"

She is currently working on her autobiography, *The Significance Factor*, to be released in 2005.

Jackie's son, Bill, is president of Amati Trust and has developed an incredible skill—he makes violins. Bill and his wife Jen live in Austin, Texas with their two sons.

Kelly is married to Gary Rostic and the happy couple lives in Springfield, Missouri, They are expecting their third child. Kelly anchors the news on KOLR-10 and FOX 27.

To book Jackie for speaking engagements, visit www.katekitchen.com. Watch for Jackie's new book on www.jackiemayer.com.

Miss America 1964

Donna Axum

Student - University of Arkansas
State - Arkansas
Age - 21   Height - 5' 6½''

Talent: Donna sang *I Love Paris* and an excerpt from *La Boheme*.

"Allow nothing to discourage or deter you. Define your goal then live it,
sleep it, dream it—keep on and on, and it will be yours."
—Donna Axum Whitworth

101

Donna Axum

Taking her firmly by the arm, pageant Executive Director Lenora Slaughter whisked the stunned, beautiful lady through the corridor and into the back elevator. Inside were six husky, very serious looking police officers.

Startled, the young woman asked fearfully, "Oh my gosh, what's happened?" An officer replied, "We're here for you." Donna Axum had just been crowned Miss America. Only then did she realize the impact this title would have on her life.

Donna Axum Whitworth holds the distinction of being the only Miss America who first held the title of Arkansas Forestry Queen. That was in 1961 and certainly is not mentioned to belittle the title she won the next year—National Cotton Picking Queen. And just a year after that, she stood on the stage in the Convention Hall in Atlantic City to become America's sweetheart in front of twenty-five thousand people. Sixty million viewers watched her crowning from the comfort of their living rooms.

El Dorado, Arkansas, Donna's hometown of twenty-five thousand, was a boomtown in 1921. It is still known as the City of Black Gold, still the oil capital of Arkansas. Donna's father was a banker, her mother a homemaker. Donna and her sister Mona grew up singing in the choir at the First Baptist Church.

In the ninth grade, Donna and two friends, Phyllis and Linda, combined their name into an acronym and became The Philadons. The McGuire Sisters were famous at the time and Donna's talented trio performed several of their tunes.

The girls sang at school and civic events and talent contests, even making their way to New York to audition for The Ted Mack Amateur Hour, one of the decade's most popular television shows. Although that particular TV performance wasn't meant to be, Donna certainly made up for it in later years, hosting and producing three public affairs shows in Austin, Lubbock and Little Rock over a period of seven years.

In the late 1990s, Donna returned to the area for a reunion and the women reminisced as they listened to their recordings from forty years past. Linda died soon afterwards and

At six months, Donna was the first baby born in El Dorado in 1942.

Donna was happy they had been able to share that time together.

She has never forgotten her roots. "Sometimes people use the fact that they're from a small town as an excuse not to achieve rather than a reason to strive to achieve. If I can help some young person realize through my own life, my own example—that you certainly can achieve anything you want to, providing you're willing to put forth the effort—then I'll have made my point."

Pageants were a popular pastime for high school girls in the 1950s and 1960s, especially in small towns in the South. She and her friends started competing in 1958, at the age of sixteen. In her first pageant, she won Union City Fair Queen, shocking all her buddies because she was so skinny. It was just something to do at first. But once the perks started to come along, Donna was hooked. At the University of Arkansas, as a Speech and Drama major, Donna won the Pershing Rifle Sponsor (Army ROTC). The group was invited to perform at a New Orleans Mardi Gras ball and parade.

"I was a very late bloomer," she laughed. "I was five feet, six and a half inches tall and weighed only one hundred ten pounds."

Regardless of her slim physique, she was quite focused, progressing to more pivotal competitions with scholarships attached. When she became Arkansas Forestry Queen, Donna learned what speaking and performing experiences might be worth to her future. She learned that a title carried with it responsibility, and she began to prepare seriously for her future role as Miss Arkansas.

With forestry being one of Arkansas' most precious resources, Donna took a year off from college to do public appearances relating to the state's industry. She humbly refers to her topic as the *The Uses of Wood* speech, but her speech

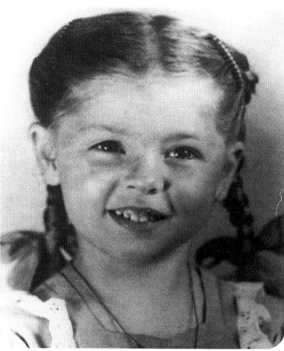
Already a beauty at five

was taken seriously enough to be recorded in the Congressional Record by Arkansas Senator John McClellan.

At the end of the year, she had given more than two hundred fifty speeches to schools, civic groups and other organizations. She had also performed throughout the year, and learned the discipline of traveling with a message. "I talked and sang my way through Arkansas," she said.

That year marked a milestone for the young woman. Donna was invited to Washington, D.C. for a very special event. Her college choir, The Schola Cantorum, had won an international competi-

High School ROTC

103

En route to New York City for the Ted Mack audition.

tion in Italy and was invited to perform in the Rose Garden at the White House. The meeting was fortuitous for Donna. It was there she met President John F. Kennedy. Although they would never again meet face-to-face, their paths would soon tragically cross—in Dallas.

Donna very nearly didn't become Miss America. At the state pageant, there was a tie for Miss Arkansas. She had won the preliminary talent and swimsuit categories. The contestants were competing on an outdoor stage at Oaklawn Race Track in Hot Springs.

She recalled, "To get back to the stage, we had to climb over a fence. We had to change our clothes in a tent. I remember looking up and seeing Jackie Mayer, the reigning Miss America. She seemed so out of place, standing in a tent, wearing a beautiful gown and her crown."

There were ten thousand people on hand to see Miss Arkansas crowned, but they had to wait a little longer for there was a tie for first place. The judges decided that in order to break the tie, they would give the talent competition priority and Donna's scores broke the tie, winning the title for her by two points. She had combined her operatic voice with musical comedy and the unique presentation had proved to be a winning combination.

"I never learned to play bridge with the other girls," Donna explained. "I was so focused on improving my performance and speaking ability, I could always be found vocalizing at the Music Building or working on my public speaking. I guess my training and persistence paid off."

And her training certainly did pay off. The next step, and it happened quickly, was to capture the Miss America title. This was the big time. She was competing for a ten thousand dollar scholarship. Her goal was to complete her Bachelor of Arts, then pursue a master's degree. And her goal wasn't far away.

"Even though I had competed in a total of fifteen pageants," Donna explained, "it certainly was intimidating to be immediately thrown into the national spotlight in front of the media. You learn to choose your words carefully. You realize suddenly that you're not only a spokesperson for yourself, but for your peers, for the sponsors and for the pageant organization. You begin to realize you are speaking to the whole country and *for* the whole country! You learn to publicly stand up for moral values and high ideals." She paused thoughtfully, "The responsibility is overwhelming."

Donna was brought back down to earth within minutes of leaving the stage as the new Miss America. "I went to the dressing room to fix my hair and re-attach the crown and Lenora Slaughter handed me a six-page letter that I was to read that very minute. The press and the Miss America ball would have to wait."

The letter was standard for the new Miss America in those days. It strongly suggested topics the women should avoid discussing, namely, her political views, anything with sexual overtones, and of course, the subject of religion. "We weren't 'restricted' from expressing our opinions," she said carefully. "It was just suggested—strongly—that we politely refrain from discussing those topics."

A hint of censorship?

"Maybe," Donna responded, "but perhaps more just a reflection of the conservative tone of the early '60s".

The Miss America Pageants, from preliminary competitions through the national level, have provided for millions upon millions of dollars in scholarships over the years to women who are believed to be representative of the best of young America. Controversy was, at that time, best avoided to keep the sponsors happy. Wholesome and refreshing have been the usual descriptors that envelope the Miss America persona.

Donna didn't object to the reasoning at the time. Now, forty years later, she remembers the dichotomy. She was surrounded by thousands of cheering fans at one moment as she stood at the end of the runway facing an enthusiastic audience, television cameras measuring her every tear, then minutes later, sat nearly alone, quietly in a room, trying to absorb six pages of instructions.

And then she was whisked into the back elevator where her six-man police force surrounded her. "That," she said emphatically, "was a life-changing experience."

The next morning, Sue Mason, her chaperone from El Dorado, packed Donna's personal effects as the new Miss America attended the awards breakfast and a press conference. Immediately afterwards, Donna was driven to New York for her first national press conference. She was met in her hotel suite by photographers and with the precision of Swiss watch makers, they pulled down a huge, makeshift blue paper backdrop and posed her in front of it. They quickly took the shots that would become the front cover of the next national, state and local pageant program books. So much had happened in just one day. Those twenty-four hours symbolized the frantic, exciting pace that would continue during an incredible year.

There were ups and downs as well as inspirational and funny moments during her tour. One happy highlight that stands out in Donna's mind is that she celebrated her twenty-second birthday on The Gary Moore Show. "Remember, television was still in black and white," she laughed.

The tragedy that surpassed all other events that decade took place on November 22, 1963. Pepsi, then one of the pageant's major sponsors, had hired Miss America to attend their national convention at a hotel in downtown Dallas. On their way to a luncheon, Donna and her chaperone encountered a shocked Dallas resident in the hotel elevator.

"Have you heard? President Kennedy has been shot!"

Miss America and her chaperone, Peggy O' Neill, walked into the luncheon and sat quietly while they all waited for the news. There were no speeches, only a prayer for the President. Waiters who could not restrain their tears placed food before them with trembling hands. The news finally came to the silent room. No one wanted to hear those awful words. "The President is dead."

Donna recalled the incident, speaking softly. "Peggy and I began to walk. We walked to our hotel room, then not knowing what to do, we walked in stunned silence out the door and down the street. We walked in and out of shops and were so completely overcome with the demeanor of the people in Dallas. Without question, they were so apologetic that this horrible tragedy could happen there."

She collected her thoughts for a moment, then continued quietly, "The very next day, the impact of what had happened broke our hearts. As we prepared to leave Dallas, we had to fly out of Love Field."

President Kennedy's body, with his widow Jackie by his side, had already been flown from that very airfield back to Washington. It was too enormous a tragedy, a tragedy that would signal forever the end of Camelot.

"And worse," she explained, "it quickly became a time of chaos, complete unrest, a beginning of transition and turmoil as the country immersed itself in the Vietnam War."

Several years ago, Donna was asked to return to Dallas to do an interview in the Schoolbook Depository - Sixth Floor Museum. The museum is dedicated to Kennedy and holds archives memorializing the assassination. She was honored to be asked to commemorate the former President in this special tribute. She vividly remembers that day in 1963 and the residents of Dallas as they apologized over and over in shock and horror for the terrible tragedy that occurred in their beloved city.

Donna continued her Miss America tour, but not without narrowly escaping death herself. A month after the Kennedy assassination,

Donna (rt) as Miss Arkansas during the Miss America Pageant.

Donna and another chaperone, Lucille Previtti, flew to Jacksonville, Florida for an appearance at the Gator Bowl. The Roosevelt Hotel was crammed with football fans from North Carolina and the Air Force Academy.

"For once," said Donna, "we were allowed to sleep in. We had no early wake up call. But the phone began ringing at seven-thirty a.m. and it rang incessantly! We tried to ignore it, but it wouldn't stop."

Lucky for Donna and her chaperone that the hotel operator had awakened them, for they suddenly became aware of dark, thick, curling smoke filtering into the room from under their door. Later it was determined that the wiring in the ballroom ceiling downstairs had shorted and caught on fire.

"We were on the tenth floor. You need to know," she said, "that the fire truck ladders only reached to the seventh floor! I can laugh now, but then it was very frightening!"

Donna and Lucille looked out the window. Swirling around them, coming from everywhere was a cloud of thick, black smoke. They quickly closed the door behind them, sealing themselves in the room, and knocked out the window screen. Hanging out the window, they began shouting for help. There were firemen on the garage rooftop next door, but there was so much smoke, the firefighters couldn't see the women.

"There was smoke coming up into our faces from the lower floors and smoke surrounding us from behind. We couldn't see anything beyond our own bodies. We grabbed wet towels and put them around our heads."

Donna suddenly remembered something about hair being a filter and grabbing her fur coat, began breathing through the mink collar to try to dissipate the effect of the chemicals in the smoke.

She looked up to see that Lucille had run to another window in the room. She quickly returned to Donna. "Lucille had bronchitis and couldn't take the smoke. She passed out and slumped over the windowsill. I kept trying to lift her and I couldn't. She fell to the floor at my feet."

Donna said, "Finally I heard a loud pounding on our door. The son of the public relations man from Pepsi-Cola was staying at the hotel. He had come to town to join his dad for the big game. He literally broke in the door and pulled us to safety."

Despite the valiant efforts of the firemen and the rescues by helicopters on the roof, twenty-one people died of smoke inhalation during that fire. Donna suffered burned bronchial

Donna with her sister Mona and their parents.

After her tour, Donna returned to the University of Arkansas and completed a bachelor's degree. Her scholarship and her experience as Miss America had given her the education she needed and the opportunities she wanted to create a successful professional life.

Donna first married at twenty-two, seeking the normalcy of family life after her frantic year as Miss America. "I think every Miss America finishes her year with that desire, plus—the expectations of what women could achieve in the 1960s was very limited," Donna explained.

tubes from the chemicals in the smoke. She and Lucille were taken by ambulance to the hospital.

"You know, the funniest things hit you in a tragic moment," Donna explained, half-laughing, half-serious. "There we stood, in this horrifying moment and just for a second, I imagined the headlines, *Miss America Perishes in Hotel Fire! First Runner-up Takes Over.*"

"Then the strangest thing happened," she said. "The firemen later discovered two people in our bathroom! They were unconscious, but quickly rescued. They evidently thought our open door was a stairwell or a fire escape and had made their way into our bathroom after we left. When we were allowed to go back in for our personal things, I found a man's shoe!"

Donna met the shoe's owner five months later while appearing at the Miss North Carolina Pageant. "A couple came up to me and said, 'We're the people who found refuge in your bathroom!'"

After the fire, Donna had gone on to Miami to ride in the Orange Bowl Parade but had been prohibited by her doctor from participating. It was a night parade and he was concerned that the damage to her lungs might lead to pneumonia. It was a rare occasion for a Miss America to miss an event.

The year of her reign wasn't marked solely by tragedy, however. Donna had many happy times as well. "I got to meet Norman Rockwell and thousands of other wonderful people."

Thinking she wanted a career, she told her mother she wanted to go into television. "Mom said, 'Oh, don't do that! You could be a teacher or secretary!'"

Donna realized she was on the cutting edge of television but she opted to marry instead.

"I didn't realize how important it was for me to get back to a balance in my life after that incredibly demanding year. I think it's very important to be sure your life is stabilized in all areas before making any decisions regarding developing or committing to a permanent relationship. You need to discover who you are first. You have to know yourself, to make yourself secure financially and professionally, or at least be in the process before you decide to tie in with the first guy who asks you to marry him."

Donna believes there are two primary things to remember in life: "You need to figure out what you want and what you don't want for your life. One of the challenges of being a former Miss America is finding the right balance in a future husband. This is a lifelong commitment that requires serious consideration. It's an abnormal year in your life. You're with thousands of people but you're socially isolated. You're not around friends. You don't date for a year."

Donna didn't have a boyfriend at the time she was crowned. "I entered the pageant thinking I could go back to a normal life as a college student. When I returned, I found that some guys were afraid to ask me out because they would be teased. Others were intimidated by the title.

"I recall as a young woman, making a list of the Christian-based characteristics that I wanted in a husband. It was just a thing you did with your girlfriends."

The list would now have to be extended. Coming from such a public persona after winning the title, Donna needed a man who was inwardly secure and strong. "My life experiences had been so accelerated over the year of my tour, I knew even then that dating a Miss America might be understandably intimidating for a young man. And of course, I still needed someone who was God centered, more than anything else."

Donna married, perhaps too quickly, seeking a quieter life coming from the pageant experience. This is a life event that the majority of Miss Americas have experienced. And as with many young marriages, she soon recognized that it wasn't going to work no matter how much effort she put into the relationship. She soon found herself on her own again, looking for a new direction for her life.

Donna was stinging a bit from her personal defeat. "When you're in the public eye and your marriage doesn't work, it's a real downer psychologically." Donna turned to her family and her church for emotional support. She moved back to her parents' home with her baby daughter.

"I did some personal appearances for a while, thinking the phone would ring, that something would happen professionally. Then I suddenly realized that I needed to pull from my earlier goal-oriented philosophy to make it happen!"

And Donna wasted no more time. Completely focused, she headed back to the University of Arkansas to work on her master's degree. This single mother taught four speech classes as a graduate teaching assistant, studied, attended classes, wrote her thesis, and graduated with a master's degree in Speech and Drama—all in one year!

But when she graduated this time, she was prepared to develop herself professionally. "I got a teaching job at Texas Tech University and at the same time started doing my first TV show."

She was booked as a speaker all over the country. She emceed and sang at pageants and performed as guest artist with several symphonies. For seven years, Donna produced and hosted public affairs shows in Little Rock, Austin and Lubbock.

Five years later, a second marriage produced a son, but ended several years after that, the result of too much strain from trying to withstand her husband's statewide political scandal.

Donna experienced a great deal of introspection and spiritual growth over the next ten years.

"When I was down and out and literally on my back looking up to God, I'd ask Him to help me, to redirect my path. Because I had discovered that every time I tried to make a decision without God being a part of it, even though I was thinking I was making a right decision—especially about mates, every time God was not a part of it, it turned out to be the wrong decision."

She had been divorced ten years when faith and fate finally intervened. Now a successful television host and producer, Donna learned to be content in whatever she was experiencing in her life. "I had wonderful friends, a great, dynamic church and life was good," she said.

Then a single phone call changed her life—again.

She was taping *Good Morning, Arkansas* in Little Rock and her guest was an executive vice president of Phillips Petroleum Company. They were discussing the current state of the oil industry. After the show, her guest approached her, "You know, Donna, there's this guy in Bartlesville who reports to me at Phillips. He's a really sharp guy. His name is Bryan Whitworth. You need to meet him. I'll be back in touch."

But Donna finally had her life in order, personally and professionally, and thought nothing of it. In fact, she had just closed on a house in Little Rock. There she stood, boxes piled to the ceiling, when the phone rang. It was her friend making good on his promise—a promise she had promptly forgotten. "Donna, Bryan and I are coming to town on business. We will

Donna and Bryan

meet you at seven for dinner."

"I need to take a rain check," she pleaded, explaining her plight. She had just moved in, was busy unpacking, trying to get her house in order, busy with her show, no time, no time—but Charlie would have none of it.

"So we had dinner, the three of us," she laughed, "and the rest is history."

How did she know this was the one?

"There was instantly a really good balance there between us. I had learned to be secure and happy within myself. I knew exactly what I was looking for." Donna had traveled a great deal as Miss America and in her television work. She had learned to enjoy travel and a culteral variety—the arts, music and generally all things good life has to offer.

"I tend to get cabin fever if I'm home too long," she admitted. "Bryan traveled a lot in his job. He enjoys the stimulation of different things, as I do. We were instantly completely compatible, and became best friends. And perhaps," she added thoughtfully, "the most important characteristic, aside from his personality and professional successes, is the fact that he is a Christian gentleman. That says it all."

And this, this above all, was the deciding factor for their getting together. Through the last twenty years, as a step-mom with a blended family, Donna admits to experiencing some bumps along the way.

"Bryan and I have prayed about things together and relationships have developed over the years, miraculous healing relationships when we personally and physically couldn't heal them, but we would step back and say, God, I can't do this by myself. I'm going to step back and listen until I know what you need me to do. "When she encounters an obstacle,

Donna still asks herself, "What would Jesus do?" She said, "He knew what His purpose was on earth. We have to struggle to find our purpose, sometimes. But we are to emulate His actions as we relate to others around us. There are such great challenges in our lives in today's society. Jesus already knew what we would face, but we still need to figure it out."

Perhaps Bryan and Donna didn't choose each other. Perhaps the Lord chose them *for* each other. Donna said, "Bryan's professional success was not as important to me as was the fact that he was a Christian gentleman. When we dated we discussed our value systems, morals, our convictions. And when he asked me to marry him, I said, 'Well, I'm not through asking you questions. Are you a born-again believer?'" Bryan's answer was an unequivocal yes and the happy couple married three months after they met. Donna believes that there is no spiritual bond between a couple if the Lord is not present in both lives.

They currently live in Fort Worth, Texas. Bryan Whitworth is a retired executive vice president and general counsel of Phillips Petroleum Company. Currently, he is of counsel to a New York City law firm, Wachtell, Lipton, Rosen and Katz. They have been married since 1984 and Donna shares her introspection as to why this marriage is successful. "Love, respect, balance and friendship. These are the keys to a happy marriage," she said. This blended family includes five children and eight grandchildren.

"The Miss America experience broadened my life tremendously, and I'm so grateful," Donna said. When she gives an inspirational talk, she often uses this quote. "Allow nothing to discourage or deter you. Define your goal then live it, sleep it, dream it—keep on and on, and it will be yours." Donna has always lived by this very premise, even as a college student.

A proud mom at her son's wedding

"I taped it to the mirror at college and every morning en route to class, this was emblazoned on my brain," she said.

She added, "I encourage people to break out of small-box thinking. I had the curiosity to look beyond my little box, to grow. And every time, I learned something," Donna said. "And I think if people follow that premise, their box will continually expand and their personal fulfillment become greater."

Donna has a passion for learning that started as a little girl in small-town America. "I frequently went to the library. I was always curious about other cultures and different countries and always wanted to travel a lot.

"I'll always be interested in learning—whether I'm learning a new skill, attending an art exhibit or a symphony performance."

This lovely woman has made a practice of encouraging young people to look inside themselves, to identify their God-given talents and to seek out opportunities that will allow them to develop their talents and skills and eventually become fulfilled.

"To me, this is a lifelong process. People need to focus on discovering their purpose, then plan their course and pursue their dream."

Asked if it was difficult to transition between being a Miss America and living in the private sector, she responded, "We have a foot in both worlds. We're a public figure but we're wives and moms and grandmas and professional women. But as you get older, you're allowed to be more yourself,

I think. Life isn't over when you hand over the crown. It's a stepping-stone; it's not the whole world. The important thing to remember is to continually ask yourself: *How can I apply what I've learned in the life I'm creating today? How can I use that?* You can't just stay in the past."

With all she's accomplished, Donna never forgets her roots. And with all her achievements, she uses her name and contacts to better the lives of others.

Donna remains active in the arts. In 1994, President Bill Clinton appointed Donna to the President's Advisory Commission on the Arts for the John F. Kennedy Center for the Performing Arts in Washington, D.C., yet another Kennedy connection in her life. Donna's committee raises over a million dollars a year to support the education programs for the Center, throughout the nation.

"I'm so convinced, based on statistics and my own

Lovely as ever, Donna chatting with a guest in the Hospitality Suite at Caesar's during pageant week 2003. Donna is on the board of directors of the Miss America Organization.
Photo by Kate Kitchen

experience that participation in the arts boosts scholastic achievement and enriches the lives of individuals—of not only those who participate but audiences as well."

Donna does a great deal of civic work in the cultural arts and education arena as well as with women's organizations.

She volunteers with passion in fundraising efforts for the Van Cliburn Foundation, which hosts the international piano competition for aspiring concert pianists. She has served on the executive committee since 2002. She is so focused on helping others through arts and education that her generous gift helped name a new fitness center in her honor at the University of Arkansas. It is used daily by two thousand students, staff and faculty.

"I find myself asking the Lord - *What am I supposed to be doing now?* I ask Him to please open doors for me that should be open and close the ones that should be closed."

Donna returns every year to the pageant to visit with her Miss America sisters. She has missed only three years in the forty years since her tour. "I still love the Miss America program," she said. In February 2004, Donna was named a member of the Miss America Organization Board of Directors.

"I remain focused on helping these young women to develop their leadership skills and earn scholarships to further their education and professional careers."

In summing up her life thus far, and reflecting on the years since she wore the Miss America crown, Donna Axum Whitworth didn't do too badly for a "late bloomer—just a skinny kid from El Dorado, Arkansas—a skinny kid with a dream."

Miss America 1965

Vonda Kay Van Dyke

Student - Arizona State University

Age - 21   Height - 5' 6''

Talent: Vonda Kay, a professional ventriloquist, sang *Together*
in a duet with Kurley, her red-haired dummy

After being urged by her chaperone to be a little more dignified, Vonda Kay thought
carefully, then responded cheerfully, "Well, today I guess I'm not being Miss America.
Today I'm being Miss Congeniality!"

—Vonda Kay Van Dyke

Vonda Kay Van Dyke

Vonda Kay Van Dyke still holds the distinction of being the only Miss America to carry a pet turtle with her in First Class during her reign—until she got caught, that is. She was most certainly the only Miss America to get kicked out of class in high school for playing a trick on her teacher. Life must never be dull around this lovely lady. She is subject to whimsical behavior and her life is surrounded with energy, a positive spirit and lots of laughter.

Although she had a rather rhythmic-sounding name, *Vonda Kay Van Dyke* proved to be a bit cumbersome when the TV Guide graphic artist tried to fit it all into one line. Vonda Kay and her agent immediately decided to rectify that situation for the future by dropping her middle name. Vonda Van Dyke now fits precisely on one line in TV Guide.

So how did this woman, who was also the only Miss America to earn the title Miss Congeniality, choose to develop such a talent as ventriloquism? It turned out to be a talent that would spawn a highly successful career as an entertainer.

When Vonda was a little girl growing up in Muskegon, Michigan, she and her family lived in a quiet, settled neighborhood consisting mostly of empty nesters. There were no children to play with. She became fascinated watching ventriloquist Paul Winchell and his wooden sidekick Jerry Mahoney on television. A

Vonda and Kurley -1965.

neighbor suggested she might enjoy learning the craft, so for her seventh birthday, Vonda was given a dummy. She remembers fondly that her first performance was for her Sunday school class. Her debut was successful and Vonda Kay Van Dyke, entertainer, was born.

Shortly thereafter, the family moved to Phoenix, Arizona and the child began to act in commercials. She was selected, along with an unknown, husky, nine-year-old singer to do a local television show called the Lou King Ranger Show. The boy's name, by the way, was Wayne Newton. Just Vonda, Wayne and Flamenco dancers—it was quite a show. Vonda was only eight at the time. The group was hired to do other events and the twenty-five dollars she earned went a long way. It was, after all, the 1950s.

Vonda's luck ran out quickly, however. One day, she ran straight out in front of a car and broke her leg. The fracture was so severe that she was laid up in a body cast for two months.

This was her first show business lesson. "I learned early on that if you're not there, the opportunity goes away. If you lose the continuity or don't pay attention to what you're doing, it's gone. You have to be at the right place at the right time and be willing to work consistently or the opportunity will vanish." Vonda did in fact lose that chance, but it didn't matter. She had enjoyed her start

Kate Kitchen

As Grand Marshall for the parade in Atlantic City (1970s).

and had already been bitten by the entertainment bug.

Before she became Miss America, Vonda earned the title of Arizona's Junior Miss. For the talent competition, she teamed up with a brand new partner. Her bald dummy donned a red, wavy wig and the team became Vonda Kay and Kurley.

The young woman became so adept at ventriloquism that she even fooled her high school teacher. On one particular warm afternoon, Vonda couldn't help but notice that the classroom windows were open. She had an idea. In addition to learning how to throw her voice, Vonda Kay had also learned how to throw a whistle.

As the class progressed, Vonda sat straight-faced and proper, then periodically whistled, looking over innocently toward the open windows as if she thought the sound were coming from outside. Classmates followed suit, searching for the source. Things would calm down, then there it would come, a loud whistle, just outside the classroom. This strange sound finally became so disruptive that the teacher became angry. "I'm going to find out who's doing that and stop it!" And outside he went. Then back inside he came. Nothing. No one was out there.

Having far too much fun, Vonda Kay waited quietly, patiently, until she couldn't stand it anymore. Just one more time. She whistled a piercing whistle, still without moving her mouth, throwing the sound outside. The teacher became really angry.

"I'm going to find out who that is if it's the last thing I do!" he said, once again storming out of the classroom. Soon after, he returned triumphant, holding a twisted metal whistle in his hand. He had crushed it by stomping on it.

Unable to contain her mirth, Vonda began to laugh. The class quickly caught on to her prank and joined her.

The next day the teacher lectured her sternly, explaining that this class was required for her to graduate and he was going to have to dismiss her. She was devastated. Crying, she turned toward the door and began to leave, when she felt his hand on her shoulder.

"Vonda Kay," he said. "You had a laugh at my expense and I just wanted to show you I have a sense of humor, too. I was kidding about kicking you out. But you need to behave. Now go back to class." She was so relieved she returned to class and never pulled that stunt again. At least not until pageant night in Atlantic City.

But Vonda had to earn her way to the title first. She competed in the Miss Phoenix Pageant and was named first runner-up two years in a row.

"An official Miss America judge called me and told me she thought I had potential. She suggested that I run in the Miss Tempe competition. So I entered the same year I had placed for the second time in the Miss Phoenix event. I won the Miss Tempe Pageant."

Vonda is remarkably candid about her win. She laughed. "I won because I was the only contestant who showed up. I stood around for a while and someone finally came up to me and said, 'Congratulations, you've won.'"

Vonda then competed for the next level and this time there was plenty of competition. She walked off the stage with the title Miss

114

From Vonda's composite during her acting days.

Maricopa County. "I had ended up competing against the Miss Phoenix I had lost to earlier," she said.

What a smart move, it was for her to enter again, because this time Vonda walked off with the brass ring.

Once she decided to enter the pageant, as a junior in college, Vonda Kay gave it her all. For the year and a half prior to the competition, in addition to attending Arizona State University, Vonda was working twelve shows a day, six days a week, at Legend City—an amusement park in Phoenix. She had auditioned three hundred jokes and timed them, including the laughter, in preparation for her two minute and forty-second performance at the pageant.

During the night of the Miss America Pageant, Vonda Kay was having way too much fun to curtail her mischievous sense of humor. After having been named Miss Congeniality and then named in the top ten, she truly thought the evening was over for her. No Miss Congeniality had ever become Miss America. She had already won enough scholarship money to finish college. How much better could it get?

Now quite relaxed, standing in a row with nine other hopefuls, she began to feel restless. As they took turns smiling, speaking, turning around and posing, she began to make wisecracks without moving her lips. Finally, Miss Texas, standing near her, whispered, "Will you please stop!? My tummy's jiggling—I can't stop laughing!" And suddenly the winner was announced—the ventriloquist had taken the prize—and the crown.

This time, it was not her refreshing sense of humor that got her into hot water during the pageant. It was her faith. Miss America contestants and winners were to stay clear of two topics—religion and politics. This was a hard and fast rule at the time.

But this one question had appeared on the application: Do you carry a good luck charm? Not a superstitious woman, Vonda wasn't sure what to write down. She answered honestly, "No, but I did bring my Bible with me."

Unaware of the pageant rule, the judges had developed the questions for the interview and Vonda Kay's question reflected their lack of awareness. "We understand you carry a Bible with you as a good luck charm. Tell us about your religion." Her reply made pageant history as the first Miss America to make a bold statement about her faith.

"I don't consider my Bible a good luck charm. I consider it to be the most important Book I own and I wouldn't consider my companionship with God as a religion, but as a faith. I believe in Him, I trust in Him, and pray that even tonight, *His* will be done."

The instantaneous applause may have reflected what the audience felt, but immediately after she was crowned, even before she was allowed to give her first press conference, pageant officials swarmed over her, sternly lecturing her about her comments. She refused to crumble. She stood firm and reminded them that others had initiated that topic, and that she had to be free to respond honestly if she were asked that question. She did agree, however, not to initiate the topic. Pageant officials would have to be satisfied with that. They agreed.

And of course from that moment on, the subject came up in every press conference. Vonda Kay was sent hundreds of Bibles that year.

Although she was used to a grueling schedule, nevertheless Vonda decided to liven up her

115

Miss America tour. She declared to Mr. Homeyer, a representative from Oldsmobile, a pageant sponsor, that she really wanted a pet so it could travel with her. Happy to please her, Mr. Homeyer complied, all in good fun. He presented her with a tiny turtle in a little plastic bowl, complete with a miniature, plastic palm tree. He had assumed she would get a laugh out of it and leave it with someone in a hotel. Vonda decided to let Mr. Ho (she named the turtle after the benefactor) travel with her.

Her chaperone, probably worn down by Vonda's earnest pleas and contagious zest for life, finally agreed with one condition. "Vonda Kay, you *cannot*—absolutely *cannot* tell anyone about this! It *must stay hidden*!" Of course, Vonda promised.

All was well until during one particularly rough flight, Mr. Ho was somehow shaken out of his milk-carton home which tipped over—in the First Class cabin. Once he was found, he was quickly adopted and promised a new home—on the ground. Vonda and her chaperone continued their journey, Vonda just a bit chagrined and her chaperone worried about the press finding out, thereby creating a major incident over a silly turtle.

Occasionally Vonda's chaperone would ask with more than a hint of exasperation, "Vonda Kay, can't you be a little more dignified?" Vonda Kay would pretend to think carefully, weigh her words, then respond cheerfully, "Well, today I guess I'm not being Miss America, I'm being Miss Congeniality."

Vonda Kay had a wide-eyed naivete about people. It wasn't until the Miss America experience that she found herself the target of petty jealousy. "I could never imagine anyone being jealous of me," she said with true humility, recalling the first time she came up against the green-eyed monster.

During a performance, she had sneaked from backstage into the auditorium to watch part of the show. She was astounded to hear two women nearby berating her for one thing after another. The conversation went on for minutes. It was very painful to hear and so unfair. But in true Vonda Kay spirit, she dealt with it head on and realized something then and there. "It had nothing to do with me. It had *everything* to do with them and how they felt about themselves." She said, "From that

moment on, I always thought that if I were doing my job and doing it well, that would be my only concern. People like those women either need to change their attitude or just go around being unhappy. It's their decision."

When reflecting on her tour, Vonda thought for a minute, then admitted, "I'm sure I was less serious than others."

What was it like to be married to this woman? Vonda's late husband David, thankfully, had a wonderful sense of humor as well. Occasionally referred to as "Mr. Van Dyke" at social gatherings, Dr. David Scoates would gently correct the person with this light-hearted response—"It's Doctor."

David was well able to handle the celebrity life his own job required, perhaps partly due to having been married to Miss America for so many years. He was president of the Dr. Robert Schuller Ministry until the late 1990s when he semi-retired and took a post in Florida. But ever since they married, David was always Vonda's protector.

According to Vonda, she had her share of Miss America *nuts*. She recalled a series of incidents with one man, in particular, that seemed to start out harmlessly enough. He worked for the postal service. Somehow, he had found out her exact schedule. His one-way courtship began as he sent gifts to her hotel—once a pound of caviar, another time a *gallon* bottle of TABU cologne! But when he started showing up at her public appearances, pageant officials began to guard her schedule more carefully.

There is a downside to everything, and this is a downside to all Miss Americas: the potential stalkers. Later on, another zealot actually threatened her life. And now, she says the fanatics are very recognizable. "They have a certain way about them. But," she added, "if someone would come up that seemed to pose a potential threat, my husband would recognize the danger right away and get me out of there."

The couple first met nearly a decade after Vonda won the title. She was hired to sing the national anthem at a Miami Dolphins game. David, a Methodist minister at the time, was asked to offer the pre-game prayer. It wasn't love at first sight, because years later, they hardly remembered meeting. It was a full five years later when someone finally proved to them that they had met before. They were shown the program from that game, the program with both their names. Several years after that auspicious football game, the fates made sure they would take notice of each other.

Two different couples invited Vonda and David to two separate dinner parties, both in the same week with the same intention, to meet one another. These two people seemed to belong together and the only two people who evidently didn't know that were Vonda Van Dyke and David Scoates. She just happened to live three blocks from the friend's home where they were to dine, and gentleman that he was, David walked her home.

Thus began a traveling courtship, as he was working at the time for the National Board of the Methodist Church. Vonda would ask her agent to book her in cities where David would be and less than a year later, she happily became the reverend's wife. Several years later, after the birth of their daughter, the owner of the Dolphins, Joe Robbie, invited the couple back to a Dolphins game to repeat their 'performance'—the prayer and the national anthem.

In 1997, after more than thirty years of performing as an vocalist, ventriloquist and all-out entertainer, Vonda Van Dyke retired. She had performed from one end of the country to another, had done television commercials for Pepsi, Oldsmobile, Maybelline and FTD. She had met hundreds of celebrities and earned several awards, including being named Outstanding Christian Witness. She served on various boards of directors and was active in charity work all her life.

But after one last performance, after singing at the Crystal Cathedral in southern California where she was participating in a women's conference, she wanted it to be over. "I was singing for three days and didn't think my voice sounded that good. I had just returned from Europe and put together this conference and was just exhausted. I remember that I sang and walked off stage at the Crystal Cathedral and thought to myself, *I don't want to do this anymore.* I went home and told David and he simply said, 'Well, don't.' And that was the end of it. I had officially retired."

During our first interview in 1998, this writer marveled at this extraordinary woman.

To speak with her even for the first time leaves you thinking you've just found a new best friend.

At that time, Vonda and her husband David Tyler Scoates, a Methodist minister, had just moved into their new home in southern California. They were celebrating twenty-one years of marriage. Their daughter, then eighteen, was attending college and subsequently graduated in theatre. Asked if she felt the empty nest syndrome, Vonda had laughed and said, "Absolutely not! We're just fixing up our honeymoon cottage!"

David retired from Crystal Cathedral that year, but decided to take another short-term pastorate in Lost Tree, North Palm Beach, Florida. It would last six months, so they could come back to southern California once it was completed. The job was different from the huge, expansive cathedral where he had been a pastor. Lost Tree was an upscale, gated community. David would be spared the normal —often monumental—duties of a church administrator; there were few meetings and he was required only to preach on Sundays in the little chapel. And then Vonda's world turned upside down.

On May 6, 2000, a normal Saturday morning, Vonda decided to make herself scarce and go shopping while David sat at the dining room table, in view of the ocean, to prepare his final sermon for the Lost Tree congregation. He had kissed her good-bye when she left.

"I had been shopping only an hour and a half," she said. "Suddenly, I came to a stoplight and the strongest feeling came over me. I felt that I had to go home. I turned around and quickly drove home."

Vonda walked into the dining room to find her husband lying on the floor. He had suffered either an aneurysm or stroke and, she was told later, had died instantly. They were preparing to celebrate their 24th wedding anniversary just one month later. And two weeks prior, David and Vonda had returned to California where he had sailed through a medical exam. She had been so relieved that he'd had a check-up.

Vonda's husband was honored in three separate memorials in the churches he had served. She traveled from Florida to California to Minnesota for all the services, grateful for the

Vonda and David

heartfelt support and the love his parishioners had shown. Everyone who knew him wanted the chance to say goodbye.

Determined to keep a promise, Vonda took her daughter and granddaughter to Europe in June, still enveloped in a fog of grief. "We had promised our grandchildren we would take them on a special trip when each one turned thirteen," she said. "I thought it was important that I keep my word."

Vonda eventually returned to their lovely home in southern California to start her life over. And thankfully, her loving husband had already given her tools to cope with during this trying time.

"The Sunday before his death, David preached a sermon on how to handle the death of a loved one. Vonda had always listened intently to David's sermons and that last one truly helped her through what she was facing.

"But I also developed some tools to deal with grief through the years," she said. "I can only describe it as an on-off switch on my control panel called life. When I'm faced with something too difficult for me to handle, I mentally pull the switch and literally hand the problem over to God. It works!"

Her life has changed in monumental ways over the past four years. But always resilient and determined to remain spiritually centered, Vonda uses her time to volunteer to help others. "I sat recently with a heart patient and thought how nice it was that I could do that without feeling rushed. And I help out at the local community theatre where my daughter is set designer. I travel a lot. I love to travel and I want to do it as much as I can while I'm still young and healthy enough to enjoy it."

As this book was going to press, Vonda was preparing for a trip to Ireland. The vacation will take place during her birthday.

"I have a theory," she said smiling. "If you're out of the country during your birthday, it doesn't count. So I try to always be out of the country during my birthday. It keeps me young and gives me an excuse to travel."

Vonda has always seemed to know who she is, where she's been and where she's going-although she may decide to take a twist or turn along the way. To Vonda, life is a joyful journey and she's never been afraid to reach out for it, to experience all that it has to offer. Her sense of humor is absolutely unparalleled.

So if you're sitting in church sometime and the sermon's just a little too dull, or you're attending a symphony concert and the music's just a bit too high-brow, don't be surprised to hear a haunting whistle from the lobby, a whistle no one can identify. You might want to look around to be sure it's not a former Miss America, sitting there with an innocent smile on her face, just wanting to stir the pot a bit.

Miss America 1967

Jane Jayroe

Student - Oklahoma City University
State - Oklahoma
Age - 19   Height - 5' 6''

Talent: A musical routine that featured her singing and
conducting the pageant orchestra.

Photo courtesy of the Miss America Organization

"I might have looked like a Miss America on the outside, but inside I felt like a hick from the
sticks and I wanted to go home! I even considered giving up the crown. Thank God I didn't!"
—Jane Jayroe

Jane Jayroe

Watching her grow up in the rural town of Laverne, Oklahoma, one might never have suspected that this young girl would one day wear the coveted crown of Miss America. And her thoughts on the subject? Jane Jayroe was too busy becoming an expert at basketball to even consider the possibility. She picked up the game from her father, high school teacher and basketball coach, Pete Jayroe. Her team placed second at state competition then suddenly, Jane reversed her focus.

She entered Oklahoma City University, declaring a major in Music Education—about as far from the basketball court as she could get. Never one to be concerned with gender stereotypes, Jane aspired to become a professional singer or musical conductor.

It was a unique era for women. While a college education was encouraged, a woman was somehow stigmatized if she graduated without a ring on her finger. Academic and career counselors were few and far between, and if a young lady were lucky enough to be counseled at all, she would most likely hear, "You need a degree to *fall back on*." There wasn't much incentive for a lady to be encouraged to find her professional niche in those days. Jane had thought she might teach, but was less than inspired by the thought. And then the roller coaster of life came along and took her up and down its own track.

During her sophomore year, Jane was encouraged to enter the Miss Oklahoma City Pageant. On her first try, she won the local competition. She became Miss Oklahoma and in quick succession, Miss America. To a nineteen-year-old in the '60s, it was a fairy tale come true. What a rush to stand before eighteen thousand screaming fans at Convention Hall in Atlantic City and be adored without people even knowing you. No one was more surprised. This lovely nineteen-year-old was not, in her own mind, qualified to win such an honor.

"I thought Miss California should have won—Charlene Diane Dallas—even her name was sophisticated."

Until pageant summer, Jane had never spoken in public to a group, she had never flown in an airplane and had never been far from home. Painfully shy and insecure, she longed suddenly to be back on the court—not the beauty queen's court, but rather the basketball

Photo courtesy of the Miss America Organization.

Jane and Tyler with their furry family - 1986.

court where in a tee-shirt and shorts she had always felt at home. *What had she done?* she asked herself as she waved at the television camera that beamed the signal to millions of viewers. Jane Jayroe, the little girl from Oklahoma, was now a celebrity and represented young women everywhere. Suddenly she felt the enormity of the responsibility.

Instead of the joy that is expected following such a highlight, Jane was overcome with the realities of living up to the title. She felt so inept and unprepared to spend the year away from family and friends and play the role of Miss America. She felt hopelessly inadequate.

"In the midst of all the self doubt, God reached out His loving hand in a simple but miraculous way," she said, recalling the moments after her crowning. "Following the pageant, Miss America is immediately protected from everyone. No telephone calls were even allowed into the room. But on that Sunday morning, a very special phone call got through to me.

"It was Reverend Leonard Gillingham, the Methodist minister who had been so dear to our family."

Jane doesn't remember the details of the conversation but knew in her heart she was receiving God's assurance through Leonard. She was certain of it.

"God was saying in a strong voice that I would not be traveling the year alone as Miss America, but that He would be there—every mile of the trip—in every speech that was given—through every moment."

Jane knew it was God's grace that had brought her to this moment in Atlantic City, and she was assured that grace would take her through the year.

Whether or not she was prepared for this honor, she wore the crown well. Taking her responsibilities seriously, she made something very special happen. For years, Bob Hope had asked the pageant to permit Miss America to join his USO tour, but he always used the position more for a springboard to a punch line than treating it as an honor, so the organization had refused. Jane was overcome with the feeling of duty, knowing while she was enjoying the luxury of her new celebrity, boys back home in Oklahoma had left their families to fight in Vietnam.

"I had to go," she explained. "I had always been inspired by the Susan Hayward movie, *With a Song in My Heart.*"

The media continued to ask her about Vietnam because of its controversy, and she kept insisting she wanted to go. The pressure from the press only served to help her cause.

So Jane, with the help of pageant officials and one of the primary sponsors, PepsiCo, (chaired at the time by Joan Crawford), initiated the USO tour. After rounding up former competitors and state winners, off she went with a professionally produced musical show choreographed especially for the American military forces. Controversial or not, this effort was for the men and women who were honoring our country's flag by risking their lives in a foreign country. The young woman—who months before had never flown in an airplane—was now leading a musical tour halfway across the world to entertain the troops.

As a news anchor at KXAS in Dallas - Ft. Worth.

To date, the memories of that two-week engagement still bring tears to her eyes. "It was so meaningful," she said. "I was the first Miss America to have the opportunity to go to Vietnam. It was so rewarding to bring honor to all the Americans there. In this country we have been so blessed, educationally and culturally. At that time we had not experienced in our own homeland the total tragedy, devastation and hopelessness that war brings to a nation.

"Miss Tennessee was on the tour. She saw her high school friend who had been severely injured. His legs had been amputated. I saw my own cousin from back home. I'll never forget that experience."

The rest of the year provided the normal whirlwind of activities scheduled for Miss America. Day after day, Jane traveled from city to city, coast to coast, performing and speaking in front of large groups with never enough rest nor rehearsal time. She still laughs when she thinks of how unspoiled Miss America is as a celebrity. She noted that when major celebrities and singers appear on tour, many send along a long list of their specific requirements such as food and beverages, dressing room amenities, and the like.

"Miss Americas are lucky to get to a city on time with their luggage and music, and rarely do we have time for rehearsal or to rest at all before a performance. And if something's not in place, we just do what we need to do."

This go-with-the-flow ability served Jane well in her later years as a broadcast journalist. "When I think of what I learned that year, being shoved in front of cameras, speaking to the media or the audience at the drop of a hat, I owe a great deal of gratitude to the Miss America experience."

It wasn't difficult at all for Jane to relinquish the crown and get back to her roots.

"I returned to Oklahoma City University, to my friends, to the church, and I was once again close to my family. In addition to the scholarship award, she earned approximately a hundred thousand dollars in speaking engagements. She worked as a spokesperson for the next year or two, in addition to attending school.

She could have gone to any college in the country. Why Oklahoma City University?

"I was so glad to be home," she said, "and the university has an outstanding Performing Arts Department. God had led me to OCU in such an incredible way, and that's where I needed to return."

At the time, OCU was a small, private Methodist University with a great sense of community, a remarkable and caring faculty, and a tradition of successful performers. Jane was the first Miss America from that school, but since that time, two other Miss Americas have attended OCU (Susan Powell and Shawntel Smith) as well as Miss America state representatives and numerous other pageant winners.

However, it was time for the post-Miss America trap that many of the women have experienced. It seems that life on the road, carrying the crown and gown persona, is so harrowing, so fast-paced, so demanding—that many of our heroines were unprepared for the toll it takes. Jane was no exception.

"So many boys were intimidated to date Miss America that they simply chose not to," she laughed. "And I was so tired of the frantic pace and always being on stage and trying to be perfect, I wanted a normal quieter life. Plus," she said reflectively, "there still was a stigma about getting out of school with a degree and no ring on your finger." Jane wanted to have what she thought was a normal life with someone who wasn't afraid of her celebrity.

"When you become Miss America at that age, what do you do for an encore? Not only did I feel a pull to be something more, but I guess, subconsciously, I wanted to subjugate that stigma of getting out of school with a degree, being single and having no particular

On the set of *Discover Oklahome* - 1998.

purpose."

Jane began dating a young fellow who was in no way intimidated about being with a former Miss America.

"He was very aggressive about dating me, and I must admit that being so young and inexperienced, it felt good to let down my guard and have someone else make the decisions. Jane met the young man in October, shortly after she returned from her yearlong tour and by February they were engaged. They were married the following August.

She had permitted herself to fall in love earlier than she should have, she admits candidly. In retrospect, she said "I think it's better when Miss A is older, after having developed her professional orientation and career skills." In the '60s, however, Jane agrees that the mentality of women was different. "I was almost relieved to have the man making the major life decisions. I could now rest, I thought."

Her husband was a law student and after they married and graduated, they moved to Tulsa. Jane still traveled a great deal as a Miss America, offering her celebrity to dedications and ribbon cuttings for sponsors. She also became involved with community musical theatre.

"I could make more money as a Miss America spokesperson than any job I could have been offered, although a regular job would have given me better structure, a healthier sense of community and would have prepared me better for the future," she said.

Complimenting one of her Miss America sisters, she explained, "Phyllis George was one of many Miss Americas who did it well. She was very savvy during her year. She was self-directed. She networked well and used her appearances constructively to build her future."

Jane, on the other hand, wasn't faring so well in her new marriage or her career.

"My marriage was troubled from the beginning. I tried to be everything I was supposed to be, but it wasn't working. He was a young attorney, totally absorbed in his career. But even though I tried to search for direction and to make our marriage better, we continued to have serious problems."

Although those problems were rapidly becoming insurmountable, for eight years Jane remained in the marriage because her upbringing had taught her that divorce was never an option.

The reality of life's unfairness hit her hard. "I tried my best. I always thought that if you did the right things and worked hard, you were rewarded. Especially when you've been everyone's darling, it's all amplified. I was failing at my marriage, trying harder and harder, and it wasn't working. The unfairness of that reality hit me so hard."

Jane began to feel totally out of control. No matter how hard she had tried, her marriage continued to dissolve. She had a strong desire to have a child. After eight years of marriage, she finally succeeded in getting pregnant. But even with the baby's birth heralded by the press, Jane knew she couldn't ignore what was going on in her life. She was experiencing total joy from the brand new life of her son Tyler, born on the fourth of July, 1976. Yet there was a cold, numbing reality brought on by the devastation and eventual death of her marriage.

"I finally went into a protective mode. I

123

needed to be in a place of emotional support and to be closer to my family."

During her years in Tulsa, she hadn't wasted her time. Having earned a master's degree in Humanities, she was at least better equipped to find a job.

"I finally sought counsel from my minister. I had been involved with the local church for two years and before I got pregnant, that faith community had begun to help strengthen me. I knew after Tyler's birth, I couldn't stay in limbo. I needed love and support."

With a renewed direction, learning finally to seek a life of her own, on her own, she packed up the baby and moved to Oklahoma City.

"For some reason, I didn't even have the confidence to apply for a job. I stayed with my sister for a while. I just didn't know what to do."

One night, feeling totally alone, Jane reached the depths of despair. Tyler had been quite ill during the night, and the young mother was exhausted from a combination of stress and sleep deprivation. After finally getting the baby back to sleep, she went to bed. Lying alone in the dark, she was suddenly overcome with a tragic sense of loss.

Her face pressed into the pillow, she found herself sobbing uncontrollably, unable and unwilling to stop. She remembered her minister telling her once that it was all right just to experience grief, to let it happen. She was so tired of struggling and so tired of being lonely in her struggle for a happy marriage only to have it self-destruct before her eyes, that she just let go. She finally let herself surrender into her grief.

"I just let go of trying to get out of the hole of sadness, and wallowed in it. Tears were streaming down my face. I was falling into despair. Falling—crying—hurting; I never knew that emotional trauma could physically hurt so much. I was pitiful."

Jane felt betrayed, betrayed by someone she had trusted, betrayed by the unfairness of life itself. She had tried to do everything right and had failed miserably.

"But suddenly," she explained, "in the midst of the darkness, there was a subtle change. I began experiencing a feeling of grace, and I was no longer falling. There seemed to be, all at once, a bottom to the dark hole." She felt something powerful overtaking her, something cushioning her. She no longer felt alone. She felt as if she were being held, supported, and yes—loved. And she knew it was God's presence, His very grace that she was experiencing.

Whatever that was, that experience in the middle of a night of terror, loss and loneliness, Jane had given up to it; and the minute she did, she experienced a state of grace as if the Lord suddenly took it over because it was too much for her to bear.

And she remembered the words Jesus said: *"Come to me, all you who are weary and burdened, and I will give you rest. Take my yoke upon you and learn from me, for I am gentle and humble in heart, and you will find rest for your souls. For my yoke is easy and my burden is light."* (Matthew. 11:28)

Jane recalled exactly how she felt reading those words again. "There was rest and a sense of peace from the sharing of my burdens. By giving into the grief, God allowed it to be shared and gave me the hope that always grows from partnering with Jesus."

By morning, her grief and loneliness were replaced by a feeling of peace that she had never before experienced. It was then that things began to change.

The change wasn't quick, she noted. "Change seldom is. This was a step-by-step process. It was a matter some days of just doing the next right thing." She added, "Healing takes time. There are no shortcuts, but the journey was no longer hopeless. No longer was I alone."

Her father, still an educator, was by her side, offering his support. "He got me a job. And I learned a big lesson. Humbling as it was in its mediocrity, this job and my new co-workers started me on the path to knowing who and what I was," she said. Jane recalls that her way back to becoming a productive, thinking, self-directed woman started with this job.

"I began to have confidence again. I was only there six months. I had a twice-a-day, forty-five-minute commute and was restricted to two fifteen-minute breaks and a forty-five-minute lunch. I was caring for my baby and struggling to budget and pay the bills on my meager income. But during those months, I began the process of healing, and it was good."

It wasn't long before Jane's progress in spiritual healing began to bear fruit. She began to produce a public affairs TV show for the local educational station in Oklahoma City. What followed was a phone call from the local ABC television station asking Jane to audition to be their first female news anchor for the six p.m. and ten p.m. news.

"Women hadn't been on late news much, not *ever* at this particular station! After an audition, they offered me a late-night anchor position at double my current salary."

Jane doesn't pretend to think the call came because of her skills in journalism. She admittedly had none. "They called me solely for name recognition, not experience. And Oklahoma City viewers were very forgiving," she laughed warmly.

Tea on the Thames - Jane and Jerry on a canal boat in Europe - 1995.

But anchors at that time were writing their own copy and Jane, having completed a master's degree that had required a great deal of writing, learned quickly. She added, "If I had known that kind of job had been available when I went to college, I would have majored in it. It's a *perfect* arena for me!"

Jane was mentored by a news director who was thrilled at her enthusiasm and quick learning skills. "This job was a real godsend," she said. "The skills it required were very compatible with skills of being Miss A—dealing with pressure, the ability to remain calm and poised under great stress. There were days and nights coming into town as Miss A—not knowing what I was going to be doing. That experience helped me in this profession." Jane added reflectively, "As a Miss America, many times, you have no prep time. The great gift in that experience is that you soon learn to function in any environment."

The hand of God always supported Jane, but also pulled her forward. It was as if Jane never felt prepared for the next step; and yet, God pulled her forward and beyond any of her expectations. Jane found her career of choice through the tough times. She would never have gone to work doing the news on television because she wasn't prepared academically for that career. She would never have chosen to work nights because it didn't fit with the kind of family life that she had envisioned for herself. And yet—God knew best, and Jane followed out of desire for a suitable income for herself and her son.

Jane Jayroe had found her niche. She was in her early thirties, had her sweet baby boy and was finally earning a living as a professional, and she loved it. She remained at the ABC affiliate for two years, then moved up the ladder to Dallas and a larger broadcast journalism market where she stayed for four years. Her Dallas news director had not wanted her Miss America affiliation promoted, realizing her skills and knowing she had paid her professional dues as a broadcast journalist. But a print reporter evidently was vying for a big by line that day and wrote "KXAS Hires Barbie Doll." Two years later, he wrote an extremely flattering article on Jane's skills as a broadcast journalist and all was forgiven.

But the lessons we learn don't stay with us forever. It seems we have to learn the same ones over and over in order to become a life veteran. And Jane did it again. She married a man she met soon after her divorce. The deci-

Jane and Jerry in Jerusalem - 1998.

sion was based in part out of fear of being alone and a deep desire for family. She especially wanted to find a good father figure for Tyler and she desired additional children. At that time, she thought marriage would fulfill her personal need for emotional security. While her career skyrocketed, her personal life floundered once again.

"I finally decided that this was it with drama and trauma, with men who wanted to come and go in my life. I wanted to plant myself in a stable environment near my family, raise my son and grow up. My focus was always to be as good a mom as possible, and I didn't think I could do it in Dallas without family. Professionally, leaving a top ten market, when they wanted me to stay, was the toughest career decision I ever made."

Tyler was in the third grade when she returned with him to Oklahoma City. She has remained there. Her career as a broadcast journalist spanned sixteen years, but changes were due.

"I could see the handwriting on the wall regarding the dilemma women face of aging on television." The camera isn't kind, adding pounds and wrinkles indiscriminately. Jane left the on-camera work and designed a program for a medical complex, doing their marketing and writing their medical news. For four years, Jane served as vice president of the

Presbyterian Health Foundation and spokesperson for the Oklahoma Health Center.

And at long last, she's truly happy with a life partner. Her husband Gerald Gamble is a commercial real estate broker. She laughs as she reflects on their relationship. "We dated a long time. I thought he'd never marry me!" It seems this match was made for the Oklahoma beauty. "He's from a small town, too, with the same religious beliefs, the same values as mine. He's a great guy."

And as with many women who finally find Mr. Right, she realizes the obvious. "During the years of totally being on my own, raising a son alone, being fully responsible for my own decisions, my own life, I finally felt secure in myself. I didn't come into a relationship with him, needy. I wanted a companion, but I was doing just fine without one."

It's a sweet love story. The two met at

With Tyler, all grown up, on the Plaza Mayor in Madrid - 1997.

How precious a gift - the first grandson.

church. She coerced a friend into urging Jerry to escort her to an event she had to attend. Her voice fills with such warmth when she talks about him that you know instinctively this is a good match. "He's very practical, and has a lot of common sense. We were friends for a year, then we dated for five years until I finally popped the question!"

She laughed, offering this sensitive reflection. "I'm very happy now. The gift of having problems is knowing how to be grateful. Life can be really tough. When you hit these smooth, wonderful cycles, I'm very grateful for them, which is not to say you don't have little bumps along the way."

Whatever bumps along the way Jane Jayroe has yet in store for her, you can bet she'll be able to deal with them from now on.

Recently Jane has been co-hosting a statewide TV show, *Discover Oklahoma*. She is working on her writing career, having been published in McCall's and is a contributing writer for Chicken Soup for the Mother's Soul. She has created a seminar for women entitled, *Living Grace-fully* and another interdenominational Bible study entitled: *Esther Women—Those God Has Called Beyond Expectations.*

Jane continues to give back to her community. She serves on various boards and works with civic organizations throughout the state. In February 1999, Governor Frank Keating appointed her Secretary of Tourism for the state of Oklahoma. In addition to this cabinet position, Jane served as the director, for a time, of the Oklahoma Tourism and Recreation Department.

Being named Cabinet Secretary for the Department of Tourism was another giant leap of faith for Jane. It was a huge job that was offered just as she thought her career was winding down. After a lifetime of being pulled by God to accept His gifts, this time Jane jumped into the challenge of that calling with both feet.

"It was difficult, but a thrill to work for the state that had given me so much opportunity," she said. The job involved overseeing a sixty-three million dollar operational budget, fifty-one state parks, more than a thousand employees and a substantial marketing budget.

This job, above all other endeavors, taught Jane the importance of spiritual discipline. Church had always been a centerpiece of Jane's life, but the necessary daily devotional in one's walk with the Lord, a devotional that requires significant personal time didn't come until this point in her life. Because of God's faithfulness in her past, Jane knew that no problem was too much to bear, but she had to be in touch with the Father to pull her through the obstacles.

Within weeks of her appointment, God brought the most incredible Christian people to surround her and help her with this, the toughest job of her career. For four years, Jane served the people of Oklahoma and brought many rewards to the Tourism Department and to the state. Jane considers the entire experience, even the difficult times, as a blessing and a giant step forward in her faith.

Jane's next step will be working with Oklahoma City University, her alma mater, and continuing her teaching and organizing of Christian faith development opportunities for women.

"My life has not been at all what I expected. It has been so much better and yet the bad times have been so much worse that I had anticipated; but regardless of the surprises, God has been so steadfast and faithful to me. I am filled with gratitude for all that I've experienced."

One of Jane's favorite scriptures sums it all up: *"being confident of this, that he who began a good work in you will carry it on to completion until the day of Christ Jesus." (Philippians 1:6)*

"I look forward to the next chapter of life, knowing that God is never finished with me."

Jane says that life is so good with a loving family, a purposeful walk, a blessed marriage, babies to love, great girlfriends, and a sassy dog named Lily PONS and her favorite young man—Tyler." My son Tyler has given me not only the cutest grandson ever, but a daughter to love as well—his wonderful wife, Elaine."

Tyler is a graduate of Vanderbilt University in Nashville and at this writing is pursuing an MBA at the University of Virginia.

Miss America 1968

Debra Dene Barnes

Student - Kansas State College of Pittsburg
State - Kansas
Age - 20   Height - 5' 9"

Talent: Debra, a pianist since the age of three and a half, played *Born Free*.

Photo courtesy of the Miss America Organization

"I'm the nurturing part of our ministry, and I attribute my skills to the Holy Spirit
living inside me, plus what I learned in the years after the pageant.
God is using me to bless people's lives."
——Debra Barnes Miles

129

Debra Dene Barnes

Since 1984, Debbie and Mitch Miles, her husband of thirty-four years, have served the Full Faith Church in Carthage, Missouri. Mitch is pastor and Debbie is the music director. For several years, Debbie helped to spearhead a group called Christian Resources Unlimited, to assist victims of domestic violence and families of prison inmates. The happy couple has two lovely daughters and five grandchildren. Debbie freely admits that she may be the most *obnoxious* grandmother ever. "I'm worse about showing their pictures than any grandma I ever met!" she exclaimed.

Debra Barnes was a child growing up in the little town of Moran, Kansas when her mother began to experience symptoms that would later be diagnosed as multiple sclerosis. During elementary school years, Debbie and her sister stayed with one grandmother during the summers and another during the school year. When they were at home, the girls watched in frustration and fear as their mother steadily succumbed to the debilitating illness that seemed to progress with each passing day.

Debbie recalls the gloom that hung around the house, the total despair that marked what should have been a normal childhood. There was no joy in the collection of happy, exciting memories. Not having the capacity for patience and caring that an adult normally has when faced with a loved one's long-term illness, Debbie found herself as a teenager becoming more and more impatient with her mother, more disrespectful as time wore on.

In later years, she would come to understand that it wasn't her mother she resented, but rather the illness that had robbed Debbie and

her sister from enjoying a regular home life. As the girls matured and were better able to care for themselves, they spent more time at home. Debbie found herself having to take over some of the cooking and other tasks that keep a household running smoothly until her very patient dad hired a woman to put their house in order once again. Debbie remembers that as a blessing.

Debbie would often later chastise herself for being selfish and immature. She carried a great deal of guilt around until one night in 1971, just three years after she won the title of Miss America, she received Jesus Christ as her Savior. "I was finally able to forgive myself, as

Debbie is music director for the church.

I was promised forgiveness," she said. Debbie lost her mother two years later.

According to Debbie, even on the night of her crowning in Atlantic City, she had left the pageant with a strange feeling of emptiness, even a lack of fulfillment.

What was out there, she wondered, that would fill this need inside her? Perhaps the stepping-stones to her fulfillment had been laid the year before when Debbie was in her first year at Pittsburg State University in Kansas. She had already decided she would major in Music.

One warm, sunny afternoon, while practicing in the tiny rehearsal room at the Music Building, she opened the window for some fresh air. Suddenly she heard the lilting sounds of a rhapsody coming from a piano in a nearby practice room. Then just as suddenly, the music stopped halfway through the piece.

Blessed with a sense of humor, Debbie smiled, placed her hands on the keyboard and continued the rhapsody. The two strangers played a duet, one taking over where the other left off, all the way to the end. A few minutes after the pianists had completed their anonymous duet, the smiling face of Mitch Miles appeared at the door to her practice room. And the stage was set for a long and healthy marriage.

But these students had other things on their minds. Mitch was already seeing someone and their first date didn't occur until the next year. During the spring of her sophomore year, Debbie and Mitch finally began to date. Shortly thereafter, Debbie became Miss Pittsburgh State. Eager to win a scholarship to help with tuition, Debbie tried twice for the local title. The second time, not only did she win the Miss Kansas crown, but she reeled in a great deal of scholarship money by winning the title of Miss America 1968.

Now she recalls how difficult the decision to compete for the title had been at the time. "If I were to win, I would have to be gone an entire year," she explained. "It's difficult when you've fallen in love. I knew I would be able to see Mitch only a couple of times during the year."

Pageant officials frowned on contestants broadcasting their romances, so Debbie had to keep her love life quiet, which made it seem as

Reminiscing

if her suitor were even further away.

One of the most inspirational moments during the year of her reign truly affected Debbie's love for all people, but especially those in her own country.

"We were putting on a three-week-long USO tour in Korea and Japan," she said. "I had never been overseas. While performing in Korea one night, we went to the installation closest to Freedom Bridge. One of the guys went out on patrol and never came back. He was shot and killed. That was the time when Vietnam was a hot topic and no one was paying much attention to Korea. I remember thinking that he died defending his country with his life. I never loved my country more than at that moment."

Debbie is still grateful for the opportunity that allowed her to travel a quarter of a million miles while representing the United States, but particularly grateful for that USO tour.

"That helped me realize that I was doing something to benefit someone, something that would be helping the guys forget, just for a moment, the dangers and fears they were facing every single day."

Mitch had waited patiently and on the night before Debbie crowned her successor, Mitch Miles asked Debbie to be his wife. They were married a few months later.

Their marriage was to be a successful one,

Debbie and Mitch

strong from the start, and especially strong through all of their future ups and downs. She attributes part of their success to this, "I knew he loved me for *me*. He knew me before I became Miss America. And there was a trust there, also, because he knew I could have dated others, especially after I had won the title, and I simply chose not to."

Mitch began his career as a music teacher and they started their family. After two daughters and thirteen years of teaching, Mitch was feeling burned out and felt the need for a career change. Debbie recalls their dilemma.

"We both asked, 'God, what do you want me to do now?'" For some reason, friends urged Mitch to go to cosmetology school. They moved to Carthage, Missouri and Mitch became a cosmetologist. They were both still searching, but they didn't know what they were searching for. There seemed to be a void somewhere and neither of them knew how to fill it.

It is said so often that the Lord works in mysterious ways. And He evidently took that opportunity to put other friends in their path, friends that would help lead the couple to their destination.

Mitch and Debbie began going to a church started by their friends, a church attended by a Christian-flavored melting pot: people from all sorts of denominations—Catholics, Presbyterians, Baptists and the like. Mitch felt called to become one of the church's four elders and as the church grew to a thriving congregation of eighty, they both became more and more spiritually committed. They had found their home.

The congregation began to realize at about the same time as Debbie and Mitch did, that he was being called to pastor that little church in Carthage. In faith, Mitch accepted the call and was soon ordained to pastor the New Covenant Church. It later became Full Faith Church. That was in 1984 and they have never looked back. Debbie became the church's director of music.

How did becoming Miss America help Debbie Barnes Miles take on the role of pastor's wife? "During my tour as Miss America, I learned to relate to people from all walks of life. I had so many varied experiences with people. I can truly look back and see how those thousands of people affected my life today. I can look anyone in the eyes and value who they are. I can relate to anyone and respect him."

Regarding their ministry, Debbie said softly, "I'm the nurturing part of our ministry, and I attribute my skills to the Holy Spirit living inside me, plus what I learned in the years after the pageant. God is using me to bless people's lives."

According to Debbie, as the years have passed, she has become more and more sensitive to people's suffering. So much so that several years ago, she helped to develop a volunteer program called Christian Resources Unlimited. This task force would minister to families of those who had been criminally prosecuted, to families of inmates and victims of domestic violence.

"Unfortunately, most of the trained volunteers began to accept full-time employment and the group had to disband for lack of staffing," she said. But for three years, this group touched hundreds of lives, and for that Debbie is grateful.

"We had initially sent out a mailing asking victims of domestic violence if they needed court procedures explained or needed someone to be with them during proceedings. The response we received was overwhelming. There was so much need. At least we could help them for a time."

Her life hasn't been without severe emotional upheaval and heart-wrenching struggles. With the generous permission of her lovely daughter, Kristi, Debbie shared this story, both of them expressing the hope that their story might help someone else.

As Kristi entered high school, she began rebelling, not unlike most teenagers. Remembering her own insolence as a teen, Debbie tried to be patient, hoping this behavior was merely reflecting an adolescent stage that would disappear in time. But Kristi's behavior grew more and more negative until her senior year when it culminated in her association with an undesirable group of friends. There was drinking. There were drugs. The relationship between Debbie and her daughter deteriorated.

Debbie with Kristi's little girl.

Ever mindful of the example they should be setting as parents, both to the church and their community, Debbie and her husband tried everything.

"We panicked, prayed, sought counsel, disciplined, bribed, cried, blamed ourselves and just came short of blaming each other. We lost a lot of sleep," she said. "Nothing worked."

Their daughter finally moved out of the house, continuing the downward spiral toward destruction for three more years.

One evening, Debbie and Mitch were sitting peacefully in the living room when twenty-year-old Kristi quietly entered the room. The girl kept silent at first, rocking back and forth in the rocking chair. Finally, she looked at them both, tears welling up in her eyes.

"Kristi?" Debbie asked, becoming alarmed. "What is it? What has you so upset?"

"I'm pregnant," was the answer. Debbie felt her heart turn to stone and the world became silent as she tried to absorb the news. She looked at Mitch and he looked at her. There were no words that could possibly describe how they felt at that moment.

This was not a happy announcement, to say the least. The father of the baby was not a promising prospect for a husband or a father.

But Kristi had been seeing the boy for two years. This was the worst possible result. The first order of business would be to offer Kristi their home and shelter, and this they did.

The next order of business was to announce to the church their dilemma to prevent a continuing rumor mill of negativity. Mitch and Debbie struggled with their share of guilt and remorse. Aside from supposedly being an example of the perfect American woman, she thought, how could they possibly minister to others "if we can't even keep our own house in order?" The only thing important to Debbie was to succeed as a Christian—a Christian wife and mother. Her talents, her loving spirit, her ability to make others feel at ease, her Miss America acclaim—none of this mattered. The only important thing right now was just how good a mother she was. She immediately felt that she had failed miserably and blamed herself, trying to figure out where she had gone wrong.

She recalled another local pastor whose family had suffered the same kind of embarrassment. He was asked to leave his position. She feared for her husband and her daughter—but most of all, their church family that had grown so strong and healthy in spirit.

And so on a cold, winter Sunday morning, Mitch took the pulpit and faced his congregation. He explained their situation and asked his extended Christian family for love and charity. He said that if we (the church) were going to call ourselves a Christian family, he needed to be honest with them, since a family doesn't hold things back. Neither Debbie nor Mitch should have feared anything, for instead of blame and judgment, their loving community not only supported them emotionally but shared their unconditional love with Kristi, and a few months later, her newborn daughter. But it wasn't a happy ending. There was more to come, much more.

Kristi worked hard to earn a license in cosmetology, took responsibility for herself and

Kristi and Karla

had spoken to her heart. He said, "I will take care of you." At that moment, she claimed the right to that promise and the right to believe He would. She cancelled the appointment to have her abortion and then was able to finally share her story with her parents.

Some time later, Debbie's daughter Kristi sang a solo in church. It was a very special song called *My Faithful God*. And Kristi shared with that loving, non-judgmental congregation her story and the promise the Lord had made. The church surrounded her with love and prayer. And the baby? A girl. Perfect—happy—healthy.

Years ago, Kristi gave up her destructive life style. Today, she has been married for five years to the son of a church elder. They have a son together. Kristi returned to college at the age of twenty-seven to work toward her nursing degree. She is now a registered nurse and as a member of the local hospital staff frequently has the opportunity to pray with patients. Kristi continually shares her testimony and her commitment to Christ with others, especially within the Christian community who never stopped loving her or praying for her—this child who was lost, then found, a child who just happens to be the daughter of a Miss America.

Debbie's daughter Karla is in the health-care

the baby, rented an apartment, and everyone began to heal, or so the family believed. But for four more years, Kristi continued down the path of self-destruction. Now twenty-five, she became pregnant again, by a man she was with for just a short time. This time, she didn't tell Debbie and Mitch.

As soon as Kristi's physician learned of the pregnancy and the father's long-term, excessive drug history, the doctor suggested strongly that Kristi abort the fetus. A second doctor was called in and agreed with the opinion to abort. Both physicians were deeply concerned about the child's strong potential for multiple birth defects. She didn't know where to turn. The young woman made an appointment to have the procedure.

Kristi went home devastated. She had reached the bottom. Suddenly, she began to realize what she had done to her life, and to this little life within her, for which she was ultimately responsible. Wrestling with the news, she reached out to the only one she knew could truly help her. Praying for guidance in her misery, she finally received her answer.

Deep in prayer, Kristi knew that the Lord

Debbie's 50th birthday celebration with church family.

profession as well. Karla is a dental hygienist and serves as local coordinator of Camp Quality, a non-profit, volunteer organization that provides camping experience to children with cancer.

Regardless of who walks that runway as Miss America, where she comes from or where she's going, perhaps there is certainly a special mystique for that one night. But beyond that, what matters is what she does with her life after the crowning. Debra Barnes Miles was just a little girl from Moran, Kansas who now considers herself extremely blessed to have had the experience that gave her the strength to learn about the human condition, to "look into the eyes of everyone, and *value* them for who they are."

Miss America 1969
Judith Anne Ford

Student - University of Illinois
State - Illinois
Age - 18   Height - 5'7½''

Talent: Judi performed a gymnastic routine on the trampoline.

Photo courtesy of the Miss America Organization

"Part of what I've learned from being Miss America is that
the show really must go on. No matter what's in your
personal life, you just don't let events get you down!"

—Judi Nash

Judith Anne Ford

At sixteen, Judi Ford entered the Boone County Fair Queen Pageant in Belvidere, Illinois. She went home a winner. That win sent her straight to the next pageant and she earned that title as well: State Fair Queen. But pageants were quickly forgotten when Judi entered the University of Southwestern Louisiana. She had become so skilled at performing on the trampoline that she was determined to be taught by the best coach she could find. According to her, that coach taught at Southwestern. She had already achieved status with two sports titles, both very important to her: She had been awarded Junior Women's National Trampoline Champion and was the first woman to win a varsity letter in a sport at the University of Southwestern Louisiana. Judi's mother reminded her that as State Fair Queen, she was not only eligible to compete for the Miss Illinois title, but had already committed to do so.

Transferring to the University of Illinois as a sophomore, Judi was ready to fulfill her obligation. She had no idea that honoring that commitment would end in her becoming the next Miss America. The impact of her new life finally struck her during her post when she went to Vietnam. It was August 1969. She was in the war-torn country nearly three weeks doing USO shows with six other former Miss America contestants. "There were seven of us singing, dancing and entertaining the troops. We would then visit the hospitals and go onto the hospital ships to visit other wounded. We felt as if we were really making a difference. They really appreciated our being there."

It all may sound quite glamorous on the surface, but as Judi explained, the experience was anything but fun and games. There were many times the girls knew absolute terror as ammunition rounds struck inside their base camp.

"We often were awakened in the middle of the night, having to run to the bunkers, but to tell you the truth, I was more afraid of the lizards!"

According to Judi, there were clusters of lizards on the ceiling on any given night and the most frightening thing of all was—"We would keep track of them. When we didn't see them anymore, we'd wonder where they went—all night long!"

Her memories of the Vietnam experience concluded with another unique observation. "The last month we were there, I began to be literally eaten up by mosquitoes. Between the lizards and the mosquitoes, I couldn't even concentrate on mortar shells anymore."

She is convinced that she handled things better because she was only eighteen. "I was used to doing what I was told. When we returned to the States, I was always with someone for reasons of security. I couldn't go out in New York City by myself to go shopping or anything, but I never thought to question that. I did miss being with kids my own age, though."

Judi remembers arriving at events as Miss America where people were waiting to greet her. Instead of chatting with them and making the required small talk per social protocol, Judi would often find herself playing with the car radio trying to find the Top 40 stations.

"When I won the title of Miss America, I had *no* idea what Miss America did or what her responsibilities were. I had planned on returning to college and being a normal co-ed again, the week after the pageant."

It was a full year later when Judi returned to the University of Illinois, her ten thousand dollar scholarship paving the way. Dedicated to earning a degree in Physical Education, Judi quickly returned to campus life. But she still managed to schedule public speaking appearances on weekends.

1980 - Judi, Brian and Brad.

This Miss America grew up fast, perhaps too fast, according to Judi. "I got married at twenty-one when I was a senior," Judi said. "But I was married sixteen years and had two wonderful sons." Brad is twenty-eight and Brian twenty-six. They both live in Chicago and are in sales. Judi's athletic skills, combined with their father's (also a Physical Education major and highly skilled athlete) became a family trait and they both excelled in sports.

But Judi's early marriage turned into a disaster. She had to recognize that her husband had another mistress—alcohol. Judi fought the fight as long as she could, perhaps holding on longer than she should have, according to her, but she finally lost the battle. As so many other Miss Americas have expressed, Judi had longed for stability and family after the year's frantic pace, and perhaps she had tried to settle down too quickly. It was a marriage that would impact her life forever.

"He remained an alcoholic," she admitted candidly, hoping her honesty would perhaps help someone else. "When we were

first married, he was so much fun. And we did have some really good years."

As do many young adults, the newlyweds entertained, went to parties and socialized a lot with friends. "But," explained Judi, "the sobering truth is that when you have kids, you need to change priorities—you need to grow up. He never did."

The marriage-gone-sour had an impact on the little ones that began before they were even school age, according to Judi. "He started his own sporting goods store but he wouldn't accept any professional help—legal or otherwise, in how to run a business, so it began to fail. The kids were three and five at the time. His drinking bouts affected all of us. For five years, I kept putting up with his personality changes, his constant drinking, his irresponsibility—all because of the kids until finally, after countless Al Anon sessions (Alcoholics Anonymous support system for families of alcoholics) and intervention efforts, I just couldn't go through it anymore. It wasn't fair to the kids—*or* me."

Judi credits Al Anon for saving her life. "He had me nearly convinced that I was going crazy, that the problem was mine," she explained. But Al Anon knew the symptoms, knew the drill, and through that support system, Judi finally realized she had done all she could do. Her husband had been in and out of hospitals several times, had tried counseling several times, but his commitment would change as often as his mood.

The final straw happened one day when Judi went downstairs to do the laundry. "We had a fridge downstairs where he kept his beer. I had

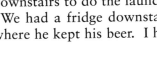

Judi playing mud volleyball.

begun to confront him about his drinking and he knew I would be counting the cans. He had started hiding them so I wouldn't know how much he was drinking."

Judi had run downstairs with a basket full of dirty clothing in her arms, and as she headed for the washer, she happened to look up. Shoved into an angle in the overhead beam was a beer can. *What is that doing there?* Without thinking, she reached for it and upon examining it, discovered the strangest thing.

"In the bottom of the can," she whispered, as if she still couldn't believe what she was looking at, "were the marks of a 'church key.' He had been *opening the cans from the bottom, drinking the beer, then stacking the empty cans in the refrigerator!"*

As she opened the little refrigerator, there they were, all those cans neatly lined up, seemingly untouched. "Now I *knew* I wasn't going crazy! And suddenly I realized—This had *nothing* to do with me." It was around this time, during his more frequent hospital visits, that she decided to seek a divorce for the sake of the children.

"After I'd talked to his parents and friends and we all tried another intervention," Judi explained, "he checked himself into a hospital for three days, then came out and went on a binge. He was so angry that I'd turned against him." The scenario happened over and over, and Judi was becoming alarmed at his behavior. Increasingly, he was becoming more verbally abusive.

Their battles over visitation became more heated. He was often under the influence of alcohol, causing their problems to escalate until finally, after totaling his car while intoxicated, the courts took over the battle, finalizing the divorce and settling the custody issue. Judi would be awarded full custody of the children. She was devastated, still, to watch someone she had loved, someone strong and healthy with so much potential as a father, ruin his life.

"He was a husband, a solid community citizen, a father and an athlete," she tried to explain, obviously still struggling to make sense of it all. "To watch someone with so much promise totally destroy himself was almost unimaginable," she said quietly.

"It got to the point that he would be drunk at work, he would let the kids see him drunk—he didn't even try to hide it anymore. His business and his life finally just went down the tubes. It was so sad," she explained. "He had been such a health nut." She recalls how her heart would ache when one of her boys would have a birthday. Either the child wouldn't hear from his father at all, or the man would send a birthday card— sometimes to the wrong boy.

Those memories are old memories now. Her ex-husband was found on the streets several years ago where his lifestyle had taken him, after having had an accident. After several days in a coma, he died.

Judi's brother is a physician in a small town in Illinois. Eventually, he thoughtfully introduced Judi to his friend, Jim, an attorney. Judi had been through so much and had lost so much trust, she admitted that her first reaction was, "That's just what I need, a man with three kids!"

But Jim was a wonderful influence on her children and a good, solid friend to Judi. Their relationship quickly blossomed into love and after dating for two years, they decided to blend their families. They were married in 1990.

"He already had a son and two

At the Schaumberg Golf Club - 1997.
Judi is second from right.

139

A rock-solid family - 1995.

daughters, really nice kids. It was an adjustment at first, but Jim is such a good role model for the way a husband and father should be. It was really good for all of us."

Time passed quickly. All five children are grown now, and thankfully for Judi and Jim—through college.

And yet, challenges are not over for the couple. Just when they were really starting to enjoy life, Jim went through a routine cancer screening in 1997, and was found to have prostate cancer.

The fact he was even tested was either a fluke or fate. Judi teaches elementary Physical Education and her school was sponsoring a wellness screening. She had thought it was to be a general wellness screening and signed him up for it, against his will. She wanted to be careful because his family had a history of heart problems and he was in a high-risk category. The testing turned out, in fact, to be a PSA test for prostate cancer. Jim was only forty-nine, an unlikely age for this disease.

Judi was at school when the call came from

her brother Don, a physician. Jim's test indicated a problem with the prostate. Within two weeks, he had seen specialists, had a biopsy taken, a bone scan done and finally surgery to remove his prostate. The prognosis was good. The cancer seemed to be contained and was not thought to have spread through the lymph nodes. They had caught it early.

Retesting continues, but after all Judi's been through, her outlook is optimistic. "We go one day at a time and keep a watchful eye on his condition. He's feeling good and we're hoping they'll find a cure.

"But—" she paused, with the wisdom she's gained through the thirty-five years since the eighteen-year-old became Miss America, "part of what I learned from being Miss America is that the show really must go on. No matter what's in your personal life, you just don't let

The whole family - Brad, Brian, Kelly, Judi, Jim , Molly and Drew.

Jim and Judi - What a gorgeous couple!

events get you down!" Jim's children are now grown. Drew, twenty-eight, has just completed fighter jet training and is in the Arkansas National Guard. Molly, Jim's second oldest, is married and has recently presented Judi and Jim with their first grandchild, Jack. "He's eight weeks old today," Judi said proudly. And Kelly is a Spanish teacher in a middle school in Chicago.

Still teaching, Judi is also attending graduate classes to work toward her master's degree. "I'm halfway there," she said, "but it's sure harder now, going back to school."

Miss America 1976

Tawny Elaine Godin

Student - Skidmore College

Age - 18   Height - 5' 10½"

Talent: Tawny played *Images in Pastels*,
a piano composition she had written at sixteen.

Photo courtesy of the Miss America Organization

"Learn to believe in yourself! If you need to change a situation
and think that you can, go for it! Give it all you've got!
But if you can't, you've got to learn when to walk away."

—Tawny Godin

Tawny Elaine Godin

Tawny Elaine Godin began taking piano lessons at the age of ten in her hometown of Toronto. She was the only child of an IBM executive and a homemaker. "Early on my mother was a fashion designer. She later worked at an advertising agency. When I was eight, she decided to stay at home."

Tawny enjoyed growing up without siblings, although in later years she found herself yearning for the connection she might have had with a sister or brother.

"Overall, I liked growing up alone. I didn't even have cousins my age. I was an *island* with adults. But my parents, too, had more freedom with just one child. I got to attend adult dinner parties and was able to travel with them frequently."

The downside was that there was no one to confide in, to share teenage fears and dreams with, and there was another, rather unusual negative. "This sounds silly, but it's true," she said. "I felt a tremendous burden to just stay *safe and alive!*"

Tawny's mother occasionally remarked that she didn't know what she would do if anything happened to Tawny. The way those words were spoken created a feeling of responsibility in Tawny that she recalls to this day. "I think with all the advantages I had of being a single child in a loving family, I determined from the feeling of that burden alone that I'd never have just one child."

Tawny's parents were always liberal with their praise. "They were very strong and gave me a lot of strength. I always had a tremendous amount of self confidence," she explained.

"I still believe anyone can do what they want to do if they want it badly enough—if they're really willing to work for something. People give up too easily. They're not willing to work for what they want. They moan and groan because life's tough, but more often than not, they've made it that way—or at least on the flip side, they've done nothing to correct the situation."

Tawny credits her becoming Miss America to the manner in which she was raised. "I was

Tawny at 9 months

able to face the challenge with equanimity. I was from the New York City area, had already traveled extensively and grew up in a world of adults.

As a youth, Tawny studied piano at the Royal Conservatory of Music at the University of Toronto. She was introduced to discipline early on and accepted that work ethic happily. She reached the highest pre-professional level in Piano Performance possible, attaining her goal in six years, rather than the twelve years it normally takes a student.

When she was sixteen, her family moved from Toronto to New York and her life was about to become much larger.

Tawny won the title of Miss Saratoga in 1975. She had played a special composition she wrote at sixteen, *Images in Pastels*. During her appearances in representing Saratoga, lovely Olivia Newton-John shared the stage with her and requested tapes of *Images* and other compositions. It was a great compliment to Tawny and well deserved.

Practiced and poised from her professional appearances, and fully prepared by years of polishing her performances, Tawny Elaine Godin, a sophomore at Skidmore College in New York, became Miss America 1976. It seemed a natural extension of who she was. At a statuesque five feet ten and a half inches, she was a picture of elegance as she walked onto the runway that night. Tawny was eighteen.

During the year of her reign, Tawny was introduced to a man who was to be her escort at a charity ball in South Carolina. "I had always thought I wouldn't get married until I was well established in a career and close to thirty!" she exclaimed. "But I fell in love, abandoned my dreams and married him six months after I gave up the crown. We had become engaged halfway through my reign."

She explained her decision with a great deal of reflection. "I had given up the crown at nineteen. I don't think, in that point in my life, that I was being impetuous. But I hadn't given myself a chance to figure out who I was. That year changed my vision of who I *thought* I was and who I *really* was! My husband was a physician from Los Angeles and of course, I moved to L.A."

As other Miss Americas have expressed, it takes a while, after that one frantic year, to get

back to the person you really are, only to find out that person has been forever changed.

Newly wed, Tawny pursued her career, and Los Angeles provided her with the professional venue she needed. For a while she took classes at the University of Southern California, but soon found that a full-time job and social responsibilities as the wife of an up-and-coming physician precluded her continuing at USC.

Unlike most others, however, once Tawny left the crown and throne behind her, she rarely made public appearances as a former Miss America.

"Once I was finished, that was it," she explained. "I didn't want any more of it, even the money." Tawny had been quite ready, "very ready!" she said, to relinquish her crown. "I was shocked to have won, in the first place. I had never had any aspiration to be Miss America—-ever!" she said. "I entered for the scholarship. It was kind of weird because I had *never* thought of myself in that role. When I entered," she explained, "I was worried about normal things—college, friends—we had just coordinated our roommate situation and apartment suite in time for fall semester. I wanted to be in the top ten, definitely, because I wanted a scholarship, but I had absolutely no aspirations beyond that. So when I was announced in the top ten, I wasn't even nervous. I had already met my goal!"

The enormity of what she represented as Miss America only overwhelmed her when she would occasionally receive a request forwarded to her through the Miss America Organization from a dying child whose last wish was to meet Miss America.

"Of course I'd go whenever I could. All of us did. But it was always heartbreaking, always hard for me not to cry, especially when the mother was there. Later, I'd get the child's death notice from the pageant office. That year, half the time I'd wish I were someplace else. People expect too much. It's just hard. But you do it."

Tawny remained in L.A., anchoring television news for twenty-three years. "I was with ABC for fifteen years. My first day on the job was May 16, 1977. I started as a weekend anchor a year later, then in 1980, became an across-the-board weekday anchor."

For years she did overseas reporting, but

curtailed the international assignments when her children came along. She hosted several magazine shows and talk shows, among them, *Eye on Hollywood* and *AM Los Angeles*. For several years, she was with KCOP-TV, a UPN (United Paramount Network) affiliate.

Television is a tough business, heavily competitive, but Tawny never shied away from competition.

"Being in television is very much like life. You've got to learn to believe in yourself! If you need to change a situation, and think that you can, go for it! Give it all you've got! But if you can't, you've got to learn when to walk away."

Asked if she ever felt the pressure of being *forever a Miss America*, Tawny answered candidly, "No, I'm very grounded. I don't know how to be anybody but myself. I can't pretend to be someone I'm not. I am who I am and I also just happen to be a Miss America."

A couple years after her first divorce, Tawny fell in love with and married actor John Schneider, who is famous for the television sitcom, *The Dukes of Hazzard*. Their marriage lasted two years. "We remained fast friends, just friends that shouldn't be married," she explained. "We both tried to make a go of it, but couldn't."

She was single a year before she met the man who was to become the father of her two boys. She was determined to make this marriage work. "He worked at ABC and we dated a few months before we married. I had known him for years."

They were married for five years before they called it quits. It's not easy for anyone to admit

April in Paris

publicly that they've failed at three marriages but Tawny Little is an exceptional person, and has within her enough character to take her life experiences in stride, think about them, learn from them, and share them in a spirit of inspiration to others. Tawny remained a single mom from the early 1990s until 2000. She said, "I *now* knew the difference in what I want and what I need. They're not the same things, and I didn't recognize that before."

She explained, "What you need is usually very, very different from what you want. I had to learn the hard way to recognize the difference. Marriage is a yin and a yang, it's a balance."

So many other Miss Americas in this book have shared this thought. "I know now what it will take for someone to earn my respect. I think having been Miss A is part of that. For that year, even if you *are* that person inside, it changes your outlook to some degree."

She thought pensively for a moment, going back more than two decades in her memory.

"I wanted to live in a small college town and be married to a college professor in the Northeast. Instead, not that I regret it, certainly—I became Miss America, married, moved to Los Angeles, and let myself get sidetracked. Then my head was turned by TV, and though it has certainly provided me with an exceptional career opportunity, television has never really nourished my *soul* the way it should be nourished."

She finished passionately, perhaps verbalizing for the first time in a long time, a goal she may have pushed aside for a while. "I still want to teach," she said quietly.

145

As for marriage, Tawny now had two little ones to focus on and she took a few years to watch them grow and to re-evaluate her own needs. "These two little people are the most important things in my life. And their father and I are great friends. We make it a point to spend quality time together with them, with no animosity. We see each other frequently and it's important for the kids to maintain that kind of relationship."

The family today

But her career eventually sapped her energy. For a long while, she didn't even think about marriage. "I was so often exhausted when I came home from anchoring the news—day after day, I was processing information. My days were filled with violence and despair. When they were young, I didn't even let my kids watch the news. Or the shows like Springer and others. I can't even fathom that kind of trash! Something's wrong. Millions and millions of people can see it, and it becomes normal. People get desensitized to it."

What does she consider her greatest triumph? The Miss America crown? Her piano composition at sixteen? A successful career as a news anchor in Los Angeles, one of the most competitive television markets in the world? Ask her, and she'll give you a two-word answer: "My kids!"

No mother can resist this question. "What's so special about them?" Tawny is no exception. "I have people tell me all the time that my boys are sensitive and wonderful, and great! People who don't even know me, whether we're on a plane or in a restaurant, they'll make it a point to come up to me and compliment my kids."

Through the '90s, that was a good solid compliment for a single mom who's a celebrity and whose children attend a private school. "I made sure they were grounded," she said. "I want them open to a whole world of different possibilities. All the years I was doing this by myself, I would get a little nervous. But I made

sure to get up with them when they went to school, and I took them to school, then picked them up—everyday!"

Tawny learned a lot from her marriages. "The first two marriages, there was no *foul,* because there were no kids involved. You just stumble along for a while. Those marriages might have lasted if we'd had to stay together for the sake of the children. But I don't believe in that, either. Children *know,* and I don't think that's fair to them. My boys were three and a half and one and a half when we divorced. They were young enough that it wasn't so traumatic. And still, he lives close by and we spend holidays together."

What's the most valuable lesson she's learned? "I think when you're young, you kind of expect other people to make you happy. I don't subscribe to that one iota!" she exclaimed. "It's *your* responsibility to make yourself happy. You must be responsible for yourself! That's the only way you can make anyone else happy."

She continued thoughtfully. "One of the main problems with relationships, with our society, overall, is that everyone blames everyone else. We're so used to pointing the finger. I wasn't brought up that way. I was taught to be accountable for my behavior, responsible for my actions."

Intent on using her personal experiences to teach her children, Tawny has spent a lot of time thinking things through, over the years, and she's convinced of one thing: "You have to respect and love yourself before you can respect and love anyone else. You have to know what love and respect are, first of all. *If we can just teach our children....*"

Life provides us all with a great many experiences and some of the lessons are very hard. Tawny has created achievements the likes of which are just pipe dreams for others. The difference is, Tawny would take a pipe dream and make it come true! She's been responsible for herself, her successes, her failures and all the in-betweens, for many years.

But one thing is certain. She recognizes one of her "careers" as the most valuable and uses everything she's got to make it work—that's the role of motherhood. J.J. and Christian —those were two lucky little boys—and now they're all grown up.

On January 1, 2000—on the first day of the millennium, Tawny was married in a civil cere-mony by an Appellate Court judge in Pasadena in preparation for a formal wedding and hon-eymoon not likely to ever be forgotten. On April 2, Tawny and her husband re-tied the knot in Paris at the American Cathedral. "You can't just go to Paris and get married. You have to be married at least in a civil ceremony, first," she explained.

She met corporate attorney Richard Welch in Los Angeles the year before. "I was on an advisory board of the Los Angeles Sports and Entertainment Commission, and was being considered for a seat on the board of directors. Richard invited himself along as former chair. He wanted to meet me. And after meeting him,

I certainly wanted to see him again!"

This was in September. On October 16, he was *set up* to escort her to a gala at the Staples Center—"a non-date," she laughed.

Tawny was given the option of not working outside the home when they married and she took that option. "Television was good to me, but I was happy to retire from it. I was burned out. Just one car chase and one violent crime too many," she said.

And a baby boy soon affirmed to her that she had made the right decision. Thomas Cole Welch came onto the scene on May 25, 2001 and his two older brothers, J.J. now seventeen and Chris, fifteen, think he's the best. "Here are these two grown-up, big strapping boys and the baby wraps his arms around their legs and coos, 'I wuv you' - and they just melt," she laughed.

Happy and fulfilled, Tawny will continue to use her professional expertise. She recently started a production company with her friend, who also happens to be Cole's godmother. It's called *Two Friends Productions*.

Miss America 1977

Dorothy Benham

Student - Macalester College
State - Minnesota
Age - 20   Height - 5' 7''

Talent: A classical soprano, Dorothy sang *Adele's Laughing Song* from the opera *Die Fledermaus*.

Photo courtesy of the Miss America Organization

"The most important thing I've learned through the years is that if you put God first, the rest of it all just falls into place."
—Dorothy Benham

Dorothy Benham

Dorothy Benham was in her third year of college when she entered the Miss America Pageant. Having studied opera for eight years, she was determined to earn a degree in vocal performance, but she needed the funds to finish school. She decided to give it one shot: from local to state to national—just one shot. Not many women have earned the title of Miss America on their first attempt, but Dorothy did just that. The goal was a fifteen thousand dollar scholarship. But she found so much more—more than she had ever dreamed possible.

"After I won the local contest," she recalled, "one of the judges came running up on stage and asked me if I'd try again if I didn't win state. I said, 'No, just one shot.'"

Dorothy was focused. She needed money to repay student loans.

The process became a series of green lights. In rapid succession, she won the local competition and the state competition followed rapidly by her being awarded the coveted title of Miss America.

During her tour, the unexpected happened. Bob Hope found out the name of the hotel where Miss America was staying and contacted her for a *command* performance. He asked her to sing for a celebration finishing off the mortgage of the Bob Hope House for Boys. But Dorothy was already heavily booked and had to say no—several times!

Totally oblivious to her response, Hope flew his private plane to New York to pick her up, then flew her to Cincinnati where Dorothy met Johnny Bench and Wayne Newton. She was stunned at Wayne's musical talent and still speaks of that moment with respect and amaze-

ment. "Aside from his singing ability, Wayne worked his way through the entire orchestra, playing first one instrument, then another throughout the forty-five minute show. Since this was a spur-of-the-moment appearance, with no opportunity for rehearsal, Dorothy selected *Summertime*, a beautiful and standard arrangement for a soprano to perform on the fly. "The things you must do as Miss

High School Homecoming

149

America," she laughed. "There was no option. I think that after that year, you're kind of unflappable."

One of her fondest memories of that special year was the Mardi Gras parade. "Phyllis Diller and I were both in the parade—in the soaking rain! We were absolutely drenched to the bone!"

Another unforgettable celebrity she met was Elizabeth Taylor. At the time, the silver screen beauty was the wife of Virginia Senator John Warner. Which star was the most memorable? She didn't hesitate for a moment. "Bob Hope. He truly lived up to his reputation. He was so kind, very down to earth and humble. He had me on his television special at a later date and had no arrogance about him at all. It proved to me that even when people achieve certain success, they *can* remain human. It was a good lesson."

Dorothy has no delusions about who she is. She enjoys recalling the humbling aspects of her reign, remembering one of her first appearances as Miss America. "I was in South Carolina at a charity event—the Heart Fund Ball. Physicians, business executives, lawyers and other prominent community members were in attendance. I was to walk into the hall to the accompaniment of the Miss America theme. It was to be a grand entrance.

"I suggested to my companion that we wait in the ladies' room because no one was to see me until the announcement. Here I am, in my crown and gown in the ladies' room, and a woman who was busy washing her hands suddenly looked up and started screaming. Jumping up and down, she said, 'I can't believe it! I just can't believe it!' When she saw that I was preparing to enter the stall, she grabbed her chest and pleaded earnestly, 'Oh, please, please don't *go* while I'm in here! I don't want to think you do that sort of thing!'" Dorothy laughed, "Talk about living up to an image!"

Although Dorothy thoroughly enjoyed her experience, the schedule took its toll on her. After eight months, the year began to show on her.

"I cried one day. I was *so tired*, I just sat down and cried. I had one day off, finally, after so long—and someone had tried to set up a television interview. I didn't want to disappoint anyone, but I was simply exhausted. I

just cried and said, 'I can't.' I still remember that day as a precious day of rest."

She remembers how badly she thought she looked and recalls the day someone else noticed how tired she was looking. "We called it the changing of the guard," she explained. "My companions would rotate on and off. I met Peggy McMahon, my new companion at the airport and she took one look at me and said, 'Girl, if I had a paper bag, I'd put it right over your head! Why, you sweet thing, just look at you! You look exhausted!'"

By the end of the year, Dorothy was quite willing to give up her crown. "I was ready for my next adventure," she confessed. "But I still found myself calling the pageant office almost daily to say hi and see how everyone was."

Dorothy had grown up in Minnesota. Her father was an older man, and had died when she was sixteen. "Mom remarried and we adored her new husband. He was my high school choral director and the best step-dad in the whole world."

Dorothy had a full family life, with two brothers and a sister, four half-siblings and two step-siblings. "My step-dad's name was Oscar

Dorothy with Russell at one month

but it was easy from the onset to call him Dad. I was very close to him," she explained.

During Dorothy's post, she dated a fellow she had known in junior high school. They had gone to separate high schools but met at a mutual friend's wedding. He was a professional hockey player. They married the next May and in twelve and a half years, produced a lovely family of three boys and a girl.

Their son Russ nearly died at the age of four months. Dorothy's voice quieted, taking her back to this painful memory.

"Russ had been sick, just spitting up a little. He had a fever. I thought he was just teething because he had just cut his first tooth. The doctor was called and we thought it might be flu." It didn't seem serious enough to keep Dorothy and her husband from their commitment to attend a benefit on that Friday night. But when they returned home, the baby's fever had risen.

Dorothy held him in her arms, rocking him until three o'clock in the morning. She finally went into the bedroom and asked her husband to take over, pleading the need to sleep for a couple of hours. An hour or so later, her husband came in to the bedroom, more concerned than ever.

"The baby's fever had escalated and he had begun to moan almost as if it were a primal call," Dorothy explained, recalling that horrific night.

Hours later they found themselves in the hospital emergency room faced with a terrible diagnosis. After a spinal tap, physicians determined that the baby had a rare form of life-threatening spinal meningitis. They were unable to offer the baby pain medication because the drugs would have disguised the brain waves that needed to be monitored. Specialists slipped in and out of the room all night long. The infant fell into a coma. The doctor couldn't even look at Dorothy, but finally pulled himself together enough to say, "I don't know how to even begin to go about telling you. This infection is so severe that I don't think your child's going to make it through the night."

Somehow, they suddenly felt the need to be with their two-year-old, at home. Dorothy and her husband knew there was nothing they could do for lit-

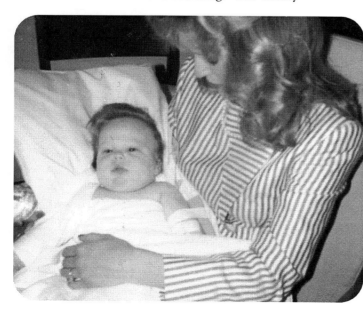

Russell at four months - in the hospital.

tle Russ but pray. The baby was in good hands. They went home to watch their other little one sleep a healthy sleep, all the while praying for the life of their precious baby, lying in a coma just miles away. They returned, weary and unrested, the next morning.

Little Russ had been given constant fluids intravenously and had begun to pull away from touch because of pain.

"The veins in his arms and legs had all been used up, and he couldn't take the pain anymore," Dorothy explained. Dorothy would try to touch him in order to comfort him and was devastated when he recoiled from her touch. They were forced to prepare for his remaining in a vegetative state if he were to survive at all. The prognosis didn't change. Dorothy and her husband rotated shifts so someone would always be with him.

Four days later, they received a good report. Nearly beside herself with joy, the doctor called to say, "I can't tell you how incredible this is. He woke up and he's starving!"

But their relief was short-lived. Soon after awakening, he began to seize again. Luckily the physicians were with him.

"I've always been able to stay calm in emergencies," Dorothy explained, "and I had already prepared myself for his death. I was accepting. I knew he was in God's hands. Within an hour, they had completed the brain scans and he stopped seizing. The tests—suddenly—were normal! The doctors didn't understand that. But I said, 'I do. It's not time for him to go home yet to the Lord.'"

The baby stayed in the hospital for two more weeks. They used sterile techniques to touch him, afraid of a recurring infection. He was in isolation most of the time. But finally he began to rally and was able to return home.

Dorothy recalls the story with a full heart adding, "Russ has grown up to become an incredible student and amazing human being.

The Lord evidently has something for him to do. But it was a life-changing experience. When something of this nature happens, you never take anything for granted again. We're so close—not just he and I, but all of the kids." The long-term result of this ordeal was hearing loss in one ear. That was the extent of the entire horrifying experience.

After nearly thirteen years, the marriage ended. But soon, too soon, after the divorce, Dorothy married a man she had known since high school. She moved back to Minnesota and together, they had two children. It was not a happy union. Eventually, it took therapy and the realization that the kind of existence they were living was not acceptable before Dorothy decided they would all be better off alone, rather than trying to live in an environment that was constantly upsetting to all of them. Sadly, the marriage ended in divorce. She discovered, much later, that the children had kept many negative things from her, not wanting to destroy her marriage.

She determined she would go on without sharing her life with a man, that her children must always come first and she needed to concentrate on creating and maintaining a wholly functional family. With six children in tow, Dorothy reminded herself that if she were to keep God first in her life, everything would be all right.

Dorothy confined her singing primarily to church and continued to do occasional television spots and public speaking. As for her major focus, however, she remained centered and very specific about her greatest joys. "I need to take more time for myself, I know. But I really adore all my children and the real joy of my life is watching as they grow into incredible adults."

Dorothy's oldest is now twenty-three. "Adam was always a good role model for the younger ones," she said. "He would take his little sister ice skating and skiing and take his younger brothers around. They all learned to take care of each other. My house finally became so happy, so much fun!" she exclaimed. "They all became very close. I'm truly blessed."

Dorothy believes firmly in the power of the Lord. She had further proof of His grace in 1986, shortly after Christmas. "My step-dad was diagnosed with cancer in September and as he lay dying, I sat on his bed holding his hands in mine. He'd seem to go far away and talk to somebody, then come back. He once said, 'It's beautiful there. It's very large and—many rooms.'" He died on New Year's Eve.

Dorothy says it was like watching someone talk to the Lord. She had learned the peace of giving one's loved one up to the Lord when her own baby's life had hung in the balance. This time, there would be a final goodbye, but it was a cherished, peaceful, bittersweet moment. Her step-dad had enjoyed a complete life, a fulfilling life.

But God had something very special in store for this family. And no one knew it, not Dorothy, not Adam, nor Russell, Ben, Mia, Maddie or Richard.

"The night my divorce was complete, I remember lying in bed and praying—

"Thank you, Lord, for this little house and all these children in it, safe and sound. We're all happy here, finally. And thank you for my job and for food on the table. Thank you for my wonderful children. I finally feel as if I'm going to have some peace.

Lord, I know I have lessons to learn from my divorces. And I leave this in your hands. But if you ever decide I need to share my life,

Dorothy's step-dad Oscar and her mom in 1986, one month before his death.

whether tomorrow or twenty years from now, please let me be open to it. But for now, Lord, I accept where I am alone and ask you for nothing. I accept what I have and trust completely in You."

And as often happens when we're obedient and faithful, and concentrate on praise rather than petition, God showers upon us His greatest blessings. Ten days after her prayer of acceptance, now in complete peace and understanding at being alone, Dorothy attended a social function that would change her life.

The older kids were off in all directions and the two younger ones were with their father. Suddenly I had an entire Saturday free. I thought I should stay home and clean the house or just relax. I have few days like that," she laughed quietly. "But I was encouraged to go on a boat with friends and I thought it was something I really should do."

The boat was large enough, that Dorothy was at the rear of the boat for the first three hours and didn't notice a handsome gentleman who was equally engaged in conversation with others on the foredeck.

"We docked and went to a restaurant for a light dinner. It was there that I met Paul Shoemaker. He was interesting, funny, tall and handsome and so very nice."

For the rest of the evening, once again at sea, the two talked, but realizing she was recently divorced and not ready to date, Paul didn't even ask for her phone number. Dorothy had had enough of men for a while, and also didn't encourage any more than a light-hearted conversation.

"Just my luck, I thought, to meet a nice man and he ends up being an attorney. I wasn't too

153

thrilled with attorneys at this stage in my life, having just gone through a horrible divorce. But then I found out that he was the son of a minister, and I said to a friend, 'Now isn't that the strangest combination?'"

Dorothy thought of this nice man off and on for six weeks when a mutual friend, Heather, hosted a political fund-raiser and invited each of them, separately.

"I kept wondering if he would be there and later found out he was wondering the same thing."

The two talked long enough to finally exchange phone numbers and later that week, Paul called to ask her out.

"I had the weekend with my children and had firmly committed God first, family second—and there was no room in that priority to allow me to leave them, so I explained to Paul that the children had to come first and he agreed!"

Dorothy was so impressed with his grace and understanding that she offered, lamely, "If you want to come over here, I'll order pizza—but there will be toys and pizza flying all around and children in and out...."

Paul responded, "I'll do that. I'd love to."

And that became the tenor of their relationship. Supportive, kind, understanding, totally secure as a man and comfortable with her as a self-sufficient, gifted mother of six, Paul won his way into the heart of Dorothy and every one of her children in record time.

"He played Candyland and he colored with the little ones. We had pizza, and it was all chaotic and fun, and when he left, he asked me out to dinner. The next weekend, I was free and we went to a German restaurant. And then the real test came," she laughed.

Dorothy had just been featured on the cover of a regional news magazine and a restaurant patron recognized her. He and his wife came over and made a big to-do about her story, and when they left, Paul asked, "Does that happen often?"

Dorothy gently explained. "It's not easy dating me. I'm the mother of six and the children come first. I'm a former Miss America and I do have strangers approach me. I'm a singer and it's a fairly small town, so everyone knows me, so anyone who wants to be part of my life needs to be able to accept it and understand

it—all!" At the risk of losing this fine man, Dorothy finally knew exactly who she was and where her priorities were and she needed to let him know she was coming to the relationship with a lot of baggage and some awesome, built-in responsibilities.

None of it scared off Paul Shoemaker. Not only was he equal to the task, he welcomed it. Earlier, he had prayed that the Lord would send someone into his life so he could have a family, and preferably—he had requested—someone musical! Paul's mom was a piano teacher, Paul was musical, and as the son of a pastor, he had grown up loving music.

As an aside, if we may, —The following was rather difficult to write, because as she described the last three years of her marriage to this incredible man, this former Miss America kept dissolving into tears, but suffice it to say that Paul and Dorothy have created together a peaceful family, happy, healthy, connected, and emotionally secure.

Dorothy's six children now range in age from twenty-three to nine. Adam, the oldest, recently graduated from St. Thomas University with a major in Psychology. He was recently commissioned a Second Lieutenant in the Air Force and is going into the Space and Missiles program in southern California.

The children were all asked, eighteen months after the two started dating, if they were in favor of Paul and Dorothy getting married and they had a private pow-wow that took all of thirty seconds for them to decide. They all were one hundred percent behind the decision. And the two were married August 28, 2001, on a boat, on the anniversary of their first meeting.

"He's truly my gift from God," Dorothy says of her husband. She laughs when she talks about the children's reactions. "My older kids will tease, 'Wow, I can't believe Paul's still here!'—He makes it a point to know each child individually. He just steps in and handles things and they love him so much. He gets up an hour or more earlier than normal to drive Mia to school. If any one of them needs him, he's right there.

"I thought for sure I'd be without a man in my life for a very, very long time, and I was accepting of it. But I think that's what happens. When you release control to God and become open to what he has planned for you, and you're confident enough in who you are and keep Him your first priority, that's when it happens."

Dorothy says she gives thanks every day for Paul. "It can't be easy for him, not being the biological father. He wasn't marrying one person—he married seven of us. You have to take that and embrace it and that's exactly what he's done. He's smart, he's wise, and the children respect him and adore him." Her voice is filled with admiration for her husband as she talks about her newly blended family.

Russell, who's now a strong, vibrant young man, said recently, "Paul's amazing. I don't know how he's done all that." When Dorothy first asked Russell what he thought of the impending marriage, Russell jumped up out of his chair and lifted her into his arms, "I think this is wonderful! He's a great guy, Mom."

Since they have been together, Dorothy has developed, under Paul's excellent capabilities as a producer and with his incredible encouragement, three CDs. "He's very supportive and we work well together," she said.

"The most important thing I've learned through the years is that if you put God first, the rest of it just falls into place."

To book Dorothy for speaking engagements and to acquire her CDs, please go to her Website: www.dorothybenham.com.

Miss America 1978
Susan Yvonne Perkins

State - Ohio
Age - 23   Height - 5' 5''

Talent: Susan sang *Good Morning, Heartache.*

Photo courtesy of the Miss America Organization.

"As I walked with my chaperone through our sponsor's office,
I saw a drop-dead handsome guy. I said, "Now, there's a 10!"
—Susan Perkins commenting on the man she would later marry.

Susan Yvonne Perkins

Susan Perkins grew up in Middletown, a small town in southwestern Ohio. She carries no sob stories about her beginnings, counting her blessings from day one. "I was so lucky. My parents had very strong values, and my childhood was so secure."

Many women who have won the title of Miss America competed several times. Susan was fortunate to have a mentor who encouraged her to try a second year. She had become Miss Miami University, her first time out, then earned the spot as first runner-up to Miss Ohio. A senior in college, Susan was earning her degree with a major in Biology when the pageant bug bit. After the state pageant, a judge, obviously recognizing potential, called her, urging Susan to try again saying, "I really think you can do this. I think you can win."

Susan's life has been built around recognizing priorities and making responsible choices. She had always wanted to sing, to perform. She couldn't get it out of her system. After she graduated, she sang for six weeks at a Holiday Inn. Realizing that while it was fun, she needed to do something more substantive, so she accepted a job with the Ohio State legislature as a legislative aide. She worked hard. There was always deadline pressure and she loved her job as she wrote speeches, did research, worked for senators, and handled all the duties an aide does in the course of a day. It proved to be an interesting position, as generic drug legislation was one of the issues of the day, and her minor had been in Chemistry.

But she still wanted one special thing, to sing on national television. And she wanted to earn enough scholarship money to get some solid, formal training from a good coach. She couldn't get it out of her mind. So she decided to compete again, for the crown of Miss Ohio, and she won! The second try paid off. A few months later, she stood before thousands of cheering fans in a crowded Atlantic City auditorium and before millions of television viewers, belted out, *Good Morning, Heartache.*

Her dream had come true. She had sung on national television. And this night, the night of the big pageant, something very special hap-

In 1997 at competition in Atlantic City with her mom, dad and sister Brenda.

157

Alan and Susan at his 10th reunion - Harvard Business School.

pened. "So many people think it's a cut-throat competition. That's such a mistaken impression," she said earnestly. She recalled when Miss Missouri and Miss Wyoming brought her a rose that night. They said, "We want to wish you luck. We think you're going to win tonight." Susan never forgot that. "I can't tell you what that meant to me."

And after all that, when she thought she couldn't possibly be happier, she won the crown! She performed all year long, during her reign, singing her heart out.

In January 1978, just four months into her year as Miss America, she was called to Boston for an office tour of Gillette, one of the pageant's major sponsors. As she walked through the offices, she saw a "drop-dead, handsome" guy and said to her chaperone, Pat McMahon, "Now there's a 10!" She laughed relating the story and admitted sheepishly, "It was totally superficial."

They were escorted into the conference room for a presentation of a shampoo, a new product that was being prepared for the market. An executive had been slated to give the presentation but had been called out of town. As the fates would have it, in walked Alan, the product manager, AKA Mr. "Drop-dead Handsome!" He gave the presentation and

later joined Susan to ask if she were busy that evening. He offered to show her Boston, having assumed the chaperone would join them.

Susan happily agreed, but when the young man came for Susan, he discovered that the chaperone had decided to spend a quiet night alone in her hotel room. By the end of this fortuitous evening, Susan had returned to the hotel and called her mom, saying simply, "I met the man I'm going to marry." Her mother replied, "That's not like you! Tell me about him."

Now, twenty-five years later, Susan was asked to describe her husband. She said, "He is a wonderful husband and father. In addition to that, he is such an optimist, a real people-person and just really fun to be with! I am so lucky to have chosen someone who is so perfect for me."

Fate intervened again the next day, and a severe blizzard whipped through Boston, stranding her in the city. Unable to travel, she and Alan had the luxury of three whole days to get to know each other. On the third day, they toured the public gardens in Boston and he kissed her for the first time. A year later, he would propose in the same garden.

Whenever she had a few days off, she was permitted to return to Boston. It may have helped that his firm was a sponsor. Regardless of the reason, Susan remains grateful. "Pageant officials were really nice. Instead of

Susan with Bert Parks in 1992.

158

making me return to Atlantic City, they allowed me to go to Boston," she explained.

During her reign, she had "the most incredible year!" She traveled a quarter of a million miles. To Susan, the USO tour was the highlight because of the friends she made. "We did the Mediterranean tour; we visited Greece, Naples, Turkey and Istanbul. Six other state winners I had competed with toured with me and we all became so close, they ended up being brides-maids at my wedding."

Brooke at 9.

Trip, 11.

the whole Miss America Pageant." And I just sat there thinking, *if you're so unimpressed, why are you here?!*

"Once you become Miss America, you're *always* getting looked over and judged," she laughed. "When the Miss As return for reunions, we talk about how we always starve before we go back, struggling to lose those few extra pounds that keep creeping back on. I wonder how many collective pounds we've lost from June to September," she laughed.

It wasn't all glamour, however. At times, people's reactions caused Susan to question why she had won in the first place. "You have to become so thick-skinned," she explained. "People say the strangest things to you. I was at an event and a woman came up to me screaming, '*You* have no *business* being Miss America! Miss Pennsylvania should have won!' People get so caught up in it. They only know the final night, not what goes into it. They still put it down, regardless of what it's done to educate women through scholarships and the whole myriad of experiences it offers."

Going to an event one night, Susan walked past an angry man on the street who exclaimed loudly, "My *sister's* prettier than her!"

A year after her reign ended, she was on a flight to New York City, traveling in coach, when a flight attendant recognized her. She said, "I'll see if I can move you up to first class."

Susan certainly hadn't asked for the favor, but thought it was a sweet gesture. The attendant was eager to do so, and there were ample seats available, so Susan moved. Some time later, the pilot came back and asked if he could join her. She warmly consented. "He then proceeded to tell me how *unimpressed* he was with

A year later, tired of traveling, tired of living out of suitcases, tired of the constant demands on her time and talent, Susan was ready to give up her crown. Alan and his brother were at the pageant. She remembers the night with mixed emotions. "A year is long enough. It was time to go on with my life and do something else. It's not all 'wonderful-wonderful.' I loved the whole experience, but I was definitely ready."

Susan's generous twenty-thousand-dollar scholarship allowed her to pursue her dreams. Moving to New York, she got a job singing at the Red Parrot, a nightclub that had taken over the clientele from Studio 54. She was accompanied by a fifteen-piece orchestra. She dressed in long, lovely gowns and gathered wonderful memories, a dream come true. With her scholarship money, she was able to take singing, acting and speech lessons. She enjoyed it all.

After a time, Susan began to realize that this was not what she wanted to spend her entire life doing. I began to see it differently," she said, "and the reality was that it was loud, smoky and crowded!"

In the spring of 1979, Susan Perkins became Susan Perkins Botsford, marrying the "10" she had seen at Gillette in Boston. But by this time, he had moved on in his career and was living in

Susan and the kids at the Berlin Wall in 1997.

San Francisco, a continent away. Susan was working in television and making appearances in New York. She remembers his patience with awe.

"He was so patient, so understanding about my career needs at the time. He had continued to make his own career moves strategically, always upward. He offered me full support in my own."

She is warm and generous in her description of the man she married. "He's kind, very spiritual, and so much better a person than I am," she laughed and added wisely, "the kids are even old enough to agree with that, now. They say I'm feisty! But not Alan. He's even-tempered and calm."

So what made her change her mind about continuing the coast-to-coast commute?

Susan explained her reasons for the shift in lifestyle.

"Something happened to help me make a decision that changed our married lives. I was working in New York with Alan in San Francisco. One night, Alan's parents and I went to dinner, then to Madison Square Garden for a horse show. We had been married two years and I adored his parents. At the Gardens, Alan's dad got up and went to walk around. We thought nothing of it. After a few minutes, an usher came to find us. Alan's dad was having difficulty breathing. He'd suffered a

collapsed lung. He died that night. He was only sixty-two.

"My mother-in-law stayed in my apartment with me that night. I remember that my sister had just flown in that night. Sitting there, still and quiet, all of us totally grief stricken, I came to realize how important family is. I wondered, "What am I doing here? Trying to get one more TV commercial? Sing one more club? Get one more job? I have a wonderful husband out there in San Francisco who I want to live with more than anything in the world. *What am I doing here?*"

Susan believes strongly that experiencing the death of someone close to you affects your thinking. She continued, "It's really important to spend time with the people you love. It's your family that counts! That was the worst thing that has ever happened to me. But I have to look at the fact that he never had to suffer through a debilitating illness or live out his later years in a nursing home. He had a premature death, and we had to accept it, but he had a great life, too.

"I was just twenty-eight at the time. A few

Susan, Alan, Trip and Brooke in Visby, Sweden that same summer.

160

weeks later, I moved, bag and baggage, to San Francisco to be with my husband. After I told Alan of my decision, he said, "I'm happy you made that decision. I didn't want to ask."

He would have been supportive of anything I'd chosen to do, but this decision made our marriage bond even stronger."

The San Francisco ABC affiliate welcomed her and Susan began working full time in television. But she soon found herself having to make another choice. "I suddenly became aware that the clock was ticking. We decided it was time to start our family. And after the birth of our first child, as I began to interview sitters, I had to once again rethink my priorities."

Again, the self-examination, the hard questions: "*What am I doing?* I kept asking myself. And my answer was, *I want to be with my husband and son!*" Susan told Alan she was committed to being a full-time mom. He expressed how happy he was that she had come to that decision, but again, he hadn't wanted to ask.

How did the Miss America experience help her determine her goals in life? "I think having that year matured me and helped me decide what I would need in my life to make me happy. I learned to prioritize life better and more quickly, but I was blessed with marrying Alan because whatever I had decided would have been fine with him. Some of my blessings might be from using good judgment but others, just plain luck. Look at how we met, and there I was, stranded in a snowstorm right in the middle of the busiest year of my life!"

The children were born in Berkeley. They both attend private schools on the east coast. Alan III, eighteen, is nicknamed Trip for *triple*, and once spoken, the name stuck. Throughout

Brooke, 16 and Trip, 18.

his youth, Trip was completely committed to golf, spending his summers on the course, from morning until night, until basketball took over some of that passion. He wants to play college basketball and perhaps to one day become a sportscaster. Brooke, just nine when interviews for this book began, was at the time working on a song, *The Lonely Goatherd* from Sound of Music. Since that time, the lovely young girl starred as Annie in a local theatre production. At sixteen, she is currently concentrating on singing.

Obstacles? Failures? Defeats? Sorrows? If everything sounds too idyllic here, it does to Susan, too. In her heart, she's still that girl from Middletown, Ohio who was excited to get a six-week gig at a Holiday Inn. There's a part of her mind that "kind of waits for the other shoe to drop. Sometimes, I just wonder when I'm gonna' get it!"

Susan attributes much of her happiness to her parents. "They're great! I was happy as a child and my own kids are happy and healthy."

Then she adds, with a serious note, "Sometimes I realize how blessed my life is and it frightens me. But looking around at the other former Miss Americas, at a recent reunion, I began to realize that a big part of what we all seem to have in common is a strong spiritual foundation.

"Even if some of the women wouldn't consider themselves particularly religious, there's still a certain strong spiritual connection that we share. Mine, I'm sure, came from being fortunate enough to be brought up in a wonderful home where there was a solid foundation. I'm really lucky."

Susan reflected on her twentieth reunion at the pageant, in the fall of 1997. "I got to talk at length with the mothers of Shawntel Smith

(Miss A '96) and Kim Aiken (Miss A '94). I realized my age and the passing of time only because those mothers are younger than I am now. I listened to them about the way they raised their girls. I became so aware of their good principles, their solid moral foundation. They both were married very young and may have had many strikes against them because of that. But they're so happy and were such good parents. I look at them and think, *This is what's important*. If I can just do half that well, I'll be happy."

Miss America 1979

Kylene Barker

Graduate - Virginia Polytechnic Institute and State University

State - Virginia

Age - 22   Height - 5' 4"

Talent: Kylene performed an acrobatic dance and gymnastics
to a medley which included *Rocky*.

Photo courtesy of the Miss America Organization

"There are just some people in life who can't be happy.
I don't want to be one of them."
— Kylene Barker

Kylene Barker

Kylene Barker was born on Veterans Day in 1955 in a small Virginia town. Galax, population six-thousand, is located approximately a hundred miles east of Bristol, Tennessee.

At the risk of sounding too much like a Norman Rockwell tribute, Kylene staunchly attributes her solid values solely to her family. She still returns for Thanksgiving and other holidays, and lovingly talks about her family, especially her grandparents, in a voice filled with awe.

"My grandfather is ninety, my grandmother is eighty-five, and they celebrated their seventieth anniversary in the summer of 2003," she said proudly.

"They are such fine role models. They hold hands and say a prayer before each meal, and after the meal, he kisses her hand."

She talks about her family with a bit of wistfulness. "They're not big business people. They're just sweet, nice, caring people." Kylene's father has worked as a butcher and a salesman for years. Her mother, Dolores (Dee), stayed home with the children during most of their youth, but worked part-time for a veterinarian several hours a week. "Mother is battling cancer and had a stem cell transplant recently," Kylene said.

She loves to share this story about her mother. "Dr. Don Fincher, the vet she worked for, came to my parents' fiftieth anniversary last summer and told everyone how impeccably groomed mother always was. He said, 'On Friday afternoons, it didn't matter if we were in the middle of an emergency surgery or if every pet in Grayson County needed to come in for treatment. Dee had to leave at four o'clock to

get her hair done!'"

Kylene learned her own discipline of being well groomed from her mother but laughs when she admits to sneaking off to the grocery store in something more casual than her mother would probably like. "Mother would never go out the door without looking perfect," Kylene said.

Surrounded by a fine supportive family and remarkable friends, there was only one more thing that would make her childhood complete, and Kylene had that treasure as well. She grew up on horseback.

"I was in the fifth grade when Dad bought me a horse named Blaze. He was chestnut color with a white blaze and three white socks. My girlfriend Cindy and I lived on our horses, Blaze and Charley."

The memory is still vivid and Kylene gets excited all over, recalling those happy days. "We used to play Roy Rogers and rode every day—all day, whenever we could. I had Blaze for years.

"Then as a senior in college, just before I became Miss America, I realized it wasn't fair to him to just spend his days in the pasture. I had less and less time to be with him.

"Mom used to look out the kitchen window and be so comforted watching him in the field behind our house, but I felt sorry for him. I thought it best to sell him. A cheerleader friend from Virginia Tech bought him." Suddenly her voice became thick with emotion.

She continued, "During the Miss America year, I was invited back to Galax for homecoming. They were honoring me with a *This is Your Life* skit. I looked up and here came

Kylene on Blaze during the July 4th hometown parade.

Blaze, right down the red carpet to me!"

But a few months later, Kylene's special year was marred by the death of her old friend. "Months after homecoming, I found out that as soon as I'd sold him, he started losing weight. The vet said later that there was absolutely nothing wrong with him, that he had evidently just gone into mourning."

Kylene was heart-broken, grateful always for the "best horse a little girl ever had." But she was in the throes of traveling, and everyone who demanded her presence also required a brilliant smile and bright eyes. Little did they know that during many of those public appearances, those bright eyes were attributed to tears for her lost companion. "I couldn't dwell on it. I had a job to do."

It was quite a lesson to learn, to be able to put her personal feelings aside and try to celebrate the most incredible thing that had ever happened to her, to be chosen Miss America.

At the end of her senior year, just months before earning a B.S. in Apparel Design and Fashion Merchandising at Virginia Tech, Kylene competed in the Miss America preliminaries and won the Miss Pulaski title. She graduated the next month in June, won Miss Virginia in July—and in September was crowned Miss America 1979. It had been a busy summer to say the least.

Kylene traveled more than 350,000 miles that year. As an acrobatic dancer, she was invited to perform all over the world.

"I remember the USO shows in Germany and Iceland where

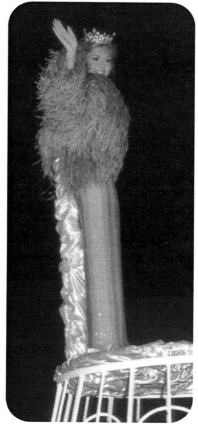

the stages were very small. I had to do back-handsprings in a tiny area. I had to keep myself fit in order to make my mark so I wouldn't fall and be hurt."

Staying fit was a daily challenge. "It was too dangerous to go out running in strange cities, away from the hotel, so I'd skip rope and do jumping jacks in the room, anything I could do to fight the results of having to eat at every event!" She even came up with a tip for people on this kind of schedule—to sprinkle black pepper on the dessert!

Kylene appeared on the *Donnie and Marie Show*, the *Perry Como Christmas Special* and was on *Regis and Kathie Lee* on numerous occasions. During the '80s, she appeared on NBC's *Today Show* as a fashion and feature reporter. Appropriately, her features included pageant news.

After the pageant, Kylene was interviewed on the *Today* show and remarked that she wanted to open her own clothing business. The owners of a building in Florida saw her interview and invited her to a ceremony to open a large parking lot in Palm Beach. She recognized this phone call as opportunity knocking. Kylene accepted the invitation.

Rather than simply cutting the traditional ribbon, however, Kylene drove a Cadillac with the Gucci-designed interior through a huge display to honor the occasion. Impressed with her promotional spunk, the building's owner escorted her and the party of dignitaries to Petite Marmite, an upscale restaurant nearby. He said, "I hear you want to open a store. I'll soon have a space available that would be perfect for you."

As luck would have it, Kylene was seriously dating a real estate developer. He looked into the real estate issues and before she knew it, Kylene had signed a ten-year lease. Her Miss America scholarship was twenty thousand dollars and she was permitted to use it for business development.

Things were happening fast, almost too fast. "I had thought about going back for an advanced degree, but so many doors open for you when you become Miss America that I just couldn't let this opportunity pass."

As if the year hadn't been frantic enough, Kylene was married in October to the real estate developer, just one short month after her tour ended. And a month after that, she opened her new store "d. Kylene."

This spunky entrepreneur never looked back. A lot had happened in a year and a half. And now the next decade was mapped out for her. Kylene dug her heels in and worked hard to make her boutique a success. She worked long hours, loving every minute of it. Days turned into weeks, weeks into months and months into years. Kylene's husband was supportive of her career and they communicated extremely well at first, but regardless of their seemingly solid foundation, the relationship began to unravel. As they grew apart, they decided, after thirteen years of marriage, to go their separate ways. In 1992 they divorced.

As difficult as it was to try to uphold the image of being a Miss America, a role model of supposed perfection, Kylene was far less concerned about that image than the family pressure she felt. "I worried so much about hurting my mother, about disappointing the folks."

But the marriage was no longer working and there was nothing to be done.

Brought up in the Church of Christ, Kylene feels that her Christian background and the solid sense of values she had been given by her family worked together to help her become and remain a positive person.

"When bad things happen, for whatever reason," Kylene explained, "I really try not to dwell on them. I'm a happy person. I always try to be prepared and I owe my positive outlook to my genes and growing up in a wonderful family and supportive, positive church." She added, "There are just some people in life that can't be happy. I don't want to be one of them."

An author, Kylene combined her observations from the Miss America Pageant to her experience from managing her Palm Beach boutique to write *Southern Beauty, a Total Fitness and Beauty Program for that Winning All American Look.* The popular book was published by Simon and Schuster.

Her television appearances once earned her a place on the hot seat of CNN's Crossfire. A Miss California Pageant contestant had held up a banner during a competition that said, "Pageants hurt women!"

A producer from CNN called Kylene, asking her to debate the issue with the former contestant. After the interview, Kylene had called her husband from the airport and asked, "How'd I do?"

The prompt response was, "You cleaned her clock!"

Kylene doesn't shy away from controversy but wonders what all the fuss about the swimsuit competition is. "Some people may regard it as cheesecake," she explained. "It's much more meaningful than that. Those comments don't bother me. The women who compete are physically fit and used to being in fitness clothes. I think too much is made of the swimsuit controversy."

In the mid-'90s, Kylene remarried, and her life was about to become incredibly interesting. Her groom was twenty-five years her senior, a Canadian by the name of Ralph Hibbard. For seven and a half years, they

Kylene on the set -1999.

shared their lives in Canada as owners of Polo Ralph Lauren, but during the bitter cold holiday months in Canada, they could be found at their winter home in Florida.

"There was never a dull moment with this man. Someone said to me, shortly after his death, 'You got a Ph.D. in how to live.' He was cultured, sophisticated, well traveled and a brilliant businessman. I grew a lot just being with him. I was exposed to things I'd never been exposed to."

Kylene credits Ralph with her new passion for golf. "He created a monster. I remember after his death, walking the fairway at my favorite golf club and looking up at the sky. I said, 'Thank you Ralph for introducing me to this game. It's a passion of mine, now, and I love it.'"

As he handled everything in his life, Ralph Hibbard dealt with his impending death with a grace that Kylene not only noted, but respected tremendously. It was a sudden ending to what had become a beautiful union.

"We were golfing in Quebec. He was walking up the steps to the first tee and couldn't get his breath. Several days later, on September 5, 2002, he was diagnosed with a very aggressive Stage IV lung and bone cancer. He was such a trouper. He handled it with such grace. He wouldn't have been the type to tolerate chemo and radiation. This was the best way for him," she said. Three short months after the diagnosis, Ralph died, leaving Kylene in shock.

She smiled, saying softly, "We were very lucky to have that much notice. The last three months were very special and very precious to us both."

One of the most comforting things for Kylene during those lonely days and nights in the hospital by his bedside were the emails she would get from her family, friends and her Miss America family.

"I didn't want to talk on the phone for fear I would disturb him, so I took my laptop into the hospital and could sit right there beside him and receive comfort from those we loved."

For the first four months, she felt nearly numb. "I was in shock, all of it had happened so fast. And being December, a time we would normally be in Florida, I found I wanted to go there right after his death. I had spent the past

Ralph and Kylene in Cannes, France - 1991.

Cutting up in a Cape Cod shop.

twenty-five winters in Florida and I needed that warmth and sunshine to help me heal."

She spent a lot of time with friends that winter, then returned to Canada in the summer to take care of the estate and say good-bye to their northern home.

With all the traveling they had done, they had always taken their "kids," Chuck and Harold. These guys were standard poodles who went with the couple nearly everyplace they traveled. In 2001, a year prior to Ralph's death, they had lost Chuck, at age ten, to cancer.

In September of 2003, as she was preparing to return for the Miss America Pageant, Kylene noticed a problem with Harold, now twelve, and took him to the vet only to receive bad news once again: Harold was diagnosed with an aggressive type of cancer. He wasn't expected to live much longer. "I went up to the receptionist and starting writing a check and asked what the date was. When she answered 'September 5th,' I got chills. That was the exact date my husband had been diagnosed one year before."

Kylene took her old friend home and cuddled up with him on the couch, just holding him and loving him.

"Suddenly, as I'm crying, it was almost as if I felt God speaking to me. I had been trying to decide what to do with my life and had thought about renting an apartment in Naples, but they don't take big dogs. This was God's way of say-ing—*Move on with your life.*"

Kylene left for the pageant days later and when she returned, she and Harold made his last trip to the vet. "I've said good-bye to lots of pets, but I really get a happy feeling when I think of Chuck and Harold, both of whom were spoiled rotten and lived an incredibly happy life. They're buried on the grounds overlooking the lake where they spent so much time playing together and playing with Ralph. It's as if they're all together again in spirit.

Where would she be had she not become Miss America? "You take bigger risks when you're younger. I probably would have opened a little shop in Virginia. But winning the title and having earned enough money to invest in my own business, I had a lot more confidence. I was thinking much bigger."

She recalls the first lease she signed, admitting, "I really hadn't thought it through. That first year I paid sixteen dollars a square foot for a building of a thousand square feet. But still, it was a ten-year lease, which was to compensate for the large investment I made to completely gut the existing space and remodel it for the 1980s. The former shop had existed since the '40s.

By the fifth year, large investors had come into the area, and by the tenth year, building space costs had skyrocketed. I renewed for another three years at seventy dollars a square foot!" She laughed, "Luckily it all worked out." She reflected for a moment, then added, "Luck—and a whole lot of hard work plus long, long hours!"

Kylene still believes that fitness and beauty go hand in hand. "The Miss A experience strengthened me in many ways. Just going through the process gives you confidence. It polishes you. This process prepares you for anything. I was always disciplined but I learned to be even more so that year, especially in the struggle to keep fit. It was—still is—so important. But all in all, the pageant experience gave me confidence to do new things, to become a bona fide businesswoman. I traveled extensively, saw so much, was not just allowed, but encouraged to think bigger—much bigger."

The five-feet-four-inch beauty still tries to work out every day. "I try to vary my workouts. Sometimes I do a thirty-minute video. She likes to work out to the popular fitness video

The Firm. I also lift free weights coupled with a session of aerobics. She often works out on her Bowflex for resistance training.

As for appetite, Kylene makes no pretense about food. "I love to eat. My husband Ralph used to say he never saw a woman eat as much as I could," she laughed. "I have a tendency to gain weight and could easily be a few sizes larger, but I work hard to keep fit." And no golf cart for this lady. Kylene uses a pushcart for her clubs and walks all eighteen holes. "I figured out that you can use up to 1400 calories during an entire game if you walk the course."

But being fit doesn't come without a price. In the 1980s, Kylene decided to run the Trevira Twosome. She ran the 10K race without having trained. "It proved to be, perhaps, not the smartest thing to do," she confessed sheepishly. "I couldn't get out of bed the next day! So the next year, I trained properly and did it again."

This time, she trained to videos, participated in exercise classes and ran three to five miles a day. The result? "I *leaped* across the finish line!" she laughed. "I've found that anywhere in life, including marathons, it's all about working hard and being prepared!"

Asked how she is handling her life now, with so many recent losses, she said, "I'm a lot like my father. He's always in a great mood. I always try to think of positive things in my life versus dwelling on the negative. And being so physically active, that helps keep me on an even keel emotionally."

Recently, Kylene met a wonderful man who had also lost a spouse and his friendship means the world to her, she said.

"His wife died of cancer shortly after I lost

Ralph and Kylene with Chuck and Harold on New Year's Eve.

Ralph, and it's wonderful to spend quality time with someone who was married for many years and who honors his wife's memory. That attracted me to him, among other things. And we share such a common bond. They began dating just before the new year of 2004, and are enjoying their friendship.

Kylene has recently undertaken some volunteer work that she's becoming quite enthusiastic about. She has become a Big Sister to a little nine-year-old girl who lost her father recently. Michelle takes dance and is interested in gymnastics, and Kylene is thrilled that she knows enough about both that she can take her under her wing and help mentor and coach her.

"It just makes you feel really good inside. After class, we get take-out and go have dinner with her mother and brother. It's a wonderful opportunity for me to share some gifts I've been given."

The child has no idea that her big sister is a Miss America. Kylene is planning to tell her soon. Can you imagine the delight on the child's face when she learns this special secret?

"The main thing I've learned, through the years," Kylene said, "is that life does constantly change and you have to take it one day at a time. But one thing I realize is that life does go on and you have to make the best of every situation."

Kylene says she has always been a believer of hard work. "If you want to make things happen, *you* have to make them happen. Even winning the Miss America title and having so many doors open, we still have to knock on those doors and be prepared when we walk inside."

Miss America 1981
Susan Powell

Student - Oklahoma City University
State - Oklahoma
Age - 21   Height: 5' 4"

Talent: Susan sang *The Telephone Aria* by Gian Carlo Menotti

Photo courtesy of the Miss America Organization.

"I think we are born into grace and that it is up to us to be responsible
to that gift—to the grace in our lives. And I also think it's very important
to listen to our own greatness along the way."
—Susan Powell

Susan Powell

Susan Powell was born in the spring of 1959. Susan and her older brother Tommy grew up in the small farming community of Elk City, Oklahoma where their extended family included a town of seven thousand. "I loved my childhood," she said.

"My father farmed most of my life and in the summertime, I worked alongside my girl-friends in the cotton fields to make extra money. It was part of the culture."

Susan's dad later left farming and started his own business as owner of a television and appliance store.

As in most small towns, social activities centered around the church and Susan's life was no exception.

"I was active in the youth fellowship programs at my church. It was just something you did as a part of your life," she said. Susan's interests varied and she played trumpet in marching band, even becoming drum major during her senior year. She also sang in the high school choir and learned early on that her voice would provide the key to her creative and professional fulfillment.

Although her parents were not wealthy, Susan was richly blessed. Recognizing her vocal talents, her mom and dad made it a priority to honor this precious gift.

"When I was fifteen, Mom began to drive me to Oklahoma City to a voice teacher at the university." Florence Birdwell was the mentor and vocal coach instrumental in helping Susan develop her clear, strong soprano voice. She carefully coached the young girl, successfully guiding her toward a professional career.

"I had boy friends and did normal teenage activities, but I really focused on music," she said. "I took piano and basically lived at the community theatre anytime I was out of school, from the time I was ten." Theatre directors noticed her obvious talent from that young age, as they cast her in her first role as a Polynesian girl in the popular musical *South Pacific*.

She followed that role by playing a dog. True story. "I got to play Snoopy in Charlie Brown when I was fourteen," she laughed. But then she quickly became a girl again the next year when she was cast in the lead of *My Fair Lady*. And the next performance would have been a stretch for the lovely young woman, but at sixteen, any potential self-esteem issues aside, Susan took the role of an ugly stepsister in Cinderella. She played that role with relish.

Celebrating her 1st birthday

Her high school teachers were ultimately supportive. "They never had the funding to do a musical, but when I was a senior, they decided to put on a little operetta for me to perform in. It was called *Little Mary Sunshine*.

Susan considers herself extremely fortunate to have parents and teachers who cared so much about her talent that they helped her prepare for what they evidently knew, even then, would be her destiny—she was to be a professional singer. Whatever this required of her parents, they did without fuss or fanfare. Susan's gratitude for their support is unquestioned.

"My parents are characters, in a way, but they're really practical. My great grandparents were Sooners—Homesteaders—who came to claim their land in the great Oklahoma Land Run of 1897," she said proudly. "Common sense and a can-do attitude is part of the heritage."

Part of her maturity, even as a youth, came from her faith. "Church was a really important part of growing up in a small community. Even if you don't totally understand it all, I think there's an innate sense of spiritual growth when you're exposed to that kind of life."

Susan considers herself a quiet Christian. She doesn't talk about her faith a lot, but believes strongly in the inclusion of everyone and the rights of all to embrace their faith. She is highly aware of her spiritual health and has a strong, consistent prayer life.

"A lot of my self-assuredness through the years has come from faith in myself and faith in others," she said. "I never have felt alone and I realize that may be through grace."

In 1977, as a high school senior, Susan competed in the Miss America preliminaries for the first time. She was crowned Miss Elk City. When she went on to the Miss

Our future Miss America in Kindergarten

Oklahoma Pageant that year, Jane Jayroe, Miss America 1967, emceed the competition. Susan was named second runner-up. She was eighteen.

"That experience encouraged me," Susan said. "Jane lived in a town close to me and I nearly worshipped her. My mom kept telling me to go up and speak to her and I was too shy. I could hardly talk," she laughed. "I had very limited verbal skills other than with my closest friends. You'd never know it now, but I was so shy in social situations. That is—until I was asked to sing. I could always sing! I understood that language."

Susan's win enabled her to attend college at no cost and it was a natural progression for this young, vibrant beauty to major in Vocal Performance at Oklahoma City University, the academic home of her dear vocal coach.

All in all, with her awards for talent performance and the runner-up position, she took away eight thousand dollars in scholarships, enough for tuition and books.

"Oklahoma has always been a strong pageant for providing scholarship awards," she said.

"This was helpful to my parents. And since they provided me with spending money, I didn't even have to hold down a job. I could focus completely on my education and my vocal studies. I had also received a small scholarship from the university for playing trumpet in the band my freshman year, so I got a free ride for almost three years."

The third year, Susan started entering pageants again. She wasn't just entering a pageant for the competition. Her goal was fixed solidly before her and she was bent on finding a major steppingstone to a career as a professional singer.

"I was destined to go to New York. I had always wanted to develop a career there."

All dolled up for church with brother Tommy.

Susan with her dad

Susan experienced one minor challenge during college that most co-eds experience, at least once. It was a bump in the road that only served to strengthen her character and her resolve. "I suffered a heartbreak and it made me decide that I really needed to keep my eyes on the future and learn everything I could so I could manage on my own. I learned that it wasn't wise to depend on someone else for my future," she said. "I became more focused than ever."

The greatest gift she was given was to be able to study under Florence Birdwell. "She was the most amazing teacher. Since I had worked with her for several years already, we developed quite a bond and she opened up for me an entire world of possibilities. Her mantra was 'the sky's the limit,' and she really believed that," Susan said.

Susan shares a philosophy that is so profound. "Sometimes parents love you so much that they may tend to hold back from being too encouraging because if you fail, they feel the disappointment equally as well, but a teacher isn't quite as emotionally invested and may push you harder. This was the case with Ms. Birdwell," Susan said. "She literally led me by the hand. She guided me, she carried me, she remained absolutely honest and true. I knew I had been given a great gift. She knew it, too, and she was there to help me use it in the most fulfilling and honest way that we could find."

With three years of intense study in Vocal Performance behind her, in 1980, Susan took her classically trained voice and entered the auditions for the Metropolitan Opera. "This was a banner year for me," she said. "I was named district winner. That year, I entered one vocal competition after another and won first prize several times. Then I entered the Miss Oklahoma City Pageant and continued to

work hard on my singing. Through good grace and hard work, everything came together that year," she said.

All of this happened by March 30, 1980. In quick succession, Susan won Miss Oklahoma City, then went on to win the Miss Oklahoma title in June.

Susan had gone off to the Miss Oklahoma competition fully prepared, but there was so much talent there that year, it was quite stressful, according to Susan. "I wanted it badly and I went to win, but it was a really hard win," she said.

At the time, talent was judged as fifty-percent of the points and being a fairly subjective category, she had no idea what the outcome would be. "I knew I'd be a great Miss America, but I had to get there to prove it!"

Her engaging charm, her incredible work ethic and discipline coupled with an enormously appealing talent would indeed make her a successful Miss America. But would the judges think so? For now, her total concentration was on winning the state pageant.

"I had a real winning combination that year. And when I won, it was such a relief! It was important for me to take one competition at a time. That's really a microcosm of how your life is—an accurate metaphor for life—just one step at a time.

"My father Wendell always said the difference between good and great is concentration. That's the key."

The summer had been difficult for Susan. After she won the Miss Oklahoma title, she happily celebrated with family and friends, but then was quickly and unceremoniously whisked away to the host's house where she would spend the summer preparing for the national competition in September.

"It was automatic," she said. "Miss Oklahoma always moved in with a host family in Tulsa."

Susan and her mom at Christmas.

The lady of the house was Frances Campbell and although they eventually came to be close friends, Susan was so lonely the first few days.

"Frances was to be my escort to the pageant; and although I was the twelfth girl she'd escorted, she had never had a national winner." It was obvious to Susan that Frances was holding back a bit on encouraging her too much because the woman didn't want to get her hopes up.

"I felt so lonely at first. I'd always been such a private person and it was hard for me to adjust living in a stranger's home."

Settled in for the summer, five hours from her family and her hometown, Susan buckled down to work and made the adjustment. "It was a challenge that I just quietly did," she said. Frances eventually became one of Susan's closest and dearest friends and remained so until her death several years ago.

"It was so hot that summer. Frances liked to take drives in the car late at night. We'd ride around and look at houses and she'd tell me stories of people who lived there. We eventually developed a very special bond."

Susan kept busy with her eyes on the task at hand. A car was donated to her for her use during the summer. She was grateful for the transportation, so she could take the two-hour drive to Oklahoma City for voice lessons and gown fittings.

She received a sea of advice from people she knew and people she didn't. "Everyone's got an opinion about every aspect of the competition—your performance, your appearance, how you wear your hair, your wardrobe—everything," she said. "But there's nobody else that knows you better than you, and I had to focus on what I knew about me that would win that pageant."

Susan did a mock judging every two weeks to sharpen her interview skills. It's so bizarre to think that since her Miss America days, she has made a successful living as a professional speaker, even having her own television talk show for nearly ten years, when her verbal skills were her weakest talent at the time.

"I was exhausted. It was just—so—unbelievably hot that summer; and there was so much stress, I had to struggle to stay focused."

She recalls the story of one particular man who participated in a mock interview with her, then went to work and told a co-worker, "If there are fifty women in the pageant, Susan Powell will be number fifty-one!"

Susan's response was one of charm and candor. "You either take the hook in your cheek and get reeled in, or you just cut the line and keep on swimming!"

Pageant week finally arrived and after the grueling heat in Oklahoma and having never seen the ocean, Susan received a wonderful surprise.

"Oklahoma sent us in a day early and paid for the hotel that extra day so I could get acclimated and relax before competing. Contestants weren't supposed to leave the hotel, but Frances let me put on a swimsuit and wade in the ocean. It was my first time ever, and I'm so grateful for that extra special day!"

The next morning, she was rested, refocused and raring to go. "It was a week of keeping my eye on the prize and knowing what I was there for. My voice teacher called to talk to me every day. She was in Atlantic City with my mom and two of my aunts for the entire week. She kept saying—'You need to be true to you. You're the strongest asset you have. If you try to be anything you're not, you won't win.'"

Susan paused for a moment then said, "That's another metaphor for life, isn't it?"

She had used visualization techniques all summer, seeing herself being crowned, walking the runway, singing her aria perfectly.

"But during the week I remember thinking

On the set of *Home Matters* with Biker Billy.

that it was just going to come down to survival of the fittest. We were all so exhausted from rehearsing and all that goes with the competition."

Susan laughed, "It was so much about just being tired toward the end, I wanted to say, 'Just crown somebody so we can all go home!'"

Susan was definitely a dark horse candidate, at least among the other girls. Not because she didn't have the class or the talent or the skills to earn the coveted crown, but simply because she remained quiet and unobtrusive all week. Focused completely on the end result, Susan didn't socialize much. "I knew all the girls, but became close to only two or three," she said.

She laughed when she remembered this story. On talent night when she sang her aria, it was projected onto a television monitor backstage. Miss Louisiana looked the screen and suddenly said, "Who is that girl?"

"I'd been so quiet, they hadn't noticed me all week!" Susan laughed.

The beautiful brunette did not show up in Atlantic City with a high-fashion wardrobe and designer ballgowns. "My wardrobe was off the rack from JC Penney. And I certainly wasn't a drop-dead, gorgeous knockout, especially at five feet four—until I sang. Then people started watching me."

All summer long, Susan had been honing her interview skills by reading current events. "I'd devour Newsweek and try to memorize facts and names of prominent people in the news," she said. But the judges evidently weren't concerned if their new Miss America knew anything about the current Iran hostage crisis or the Shah of Iran's downfall. They asked, 'What makes you laugh? What kinds of summer jobs have you had?' — and the like. Susan was so overly prepared that although the questions didn't seem highly important at the

time, she was later told that this was when she began to win the title.

The highlight of the event, as Susan Powell blazed a trail onto the runway in Atlantic City, was her rendition of *The Telephone Aria* by Gian Carlo Menotti. The audience and the judges were blown away by the beautiful soprano voice coming from this poised, petite body. Since that time, this aria has become a favorite of local and state contestants.

When Susan's name was announced, no one was more shocked than her mother. "My whole pageant life, she had told me I was too short to win. I think this is the way parents insulate themselves from disappointment, because they're so involved in what makes you happy, that when you don't make it—they feel the hurt every bit as deeply."

Susan's parents divorced when Susan was sixteen. But both were in the audience and she credits them for having enormous integrity.

"I must be the freakiest kid whose parents ever divorced, because the way they dealt with it, they were sure that it wouldn't affect me. They were brilliant. They never spoke negatively about the other one and they both let me know they loved me very much. We just didn't have the trauma a lot of families undergo in that situation. And it made nights like this even more special. My dad said he was never more proud of me than he was at that moment."

Susan got right to work as Miss America and one of the benefits she will always remem-

As host of The Discovery Channel's *Home Matters*. *Photo by Photo Bureau, Inc.*

ber with fondness was working with Bob Hope. "I got to work with him three times," she explained. "It was an election year and I went to Hollywood. We did a skit where Bob was the presidential candidate and I was his running mate for vice president."

When Susan first appeared on stage for rehearsal in her crown, Hope snipped, "You look like the Imperial margarine girl," (from a TV commercial) so Susan immediately lost the crown.

Luckily, Susan had been asked by pageant officials what she wanted to do as she traveled. She had a one—word answer—"Sing!"

And sing she did, all over the country—several times around. "Traveling was a big highlight for me and I became a travel guru. I love meeting people and the country has never lost its fascinating allure for me." Susan said that while some may not relish the idea of standing in a drugstore signing autographs for five hours, she loved it because she met rock-solid people and learned so much about human nature. "I wouldn't trade all that for anything," she said.

A great highlight was when she sang with the Air Force Orchestra at Constitution Hall in Washington, D.C. on the day our country's hostages were brought home from Iran. She had been delayed in a snowstorm (with Les Brown, who also was slated to entertain at the function) and with no rehearsal, Susan had to

sing four arias that day. It was a memorable afternoon.

Susan was mindful of the occasional barb she received from the media, but with our American phenomenon of celebrating everything we do by eating, it was no wonder Susan gained an extra twenty pounds during her tour.

"Everywhere I went, food was served—good food! It was really easy to put on the pounds," she said laughing. "That's how Americans say hello and I'm an American, too!"

Naturally a reporter picked up on it and was quoted as saying, "Well, there's more of her today than there was when she was crowned."

Just like any other challenge Susan had faced in her life, she took care of business and slimmed down.

"I loved being Miss America. I loved every minute of it. I knew what it was; I knew that it was only for a year and I wanted to be as good at being Miss America as I was disciplined and focused on getting there."

Susan's extra benefit was the twenty thousand dollar scholarship that paved the way for her to move to New York to study with the greatest teachers she could possibly find.

The example of how Susan has continued to deal with life should be noted by every one, especially young people, and not just Miss America hopefuls. Today, twenty-three years later, Susan still maintains her weight and her health. She reads everything she can find about proper nutrition and she works out an hour a day, six days a week—without fail.

"I figure if I can watch TV for an hour, I can certainly work out for an hour and spend that time doing something constructive for myself."

The regimen isn't easy and it isn't fun for Susan, but she has always had a no-nonsense level of maturity that moves her forward. "I usually hate working out but I have to do it. I

As Adele in *Die Fledermaus* with the Seattle Opera.

try not to think about it, I just do it. Once I start negotiating about it, I know I'm lost, but I'm much more motivated than most. In show business, I just won't get jobs if I'm heavy. I'm forty-five now, and I love my work. But being overweight definitely cuts off opportunities for me."

She attributes her professional success to the same level of commitment she used to gain the crown. "There's no substitute for skill. You have to do the tedious hard work that no one likes to do to gain the reward."

The day after Susan crowned her successor, Elizabeth Ward, she flew to Seattle to start rehearsal for a six-week run as Adele in the opera *Die Fledermaus*.

"I had so little professional stage experience, people wondered if I could handle it, but it turned out to be a great springboard for my career. The media covered it extensively, including Newsweek and People." Susan was so fortunate to have two performers in that opera who were already deeply steeped in show business—Buddy Hackett and Paul Sorvino.

"My voice teacher from Oklahoma came out to be with me for a while to be sure I was okay," she said. "She had lost her eighteen-year-old son a year before, and I think being with me helped her as well."

Susan was so grateful to be *normal* again and be working professionally in theatre. As busy as she was, she was now able to make decisions about her personal time that she hadn't been able to do during her entire tour as Miss America, where she had been constantly

accountable to a chaperone. She sorely needed some private time.

"Paul Sorvino is so neat. He asked my voice teacher and me to have dinner with him one evening, but I begged off to wash my hair and relax." It was important for Susan to find her *self*, once more, and that one night, she luxuriated in the simple mundane task of washing her hair. It was just what she needed to feel grounded again.

"I was invited for two more seasons to Seattle by an impresario who thought I was great. What a wonderful year!"

At the end of the run, Susan returned to her new home in New York City. "I came back to the biggest pool of all," she said. She soon left the Big Apple for two months to sing the lead in a *My Fair Lady* production in the Philippines, but returned to her favorite city at the show's end and has been a resident there for nearly a quarter of a century.

Since that time, she has worked on stage with hundreds of stellar performers and she hosted a show called, *Home Matters* that ran on The Discovery Channel for nine years.

Susan's town has never forgotten the diminutive woman with the powerful voice. She was honored during her tour as Miss America with a highway sign on Highway 40 that makes this proud claim: *Home of Susan Powell*. In the spring of 2004, she performed a concert in Elk, Oklahoma in the *Susan Powell Fine Arts Building*, dedicated in 1981.

In the 1980s, while doing *Laurie and Curley* with the Cincinnati Opera, Susan met a wonderful young man by the name of David Parsons. They dated for two years before tying the knot in 1986. "He was a great guy from a strong family in Michigan," she said. "He was one of six children and his parents were married a long time. The family was large and really solid, and it was wonderful to have that in my life."

For many years, the marriage was great, according to Susan, but show business, especially in a frenetic environment such as New York, takes its toll when both partners are struggling to find the next good role, traveling, performing day after day. It's a stressful career for one to manage, but when two people are trying to maintain a close relationship, much of which is over long distance, it's extremely difficult. The couple eventually divorced in 1999.

"It was a difficult decision." But on a positive note, she said, "I cherish all the love I've had in my life."

At this writing, she has been involved in a close relationship for three years and is quite happy to be sharing her life with someone very important to her.

"Richard is in the business as well," she said. "He's a singer, too, and is currently on national tour of a Broadway show. The voice of this special guy can be heard as Gaston in the movie - *The Beauty and the Beast.*

"I connect more with artists," she said wisely. "I've tried to fall in love with businessmen and professional men like lawyers and doctors, but people in show business understand the pressures of it. It's a unique career. We live at night, plus there's a big travel element. Being apart and learning to prioritize your time and effort—some men who aren't in my profession just can't understand it and don't take it seriously as a viable career. That becomes a point of huge contention when you date someone outside of the business. I was always the one being asked to sacrifice my career to stay home. But I like earning my own money and having my independence. You have to know who you are."

Asked her thoughts about marriage, she said, "It's not for everyone. We're dealt this incredible hand of cards from society or our moms that the true route, possibly the only acceptable route, to happiness is through marriage and children. I think we've done a great disservice to teenage girls by telling them that's the only option."

She offers sage advice to the young women who are just beginning to outline the goals for their lives. "First, figure out where your talents lie, what you're passionate about and what you're willing to work for. Education is the most important thing. You need to develop skills in anything you choose to do and that takes lots and lots of work and a tremendous amount of discipline. But you need education so you will be able to support yourself. Then you need to get your spiritual life in order. Anything that happens from all this is going to be right and serve you well."

Susan Powell has exemplified those words throughout her life. And lest anyone think this road has been easy, she should think again. "It's so hard. Sometimes I think I just can't go another day. When I was still in college I chose this life and it's one of the most difficult and challenging businesses there is, show business.

Susan with Richard White in the park in New York City.

Susan and Jackie Mayer(1963) cutting up at Caesar's Palace after the pageant in September 2003.

Photo by Kate Kitchen

To make it and make a consistent living means you have to constantly improve yourself—working, rehearsing, struggling, looking for that next job and keeping your head straight. But the rewards for me have been exhilarating.

"Grace is happening—and today I'm once again doing fulfilling work. I'm singing a lot. I'm envisioning my future: I enjoy television. I'd really like to host a travel show or a live talk show."

Susan reflected for a moment, then said quietly, "I think we are born into grace and that it is up to us to be responsible to that gift—to the grace in our lives. And I also think it's very important to listen to our own greatness along the way."

She thought suddenly of a particular author's philosophy she has embraced. "In M. Scott Peck's book, *The Road Less Traveled*, he cited that with patients who have the same diagnosis, the difference in the one who recovers and the one who doesn't may be due to grace. I think I've always been tuned into my own grace."

Susan compares life's mysteries: "Every year, more doors open. It's like peeling an onion. Another layer gets revealed. I think the key to success and to living life well is summed up by these two things—gratitude and grace."

Miss America 1985
Sharlene Wells

Student - Brigham Young University
State - Utah
Age - 20   Height - 5' 8''

Talent: To honor her birthplace of Paraguay, Sharlene wore a bright pink skirt and white peasant blouse and sang a Spanish folk song. She accompanied herself on the Paraguayan harp.

Photo courtesy of the Miss America Organization.

"One thing I always hated more than fear of failure was regret.
I never wanted to say, what if …?"
—Sharlene Wells Hawkes

Sharlene Wells

How does a woman born in Paraguay become Miss America? And what could a former Miss America possibly know about failure?

Sharlene Wells was number five in a family of seven children. For her first twelve years, Sharlene and her family lived in South America. Her father was an international banker-turned ecclesiastical missionary for the Church of Jesus Christ of Latter-day Saints.

When asked about the pressures of living up to the Miss America image, she laughed, "You think that was pressure! Try to live up to the standards set by the equivalent to an archbishop in the Mormon Church!"

Nevertheless, Sharlene appreciated the standards and moral values taught in her home. And that set of strong values offered her a healthy will to succeed. They taught her that it was all right to fail—*if you were trying*! And try she did!

Most of Sharlene's schooling was in Buenos Aires, Argentina, and included just about every sports activity imaginable—from volleyball to swimming, from softball to track. She lettered in all of them and was named captain of the track team. She learned early on that to succeed and continue to grow, you have to constantly push the envelope.

"You can't stay in your comfort zone and get anywhere. I failed at so many things that failure became part of my life. But if I had been more afraid of failing than afraid of the risk of trying, I wouldn't have constantly pushed myself beyond my own limits to succeed."

The family moved back home to Salt Lake City in time for Sharlene to graduate from high school, then go on to Brigham Young University.

She is willing to share her fears even today with anyone who will listen, because she believes she has learned more about herself through her failures than through her successes. "Failure actually led me to success," she said. "I was never a natural performer. Speaking in public, even now, still makes me nervous. I've tried out for performance groups and not made it; for choirs and not made it; for musicals and not made it. I kept taking voice lessons because I liked to sing—I always have. My poor teachers!" she laughed.

"I should have put on my resume *Can't sing, can't dance!*" For a woman so brutally honest about her shortcomings to compete at all seems an amazing feat in itself.

However, as a college freshman, she put herself into the most uncomfortable position of all.

"My roommate wanted me to try out for a popular performing group at BYU," Sharlene explained. I said, "I can't sing and I can't dance. What if I try out and make a fool of myself?"

Her roommate studied Sharlene for a moment, then blurted out, "What if you *don't* try out?" That was all it took. And that comment became the concrete stepping stone to her title as Miss America.

She still remembers the painful process with chagrin. "I made myself go through the whole audition, singing and dancing. I gave it all I had—for four whole bars." The director interrupted her, instructing her to go to the next song. Two measures into the next song, he stopped her again. "Why are you trying to sing soprano when you're an alto?" he demanded. Sharlene had always mistakenly assumed she was a soprano.

"I was so naïve, I really thought you could just pick the range you wanted to be," she admitted candidly.

The second part of the audition was dance. She tried desperately to follow the choreography, but knew it was hopeless. "I tried so hard to learn the steps but just didn't have that kind of talent. I forgot the routine and thought I'd have fun and try not to take myself so seriously. So I clapped, stomped and grinned my way through the routine and at the end, knowing I'd failed, just slumped over and allowed myself for a moment to feel stupid and dejected. I was *shocked* to hear my name called for the third round."

Against all odds, Sharlene had made the cut. She still wonders today if the people who auditioned her felt sorry for her or simply admired her bravado.

She became a member of The Young Ambassadors and traveled all over New England with that group. In addition to performing, she was given the assignment of public relations spokesperson and soon learned how to use a microphone, how to use the camera to her best advantage, and eventually became quite skilled at public speaking.

But now back in school, reality faced her. She needed money. Her family was a large one and she wanted to take responsibility for her own college tuition.

Having lived in a foreign country, she had never seen the Miss America Pageant. Her only reference to it was on the night of her high school prom as she nearly floated down the steps of her home in her lovely dress. Her father stood at the bottom of the stairs, serenading her with, *"There She Is—Miss America!"* He couldn't possibly have known how fortuitous that moment would be.

"Mom suggested I compete for Miss Salt Lake Valley, so I did. I won, then went to the Miss Utah competition. I was second runner-up

there. But I wasn't disappointed—I was actually ecstatic! I didn't think I'd get that high. I had an academic scholarship, but I needed funds to cover room, board and music books. I was just looking for a couple thousand dollars."

One of the pageant judges called Sharlene immediately after the competition, encouraging her to try again. "No, I don't think so," she responded.

Then she remembered her self-taught lesson about reaching beyond your comfort level and not being afraid to fail. "So I did it again. I tried again the next year."

Now a college sophomore, at the age of twenty, Sharlene suddenly became, in rapid succession, Miss Utah Valley - then Miss Utah. She was ready to compete for the 'big one.'

"I think I was competing with myself more than anyone else," she explained. "I had always wanted to be in some sport in the Olympics; and from the start, I had always tried to outdo my last performance."

Sharlene describes her experience in Atlantic City as "a really great time! I tried hard, but already had won scholarship money and didn't need to win the title, so at that point, I didn't worry about winning anymore. I felt confident but didn't feel any pressure. I mean, how often do winners come from Utah? I definitely was a dark horse!"

Sharlene competed the year after Vanessa Williams resigned, and with all the scandal surrounding the issue of nude photographs in a nationally circulated magazine, she found the media to be circling the waters, definitely after larger fish.

"They ignored me all week," she said. "The press corps was huge that year and they were so busy trying to figure out what kind of girl the American public really wanted. They were running around creating all sorts of stories about the competitors—just not about me. So the pressure was off of the 'girl from Utah' and I just had a good time!"

Then wonder of wonders, the title became hers, and when all was said and done, the girl from Utah had won the crown.

Sharlene sheepishly admits that during her reign she created "lots of problems for pageant officials." Confessing to really not liking the limelight, Sharlene figured out a way to sidestep at least one requirement that made her feel like "a stupid little doll."

She shared this story, trying to suppress a mischievous laugh. "I really didn't want to wear the crown during appearances, so I would just temporarily lose it."

She recalls one major faux pas that nearly cost the pageant a sponsor. "Once I got a call from a pageant official telling me that one of the sponsors had threatened to pull out and it was my fault! I was at an event and was so excited to see some of the girls from the pageant, I spent too much time with them and inadvertently ignored the sponsors."

Properly scolded, she never repeated that mistake again.

Her reign certainly wasn't all roses, according to Sharlene. Even Miss Americas suffer love lost. While a guest on David Letterman's show, Sharlene was asked if there were a special guy in the picture. Without mentioning his name, she answered honestly that a special fellow did exist, but the announcement must have been too much for the young man because "he quickly and unceremoniously *dumped* me."

The greatest moments came, however, when she met President Ronald Reagan and Robert and Elizabeth Dole, although she equates her meeting with Muhammed Ali as equally inspirational. Prior to Reagan's Inaugural Ball, Sharlene spent ten precious minutes talking to Ali and cherishes that memory yet today.

After she relinquished her crown, she returned to Brigham Young University and was hired as a sideline reporter for BYU football games. She "knew zip" about football, but her strong athletic background in sports and four hours a week spent with football coaches helped her to learn quickly.

She didn't listen to the critics who panned her for getting the job because of her title. She openly admits that being Miss America opened doors for her, but she did the work and took her responsibilities seriously. Throughout her college years, she continued to be a sports reporter until she graduated with a bachelor's degree in Communications.

A year and a half after her tour had ended, Sharlene, still in college, coincidentally met her former boyfriend's roommate in Sunday school. Taking an instant liking to him, she accepted an invitation to go dogsledding. Today, more than a decade later, her voice still fills with warmth when she describes the actual moment when she knew that Cupid had struck.

"I felt immediately secure with him. He's a strong and quiet guy. I remember that we went downtown to see the Christmas lights and he placed his hand on my back as we walked together. I felt so warm, so safe. Three months later, we got engaged and three months after that, we were married. He's great. I really lucked out."

Sharlene reflected on her decision, admitting that selecting your mate is "one of the scariest decisions you can make in your life." And in line with her religious background and spiritual center, she turned to prayer to make that decision.

"That's one time I really was focused. Before, with other guys, it didn't feel right. And I didn't make a mistake this time. The Lord gave me the answer. I felt calm. I had called my mom and told her that I hardly knew this guy, but I knew this was absolutely right."

She attributes prayer to many of her successes, saying, "I don't have to rely on just *me*. Rather, what is the *Lord's* will?" The secret, according to Sharlene, is to listen. "After I ask Him, then I have to be quiet and listen."

One of her favorite scriptures is *"Be still, and know that I am God."* (Psalms 46:10)

True to her values, in 1997 Sharlene put her spiritual beliefs into a book entitled, *Living In - Not Of - The World.* Her musical talents were also put to good use in two Christian CDs she recorded: *When All Will Believe* and *Song of the Morning Stars.* Sharlene wrote the music for the second CD. Not bad for a Miss America with the self-imposed title, "Can't sing, can't dance."

A more recent endeavor is a book released in January 2003: *Kissing a Frog - Four Steps to Finding Comfort Outside Your Comfort Zone.* This insightful book is published by Shadow Mountain and is available on www.amazon.com.

Sharlene expresses delight when describing her own family's current penchant for sharing musical evenings at their five-acre home in Utah. I took violin lessons several years back with my two younger daughters," she laughed. "They were better than I was!" The violin trio eventually disbanded, however, when the oldest daughter put aside the violin after playing for seven years to pursue a more exciting pastime. She quit to play softball—her mother's daughter.

Sharlene's husband Bob is a physical therapist and sports medicine specialist who operates his own clinic, the largest in the county.

The couple completed their family in December 1997 when Sharlene gave birth to their fourth child and only son.

Even four pregnancies could not deter Sharlene from working to maintain her physical fitness. Sharlene consistently works out—at least five times a week. She uses the Stairmaster, she bikes, walks and jogs, does an occasional step routine and even lifts weights.

Safely and firmly ensconced in her family life, she looks back at the pageant and the year of her reign with great fondness. How did being Miss America help her with life's challenges?

"It's nice to know that I had what it took to be at the top once, completely outside my comfort zone."

Sharlene attributes much of her confidence to the Miss America experience, adding that the year of her tour gave her the exposure in public speaking that helped guide her through several years as a sports broadcaster. "That experience especially helped me every time I stumbled."

She admits candidly that even being Miss America cannot assure women from failures. "I've had a lot of bad times on television, for instance," she explained. "I've really messed up, royally. At times I thought I was flat-out going to be fired. I totally messed up! For three days afterwards, I'd be shaky. Then I'd get back on the horse."

She even told her husband once, after doing live TV sports for six years then hitting a slump, that she'd rather go through labor than go back on live television. But her determination brought her through the hard times, even being called on the carpet by producers for indisputable, on-air errors, and she still pursued that career.

Sharlene worked for ESPN contractually for seven years. And throughout her television career, whether on assignment, by contract, or as a free-lancer, Sharlene covered everything from high school sports to college football and championship boxing.

Her ability to interview celebrity sports figures in Spanish was a definite asset as a sportscaster. She also covered prominent events such as the Kentucky Derby, World Cup Soccer, college football and the French Open. After watching an interview by Sharlene in Spanish, NBC Sports executives invited her to New York, offering her a high-profile position, but it would require her to work Saturdays and Sundays.

Time out, she thought. It was time to make a decision. Sunday was a family day and a big sports day. She knew she couldn't commit to both. But as her family was growing and she had already realized so many dreams, she decided that there was too much travel involved, too much time away from home. She wasn't willing to lose so much precious time with her husband and their very young children. Sharlene had enjoyed a thirteen-year run covering sports, had met celebrities coast to coast, had traveled around the globe, and had worn the crown of Miss America. It was time for her to focus on family.

Currently, she is a member of the National Speakers Association and still tackles, head on, the fear she once had of public speaking. As a professional motivator to large and small corporate audiences, she still

feels nervous right before going on, but then almost immediately realizes that nerves are just part of life.

"Now, I like nerves! It means I'm on my toes, that I'm growing and still challenging myself!"

She admits that every time she steps out of her comfort zone, even after all her experience in the spotlight, there's still a lesson to be learned, and professional growth is the result.

As time permits, she enjoys returning to the main event in Atlantic City in September, and during the pageant in the fall of 2003, not only was she an emcee for one of the preliminary competitions, but she performed the song, *I Believe I Can Fly*, accompanying herself on the piano. Her performance was seamless and one has to watch her, then wonder: Is *this* the woman who says she lives outside her comfort zone? On that special night, Sharlene's talent, poise and professionalism were unquestioned.

Monica, at 12, enjoys an event with Miss As after the pageant in 2003. Back (lt to rt): Maria, Katie, Jackie and Heather. Center: Sharlene. Front: Monica and Lee.

Currently, Sharlene is working on completing a master's degree in Integrated Marketing Communication and expects to graduate in the spring of 2005. As if she doesn't have enough to do, her professional reach has expanded and accelerated as well. She is now vice president of communications for an international weight management company, Monarch Health Sciences.

Sharlene Wells Hawkes is still very much her own person; but 'misplaced' crowns aside, her rebellious nature doesn't extend far. According to her, the most rebellious thing this missionary's daughter ever did in her life was to get a second hole pierced in her ear. This kind of behavior doesn't provide much fodder for the scandal-hungry media, so her image has remained untarnished.

"I still tend to over-practice for a keynote address," she confided. "Sometimes I work on a presentation from thirty to forty hours."

Highly disciplined, Sharlene doesn't like to leave anything to chance. If you're looking for Sharlene, you won't find her in her comfort zone. Look for her—way beyond her limits. But you might have to keep looking, because her limits keep expanding!

To contact Sharlene, visit www.sharlene hawkes.com.

Miss America 1987
Kellye Cash
Student - Memphis State University
State - Tennessee
Age - 21   Height - 5' 8½''

Talent: Kellye sang a blues tune called *I'll Be Home*.
She accompanied herself on the piano.

Courtesy of the Miss America Organization

"Now I knew why God gave me such a loud voice—because He was also to
give me a hearing-impaired son who *needed* to hear me!"
——Kellye Cash

Kellye Cash

Kellye Cash's initial claim to fame began with her birth, a rather unique and auspicious beginning. The physician who delivered her was the husband of the late Barbara Walker Hummel, Miss America 1947. He must have had a magic touch because Kellye's destiny was to wear the crown forty years after his own wife had won the same title. There were no other winners from Tennessee in all those years. Sadly, to make the circle complete, Kellye was asked to sing *Amazing Grace* at Barbara's funeral in 2000.

Kellye's family was rather nomadic during her childhood. The proud daughter of a U. S. Navy fighter pilot, Kellye's family moved thirteen times - through eight states and four foreign countries. But the changing environments did not hamper her education. Her mother Billie saw to it that Kellye was provided with ten years of classical piano lessons as well as voice training, and added two years of acting and jazz dance lessons for good measure. Kellye was a pianist for her church and taught piano to younger children.

After graduating from Poway High School in San Diego, Kellye decided she would have to create a stable hometown for herself so she could attend college without having to move halfway through school. With her dad, Roy, still in active duty, she hesitated to start college in California only to have to transfer with the family. She decided to attend Memphis State so she could live with her grandparents. Her family moved on to Virginia.

She was introduced to the Miss America Pageant at Memphis State. "For some reason," she explained, "my friends and I had never paid attention to the pageant while I was living in California. I knew nothing about it."

In Kellye's sophomore year, a member of Pi Kappa Alpha asked if his fraternity could sponsor her in the local pageant. She responded candidly, "I'm afraid I gave them a very offhanded California-type answer. I said, *No way*!"

Her curiosity piqued, nonetheless, Kellye soon found herself attending the Miss Memphis State Pageant.

"I was blown away!" she said. "I didn't know you could win scholarship money!

Kellye in grade school.

Kellye with Uncle Johnny.

Contrary to what I had thought, it wasn't a beauty pageant at all. They were stressing good grades and were looking for a well-rounded, wholesome girl with talent! *I can do this*, I thought."

Kellye considered herself a typical student, paying her own way by working two jobs. "By winning a scholarship, I thought I would be able to drop one job and have more time to study. I never dreamed how far I could go!"

So she set her sites on "a little scholarship money" and entered the pageant as a junior in college. Six months later, she found herself walking the famous runway in Atlantic City, having just earned *thirty-six thousand dollars in scholarships!* Her further earning potential for the year of her reign would total approximately one hundred, seventy-five thousand dollars in personal appearances. She could definitely drop one job!

The sailing wasn't smooth at the onset, however. Thus began her first real lesson in building character.

"I had entered the pageant for Memphis State in March and was first runner-up. I felt I had done everything right, but I just wasn't happy with the results. I hadn't accepted my defeat with grace. Two weeks later, I had the opportunity to enter the local pageant in Milan, Tennessee. But this time, I went into it with a true Christian spirit and an attitude that I would accept the results no matter what they were."

Kellye's lesson in faith became a cornerstone to her spiritual growth as time went on, because although she had been blessed throughout her life, she has certainly, like anyone else, been tested. She had learned a lesson in acceptance and humility and in just a few short months, it had paid off in a big way.

She credits the town of Milan for supporting her. "The whole town rallied around me. I had no car, no pageant clothes—I was just a typical college student. Ramzy's, a local store, sponsored my wardrobe and someone loaned me a car to use during the pageant. The Music Minister from the local Methodist Church coached me vocally and I won the Miss Tennessee Pageant."

When she competed for the national title, her entire family was in the audience at Convention Hall in Atlantic City with the exception of her father who was captain of a ship in the North Atlantic.

She describes that special moment. "I remember Gary Collins standing there. It was so surreal for several moments. I remember saying, *Oh, my God!* I certainly didn't mean that to be irreverent—I was just overwhelmed. By the time I got to the end of the runway, I was looking for my family, but my mom had already been ushered backstage. She didn't get to see me walk the runway. But my grandmother refused to let them catch her," she laughed. "Nana had made a beeline for the runway, and security couldn't have stopped her if they'd tried!

"I got to the end of the runway and thought of my dad. I had the presence of mind to look right into the camera, hoping he would see it and mouthed, "I love you, Dad."

Those in the military are aware that there are only two basic methods of getting a message to a ship: birth or death. A friend who knew this fact coyly teletyped a message to Kellye's dad.

The message read:

*Congratulations, you have
a beautiful daughter!*

The teletype was delivered shortly after six a.m. Feeling sorry for their skipper, stuck at sea, the men knew exactly what to do to boost everyone's morale. They decided to celebrate by dressing up like women and held a mock beauty pageant. They crowned their captain *Miss America*. A week later, he received a video of the pageant and Kellye said mistily, "We were told he dissolved into tears!"

Kellye's father has another claim to fame. He is the eldest nephew of the late country western singer Johnny Cash. "Johnny sent me flowers and one of the most touching letters I have ever received."

The note said- *It's nice to see a Cash gain the fame without the shame. Love, Uncle Johnny.*

Kellye has used her famous uncle's own testimony in fighting the demons he fought with drugs and alcohol to speak to groups all over the country. She feels blessed that she has been able to learn from others' mistakes.

On the Monday morning after she was crowned Miss America, she inadvertently launched her self-appointed platform on a national level with her appearance on *Good Morning America*. Stone Phillips asked her if there were a woman's issue in which she was interested. At the time, Miss Americas weren't required to be such strong advocates for a specific cause, but this was a perfect opportunity for her to do some good and her family's experience with drug abuse prompted her to become a spokesperson for the issue of drug and alcohol abuse. Even today, thanks to Kellye, each newly crowned Miss Tennessee becomes the official spokesperson for that program.

Kellye's experience permitted her to be one of the first Miss Americas to develop a solid civic platform. This became a springboard for the pageant officials to require the contestants to develop a platform as part of their social responsibility.

"My parents raised me to love God and put that before everything else. With my personality," she laughed, "that's important because I would otherwise be tempted to rebel."

She is fond of claiming during her speeches that she, too, had a drug problem, saying, "I was *drug* to church every time the doors were open!"

Asked how Carey, her sixteen-year-old brother dealt with her sudden fame, Kellye said, "He was so embarrassed. He said he wanted to meet the 'real' Miss America, the one before me. The funny thing is," she continued, "the next year, when Kaye Lani won, her sixteen-year-old brother Nick said the same thing—that he wanted to meet the *real* Miss America. And that was me!"

Kellye has found great symbiotic comfort in her Miss America sisterhood, especially with Kaye Lani Rae Rafko, the woman who succeeded her. Kaye Lani and Kellye were both married in the same year on the same day.

"The day Kaye Lani's brother died, I called her and we cried together on the phone. Our brothers were both sixteen when we won and they both were football heroes. I remember watching her brother play in the Rose Bowl."

During her reign, Kellye experienced several inspirational moments, but being a typical college student, hadn't realized how much one person can make a difference. This is one lesson she took home with her.

A month after she won the title, she had attended a youth rally at a Christian college. "I just sang a song, that's all," she said humbly.

But there was a very special evangelist at the pulpit that day, a minister by the name of David Ring. Ring is a celebrity in his own right. This man has a phenomenal spirit and his message is even more meaningful because he is challenged with cerebral palsy and articulates with great difficulty.

Kellye listened to his message and was moved to tears. "After he finished," she said quietly, "I watched as two thousand young people came forward to rededicate or give their lives to Christ." She was overcome with the fact that David Ring is just *one person*.

"I knew then that I wanted to be *used* by God. It made a huge impact on my life, then and now."

On a lighter note, Kellye had one very special dream come true that most Miss Americas probably don't wish for—she flew with the Blue Angels.

"I never dreamed about becoming Miss America when I was a kid," she said. "I just wanted to become a fighter pilot like my dad!"

Kellye with her mom,
Billie Cash.

She loved every minute of the aerobatics and was happy to report she didn't get sick.

Asked if she was ready to relinquish the crown at the end of the year, she said, "I was so ready! I tend to use dry humor and every time I'd say something during my tour, the media would take it out of context or misquote me."

The year Kellye won, she was fair game for the media. Knowing she was a devout Christian, they looked at her with great skepticism. It was the year of the fall of the great televangelists. She was ready for a break from answering questions that had absolutely nothing to do with her.

Upon returning to school, she quickly realized she had to cut back to one class when she was offered a job with the governor's office in Tennessee. She became the spokesperson for "Drug Free Tennessee" and that year kicked off the exceptional program that is still successfully running. "I would travel all ninety-five counties, sometimes visiting eight schools a day."

And on to the love interest. Since high school, while living in San Diego, Kellye had been smitten, "like all the other girls," she adds, with a young man by the name of Todd Sheppard. "He was two years ahead of me. We didn't date, we just kind of knew each other."

After winning the Miss America crown, Kellye had the opportunity to return to Bethel Baptist Church in Escondido, north of San Diego, to perform.

"They hosted me for a weekend—a concert, lunches, dinners; and all weekend long it seems like every time I went somewhere, Todd was there and an empty chair was beside him. So I sat with him all weekend," she said.

Kellye was amazed when after her concert, this handsome, mellow, laid-back fellow got in line with the others to get her autograph. "I couldn't believe it! I looked at him and thought it was about time that I let him know I liked him."

She laughed when she recalls her lack of decorum. "My mom just about had a hissy-fit," she declares with her down home Tennessee candor.

She wrote this on her photograph—

To Todd,
Will you marry me?
Love,
Kellye Cash

"He thought I put that on everyone's picture, and he went around the room looking at photographs to see if I had!"

Over the next eighteen months, whenever Kellye could return to San Diego, she and Todd would hook up for an occasional movie, or just stroll the mall together. But she finally realized that their relationship wasn't progressing as quickly as she wanted it to.

"I finally told myself to just forget it. I was so frustrated! Once, he even wrote to me and I purposely filed his letter with no intent of answering it!" Then she smiled as she said, "He finally redeemed himself and we were married in 1989!"

Kellye immediately moved to San Diego and began again to work on her degree, this time at

191

With Newt Gingrich, former Speaker of the House.

San Diego State. Life was good and they were a happy couple.

Life was about to create another opportunity for character development for Kellye. But it would take her several years to realize there was even a problem to deal with.

Brady, Kellye's oldest child, was in kindergarten when he was tested for hearing loss. He was found to be severely hearing impaired and evidently had been so since birth. The impact of that realization for Kellye and Todd was heartbreaking.

Kellye remembers taking Brady home after the visit to the doctor, getting into the car with him, and breaking into tears. She hadn't known why he hadn't sung at the programs in pre-school. She hadn't known why he had chosen to not follow directions at home or at school. She hadn't known that he had naturally forced himself to compensate for his hearing loss by learning to lip-read. She simply hadn't known.

Kellye's frustration spilled over in tears that streamed down her face. How many times, she wondered, had she asked doctors to examine her precious child to see if he had a hearing problem? She had suspected something, but didn't know what to do. They kept assuring her that nothing was wrong.

As she drove Brady home, still sobbing, he asked, "What's wrong, Mom, why are you crying?"

She stammered through her sobs. "Because, Brady, I—I hear *everything*, and I'm so sad because *you don't* hear everything." She looked into his sweet face, wondering how many times she had offhandedly said something to him without facing him, something he should have heard but hadn't.

He looked at her with clear eyes and an uncomprehending expression, "But Mom," he said matter-of-factly," I can hear *you!*" Brady told her that *he* could hear. "It's the people who talk with their hands who can't hear." He had never considered himself handicapped.

It was as if a piece of a puzzle had suddenly fallen into place. Kellye has a naturally strong musical voice, a voice that reflects her colorful personality. Many were the times her mother would tell her through the years to speak more quietly.

"Now I knew why God had given me such a loud voice. It's because I was to be given a hearing-impaired son who *needed to hear me!*"

Hearing aids now help the child, but Kellye and her husband are facing the dilemma of what to do as he matures. He is interested in sports and their challenge is to find ways to help him hear his coaches. "When he first got hearing aids, as a five-year-old," she explains, "he was diagnosed with shingles. All this on top of a child that only had fifty-five percent hearing. He was so stressed, he actually got a nervous condition! But God has been faith-

Kellye with Vince Gill.

What a gorgeous family!

ful," she said quietly.

"You know, I'm just like any other mother. Thankfully, special education programs help us. And Heather was so helpful to me. (See her story: Heather Whitestone, Miss America 1995. Heather is the only deaf woman to have won the national title.)

As Brady learns to deal with his infirmity, he is learning sign language as well.

"We have a deaf ministry at church," Kellye said, "and he knew enough to interpret for me on a trip. Here he was, six years old, and the Lord was already *using* him."

Kellye has the typical struggles of any wife and mother, juggling all the personal commitments with professional ones. She still can't talk about her husband without expressing her love and devotion for him. And as for the little town that sponsored her in the pageant, that little town with the population of seven thousand-plus, it has become the hometown for Kellye and her family. Their children, Brady, Cassidy and Tatum, are happy and healthy.

As if her husband and children don't keep her busy enough, Kellye still does about fifty

concerts and speaking engagements each year. She continues to give testimony to her Christian faith.

In recent years, Kellye has starred as Patsy in the musical, *Always...Patsy Cline* - throughout various productions including two separate national tours.

Tragedy struck the family in 2003, and Kellye still feels a great sense of loss. With her father and her so close to Johnny and June Carter Cash, Kellye was grieved to learn of the death of Johnny's oldest sister in the spring. At the funeral, June Carter Cash was remarking casually about how she was scheduled to go into the hospital for a heart-valve replacement in May. "I gotta' get my ticker-tock fixed," was her matter-of-fact comment.

But during the surgery, June's heart stopped for nearly thirty minutes. So many family and friends were praying for a miracle, but it wasn't to be.

Kellye was in Branson starring in *Joseph and the Amazing Technicolor Dreamcoat*, and had asked people around her to let her know if anything was heard on the news. She didn't want the media or an audience member surprising her with bad news. After she learned of June's death, through a phone call from her dad, she was able to take off time for the funeral.

Kellye's memory of the event is particularly poignant. "I could tell that Johnny's hand was in the arrangement of the event because the music and words spoken were all so Christ-centered," she said. "Some very special people, the Oak Ridge Boys and Larry Gatlin, sang. It was quite moving."

People were concerned about Johnny, and Kellye remembers the moment her dad, Johnny's nephew, saw him. "It was so touching. Johnny was very frail and in a wheelchair. But the experience was so beautiful and so moving, I was honored to be seated so close to the family and to be a part of it. I hadn't realized how much Johnny and June had impacted other peoples' lives. So many people spoke about that, from Kris Kristofferson on. Jane Seymour even spoke about how when she saw June on the set of *Dr. Quinn-Medicine Woman*, she saw God in June. It was all so touching."

Johnny was so heartbroken at losing his long-time love that he did not want to leave the graveside. Kneeling by his side, Kris Kristofferson comforted him and Johnny's oldest daughter started singing, *May the Circle Be Unbroken.*

Finally summoning up the strength to leave, Johnny was heard to say, "Well, I'm going to go home, get strong and get my house in order." And as frail as he was, soon thereafter, Johnny Cash began recording his last songs.

Johnny had been in ill health for some time and in September, after a bout in the hospital,

FEBRUARY 19 – MAY 8 ADVENTURE THEATER

Kellye as Patsy Cline.

was discharged. He had expressed disappointed in missing the MTV awards in New York due to his failing health, having been nominated for an award for his video: *Hurt.*

"He had just gotten out, and a day later, had to go back because he became short of breath. And very early in the morning, around one or two, he died. And his death was absolutely shocking. We didn't expect it," Kellye said.

Kellye had often visited him in the hospital, but during the last time, he had acquired an infection and she was unable to see him. Kellye was back at the show, performing again in *Joseph* when he died.

"I got a phone call at six a.m. from the Miss America Organization asking if my schedule were going to change for returning to the pageant the next week, and I couldn't figure out why they were asking. Then I was told that Johnny had died during the night. I didn't even know."

In a period of months, Kellye had lost three members of her family and the sadness was overwhelming, but she continued with her public and private responsibilities and even returned to the pageant in September, shortly after Johnny's death, to perform there as well.

"I'm still moved to tears when I see videos of him. They play the song, *I Still Miss Someone* as a tribute to him, and it's so special because my dad wrote it."

She feels a tremendous kinship with her Miss America sisters and has returned to the pageant nearly every year.

She's always the one whose low, gospel voice you hear start that song in the Miss America hospitality suite in Atlantic City. Suddenly the room quiets down as talking becomes more hushed, then dies out altogether, replaced with the sweet song, *Amazing Grace.* And one voice after another joins in until the room is filled with the spirit of the Lord.

She has produced a CD, *Real Life*, and is completing a country CD, which will be released in the fall of 2004. It is entitled, *Back Home, Back When.*

To book Kellye for public appearances or to acquire her CDs, see: www.kellyecash.com.

Miss America 1988
Kaye Lani Rae Rafko

State - Michigan
Age - 24   Height - 5' 10''

Talent: Kaye Lani performed a Hawaiian-Tahitian dance

Photo courtesy of the Miss America Organization.

"You have a power in that rhinestone crown to touch people, to make a difference in their lives. It's not the most important thing I have done in my life, but it was something I will always cherish and I'm so appreciative."

—Kaye Lani Rafko Wilson

Kaye Lani Rae Rafko

Sometimes, the most casual statement can come back years later to memorialize a moment in time where fate may have played a hand. This was such a moment. When Kaye Lani was a newborn, her grandmother Mimi held the precious baby in her arms while watching the Miss America Pageant with her own daughter, Jacqueline. Jacqueline, Kaye Lani's mother, is a beautiful woman with striking dark features.

The family watched as Jackie Mayer, Miss America 1963 relinquished her crown to her successor. Mimi cuddled the newborn and said, "That's Jacquelyn, Miss America, but it's not *my* Jacqueline! This one," she said, looking down at the child, "will be *my* Miss America!" How could she have known that she was looking into the eyes of *Miss America 1988*?

Born and raised in Monroe, Michigan, Kaye Lani still makes Monroe her home. The oldest of four children, she grew up knowing the importance of roots and family values. She still attends St. Mary's Catholic Church, the same church she belonged to as a child. The mother of three little ones, she is happy to share her story of first love. It's a story that resulted in a beautiful marriage to Chuck Wilson, a hometown boy, now senior systems analyst for a firm in Ann Arbor.

"We met in 1982," she said, settling comfortably into her story. "Mom and I used to go to the berry patch every summer and pick strawberries. Chuck was working. I was nineteen and had had my eye on him for two summers. He's two years older than I and I really wanted to meet him," she laughed.

Kaye Lani's mother provided the catalyst.

"If you don't say something to him, I will." So Kaye Lani approached the friendly young man, her tee-shirt torn, no makeup on, hair pulled back into a ponytail. He wisely took the hint.

"He helped me carry all the flats of berries we bought to my jeep," she laughed with delight, still remembering the warm summer afternoon. "I told him that he had the most beautiful blue eyes I'd ever seen. I gave him my number and told him if he ever wanted to go out, to please let me know."

A moment later, she understood why he hadn't approached her before. He was startled. "How old *are* you?" he asked. He had thought she was about thirteen, dressed as she was, with her ponytail and sporting tee-shirt and shorts. But he recognized her name from local pageants and knew who she was.

Once the momentum had started, she couldn't seem to stop it. She found excuses for going back to the berry patch twice more that day, the last time with the pretext of collecting berries for her aunt, and finally—Chuck asked her out.

Kaye Lani still cherishes that special memory. "It may not seem like much to anyone else, but there's a Friendly's Ice Cream Parlour in town that was so neat, and I really wanted to go there. When he asked me to go to Friendly's for ice cream after his softball game, I was thrilled!"

When her new suitor picked her up at the door, he didn't recognize her. She had dressed up. She was obviously not thirteen!

Although she had entered and won pageants throughout her school years, those competitions had served a serious purpose for this natural beauty. Kaye Lani explained, "I needed money for school. I had been accepted to St. Vincent's School of Nursing in Toledo and had just signed up for student loans that amounted to seven hundred fifty dollars for tuition alone, just for classes one day a week. I read that the Miss Monroe County title would earn exactly that. But even if I won that, I still had to figure out a way to come up with the rest, for the other four days a week, for the science and psychology courses."

Nick doing what he loved best

She recalls that when telling her dad about wanting to enter her first pageant, he was firm about refusing to permit her to do so. "No way," were his exact words. But her parents were struggling to put the other three kids through parochial school and he found himself rethinking his decision. Her dad owned a junkyard, referring to himself as Lonny Rafko, M.D. (Metal Dealer). He worked hard to provide for his family and did not want his children to have to work while going through school.

But it was just too hard, financially. Kaye Lani has always been brutally honest about her academic limitations at that time, admitting, "I wasn't good enough to get a scholarship on grades alone."

So he relented and the young woman began to weave her way through the pageant system, eventually earning a total of forty-five thousand dollars in scholarships over a period of six years throughout fourteen pageants! The scholarship money paid for her student loans and her education. "Even if I won a hundred dollars," she said, "it went to my schooling, but along the lines, you learn to recognize the other opportunities you're being given. The pageant system really provides the launching pad for

young women to reach bigger and better things for their lives."

Kaye Lani said, "We all have awesome dreams and goals we want to achieve. I wanted to be a nurse, to open up a hospice program, to marry and become a mother. The doors opened more quickly for me as Miss America than if I were just Kaye Lani Rae Rafko."

She continued, "You have a title that everyone in the country over five years of age recognizes. People listen to what Miss America has to say. You have a voice. They sit on the edge of their seats to listen. You have a power in that rhinestone crown to touch people, to make a difference in their lives. It's not the most important thing I have done in my life, but it was something I will always cherish and I'm so appreciative."

In 1985, Kaye Lani graduated from nursing school. She became a registered nurse and worked in oncology/hematology. In 1988, she donned a different kind of cap, a rhinestone crown. She was the only nurse to ever be crowned Miss America. But she never forgot what she was about.

"Every day, I thank the pageant for what they've given me," she said. "The gifts go way beyond the wardrobe, the car, the money. My best gifts were the platform I was afforded as Miss America. I would receive thirty-five to forty letters a day. My mom acted as my secretary, for which I was grateful."

Kaye Lani shares a special story about a desperately ill twelve-year-old girl who was dying from cancer. "Mom received a letter that she was in the Cleveland Clinic. I happened to be in the area. She had wanted to be like Mary Lou Retton, the Olympic gymnast. But the doctors were planning to amputate her right leg from the hip down, just to give her a fifty percent chance to live."

Kaye Lani was scheduled to appear in Cleveland at a fashion show and while there, asked the store manager to help her get to the Cleveland Clinic. No one knew she was coming. She simply stopped at the front desk of the hospital, asked for the room number and went to the room. It's hard to believe no one recognized her, but Kaye Lani said, "I'm just average looking, I wasn't the best-looking contestant. People don't recognize me in public."

Kaye Lani and Chuck with Nicholas and Alana

Making her way through the hospital corridors, she entered the room. Well trained in dealing with the effects of cancer, she wasn't prepared for this emotional moment. She still remembers the instant she first saw the little girl.

"She was nearly bald from the effects of undergoing chemotherapy. Tears started falling down my face. The child had surrounded herself with Miss America photos and articles. They were taped all over the wall."

The nurse, busy changing a dressing, looked up and asked crisply, "Can I help you Ma'am?"

The child looked up, caught her breath and shouted happily, "I knew you would come to see me!"

Kaye Lani responded to the girl's wide-eyed amazement. "Amy, it's so nice to see you," she said softly. She moved quickly to the child's bedside.

Amy explained who she was to the nurse by saying, "That's the best nurse in America!"

Kaye Lani kept in touch with the little girl. Amy had her leg amputated a few days after they met. She died a year later.

Kaye Lani's platform remained the same—

nursing and hospice—only as Miss America she had more of a voice than she would have had as a nurse. She focused on opening a hospice program called the Hospice of Monroe. She met with Amicare and her local hospital, Mercy Memorial Hospital, and got things moving. After doing a feasibility study, they decided to set up a program and administrative office through which they would train nurses and volunteers.

During her tour, Kaye Lani had talked about the need for a hospice program, and during her homecoming, the community presented her with ten thousand dollars for that purpose. They raised the money in just thirty days.

But she had other things on her mind, as well. She and Chuck had begun dating five years before she won Miss America. They both were going to school in different cities. "During the pageant year, my phone bill ran about a thousand dollars a month," she confessed sheepishly.

In 1994, Kaye Lani was thinking her life was perfect. Happily married to her first love, each day they celebrated life with their wonderful son Nicholas, two years old. He had been named for Kaye Lani's very special brother. The two had always been close. Nick was twenty-three, a husky, healthy man, a former football star who had even played in the Rose Bowl. Everyone in town loved Nick.

One night in June, Nick was leaving his fiancee's house. It was late. It had been a day of celebration. Their mom's birthday and a wedding had brought the family together.

While stopped at an intersection, he was suddenly broad-sided by a pickup truck. He was killed instantly.

Kaye Lani remembers with great detail the pre-dawn hours when the safety of her world

The family 2004.

shattered around her as her dad called her to break the news.

'Everyone loved him, everyone," she whispered, the grief still so close.

Not even time will completely heal the wound left in her heart. But Kaye Lani put her love for her brother into motion to do something good for others.

For the past several summers, Kaye Lani has coordinated an annual local golf tournament in Nick's memory to raise funds for scholarships for students.

"People still come to me with stories of the little things he did for people that he never told anyone," she said proudly.

She's learned a lot about life and its values, especially how fleeting life can be. But Kaye Lani has an incredible strength of spirit and a Christian faith that keeps her centered, and she's grateful for every moment she had with her brother.

In 1996, just two short years after her tragic loss, Kaye Lani and Chuck were blessed with a second special little angel, Alana Rae. But happiness was interrupted once again in the spring of 1999 as Kaye Lani's father became ill and died from diabetic complications after suffering a stroke. A year later, little Joseph followed his sister and brother into the world. And the cycle of life continues.

"We live on eight acres in

a house right next to Mom, so we can literally walk next door," she said.

Kaye Lani wasn't by any means finished with grieving or learning. After a pregnancy that lasted twenty-five weeks, she prematurely lost their precious baby Gabrielle. He only lived outside the womb for forty-six minutes, but in those hours that followed, Gabrielle taught Kaye Lani more than she could have learned in years of Sunday Schools. "We took turns holding and kissing him and somewhere between being held by his siblings, his heart took its last beat," she said quietly. "But I'm so glad we were chosen as his parents. It would have been so much harder on a first-time mom. I held him all night long. An hour and fifteen minutes after his death, I suddenly felt his spirit leave us and that was the first time I broke down. The room was so full of love all the time he was there. We baptized him

Kay Lani with her little ones at the 1998 pageant.
Photo by Kate Kitchen.

and took his footprints and handprints. He was perfect."

Kaye Lani has done so much bereavement work that she understands the process of grieving, perhaps more fully than most. "I think it's important to not hide your emotions. I asked that the student nurses and doctors be brought in to see him. This was the best way for them to learn the cycle of life."

Although Kaye Lani had prayed for a miracle when she first found out the baby had complications, she understands God's larger plan. "The miracle may not have been for God to heal him and let him live, but perhaps to make Gabrielle's life stand for a higher purpose. This baby came to Chuck and me and to our family with an illness and in his one hour of life, he was told over and over how much he was loved. And from his miracle of birth will come a greater understanding for all of us."

Chuck and Kaye Lani were married in 1989, and after all this time, the two lovebirds are still just that. He must have called the house three times during our initial interview for this story, just to connect with his *bride.* "We love each other so much," she laughed happily, as if an explanation were needed.

To book Kaye Lani for speaking engagements, contact Kate Kitchen through the author's Website: www.thestrengthofgrace.com

Miss America 1989

Gretchen Carlson

State - Minnesota
Age - 22
Height - 5' 3½ "

Talent: Gretchen, a classical violinist, played *Gypsy Airs.*

Photo courtesy of the Miss America Organization.

"If you don't give one hundred percent, you must one day look
in the mirror and say to yourself, I didn't deserve to win."
——Gretchen Carlson

Gretchen Carlson

For twelve excruciatingly painful minutes, standing before a live, national television audience that numbered in the millions, Gretchen Carlson, Miss Minnesota, and the other contestants tried to maintain their poise and keep their smiles fresh. They were awaiting the judges' decision on the tiebreaker between the second and third runners-up that would allow them to proceed with the announcement of the new Miss America. Those moments made Miss America history, as did Gretchen for becoming the first classical violinist to ever hold the title.

As a little girl of Swedish-American descent, growing up in Anoka, Minnesota, Gretchen Carlson had only one thing on her mind—classical violin. Her father owned a car dealership in the small town and her mom was a teacher for a time, although she eventually left the profession to become a full-time mom and community volunteer. With two younger brothers and an older sister, Gretchen enjoyed a happy childhood in the Minneapolis suburb.

Since the age of six, Gretchen Carlson had dreamed of becoming a concert violinist. As a small child, she practiced three to four hours a day. It wasn't enough to be good; she wanted to be the best! And she realized early on that there was only one way to be the best—with solid commitment. "All I can remember is wanting to be a pre-eminent, world class artist."

Although her parents had wished a normal childhood for their daughter, they recognized her talent early on and struggled with the option of sending her to New York to study at the age of twelve. Faced with that decision,

Gretchen thought about it a long time before finally choosing to stay home. However, she did attend summer music festivals in Aspen. Those events were sponsored by the Juilliard School of Music. From age ten to seventeen, her summers were filled with the finest musical opportunities possible.

"I remember when I was ten and eleven and the others in the orchestra were in their twenties, but it didn't matter." The prodigy took her work seriously and became extremely proficient in classical violin.

Suddenly at the age of seventeen, she jolted

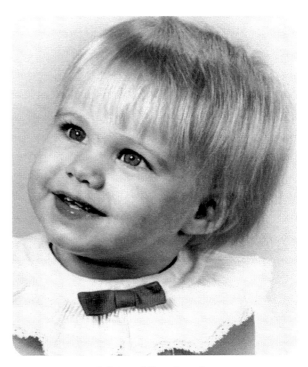

A future Miss America

Kate Kitchen

Gretchen with her sister and their pet bunnies.

her parents' world with the simple statement, "I quit."

She told her mother that if she couldn't be the best, she didn't want to do it anymore. Now there were other interests. She was participating in sports, in drama, and becoming interested in law. She realized that she would have to continue to sacrifice every other interest in her life to become the best violinist she could possibly be. The sacrifice was too much for her. She was already becoming well rounded in other social activities and academics. It was time for her to move on.

Gretchen explained, "My mom and dad struggled with my decision for a while then said it was okay, but wisely advised me to find another goal, one I could achieve by using my violin as a stepping stone. It turned out to be exceptional advice."

She enrolled at Stanford in California. Her mother had told her about a pamphlet she had read about the Miss America Pageant. She had discovered that fifty percent of the points earned were given for talent. Gretchen had been rather athletic and considered herself a tomboy as she played with her brothers outside whenever she wasn't practicing violin. "We'd play army and football. I never saw the Miss America Pageant growing up, so I didn't know what it was all about," she admitted candidly. In high school, however, Gretchen had experienced a taste of it. She had entered the Miss Teen Pageant and had become first runner-up in national competition.

Always analytical, she began researching the Miss America Pageant by observation rather than by immediately participating.

"I went to Oxford, England to study in my junior year," she explains. "Mom called and strongly suggested that I come home to make a try for the local pageant. It was for the title of Miss Cottage Grove. The contest was held in August and I won. The following June, the state pageant was to be held."

As was her nature, Gretchen committed fully to preparing for the state pageant. Unlike most contestants, she took a leave from Stanford to groom herself for the competition. It made perfect sense to her to do this. "If you don't give one hundred percent, you must one day look in the mirror and say to yourself—I didn't deserve to win."

Perhaps the worst moment was when Gretchen had to face the Dean and say, "I need to drop out of school for a year because I'm going to try to become Miss America." That must have sounded ridiculous in an academic environment, for the Dean actually looked at Gretchen and told her what a stupid idea that was.

Her parents, always supportive, jumped into the fray and helped her prepare for her competition.

"Mom and Dad set up tons of mock interviews for me with community members. They would videotape them, then we would critique them. Our family has always been close and when one of us is involved in something, all of us are involved. As you get older, you realize how important that is."

Along with helpful strategies sometimes come ideas that aren't so good. One was from a swimsuit designer in Texas who realized that Gretchen was under five feet four inches and suggested she present herself as "perky" by

A formidable athlete.

"fiddling."

"She's short, she needs to fiddle!" the woman suggested. From classical violin to *fiddling*? Gretchen passed on that idea.

She went to South Carolina to visit a designer well known for creating wonderful dresses for the Miss America competitors. From there, she went to The Butcher Shop in Texas to groom herself physically. Most women know that in swimsuit competitions, shorter women have a more difficult time looking slender. Gretchen was determined to look her absolute best.

"I was doing everything I could do to prepare for this," Gretchen said. "I read current events constantly. I gave serious thought to issues of the day and considered how I truly felt about them. I compiled notes and organized them on my computer. I developed stands on particularly sensitive issues. What I figured was that once you win the state title, you don't have time to prepare for the Miss America Pageant. It's usually only three months away. I would need to do all the grunt work, all the necessary preparation before competing for the state title."

Gretchen became Miss Minnesota in June and was satisfied she had been so astute as to prepare herself ahead of time. "During the three months prior to the Miss America Pageant, I constantly traveled the state of Minnesota. It turned out to be a good thing to already have my strategy in place."

During the evening gown competition, Gretchen, after all her planning and preparation and serious thought, found herself transfixed on one thing: the brilliant, white teeth of emcee Gary Collins. "I was so short that my eyes came up to his teeth. I didn't even hear his question to me. His smile was so big and beautiful."

But at the end of the evening, everyone was awaiting the results. "I remember looking down at the judges, seeing them actually thumb through the pages with our photos, look at mine and shake their head. I knew I'd lost at that moment."

Gretchen also knew she had several minutes left on stage to enjoy the moment, to recognize how unique and wonderful an experience this had been, how much she had grown. "I'm not going to win this, I thought. It was an agonizing time, a reflective time. But even though I knew I wasn't going to actually win the title, I thought I was still a winner."

The proceedings started up again and Gary Collins (with his big, beautiful smile) announced the fourth, the third and the second runners up. The top ten women were still standing onstage in a line.

Then he announced the top two point-getters (Gretchen and Maya Walker, Miss Colorado). Gretchen reached over to hug her compatriate

Practice makes perfect

205

Miss America with her family

and laughed, "I can't believe it's the two short ones!"

Suddenly Gretchen was introduced as the new Miss America. All her serious work had paid off.

Asked about the reign, Gretchen described her year in two words: "Grueling job." Her sense of responsibility continued with an increased effort of purpose.

She said, "I tried to exemplify the fact that women involved in this program are more than pretty women with crowns on their heads. This is a *quality* program for women. I always tried to perform with my violin whenever I made appearances. But I refused to wear the crown. When I was in front of people and discussing serious issues, I couldn't do that with a crown. People cannot take you seriously with a crown on your head. Since that time, I believe cover shots show Miss Americas holding the crown rather than wearing it."

The lives she touched during that year offered precious memories to her. She recalled one incident where she was signing autographs in Buffalo, New York and three little girls approached her. "Miss America, you've given us hope!" they shouted. "*You're* short, too!"

Gretchen remembers her grandfather and mentor telling her, "I believe in you. But you can't win, because you're too short."

Being the scholar she is, Gretchen had gone immediately to the library to research the heights of former Miss Americas. "I found out that Margaret Gorman was only five feet one. (Gorman was at sixteen the first Miss America, in 1921, and may not yet have reached her adult height.) Height never again became a consideration for Gretchen.

From being a short violinist to a poised, regal Miss America, Gretchen could never have dreamed that one day she would sit in the Oval Office with President Ronald Reagan. "He was planning to build a presidential library at my school, Stanford. We talked a lot about that."

Gretchen also met Bill Cosby and has special memories of their sharing sushi together. She was one of the lucky ones who got to go behind the scenes of his television show.

But she will never forget her stint on *Bloopers and Practical Jokes*—Gary Collins and those famous teeth were responsible for her being set up.

"Gary and Mary Ann Mobley (Miss America 1959 and wife of Gary Collins) were accomplices," she said.

Gretchen still laughs at the memory. "The show was shot in Denver. It was just one week after I had won. There was supposed to be a lecture for five thousand engineers in D.C. to introduce a new satellite system called, "The Miss America." We were on the set and Gary was suddenly called off the set for an emergency phone call. Then Mary Ann got called off the set for a supposedly bad microphone. They left me alone to do the telecast. I couldn't believe it!"

Just remembering the fear of that moment, Gretchen took a deep breath before continuing her story. "The director said, 'Just talk. We're on!'"

Poor Gretchen found herself having to ad lib on television for fourteen minutes on a topic she knew absolutely nothing about.

"Cue cards were dropping onto the floor, or the crew would hold them upside down. Gary and Mary Ann wouldn't come back onto the set, and I just knew I was doing such a poor job I'd be fired from being Miss America. Then suddenly, I heard a voice boom out, 'You are on *Bloopers and Practical Jokes*!'"

If serving no other purpose, that experience was perhaps the catalyst that led to successful extemporaneous speaking for the rest of the year, perhaps for the rest of Gretchen's professional life.

After her tour was completed, Gretchen continued to travel for several months, accepting various speaking engagements until she felt it was time to return to Stanford and resume her studies.

Photo courtesy of the Miss America Organization.

on a daily basis and was scared to death all the time." But she learned on the job and was there two years before moving on to Cincinnati for two years, then to Cleveland as an anchor.

Shortly thereafter, she moved on to Dallas, also as an anchor, then in the fall of 2000, was hired to her current position with CBS News in New York. Gretchen was promoted to host the CBS Early Show in April of 2002. She has certainly found her niche in the news business.

"It was an unusual experience because my friends were gone, but still, I welcomed it."

Gretchen designed her own major in Organizational Behavior, combining Pre-law and Industrial Engineering, with the goal of becoming a corporate problem solver. After two final quarters, she graduated in 1990 with a Bachelor of Arts in Organizational Behavior.

The experiences she had gained as Miss America, however, were already pulling her in a different direction and she heard there was an opening in television in Richmond, Virginia at the ABC affiliate. Upon calling the news director at the station, she was told, "My wife doesn't even let me watch Miss America on TV. I don't think I could hire you."

Gretchen did not let his comments deter her. She requested that he view her tape. He eventually hired her as a reporter. Her new boss soon left, however, and the new news director put Gretchen in a position as a political reporter. "I was one of few women in a pool of twenty-five reporters. I covered the governor

"This is the kind of show I've always wanted to do because it's the kind of show where you can do a combination of hard news and features. You can still interview the President of the United States but in the second half of the show, you can showcase your personality. All the hard work is paying off," she said.

And along the way love came calling. "I met my husband, Casey Close, on a blind date in Ohio. I hadn't been dating for a while and a real estate agent and friend set us up, saying, "I think I've got a perfect guy for you."

Gretchen's response was totally '90s as she responded casually, "Whatever."

She was busy, successful, not really interested. But neither was Casey, her intended. An agent for baseball players, he has a busy career as well and wasn't particularly looking for anyone, although he did finally call her.

"He made me laugh and our first date was so-so. Our second date was okay. After our third date, I called my mom and said, 'This is the man I'm going to marry." She decided that the only thing they argue about is sports. "It's a good thing I loved sports before I met him;

we'll fight over whether to watch Cable News or breaking news or getting the baseball scores!"

They understood each other from the very first. "Casey was highly disciplined as a child, only his dream was baseball and mine was the violin. We understood sacrifice, goals, and the need to work for what you want."

After dating for a year, they became engaged and Miss America became a bride October 4, 1997. "We were married in Minnesota by my grandfather. He was eighty-five when he officiated at our wedding and he recently baptized our baby girl," she said. Kaia was born in May 2003. The name is Scandinavian. "She's one hundred percent Swedish, and the name means wise woman. It's not that common," Gretchen said.

Gretchen had always worked so hard on staying fit and trim, she even worked out hours prior to the birth.

Of her marriage, she says, "We both travel a lot. I've always been so dedicated to my career, but I always wanted to be a mom, too. We're so fortunate I was able to have a child at thirty-seven."

As for what she took away from the Miss America experience, she shared this: "I think the ability to communicate with all kinds of people is wonderful. There's an arena of different people that you meet on a daily basis. I remember especially an experience at a Veterans hospital. A patient said to me, 'You know, we both served America. Just in a different way.'" She paused, cherishing that special memory. "You know, that was so cool!"

Gretchen has a solid set of values, an affirmation of the way she grew up. "I grew up in a religious family. My grandfather was a Lutheran minister and church played a huge part in my childhood." She spent hours in

Casey and Gretchen

church participating in youth groups, playing piano or violin and singing in choir. "It was great to go to church but what made it more special was when you could see your own grandfather in the pulpit. Those are special moments when the messenger from God is your own grandpa," she said. "When he gave me communion, he would brush my face with his hand."

Gretchen's father was fond of telling her that people will know you're a Christian by the way you treat others. Gretchen carried that message with her to the pageant. "And I honor that as well today, especially in my career. I am in an extremely competitive environment where sometimes people feel very important and forget how to treat others. It's very important to me to keep my feet on the ground, and my faith has a lot to do with that," she said.

Gretchen says it's in her nature to question everything. "The one thing I don't question in my life is my faith. I feel completely at peace and comfortable with that. When you have faith, you always know there is someone with you even when you might feel alone. Before playing the violin on stage at the pageant, I stopped for a moment and thanked the Lord for getting me to that point. Prayer sets the stage for me. That's the way I live my life, and I do that on a daily basis with any sort of trial or tribulation."

Gretchen says it is equally important that their daughter be raised that way.

"The biggest lesson I learned from Grandpa about being humble is a verse he quoted frequently: ...*From everyone who has been given much, much will be demanded;...* (Luke 12:48)

"And I try to live like that. Holding on to your faith is the most important thing. For us it was important that we see eye-to-eye on those values before we got married."

The happy couple welcoming Kaia into their lives.

According to Gretchen, one of her values as Miss America is that she felt she had an impact—especially on children, teaching them to set goals, to put time and effort into their talents.

"That helps them develop a sense of who they are on the inside," she said warmly. "It's more important to develop the inner person. Then if the child wants to do pageants, fine. It's not about looking pretty with bows in your hair and blowing bubbles for talent. These women have spent years cultivating their gifts and personalities."

If Gretchen holds an issue with anything controversial about the pageant, it's about swimsuits. "I'm adamantly opposed to swimsuits," she says firmly. "Women will never be taken seriously in a swimsuit."

What would be a good substitute? Gretchen thinks there should be a more prominent scholastic category for academic achievement.

"After all, the reward is based on the fact that this is a scholarship program," she said.

"I'd have to think about how to do it," she said reflectively, the wheels already turning.

An incredible talent, a brilliant mind, a generous heart—these are just a few of the characteristics that made Gretchen Carlson a very special Miss America. And they are the characteristics that make her still a very special woman.

Miss America 1990

Debbye Turner

Student - University of Missouri-Columbia
State - Missouri
Age - 23   Height 5' 7½"

Talent: Debbye played *Flight of the Bumblebee*
and other selections on the Marimba.

Photo courtesy of the Miss America Organization.

Walking into a television studio where there was heavy competition for on-air spots,
Debbye sensed the friction. "Knowing how to spay a dog wasn't going to help me now!"
— Debbye Turner, DVM

Debbye Turner

Determination—that's what Debbye Turner is all about. After seven years and eleven attempts in two states, this tall, elegant beauty won *the* crown. One after another, her placements in all the competitions meant only one thing for Debbye—they allowed her to continue her education at the University of Missouri-Columbia.

Debbye was a student of Veterinary Medicine who learned early on that the higher she placed in pageants, the more scholarship money she could earn. Becoming a vet was an expensive proposition and Debbye Turner was determined to accomplish this goal herself. She had watched her mother struggle to work her own way through college.

Debbye, the daughter of a military serviceman, was born in Hawaii and in her first five years, had moved six times, finally ending up in Jonesboro, Arkansas.

"It was a sleepy, safe southern town," Debbye said. After such a nomadic existence, it was nice to settle and Debbye, Suzette, her older sister, and their mother soon found roots in the friendly community where Debbye lived until she went to college. Debbye's parents had separated shortly after the move and Gussie, her mom, returned to college herself so she would be able to better care for her daughters.

"Mom taught me the discipline I have today by her example," Debbye said. "I remember that she seemed to be up twenty-four hours a day. If she wasn't working or taking care of us, she was studying at the dining room table."

Debbye remembers fondly her mother struggling to stay awake far into the night, after the girls had been tucked safely into their beds.

"She worked on her undergraduate degree in Sociology, then earned her master's in Rehabilitation Counseling," Debbye said quietly in a voice filled with respect. "The only way she could stay awake to study all night after a hard day's work was by chewing bubble gum. I remember to this day her sitting there surrounded by books, all settled in for the night, with a sack of Double Bubble on the table in front of her."

Debbye at the age of one.

Debbye had to say goodbye to her mother several years ago. Diagnosed with cancer, Gussie died-not from the disease, but from complications brought on by radiation treatments. She was only fifty-five. Debbye had lost her role model, her support system and worst of all, her prayer partner. Gussie, the personification of the best of all possible single parents, the woman who had provided well for her daughters, never complaining, always smiling, had struggled

Photo courtesy of the Miss America Organization.

teen. She was vying for the Miss Jonesboro title. After the competition, a judge suggested that if she didn't win the Miss Arkansas title this time around, she should run again the next year. Debbye hadn't given it a thought-to compete again.

"I wasn't a tomboy, but neither was I the frilly type," Debbye laughed. "I was just a drummer in the school band who happened to want to be a vet."

When the judge heard that, the carrot was dangled in front of Debbye—scholarships! The discovery that she could earn college scholarships just for competing changed her mind immediately and she continued from pageant to pageant.

for years to raise her family up from a lower middle-class existence. Unbelievably, Debbye was never made aware of any limitations. There was no martyrdom in this household, just lots of love, constant reassurance and good, hard work.

Speaking of her loss, Debbye affirmed her faith. "I don't know how anyone could get through such an intense grief without an abiding faith. It was only through the grace of God that I managed. Her death blew a big hole in my life. Everyone who ever met her was adopted by her, everyone who met her was touched or changed in some way."

Debbye affirms that she lives and will always live the life lessons and Christian values Gussie taught her. She wrote a friend about her loss, saying, "I remember her constant smile more even now than I did when she was alive."

Gussie was more than a mentor. She was a Christian counselor and friend to all. This woman was quite a role model for this proud daughter to live up to, but the former Miss America long ago accepted that challenge and is happy with the result.

Debbye's first pageant was at the age of six-

After trying for seven years to win the title, Debbye had just placed as a runner-up for the second time in the Miss Arkansas Pageant.

"This was the first time it hurt," Debbye said. "I was primarily encouraged to become involved in pageants for the scholarships and I certainly welcomed them. I was already more than satisfied with the financial rewards. But this time, I really thought I had it."

Debbye was heart-broken. She had competed eight times in Arkansas and had put so much effort into the process. But Gussie, always finding something positive, even now, surrounded by the sea of sadness that enveloped Debbye and her close friends, came up to her daughter. Smiling her great big loving smile, she leaned close to Debbye's face. "You know," she whispered, "there's always Missouri."

"Something just clicked in me then," Debbye said. "Aside from the scholarships, now I really wanted to be Miss America!"

Debbye's initial goal of wanting to teach and practice at a veterinarian school was rapidly becoming priority number two. She already had earned a Bachelor of Science in Agriculture.

The universe evidently had greater plans for her than to be a vet, at least for the present, because the next year, as a graduate student at University of Missouri-Columbia, Debbye competed in the Missouri Pageant. She became Miss Columbia, and shortly thereafter, Miss Missouri—and in September, this regal beauty captured the Miss America crown.

Her world suddenly exploded with possibilities and opportunities. Although she returned to school after her tour to complete her degree as a Doctor in Veterinary Medicine, Debbye had discovered that her medical practice would have to wait.

During her tour as Miss America, Debbye kept running into the oddest situation. "For some reason," she explained, "people could not come to realize that I was Debbye Turner. Strangers kept coming up to me, saying, 'you know, you look just like Debbye Turner!'" After a while it became so silly, Debbye made a game of it, agreeing with them, and even adding her own dialogue, "I know, I've been told, but I think Debbye's a little taller," or she'd say, "Yes, but I think Debbye's hair is shorter," or anything else to carry on the conversation. "For some strange reason," she said laughing, "the people could not believe I was Miss America. Once, I just gave up and went out into my car and got the crown to show them I was, indeed, who I said I was. I guess it kept me humble."

When she won, Debbye's mother had said, "This is *your* year. You must learn to ask for what you want."

Debbye remembered that statement in a flash when she met Oprah Winfrey. "She was so gracious," Debbye said. The two had been introduced at an awards ceremony and Debbye made a suggestion that would change her life. She told the megastar that if she ever needed her as a guest on the show, to call her. That comment must have planted a seed, for when Oprah's producers began planning a show on celebrities and their mothers, the Miss America organization was contacted. Debbye and her mom Gussie were invited to appear. What a

treat it must have been for that hardworking single mom from Jonesboro, Arkansas to escort her daughter onstage for an appearance on the Oprah Winfrey show.

Debbye learned a very important lesson that year from Oprah, a lesson she recalls fondly, grateful for the exercise in humility.

"On the evening prior to the show, Oprah generously took my family to dinner. During the entire evening, Oprah was interrupted by people who would come up to her and blatantly ask for an autograph, a hug or a handshake. I watched in awe as Oprah patiently, warmly—accommodated each and every one of them—all evening long until finally, I asked Oprah, 'Aren't you tired of this?' I'll never forget her response."

"I have to remember," said Oprah thoughtfully, "that I have what I have because of these people. And even though it may be my thousandth time in the day, it's their first. I need to show respect and act as if it's my first, too."

Debbye said, "After that, my attitude toward fans has never wavered." She never forgot that lesson. And she felt renewed at the time as she went on to complete her reign, shaking thousands of hands herself. She has continued her career in the public eye and if she ever feels tired or feels the need for privacy, she still recalls Oprah's words. "She helped solidify my love for people and my commitment to humanity."

Another inspirational moment during her tour came from an at-risk teenager, certainly not a celebrity, nor a person of privilege. But one who was equally responsible for teaching Debbye the importance of reaching out, regardless of who you are.

On a trip to the pageant office in Atlantic City, Debbye was slated to speak at a Females in Transition program to at-risk young women. Some of them had already experienced a fairly rough life and Debbye was trying to figure out what she could possibly have to say as a Miss America that would relate to them. Although she certainly hadn't been born with any financial advantages, her mother had created in herself an exceptional role model. Against all odds, she had become a professional woman. Debbye had grown up in a house where education and community service were respected. There were no drugs, no abuse, no alcohol

Debbye with a client.

problems.

"But who was I," she recalled asking herself, "to go in there and stand before these young women who had had such hard knocks? What could I say that would reach them?"

Then she remembered something—the fact that it had taken her seven years and eleven attempts to become Miss America, all because she needed that scholarship and *refused to give up*! So she did what she does best. She talked on their level about developing goals and having a sense of determination. "We basically ended up having a rap session," Debbye said.

She evidently got through to them because after it was over and they had met this famous Miss America, she was walking out of the room and suddenly heard a "Yo! Miss America!"

She turned around to face a seventeen-year-old, street-wise girl. The young woman said, "You know, when I heard you were comin', I coulda' cared less! Now," she paused, as if it were difficult for her to confess, "even though I made mistakes in my life, I know I don't have to keep repeating them. I can be whatever I want to be." They looked at each other and spontaneously hugged.

"Yes—you can." Debbye whispered to her. Remembering the moment as if it were yesterday, Debbye said, "There were tears—on both sides."

The two kept in touch for a brief time. A year later, Debbye met with the young woman when she returned to Atlantic City to relin-

quish her crown. She invited her protegee to the pageant. The girl had left the teen program because she no longer needed it. She was staying clean, she was working, she was on the right path.

"And best of all," Debbye said proudly, "she felt good about herself."

Debbye never forgot that lesson. "You'll never know whose life might be changed by your words, your actions, no matter who we are. It's our responsibility to reach out, to be compassionate. We may never know what kind of impact we've had. The point is, we must reach out."

Debbye loves to get letters from teens and young adults. She speaks at youth organizations and colleges whenever she can. She tells the story of a college student who attended one of her lectures. Debbye was speaking on determination, on not giving up. She never knew at the time what a monumental impact that talk would have on one young life.

Two years later, she received a letter from a young man who had attended her lecture. "You don't know me," it began. It turned out that the young man had been getting poor grades, was no longer motivated and was close to dropping out of school when he happened to hear her speak. As a result of her message, he not only refused to give up, but turned himself around, began to study and get good grades. He soon graduated from college and wrote Debbye just after receiving an offer for the job he really wanted. "I have everything I want," he said as he thanked her for caring. The most important thing he had attained, thanks to Debbye, was a feeling of genuine self-worth.

The night Debbye passed on her crown, she certainly felt more of a sense of overwhelming responsibility than she had a year before when she became Miss America 1990.

"The most intimidating day in my life," she explained, "was the day I gave up my crown, because you have to live up to the legacy of former Miss Americas—and they've done it spectacularly! I think the group of former Miss Americas is one of the best-kept secrets in the country. What a wealth of experience!"

And yet, what is focused on when something goes wrong? The title is used often to sell papers and secure ratings under the guise of news. Debbye was distraught to hear, a few years ago, about the troubles of a Miss America sister. She recalls the day Bess Myerson, Miss America 1945, was headlined in a major legal battle in New York City.

"It had been forty-five years since she won the title, and yet it was a negative story and the headline started with, *Former Miss America—!* The news had absolutely nothing to do with Miss America." It's a double-edged sword that each woman carries around with her for the rest of her life.

"What I've learned about my sisters, she continued, "is that in order to compete in such a highly intense situation, they each have a solid spiritual grounding, a set of moral values, and an inner strength. And it's something you have to have going in."

Debbye explained. "You cannot win the crown and then try to find those things. In order for you to win, you need to have those resources already within you."

People who may not have had the pageant experience, assisted by the media, frequently suggest *cat fights* and other interesting headline grabbers. Debbye has never, in all her years of competing, found that to be true. "Although," she said, "I'm well aware that in every walk of life, whether in the corporate or pageant environment, there are idiots who want to play their games. But who has time for that? I don't bother with them."

After her tour came to an end, Debbye realized she could reach more people by motivational speaking than she could as a vet. (She still plans on using her education and skills in veterinary medicine later in life.) After finishing school and becoming Debbye Turner, DVM, she found a way to combine both worlds. She accepted a position with Ralston-Purina in St. Louis as a spokesperson for their pet education program, *Caring for Pets*. For two years, she served the company in that position as well as accepting speaking engagements on her own. Then in 1995, she was offered a position as host for *Show Me St. Louis*, a popular TV program. She remained a host with that show for almost six years.

When asked about a potential love interest, Debbye didn't hesitate before using her favorite sound bite. "Who has time?" she laughed. "No boyfriend, no husband, no time!"

So this accomplished woman entered the world of television as a Miss America and veterinarian.

"What a combination! I walked into an environment where people had master's degrees in Broadcast Communications. And here I was. And I got there by being fired," she laughed, adding,"You know the saying. When God closes a door, He opens a window!"

Debbye's agent had seen her do a pet segment on local television in St. Louis, and arranged an audition for a pilot of a show targeted for national syndication. The producers loved her and signed her immediately. Contract in hand, Debbye was only waiting for the show to be audience tested. The result was negative.

"Oh, they loved the show—and me!" she laughed. "But they couldn't get past the fact that I was a former Miss America and it was too distracting, so I got fired before I even got to do a real show."

But Debbie's discipline and persistence came to her rescue again. Someone else viewed her pilot and her national television career began. Walking into a television studio where there was heavy competition for on-air spots, Debbye sensed the friction. "Knowing how to spay a dog wasn't going to help me now," she said wisely.

"These are things you just need to work through," Debbye explained. "All it meant was that I just had to prove myself again. And now some of those people are my closest colleagues and dearest friends."

Since 2001, Debbye has been a contributor to CBS -The Early Show. She currently lives in New York City.

Debbye does a great deal of motivational speaking and has addressed more than half a million students throughout the country. She has spoken to corporate executives and been honored in civic and academic circles. But of all her topics, her favorite inspirational speech is her Christian testimony.

Debbye serves on multiple boards of directors. Her civic involvement has included the Children's Miracle Network and the National Council on Youth Leadership among others. Currently she is a member of the National Advisory Child Health and Human Development Council, which is under the auspices of the National Institutes of Health.

That's life to Debbye Turner, and it's a good lesson that she shares. According to Debbye, life is all about continuing to prove yourself and remaining focused on the goal.

Asked if she is truly happy, Debbye pauses, responding warmly, "Sickeningly happy," she said. "Not because life is perfect, because it never is. But I'm happy because there is no greater and sweeter success than fulfilling your own divine purpose. I feel that I'm doing what I'm supposed to be doing, so on my worst day, it's still all right. More than all right. It's a true miracle of God to feel the contentment I feel."

When Debbye was a little girl, she came to know the Lord. Her mom once said to her, "You know, you can't get to Heaven on my apron strings. You have to have a relationship with the Lord yourself." Debbye was only seven when she accepted Christ. And her faith has never wavered. Gussie would be proud.

Debbye is currently working on her autobiography. To watch for her book or to contact Debbye for a speaking engagement, go to www.debbyeturner.com.

Miss America 1995

Heather Whitestone

Student - Jacksonville State University

State - Alabama

Age - 21   Height - 5'4"

Talent: Heather performed a ballet to Sandi Patty's vocal rendition
of *Via Dolorosa*, depicting Christ's agony and love for us
as He carried the cross to Calvary.

Photo courtesy of the Miss America Organization.

"I simply trusted God and focused on Jesus. The voice in my heart said,
'*Don't worry, Heather, I'm in charge. Relax. Dance for me.*'—and so I did."

—Heather Whitestone

217

Heather Whitestone

Heather Whitestone will forever be remembered as the first Miss America with a disability. She has been profoundly deaf since childhood. But those who look deeper will find a young woman who is even more profoundly a Christian dedicated to serving God through her time and talents, from her whole heart and the depths of her soul.

On September 14, 1974, at eighteen months of age, Heather awakened with a slight fever. Her mother and father, Daphne and Bill Whitestone, had already taken Heather's older sisters Stacey and Melissa through their brief stages of childhood illnesses and were not alarmed—at least not at first. When Heather's fever climbed to an alarming 104 degrees, Daphne rushed her baby to the hospital.

In order to save the child's life, physicians administered two different, strong antibiotics. There was a risk but there was no choice. Weak and disoriented from the massive infection, Heather eventually came home to resume a happy childhood, her parents thinking nothing had changed.

Around Christmas time, the family discovered Heather's illness and resulting antibiotics had unknowingly done irreparable damage. Daphne was scurrying around the kitchen preparing a traditional holiday dinner when she suddenly dropped a stack of pots of pans. As they fell onto the kitchen floor, they banged and clanged with a noise that alarmed everyone in the house. Everyone, that is, but Heather. The child sat on the floor by the Christmas tree, completely unaware of any commotion.

But her family noticed and as her mother stood behind Heather, banging on a pot with a wooden spoon, Heather played, oblivious to any noise.

It wasn't the holiday the family had hoped for. After extensive tests, Heather's parents were told their daughter was now profoundly deaf. Then they were given even worse news: that Heather would most probably not be able to develop good verbal skills, that she probably wouldn't develop academically beyond third grade. The doctors recommended that Bill and Daphne begin to consider eventually sending Heather through some sort of vocational training.

Refusing to listen, Heather's mom and dad never lost hope that their little girl would grow up to be a fully functioning young woman, able to use any special gifts that God gave her. As ambitious as these hopes were, they still reflected an understatement of the child's potential.

And because of their faith, lots and lots of hard work and sacrifice, and the support of Heather's sisters and extended family, they all were able to watch a miracle unfold twenty years to the month after those noisy pots and pans first signaled the end to a *normal* life.

For in September 1994, beautiful Heather Whitestone, a unique spirit and young woman of great poise and grace danced before a television audience of forty million as she performed a ballet to *Via Dolorosa* –and moments later walked the runway in Atlantic City with the Miss America crown sparkling brilliantly on top of her dark, upswept hair. And while all week, during preliminary competition, she had identified her family in the crowd by their holding up their hands to sign "I love you" – on this night she could not find them because people throughout the audience were holding up their hands and signing I love you! And after a lifetime of feeling like an outcast, Heather finally felt accepted. The love in that auditorium transcended the barrier of silence that had raised so many obstacles for Heather through the years.

The struggle had been a long one. Even with a hearing aid in her left ear, Heather had experienced a 90-decibel hearing loss in her left ear and a 120-decibel hearing loss in her right ear. Without her hearing aid, she could hear nothing.

As an elementary school child, Heather always felt different. She wore an ugly black wire that ran from her belt to her hearing aid. She

Photo courtesy of the Miss America Organization.

expressed her concern one day to a teacher who kindly told her that the children might think it was a radio. But Heather knew differently.

While her sisters were permitted to leave the dinner table and go out to play after homework, Heather had to stay in and work on her speech. It took her six years to be able to pronounce her name correctly. The discipline that this took, day after month after year, helped Heather develop into an independent and strong-willed young woman. It became clear the Lord had work for Heather to do and He needed her to be strong and independent, but full of grace.

Having grown up in an Episcopal Church, Heather was always aware of the Lord and His love for her, but never understood the meaning of being one of His own until high school. Through isolation caused by an inability to communicate well, Heather found herself at school in the cafeteria either eating alone or trying to keep up with the laughter of the others' regardless of the fact that she could not understand all the teenage girl chatter. Hearing aids don't direct a single sound; they pick up noises indiscriminately. Surrounded by a group of girls, Heather was totally lost as to what they were saying. She just didn't fit in.

When she was eleven, Heather's parents gave her an incredible opportunity. She was enrolled at the Central Institute for the Deaf in St. Louis, Missouri. When she left her home in Dothan, Alabama, she was reading at only a second grade level. When she left CID three years later, and normally would have been prepared to enter the eighth grade, she was now academically proficient enough to enter the ninth grade. Those years of multi-cultural experiences in this international school taught Heather the value of academics, the value of cultural inclusion, and a greater independence than she had ever experienced.

One person in particular was responsible for leading Heather through a unique path to self-sufficiency. Not only did Jim Marco, the physical education teacher, introduce her to a myriad of sports, but he coached her through her favorite sport, orienteering, which Heather found she could do quite well. This is the sport of dropping off students in the woods, unfamiliar territory, armed only with a map and compass. The participant must find her way through a series of checkpoints to the finish line in a timely manner.

Being in the woods was the same to Heather as being in God's house. "I never felt alone because the woods are like a cathedral," Heather said. "God's presence is so strong."

Heather never got lost and happily, she found her niche in competing, winning the state orienteering championship. "My self-confidence grew by leaps and bounds," she said. The competition was a giant step toward Heather's discipline and willingness to prepare for her goals that would eventually take her to the Miss America Pageant in Atlantic City.

Upon her return to Dothan, after her three years at CID, she felt isolated. Her sisters were involved in other things and her friends had moved on. In addition, her high school was having racial problems and fights were breaking out constantly. She had moved back home from the big-city environment of St. Louis where CID was based in a not-so-nice neighborhood right downtown—to her little town of Dothan where the school was packed with bullies and people picked fights because of the color of someone's skin.

"And that's when I really began to deal with reality," Heather said. "For the first time, I realized that dangers are not confined to places 'out there' and that you can be in danger no matter where you are."

Heather used ballet to deal with her feelings of isolation and frustration with the hearing world. "I was determined to keep a positive attitude, not bow to other people's low expectations," she said. "I just had to work extra hard to move the music from my hearing aid into my heart."

Other things had changed on the home front as well. Heather was distressed to find out that her parents were divorcing. It was quite a shock to find out that her family would from this moment on be forever divided.

Heather's mom decided to move back to her hometown of Birmingham. Trying to make the best of everything, Heather looked into the new possibilities of living in a larger city. She knew that the Alabama School of Fine Arts was based in Birmingham. It was a public school, not a private, expensive arts school, another plus.

Heather's reputation as a ballerina had preceded her and the teacher admitted her without an audition. "It was like winning a gold medal," Heather said. "Sonia Arova was the teacher. She had danced with Rudolf Nureyev. I was thrilled to be dancing three or four hours a day."

The academics, however, proved to be difficult for Heather. The classrooms were noisy and it took Heather, her mother and her Aunt Stephanie to get her through the next several months of schoolwork. At the end of the year, she decided to transfer to Berry High School. Rechanneling her dancing, she began to perform ballet at the Briarwood Presbyterian Church.

"Barbara Barker founded the Briarwood Ballet as a Christian dance company. She was dedicated to teaching and performing as a form of worship."

Heather was nearly ecstatic. She had always wanted to dance for the Lord. As a young girl, one night, she danced around the family Christmas tree, pretending to be the Virgin Mary and holding a doll that was baby Jesus in her arms. She danced for God then and from that night on, performed her little ballet for Jesus during every Christmas season.

Dance aside, Heather was still feeling like an outcast at school. But she discovered a way to be included—with a different group.

"I had joined a youth group at Shades Mountain Baptist Church. Someone asked if I had been baptized. I responded positively, that I had been baptized as a baby in the Episcopal Church. I had assumed I was *saved* all my life."

Heather began to spend more time in prayer and in the Word. She realized that she hadn't been baptized after the age of reason and began to learn scriptural teachings that moved her to ask Jesus to come into her heart and take over her life.

"I learned that just being good wouldn't cut it with God. I needed to trust Him completely and give myself over to Him."

Having the Lord constantly with her helped Heather overcome the isolation she was feeling at school. "This habit of withdrawal is one I've never shed," she said. "As a deaf person, the struggle to fit in is lifelong."

Heather felt a sense of overwhelming jealousy when she watched the popular girls laugh and play at lunchtime. And then she would feel guilty from the jealousy. She felt she needed to be worthy of their friendship. Little did she know that she only needed to concentrate on how much God loved her. And worthy or not, He showed her He did. God opened a door for Heather and she stepped through, on her way to learning yet another life lesson.

While looking at the school's annual yearbook, she realized she wanted to have something special to show her own children in years to come. She didn't want to be remembered as —*the deaf girl*. She noticed that several girls had a title next to their names marking their participation in the local Junior Miss Pageant.

Heather decided to enter her first competition.

"It was the Shelby County Junior Miss program and I placed as second runner-up." More than anything she had done, this effort helped ease her feeling of isolation. She was beginning to be able to relate to other girls her age.

As she helped other girls with the mandatory choreographed routine, they took note of her willingness and on the final night of the pageant, the girls awarded Heather *The Spirit Award*. It was a college scholarship for fourteen hundred dollars! In addition, she won the talent competition. "I learned that God has His own way of praising His children," she said.

She had offered herself in service to others and God had seen fit to reward her.

The young beauty had one more obstacle to face before graduating from high school. She didn't want to miss her senior prom and boys weren't exactly knocking down the door to date this deaf girl who didn't seem to fit in.

Heather decided that in order to attend the prom she would have to take matters into her own hands. She found a "nice Christian boy" and asked him if he would like to go to the prom. She insisted they didn't have to go to dinner, so they could save money.

Nervous and shy, they both stammered through the moment. To make matters even more awkward, she penned a note to him, sharing her belief that she was committed to saving herself for marriage and did not want any problems to ruin the evening.

Thankfully, (probably relieved)—he agreed. And he even invited her to go to dinner.

By now, the pageant bug had bitten and Heather had discovered that these competitions were not only a way to make new friends but a decent way to earn scholarship money. The added bonus was the most important thing of all: she could use the talent portion as her Christian testimony to the Lord. She would dance for God!

After struggling through the Miss Deaf Alabama Pageant, which was a disaster on several different levels, none the least was that they offered no scholarship program and the girls spoke in ASL language instead of Heather's learned SEE language, Heather refocused her efforts on college and the Miss America preliminaries.

"All my life, I had been discriminated against by hearing people. Now I found that I was being discriminated against by deaf people. They were unhappy with my attempts to sign in SEE, and more than unhappy with my trying to speak normally. They were, for the most part, willing to live in a world where signing American Sign Language was the only acceptable communication."

The sadness that evolved from that experience could only be soothed by her continuing walk with God. As Heather continued to read the Word, she ran across the passage where Jesus told Thomas, *"...blessed are those who have not seen and yet have believed." (John 20:29)*

Heather said, "I realized when I read that that *no one* can hear Jesus or see Him. Everyone has to feel Him and hear His voice in his own heart. In God's eyes, I was just like everyone else. How reassuring! I spent hours in silence, reading my Bible and listening for the voice of God. And I heard it. Not audibly, but in the same way I hear music—in my heart!"

Heather chose to attend Jacksonville State University in Jacksonville, Alabama where deaf students are mainstreamed into regular classes. In addition, Jacksonville offers a sign language interpreter for each class. Heather was a little nervous about that added barrier between her and the instructors.

"When people are signing for you, often you are spoken to in the 'third person' and not spoken to directly. That was always a difficult adjustment for me," Heather said.

When she arrived at JSU during her senior year in high school, she went to the recruiting office where she met Teresa Strickland, a former Miss Alabama and a first runner-up in the 1979 Miss America Pageant. When she arrived on campus the next year, she was taken under Teresa's wing and was happy to have a mentor whom she respected so much to help make the transition easier.

Home from college for a weekend in September 1991, Heather and her mother watched the pageant as Carolyn Sapp, Miss Hawaii, was crowned. She looked at her mother and told her she wanted to perform her ballet on television. "I can earn scholarship money, maybe even be offered a slot with a ballet company," she said.

Heather's mom could see that her daughter

was fully committed and they both knew that finances would be the only obstacle: gowns, talent coaches, transportation—there were so many costs associated with a pageant on this level. Daphne once again made a sacrifice for her daughter that Heather will never forget. "Mom took another job and even worked three jobs during the years I actively competed."

The two were extremely creative in trying to save money. For the Miss St. Clair Pageant, Heather found a gown on sale. For the interview process, she wore a business suit she had worn before for the Shelby County Junior Miss Pageant. "In the talent competition, I wore my old ballet costume, so all in all, this pageant didn't cost my mother too much," Heather said.

Teresa, by now her close friend and mentor, had been a little hesitant about Heather competing in ballet. She had no idea how experienced Heather was. But when Heather showed her the photograph of her dancing *en pointe*, at the Shelby County Junior Miss Pageant, Teresa was astounded. "I had no idea. I just couldn't picture a deaf girl dancing—until now."

"The music," Heather explained, pressing her hand to her chest, "is in here. I listen with my heart."

Heather couldn't find a suitable practice room on campus, but she discovered an empty room in the basement of her dorm. Cold, ugly, with a slippery floor, this room became her practice hall and Heather practiced ballet five days a week, two to three hours a day.

The interview was a disaster. Heather had tried to enter the pageant without letting the judges know she was deaf. They didn't understand that she had to see their lips to read them. And Heather didn't know enough about asking for what you want to tell them. Initially she told herself she didn't place because she was deaf.

"Later I realized it wasn't my deafness that made me lose, it was my inability to master the situation. It was my family who coached me through that thought process." This was yet another challenge Heather would need to deal with.

A few weeks later, Heather was seated at another interview table. This time, she was competing for Miss JSU. Having learned from her inexperience, she took charge of the situation.

"I walked to the empty chair, sat down, and looked each of them right in the eye. I introduced myself and told them I was deaf, that I could read lips and if they would just speak slowly and look at me, I could understand them."

She charmed the judges with her openness, her sincerity and Heather sailed through the interview process. She danced for God that time and was rewarded with a scholarship as winner of the talent competition. The scholarship gave her free tuition for an entire semester. A few minutes after that welcome announcement, Heather was surprised to feel someone tap her on the shoulder. She had won the title! There would be more scholarship money coming her way.

Heather entered the Miss Alabama Pageant three months later. She walked away as first runner-up. Her desire to go all the way to nationals was fueled by her win and she determined to spend the next year preparing just as hard as she had for this year's competition. Scholarship money was really easing the strain on her mother and Heather was growing personally and professionally—but best of all, spiritually.

The next year, for her preliminary competition, Heather went to Decatur for the Miss Point Mallard competition.

It was during this time that Heather faced another challenge, learning to be a good leader. She was reminded of Jesus' admonitions to serve others when she began to fail at a task she had undertaken at a community service project. She had been escorting choir groups to events and signing for them when she realized the group was becoming disgruntled. In discussing her problem with a professor, she was reminded of those words. She learned quickly that cooperation works better than inflexible delegation and came away from that experience with a new humility. She had become a better leader. And everyone involved was getting along. She had asked the Lord for direction and again, He had not failed her.

"God brought me to Matt. 23: 11-12, and I was reminded that those who exalt themselves will be humbled, and those who humble themselves will be exalted," she said. "It was a lesson I needed to learn."

Heather entered the Miss Alabama Pageant for the second time and for the second time, her name was announced: Heather Whitestone—First Runner-up!"

Heather was so disappointed that she could hardly walk to her position.

But the Lord once again was using her for His service and trying to teach her the grace of humility. She had worked so hard and really had wanted this prize. She thought she wouldn't try again, and then she received a letter.

A woman had been in the audience the night Heather had placed as first runner-up. She told Heather that a deaf man had come to her asking for a job but she was hesitant to hire him. After watching how Heather had overcome her disability, she had decided to do so. It didn't matter what position Heather had earned that night onstage. She had changed someone's life on the Lord's stage.

The third time's the charm, they say. And for Heather, it was. Heather developed a platform she named STARS: "Success Through Action and Realization of your dreamS."

With her family's support, she identified five guiding principles that had helped her overcome challenges and find success.

STARS stands for five principles:
·Have a positive attitude
·Have a dream
·Be willing to work hard
·Face your limitations
·Develop and use an effective
  support system

The next September, Heather, her mother and her aunt went to the Miss America Pageant and standing outside Convention Hall, Heather looked into the eyes of a man selling pageant cards. He looked straight at her, paused for a moment then said, "You come back next year. You'll be Miss America."

Energized by the entire experience, Heather returned to Alabama and recommitted herself to the following year's event. She began to work harder than ever and this time, she was adjusting to a different school. She had transferred to the University of Montevallo because of its excellent Accounting program. "But I knew no one there," she said.

Heather worked so hard, the year flew by. In addition to adjusting to her new school and maintaining her scholastic standing, Heather danced several hours a day nearly every day of the week.

Her drive and discipline paid off because in June 1994, she was crowned Miss Alabama. Since contestants can only be a state winner one time, she knew this was her one and only chance of realizing her goal, the goal she had held close to her heart ever since she was a little girl.

Now she would dance for Jesus on the stage in Atlantic City and offer her personal testimony to the Lord as a living sacrifice through the tender beauty of ballet. And even more poignant, she would dance to Sandi Patty's *Via Dolorosa*—the song that depicts Christ's journey along the path to Calvary.

All the turmoil, the endless hours of work and struggle, all the sacrifices her parents made to help Heather get to this point, all the disappointments—everything in her past seemed to culminate in this one effort. Strangely, it was during all this pressure and upheaval that Heather suddenly found peace. She knew this was what God wanted her to do. And in her heart, she heard these words: "Don't worry, Heather. I'm in charge. Relax. Dance for me." —and she did..

A well-meaning adviser suggested that Heather select something other than a Christian song for her talent if she wanted to win the crown. But Heather Whitestone has always had the courage of her convictions. After all, it was the Lord who gave her life, the Lord who gave her talent, and the Lord who loved her so much he gave His own life for her. Heather would dance for Him.

She realized that by winning this crown, she would place herself on a world stage that would allow her to tell people about another crown: the crown of Glory.

Heather didn't intend to hide her witness and knew that if God wanted her to speak about Him to others, that he would use her and her gifts, even her hearing challenges to do so. And suddenly she was overwhelmed with the enormity of it. Being Miss America was a huge job, she thought.

The pressure of being constantly on stage for an entire year with people who weren't cog-

223

nizant of how to speak to her would be her greatest challenge ever. It was one thing to be isolated and dance on a stage to a work she had rehearsed hundreds of hours, but to be thrown into the midst of crowds, reporters, well-wishers and perhaps those who might not have her best interests at heart—how could she handle all that and do a good job?

Heather needn't have worried. She went to the Lord with her concerns. Focusing on Him, she sailed through pageant week interviews and competitions to place in the top ten and when she performed the *Via Dolorosa,* she became America's sweetheart.

And standing at the end of the runway, tears glistening and waving the "I love you" sign, Heather whispered from her heart, *I really need you, God. You'd better come with me now.*

Heather Whitestone became the first Miss America who had any sort of disability and she knew she had a tremendous responsibility before her, not just reaching out to middle America, but speaking for those who couldn't, building up those who needed to understand and overcome their challenges, and helping others realize that although some may have tremendous obstacles to face, we're all loved by God and all the same in His eyes.

"There are forty-eight million Americans with disabilities, and I knew I had a lot of work to do," she said. She knew she could offer those with and without disabilities a greater understanding of the human condition and this would be her living sacrifice to the work of the Lord. Whether reaching them through dance or through her STARS program or her example, Heather was now prepared to face the challenge.

Heather was immediately taken into the hearts of the country and the flurry of media activity was incredible. This beautiful young woman had overcome so much. She spoke, she lip-read, she danced the most beautiful ballet, and was so grounded in her faith, Heather exemplified inspiration. In her first forty-eight hours as Miss America, Heather appeared on *Live* with Regis and Kathie Lee, on *The Today Show* on NBC, on *The Tonight Show* with Jay Leno, and America absolutely fell in love with this sweet young woman from Dothan, Alabama—at least, most of the country did.

And then the media, fueled by controversy from the deaf community, began to ignore her platform and challenge Heather to explain herself. For a little deaf girl who had struggled for six years to learn to pronounce her own name to be criticized by the deaf community for learning to speak instead of sign, Heather was devastated. All the old feelings of isolation threatened to overcome her once again.

"No matter how hard I tried, every time I tried to bring hope to the deaf community, there seemed to be negativity. I even thought of resigning my title. I didn't know what to do."

For devout Christians, during times such as these, it becomes evident that the enemy is at work and Heather, from the beginning, was up to the spiritual warfare. She decided she would continue to honor God in everything she did and let the chips fall where they may. Although often deeply hurt by the continuing controversy, Heather determined to rise above small minds and to continue her work, no matter what.

The powers-that-be in Washington noticed Heather. She was invited to become a member of the President's Committee on the Employment of People with Disabilities. She also met with her state's congressional delegates who helped her launch her STARS program through a national press conference. Through her platform and commitment, various entities cooperated, from corporate to political, to provide scholarships to students with hearing impairments. Heather met Senator Bob Dole and later, Elizabeth Dole. This was a symbiotic relationship that would continue for years to come.

Try as she might, to please everyone, Heather was the target of so much ill will that her traveling companions had to constantly reassure her that she needed to remain above it all and just move on. It was difficult to not be sensitive to all that people were saying. Sometimes standing before a crowd, she would notice deaf people signing negative comments about her for speaking. And she could, of course, read the lips of others who frequently stood in the audience whispering things that hurt as well. Being able to speak, sign and lip read was definitely a Catch 22 for Heather.

And something she never got used to and certainly never asked for was misplaced idolatry. "I didn't want people to think I was this

Heather autographing a program book at the '98 pageant.

Photo by Kate Kitchen.

perfect little angel, because I'm not."

Heather has always been spirited and independent, which is one of the reasons she was able to excel in her life. And she has always been the first to admit that she's not infallible. And so when women followed her into the public bathrooms during appearances, even at one point shoving her, and at another point, sticking a piece of paper under the stall, all to get an autograph, Heather found herself at times becoming angry.

"At the beginning of my tour, I would sign my name and try to think of a special scripture, but they began shoving the paper back to me and asking for an autograph without a verse, so I stopped," she said. But her Christian testimony did not stop, popular or not. This is who she is and she would not, will not compromise on this issue.

Six months into her tour, Heather found herself in the Washington, D.C. office of Congressman Newt Gingrich, waiting patiently for a meeting with him. Gingrich had been highly supportive of the President's Committee and Heather wanted to thank him. She was introduced to his legislative aide, John McCallum. Although three years her senior, John was so youthful in appearance, she questioned whether or not he was old enough to work in a congressman's office. John kept her company during her forty-minute wait. Their talk was professional, sincere and uneventful—or so she thought.

Shortly thereafter, the Miss America office forwarded to Heather a letter from the young man. Heather's traveling companion, Bonnie, was thrilled to see that John was asking for a dinner date the next time Heather was in Washington. Especially intriguing was the fact he had announced to her that he was an honorable man and a Christian.

Heather, a bit cynical after meeting too many insincere politicians, and too many young men interested only in meeting the celebrity, hesitated. "I don't have time to date. I'm too busy," she pleaded.

Bonnie wouldn't take no for an answer. Finally managing to get Heather's approval, she wasted no time. Bonnie called John's office and left a message. The next time Heather was scheduled to visit Washington, D.C., they would contact him.

After a couple of false starts, due to his schedule, not hers, the two finally arranged to have dinner and although it all went very well, Heather found herself stranded at the table of a lovely restaurant for a long time. Thinking he had become ill, she chose not to embarrass him upon his eventual return, so said nothing.

The poor fellow had evidently been so enamored with her, he had felt the need to go to another table where she couldn't see him and write her a lovely note. Later, when she was back in her hotel room, he slipped the note under the door.

His sincerity was unquestioned. But the two were so busy they scarcely had time to see each other during the last six months of her post.

The year was exhausting and although there were hundreds of highlights and moments to remember, she laughs when she shares one of her favorite times from that entire year.

"I was in Chicago making appearances. I

had mentioned how tired I was of banquet food and John Healy invited me home to share peanut butter and jelly sandwiches with his family. I did, and it was the best meal ever!" Miss America sat at a kitchen table with John Healy and his wife, a table overflowing with five children, and ate delicious peanut butter and strawberry jelly sandwiches—on soft, fresh white bread! What a respite!

Heather with Bonnie Sirgany, her former traveling companion, at the pageant in 1998.

Photo by Kate Kitchen.

The night Heather returned to crown the new Miss America was the seventy-fifth anniversary of the pageant. Forty-one returning Miss Americas had committed to come back to the pageant and Heather felt enormous pressure to perform well. They had asked her to dance again, but had decided she should dance with men; and one thing after another happened in rehearsal during the preliminary nights to discourage her. From a twisted ankle, to being dropped, to a bruised rib from being held too tightly, Heather was nervous about the performance. She didn't want to disappoint pageant officials. She needn't have worried. The performance went beautifully.

And after taking the last walk, she paused at the runway one last time, saying, *Thank you Father. It's over.*

"But then I heard just as clearly- *It's not over. I'm not finished with you yet.*

Heather had invited John to the pageant for her special night, and no one but her family knew that he was her special friend. But two months later, they met in Washington, D.C. and when he proposed, on one knee in an office of the Capitol building, the world was allowed to learn the truth.

People magazine helped spread the news as they did a story on the couple's commitment, not just to each other, but regarding their vow of celibacy during their courtship. The two had chosen to wait until marriage to share the gift of intimacy. Heather thought it funny that of all the celebrity news the magazine prints, the editors chose this as a story.

Continuing to work post-pageant for issues surrounding the hearing impaired, including a hugely successful program to enlighten the public to the necessity of early detection of hearing loss on children, Heather stayed busy. To begin working on her first book, *Listening with My Heart*, and because of so many scheduled speaking engagements, Heather decided to postpone her return to school.

And although she had always thought she would establish her career several years prior to marrying, the Lord evidently had chosen a partner and protector He wanted in her life. They listened to the Lord and Heather and John were married in a small, private wedding on June 8, 1996 at Christ Church on St. Simon's Island off the Georgia coast. She was twenty-three when she became a bride.

Relocating to the Atlanta area, John became the Executive Director of the Technology Association of Georgia Foundation and works in the development of Georgia's charter schools.

In January 2000, John and Heather were blessed with a baby boy they named John. A year and a half later, their son James entered the picture.

And after years of answering questions about whether or not she believed she would ever have a cochlear implant, Heather finally decided, after a great deal of research, to undergo that surgery.

"One afternoon, I saw John go over and comfort my oldest son. He had fallen in the backyard and was crying. I didn't hear him cry. And I realized that with my family being my first priority, I needed to take that step."

In August 2002, Heather underwent the procedure at Johns Hopkins Hospital in Baltimore, Maryland. A month later, she heard through her right ear for the first time. And now, with a hearing aid in her left ear and a cochlear implant in her right ear, Heather is learning to hear and interpret the new and beautiful sounds of her children's voices and the world around her.

"I heard the audiologist clapping! I thought it was a dream. Then she clapped again and I realized it was true. I immediately began weeping," she said.

She was certain it was the right thing to do, even though once again, part of the deaf community was critical of a deaf woman trying to hear. One day she heard water rushing into the bathtub and went into the bathroom to find her two little boys filling the tub to play, a disaster waiting to happen. Yes, it was definitely the right thing to do, she thought gratefully.

"My older son sometimes used to have to repeat things ten times before I understood what he needed. Now I am learning to understand speech well enough that he only has to say something twice."

Heather was asked once that if she could hear perfectly for one full day, what would she choose to hear? Without hesitation, she responded, "I would like to sit on a beach and listen to John's precious voice."

Heather accepts engagements through the Washington Speakers Bureau. She has authored four books:

Listening with My Heart - Doubleday
Believing the Promise - Doubleday
Let God Surprise You - Zondervan
Heavenly Crowns - Zondervan

For more information on Heather, visit www.heatherwhitestone.com.

Miss America 1996
Shawntel Smith

Marketing Director - Northeastern State University
State - Oklahoma
Age - 24   Height: 5' 3''

Talent: Shawntel sang *Woman in the Moon*
from "A Star is Born."

Photo courtesy of the Miss America Organization.

A former judge once said to Shawntel's mother: "Your daughter's a nice person,
but she'll never be anything more than an average contestant. She should find another
hobby."   Shawntel's response: "I wouldn't have stopped competing then for anything!"
—Shawntel Smith

Shawntel Smith

Shawntel Smith was crowned Miss America on her twenty-fourth birthday and the seventy-fifth anniversary of the Miss America Pageant. Growing up in Muldrow, Oklahoma with a population of three thousand-plus, and one stop light, the diminutive, red-haired, freckle-faced, blue-eyed beauty never dreamed she would one day be the town's favorite celebrity. Her renown went far beyond that vision, for she would later become known as America's sweetheart.

Shawntel's family roots were strong, her work ethic determined by her parents. Her father owned a furniture business for nineteen years. Throughout their school years, Shawntel worked with her sister and brother in the store after school and on weekends. The little lady who would become Miss America started her career cleaning her father's furniture store.

Learning every aspect of the business, literally from the ground up, she swept, she cleaned, she stocked and restocked the floors— even delivering furniture to customers. Finally, she began working in the marketing end of the business and found she really loved creating interest in a product. As a junior in high school, she began to focus on marketing.

"We live in a global economy. I thought— why not go international? I realized even then that you have to learn how to compete globally."

During her senior year, Shawntel and her friends were encouraged to enter an upcoming pageant. Aside from competing for college scholarships, it was a fun event and the girls enjoyed it.

The first pageant Shawntel entered, she won the title of Junior Miss in Muldrow. During her second semester in Community College in Arkansas, she was determined to assist her family in paying for her college education so she decided to compete in the Miss America scholarship program. This time, she became second runner-up in the Miss Westark Pageant. She liked the results, having already won a year's scholarship. Realizing the fruits of her efforts and appreciative of the opportunities presented to her, she began to concentrate on pageant competition.

She was involved two years in a row in the Miss America preliminaries. Although she didn't win a title at the top, Shawntel was more than satisfied, having earned enough scholarship money to pay for two years of community college.

The third time became the charm for this persistent lady. Shawntel transferred to Northeastern State University where she com-

Daddy's little girl.

pleted her bachelor's degree, but had her eyes set on an advanced degree. But that would cost more money.

Shawntel speaks candidly about her trials and about rejection. "Anytime you put yourself on the line to be judged, it's essential that you are mature enough to handle the process. You need to stand back and take a good, hard look at the whole picture. You need to remember that there are five or six judges with different opinions, and it may not be that you necessarily did anything incorrectly. My perspec-

What an adorable tomboy.

tive was to remain focused on the goal of paying for my education by obtaining scholarships and becoming a better person. I had to remember that the pageant was intended to be a confidence builder, not a self-destructive event."

Shawntel explained, "After I had experienced a couple of years in local Miss America competitions, Mom, who was literally my best friend, and I seriously talked. We decided that if I were to continue competing, we should call someone who had judged me in a previous pageant. I really wanted to identify the areas that I needed to improve on, then work on those areas."

Trying to be helpful, her mom, Karen Smith, placed the call. Little did either of them dream their inquiry would elicit such a negative response. The judge said, "Your daughter's a nice person but she'll never be anything more than an average contestant. She should find another hobby."

"In other words," Shawntel laughed, relating the story—Keep your day job!"

Many girls would have been humiliated, discouraged, perhaps even quit. Shawntel is convinced that her red hair must have been responsible for her becoming more determined than ever. She refused to listen to that negative comment and have it change her life, except for the better.

"At first," she said, "I was devastated! In the long run, however, that comment may

have been the best thing that ever happened to me. I wouldn't have stopped competing then for anything! So lesson number one was that you shouldn't listen to negative comments. You shouldn't let negative people destroy a positive attitude!" Because of her positive attitude and persistence, she ultimately won more than seventy-five thousand dollars in scholarship money.

Her second lesson came when she began to realize that there was a whole lot more to the Miss America protocol than scholarships. "I learned when I became Miss Oklahoma that with a title, even a local one, you have a powerful position that gives you a voice! This pageant gave me a voice for the cause that I was passionate about and the opportunity to use it."

The bombing in Oklahoma City had occurred within a few months of Shawntel's becoming Miss Oklahoma, but the emotional aftermath would continue for years. After visiting the site of the bombing, standing in that quiet place of devastation and loss, she gained incredible perspective. As a private citizen, she would have been just one of thousands, but as Miss Oklahoma, it became possible for her to call the governor. She earnestly asked

Every little girl's dream.

Governor Frank Keating one simple question, "How can I help?"

Shawntel was moved by a book written by Kathy Keating, the governor's wife—a book that helped put the bombing in perspective. Months later, after Shawntel became Miss America, she was invited to travel with Governor Keating in a five city *Thank you, America!* tour. They wanted to call attention to heroes from everywhere, from all walks of life.

On a family vacation with her parents in the fall of 1998.

People had come from all over the country to assist in rescue efforts. Many had put their own lives at risk. After the bombing, it had started raining, creating fear that the building would collapse. Workers appeared on the site every day from other parts of the state, from every state in the country. They had all been moved to action by the tragedy of lost lives, lost children and families irrevocably destroyed. And no one seemed to care that he or she was at risk. Volunteers just kept coming.

Shawntel remembers somberly, "We went to Washington, D.C. with Governor Keating and shared the podium with President Clinton. We were trying to reach out to those who had helped, trying somehow to fully thank those people who had shared so much with us, those who had seemed to reach into our own hearts with their helping hands and shared our loss, our tragedy.

"With nearly overwhelming love for our country, I placed a wreath at the Tomb of the Unknown Soldier. It was such an emotional experience, so memorable. I felt such tremendous respect for those who lost their lives fighting for our country. And I realized that those who had come to Oklahoma were fighting for their nation, too—fighting to regain the respect and dignity for our people and our country that they felt was lost there by this one act. That one simple devastating act of a terrorist—it was heartbreaking."

To have one's pageant year associated with such devastation and sorrow would not be the choice of any Miss America. But Shawntel will always remember this part of her reign with special thoughts as she witnessed men and women band together in unity for a common cause.

Photo courtesy of the Miss America Organization.

Her platform during the pageant nearly, as she tells it, brought groans of boredom from officials and the media. That is until she began educating them. And to that end, she adopted the school-to-work program. Why such a yawn-producing platform? According to Shawntel, as marketing director at Northeastern State University, she began to realize that the country needed a more seamless approach from school to work, a transition that would make it easier for students to relate their studies to work, and to be trained for work in their particular areas of interest.

Her interest and commit-

231

ment sparked an intention to see the entire nation adopt a philosophy of reality-focused education. But until she made the topic come alive, it had never been considered as a worthy platform for a viable contender. That commitment eventually led to Shawntel being asked by the U.S. Secretary of Education and the U.S. Secretary of Labor to become America's Ambassador for School to Work. Richard W. Riley, former U.S. Secretary of Education said, "Shawntel has spotlighted what we can do to make sure students are prepared for higher education and the employment needs of the 21st century. She has been a dedicated and effective champion of this initiative."

Shawntel's passion and efforts were also recognized when being named by Congress as one of the Ten Outstanding Young Americans in 1998.

Shawntel awoke the morning after she was crowned Miss America to the crash of thunder accompanied by terrifying lightning. This was an auspicious beginning for the new Miss America who was slated for the traditional early morning press conference on the boardwalk by the ocean.

With thunder in the background, Shawntel, dressed in a yellow slicker and hat, holding on to an inside-out umbrella, jumped at the sound as rain poured over her, lightning striking the waves beside her.

"Are you sure you want to do

Celebrating Shawntel's birthday at the 2002 Pageant with Debbye Turner (1990) and Jackie Mayer (1963).

this?" a pageant official asked tentatively. No one wanted to call off the event, but no one wanted the new Miss America struck by lightning either. Setting her fears aside, Shawntel agreed to proceed. Part of her decision rested on tradition and all it meant to the public, but if the truth were told, after spending a week indoors in competition, she was just so grateful to be outside, she would have weathered any storm!

"We had been inside rehearsing every single day. And I'd been up until three-thirty in the morning, and then only got about an hour's sleep. A little wind and lightning wasn't going to keep me inside one minute longer," she laughed. "But they would have let me off the hook." She remembers fondly one lady bringing her the rain slicker. And a year later, just before Shawntel relinquished the title, as she rode in the Miss America Parade with the new contestants, it rained again. She remembered

Shawntel singing at the Capital Dome dedication in Oklahoma City. Former Miss Oklahomas and Miss Americas Jane Jayroe and Susan Powell were also part of the event.

the lady who had been so kind to her the year before and sent her a little note that said, "Thanks for not letting it rain on my parade."

The pictures in the press were priceless - the petite young woman in the yellow rain slicker, grinning ear to ear, every bit the Miss America we all would have chosen.

All night long, back home in Muldrow, the fax machine located in the town's single bank had been cranking out sheets of paper with urgent queries from the press. "Who *was* this five-feet-three-inch, freckle-faced redhead?" They all demanded a response. She seemed to have slipped past the 'hardcore' media without anyone taking much notice—their mistake. The town's billboards, purchased courtesy of the mayor, would have to be changed—again. They had stated that Miss Oklahoma was Muldrow's claim to fame. The billboards were already outdated. The small town of Muldrow now had a Miss America.

During her reign, for several nights during one very special week, Shawntel had found herself tossing and turning, unable to sleep. She was about to meet one of America's finest leaders, General Schwartzkoff.

She recalled fondly, "I was nervous about meeting celebrities and dignitaries. I had grown up in such a small town where everyone knew everyone else, where the people you saw in the movies and on television were not people you met in real life. During my year I met many notable people and I did all right meeting them, but somehow when it came to General Schwartzkoff, I was incredibly nervous and couldn't sleep for several nights. What would I say to him? When the day came, I found him to be the nicest man! From his down-to-earth manner and wonderful sense of values, I learned to not be nervous anymore about meeting someone of notoriety. Now I can meet any-

Photo courtesy - Memories by Jody.
Wedding day - December 14, 2001

one and enjoy their company instead of being concerned about what to say."

In speeches, Shawntel always pays tribute to her meeting with the general, quoting his own definition of leadership: that "It takes two things to be a true leader. You have to always do what's right, and when placed in command, take charge!"

Shawntel learned a valuable lesson from the anxiety she experienced over that meeting, a lesson she shared with those she met throughout the country during the national tour on her special platform of school-to-work.

"We get so caught up in life, we forget about the things that are most important. Each of us has things to share, whether we're celebrities or not. We all have a common bond. I think the people in the spotlight are probably the loneliest people on earth because they hunger for companionship; they hunger for someone who wants to be with them on the *inside*. To know them for who they really are."

Her faith, like that of many Miss Americas, is strong. She delights in returning to the pageants and particularly noticed the spirituality of her Miss America sisters. "These women, beautiful on the inside as they are on the outside, are spiritually grounded in their faith. I know God uses them to impact young people as He uses me." She explained, "I remember a teenager who ran up to me after an interview and thanked me, not just for my spoken message, but especially for my Christian outlook. It brought tears to my eyes and I knew we had connected."

Leonard Horn, former President and CEO of the Miss America Organization said, "I think Shawntel has probably been one of the best Miss Americas we've ever had. I think what's truly unique about Shawntel is her enthusiasm for the job and for people. In 1999, that popularity led to Shawntel emceeing

233

the Miss America preliminary events. Shawntel returned to the pageant with her mom who also acted as her business manager. "I was so fortunate. It was a really special time and an honor. And being able to share every moment that week with Mom was such a beautiful time."

Shawntel's happiness soon turned to sorrow, however, when just two days after returning home from the pageant, her mother was in a car accident. After multiple surgeries and two horrifying weeks for the family, her mom died from injuries sustained in the accident. She was forty-six.

Because she is secure in her faith, Shawntel has been able to deal with her grief with tremendous grace. However, she admits that special events still come up where she especially misses her mom—the pageant reunions, the day-to-day business of being a former Miss America and the speaking engagements and travels that go with the continuing job and now, the most special thing of all. At this writing, Shawntel was two weeks shy of delivering a baby boy who was due to make his birthday appearance on July 4th. He has already been named—Brennan Keith Wuerch! What a wonderful day that would have been for Shawntel to share with her mom. "I know she has a window from Heaven," Shawntel said, "but of course, I would love for her to be here."

Shawntel says since that fatal accident, her father has been "absolutely incredible. He's calling me every day from Oklahoma. He's such a hero, he really is."

Although she wasn't looking for him, Shawntel found her love in line at a store in a shopping mall. "I had a young lady with me from Big Brother-Big Sister. We were Christmas shopping."

The happy family at the beach in Alabama - 2003.

The strikingly handsome Ryan Keith Wuerch was standing behind her and chimed in when he noticed Shawntel and her friend cutting up with each other. "Aren't you Shawntel Smith?" he asked, adding, "You know my sister!"

And it wasn't a line. Shawntel had appeared on BET television with Ryan's sister, who has a music ministry and was providing the entertainment for the show.

But Ryan lived in Nashville and Shawntel in Tulsa. She thought nothing more about their meeting.

And then she participated in a class for Christian Women in Tulsa - *Victory by Virtue.* "I was still going through quite a grief process over losing Mom and trying to make business decisions about my career. It was so different because everything I was involved in involved her. I was hoping God would reveal Himself to me, to direct me on what He wanted me to do."

Shawntel went to a women's retreat by a peaceful lake several months after meeting Ryan. On the first evening, when she went to bed, she began praying for guidance. "I guess I was petitioning the Lord to help guide me, to show me what I was supposed to do, where to go, how I was to be used for Him. I wasn't asking for a relationship in my life, just direction."

And for those of you who walk closely with the Lord, you will understand that when the Lord speaks to us, although we may not hear His voice through our ears, His words are just as clear to us in our hearts. And what the Lord was telling Shawntel was that her mission wasn't yet over. She was to continue her Christian testimony in her speaking engagements. The next morning, as she awoke, she felt she was seeing a vision of a scene surrounded by white, a scene that included music—wedding music, and she knew she was experiencing a wedding. And she was "told" —*Ryan Wuerch will be your husband.*

"At the time, I was very focused," Shawntel said. "My sister was having a baby and I was still traveling full time. And of course, being a realist and already doubting, as we do, I thought, Well, God, he lives in Nashville and I live here and I haven't seen or spoken with him." Shawntel felt she was urged to continue to pray for Ryan, and she did, obediently, — every day.

Several months later, Ryan called Shawntel and although they didn't share this with each other for some time, he had received the Word of knowledge about Shawntel as well. When he asked her out, she asked about his intentions. Determining that he was a gentleman, she arranged for them to meet in Tulsa for their first date.

Three months later found Ryan Wuerch down on one knee, proposing to this beautiful young woman, and in December 2001, they were married.

And they both laughed when they realized what a sense of humor God has. Shawntel explained. "I had always said that I'd like to have a child by the time I was thirty. Ryan proposed to me on the last day of my twenty-ninth year. The next day I turned thirty and was immediately blessed with two beautiful young boys." Ryan was a single father raising two wonderful boys named Braden and Barrett. Those sweet, special boys now have a Miss America they call Mommy.

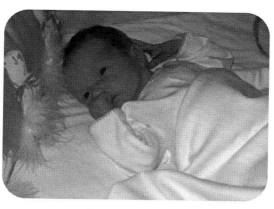

Stop the Presses!
Brennan makes his appearance on July 2nd!

How blessed is this Family!

Shawntel moved to Nashville where they started a started a business together called, PowerByHand that is today the leading mobile content and solutions company globally.

PowerByHand currently has over twenty thousand software developers worldwide and over sixty thousand digital media titles for mobile phones and handheld devices. In addition to the millions of customers that download software monthly from their Internet sites, they have an impressive stable of customers such as Verizon Wireless, Amazon and PalmOne.

"In the last three years, God has taken Ryan and me from started starting a company in Nashville to now having a worldwide company with offices in San Francisco, Raleigh, London, Beijing and Shanghai. We are seeing that the vision that began in 2001 is now impacting millions of people monthly and some of the largest corporations in the world," she said.

Shortly after the new baby comes in July 2004, the family will move to Raleigh, North Carolina where Ryan and Shawntel are relocating the headquarters of their highly successful company. Ryan is CEO and Chairman of the Board of PowerByHand and Shawntel is Executive Vice-president. (www.powerbyhand.com.)

To book Shawntel for speaking engagements, please visit: www.shawntel.com

Miss America 1997
Tara Dawn Holland

State - Kansas
Graduate Student: University of Missouri - Kansas City
Bachelor of Music Education - magna cum laude
Age - 23

Talent: Tara sang *Ou va la jeune Indoue* from Lakme' - an operatic aria by Delibes

Photo courtesy of the Miss America Organization.

"God has opened so many doors for me to be able to use the title of Miss America to promote a positive message. And if I had to go through seven years in the pageant system so I could encourage even one teenage girl, it was worth it."

—Tara Dawn Holland

Tara Dawn Holland

Tara Dawn Holland was born in 1972 in Mobile, Alabama. Her father was an incredible role model, working his way up from stock boy to division vice president during a thirty-year career in food service.

Tara was an only child and can only talk about her childhood in glowing terms. "Mom was a homemaker and because she was there for me when I came home from school and later, from dates, we developed a closeness that was absolutely precious. I never wanted to let her down, and if she hadn't been at home as much, it would have been a different childhood."

Tara's musical talents began to surface at a young age. She started taking classical piano lessons at age six. "I was always involved in the music programs at church, singing and playing the piano," she said.

Her dad's frequent transfers and promotions created a fascinating challenge for the family as Tara and her parents moved six times by the time Tara was five years old. From Mobile to New Orleans and onto Slidell, Louisiana, Illinois, Kentucky and Mississippi, Tara and her mom went faithfully, adjusting to each transition. It didn't matter where they were. Their family was whole and happy and healthy.

Tara's faith grew from a strong Christian influence that was nurtured during her elementary school years by the Missionettes program at church. "It's like Girl Scouts, only church based," she explained.

After two years in Nashville, the family moved to the Orlando area where they settled for Tara's high school and college years.

Even as a child she didn't mind the moves.

"They were a growth experience for me," she said. "There was a time when I was so shy. But you have to become social when you move a lot, and being forced to meet lots of new people and adjust to new situations actually prepared me for my later role as Miss America," she said.

Tara's Miss America dream started for her when she was in seventh grade. She didn't just daydream about it. She made it a life decision. But it wasn't until her senior year of high school that she became involved in the pageant system.

"In the seventh grade, I had a brilliant English teacher who required us to read an autobiography in order to do a book report.

Tara—Christmas surprise.

237

Family photo - Tara at age five.

However, this book report was a bit different. We had to come to class and present it as if we were the person we'd read about."

Tara had seen Cheryl Prewitt, Miss America 1980, perform in concert. Cheryl is an evangelical Christian and inspiring role model; she had autographed her book for Tara after the concert.

Tara decided the book report assignment would provide the perfect opportunity to read and share Cheryl's story. "I knew from her story that it was possible for a normal, average kid growing up in the South—not with a silver spoon—to become anything she wanted to

through perseverance, if God called her to do it. I knew then that all things are possible with God!"

The time came to give the report. Tara fashioned a crown out of cardboard, covered it with aluminum foil and added glitter. Then she made a banner with glitter on it that spelled out *Miss America*.

"I wore my Sunday best to school, I took a fake rose and I stood in front of my peers and said, "Good morning. I am Miss America!"

A taste of the title was all she needed. Tara concentrated on her schoolwork until she had it well in hand, and in her senior year of high school, she began the process of competing in local pageants. Every time she placed as a runner-up, she walked away with additional insight and a better understanding of who she was and what she needed to do to prepare for the greater challenge. At one point, during the Miss Gulf Coast Pageant in March 1990, she stood in an evening gown and stumbled and mumbled her way through the interview question until even her adoring father whispered quietly to her mom, "Well, there goes that one!"

Tara walked off the stage so completely humbled that she prayed, "Lord, I know now if I win this thing, it's of You, not me. And if I

At three.

don't, that's exactly what I deserve, and I accept that."

But minutes later, the Lord evidently wanted to remind her that he had a sense of humor, because Tara's name was announced along with the title: *Miss Gulf Coast.*

Tara prepared for the Miss Florida pageant, which was to take place two weeks after her high school graduation. However, even the best preparations cannot protect contestants from unexpected illness. "I sang light opera for that competition," she said. "I performed *The Telephone Aria* and somehow, even with severe tonsillitis, God gave me the strength to sing it."

Her loss was far from a disappointment. No one was more shocked than seventeen-year-old Tara when she was named first runner-up and earned a hefty six thousand dollar scholarship.

Tara entered Florida State at Tallahassee that fall and decided to major in Music Education. She had already taken ten years of classical piano and had always thought that eventually she would be onstage competing for the Miss America title as a pianist. But during her junior year of high school, she discovered she had a powerful voice and began to sing more than play the piano.

Throughout most of college, Tara was too busy with her studies to compete in Miss America pageants.

"I think I knew I wasn't ready to be Miss America and I didn't want to compete again until I was sure I could handle the job as well as I thought it should be done," she said.

Tara had been advised by Delta Burke's mother, Jean, to consider waiting for a while before re-entering the pageant system. Delta had competed in the pageant and was eighteen when she won the Miss Florida title. Delta's mother, according to Tara, had always felt that her daughter might have competed too soon.

"I wanted to wait until I felt prepared enough to go to Atlantic City," Tara said, acknowledging that the advice she had received was both welcome and sound.

In the spring of 1994, nearing the end of her senior year of college, Tara entered the Miss

7th grade.

Florida State Fair Pageant and won. She was now twenty-one and both she and her voice had matured.

"So I returned to the Miss Florida pageant, having just graduated from college. I remember telling God that this was a wonderful time for me to win, but in His wisdom, He evidently disagreed, because I came in fourth runner-up," she laughed good-naturedly.

Tara was determined, however, to continue competing for the title of Miss America. She said, "I was either going to win or continue trying until I had reached the maximum age to compete."

She spent her first year out of college singing professionally in the Orlando area and substitute teaching.

In the spring of 1995, Tara won the Miss Immokalee Pageant in south Florida and returned once again to the Miss Florida Pageant.

By this time, Tara's intent was clear. Through the years she had thought a lot about why she felt the need to compete in the pageant system and why she wanted to become Miss America.

"Even on the local level, I began to understand the impact of the title. I realized that my gifts, professional and spiritual, lined up with the pageant system. And that even on that preliminary level, although I was still struggling to become more comfortable with public speaking, the title would give me more of a voice through which to share my passion on the issue of literacy. I realized that this title would follow me for the rest of my life, giving me an opportunity to hopefully impact the lives of others on many issues—including, of course, literacy, as well as abstinence, motivation, confidence, and the message of Jesus Christ. I wanted people to hear what I had to say and this would give me the format with which to say it. I know of no other opportunity for a seventeen to twenty-four-year-old woman to become a national advocate for such an important issue. And I knew this was where God wanted me to be."

The strangest thing about Tara competing in the first place was that early on, she was petri-

After being named 1st runner-up at Miss Florida 1990 (age 17)

fied of public speaking. "But through our weakness, the scripture says that He is made perfect, and I know God shows Himself in our lives. If He created us, He can certainly give us gifts we weren't born with. He can do it instantly or over time. Certainly the latter is more painful," she laughed, "but that's what He chose to do in my life. And it was my responsibility to hone those skills and use them to honor Him."

Once again, Tara was a runner-up, albeit first runner-up. "I didn't win that year, either. I had already auditioned and been accepted at the University of Missouri - Kansas City (UMKC) before I went to the Miss Florida Pageant in 1995. I knew if I didn't win, I'd go to graduate school. I moved to Overland Park, Kansas and started school."

The next year, Tara was working on her master's in Music Education, quite happy that her graduate school was being paid for by scholarships from earlier pageants. That year, she became the National Sweetheart Pageant winner and the recipient of the Miss America National Community Service Award.

On her dad's birthday in 1996, Tara won the title of Miss Flint Hills. This title took her to the Miss Kansas Pageant in the summer and nothing could stop her now. In September, Tara Dawn Holland realized her dream as she walked the runway in Atlantic City as Miss America.

The week preceding the national competition, Tara realized God's timing was indeed perfect. "That's when I learned the meaning of the scripture verse: *The peace that passes all understanding.*"

She couldn't have been calmer. "I didn't know I would become Miss America at the end of the week, but I knew in my heart that I was right where God wanted me to be and I clung

to the Word in Psalm 139:16: *All the days ordained for me were written in Your book before one of them came to be."* (NIV)

"I understood that God knew who was going to be Miss America 1997 before I was born, so what did I have to worry about?" she laughed.

Then something happened that made Tara really take stock of that verse. She fell during a production number in a high-kick line, landing hard on the palm of her hand. She came back to the competition that evening with her wrist tightly bound. After the night's preliminary competition, she was taken to the Emergency Room. Doctors were unable to determine whether she had sustained a fracture because she had broken the same wrist as a child. They could not determine a precise diagnosis by X-ray.

Throughout the remainder of the week of competition, Tara removed her bandage every time she appeared on stage. Reporters kept noticing during rehearsals that something was amiss, but she chose not to discuss it.

Due to her injury, she never would have been able to play piano, and Tara thought it ironic that with all her classical piano training, the fact she switched her interests to voice in her junior year in high school was a good thing. "God knew what was going to happen to me. I wouldn't have been able to play that night," she said.

Trauma aside, Tara finished the preliminary

competition that night like a trouper. She had already won the swimsuit competition the prior evening.

During finals on Saturday night, Tara kept praying that she wouldn't be in pain. "For two and a half hours, during the pageant, through clothing changes and everything, God removed all the pain. But right after I won, my wrist started throbbing again!" She was certainly grateful for the evening in more ways than one.

After her crowning, Tara rushed into the responsibilities of her tour and had little time to think of anything but fulfilling her destiny as Miss America. She had worked for seven years as a literacy advocate and she knew this was just the beginning. She now had a lifetime title that would provide the format to allow her to reach others with multiple messages, including young women who needed to hear her message of faith and abstinence.

Miss Americas receive their schedules on the first day of each month. Shortly after being crowned, Tara began to think how wonderful it would be to be scheduled someplace really romantic for Valentine's Day. "I thought how neat it would be to be Miss America on Valentine's Day in an exciting place, like Washington, D.C., for instance."

She was thrilled when she first saw her schedule on February 1. "I was to speak in Washington, D.C. at the New Zealand Embassy on February 13. Then I turned the page of the schedule—I was scheduled to leave D.C. in the morning of Valentine's Day. I would be spending the day in Omaha, Nebraska."

Not to disparage Omaha, Nebraska, but it may not be the most thrilling place to be if one is looking for a romantic venue. But Tara soon forgot her heart's desire and took care of business. She spoke at the Embassy on the 13th of February and like a good, responsible Miss America, rode with Mickey, her traveling companion, to Reagan International Airport on the

Tara with sponsor gift - 1998.
Photo by Kate Kitchen.

morning of February 14.

"I put on my red suit as if I were really excited about where I was spending Valentine's Day," she said.

She and Mickey were commiserating slightly about being two single ladies who were spending time on a plane on Valentine's Day—together.

"Later I learned that this guy had been watching me at the airport. He wanted to talk to me, but he saw me go into the ladies room. So he went into the men's room next door, thinking we'd bump into each other on the way out. But I guess I was faster than he expected, because I left first."

She was later told by this mysterious gentleman that he had come out of the men's room, looked for her and having lost her said, "Guess that's not the one, Lord."

Tara boarded the plane bound for Omaha, her Valentine's destination, and chatted with Mickey en route to her scheduled city. The gentleman had ended up on board the same flight and had happily noticed that she was seated several rows ahead.

Since Tara was to be whisked straight from the airport to her speaking engagement, she thought she should freshen up before deplaning, so she headed off to the restroom in the back of the plane.

"When I came out, I tried to go back up front to my seat but this guy was sitting in an aisle seat in this nearly empty plane with his arm stuck straight across the aisle. I thought- *What is he doing?*

"As I approached, he looked up at me and said, 'I'm on this flight every weekend and I've never seen you on this flight. What takes you to Omaha?'"

Within minutes, Tara found out the handsome self-assured, very personable young man was a U.S. Congressman with the House of Representatives. He was commuting to his

Kate Kitchen

After a speaking engagement with youth "—doing what I love!"

home state. And on this particular weekend, he was scheduled, as she was, to speak to a school for a "Celebrate Literacy" program. "Seventy people were doing the same thing in various schools all over town," she explained.

"Within sixty seconds, literally," she said, "I knew we shared a common faith in Christ. I knew he was respectful, a man of integrity. I just knew he was okay."

As only God could orchestrate, there were only about twelve people on this particular Midwest Express flight and the aisle seat across from him was empty—perhaps another *God thing*. Tara sat and talked with him for quite some time.

"At the end of our conversation, he mentioned that it was Valentine's Day as well as Friday night and asked me out," she laughed.

"I always tell students that they should *never* accept a date with someone they just met. However, this man was a U.S. Congressman. If he tried something on Miss America, I had leverage. So I decided it was safe and agreed to meet him."

When Tara finally returned to her seat, Mickey looked at her as if she were a long lost child. Discreetly, Tara leaned her head back against her seat so he wouldn't see her talking about him and whispered, "Mickey, I just met a conservative Christian United States Congressman and I'm going out tonight."

Mickey looked at her, startled, and said, "You just went to the *bathroom*!"

Tara's night was special but certainly no Cinderella story. She couldn't help but laugh in retelling it. "Here I am, Miss America, now used to being squired around in stretch limos and first class air travel and Jon came for me in a pick-up truck, complete with a gun rack in the back and the biggest dog kennel you've ever seen."

And their first date consisted of a fish fry in the basement of a Catholic church where Jon unceremoniously placed a pot of coffee in her hands and asked simply, "Would you like to pour?"

"It was a perfect example of an evening with a politician," she said. I'd known him for fifteen minutes and found myself pouring coffee for his constituents."

They rushed in, rushed out—then went to a hockey game. After hockey, they visited a young boy who had been injured in a horrible car accident. "He finally fed me at ten o'clock when he took me to a steak house, but it was so late to eat dinner, we shared a steak."

Jon Christensen took his charge back to her hotel and wrote in his journal, "I've just met the woman I am going to marry."

And once again, God's timing was perfect. Tara was twenty-four and had she not waited until "later" to compete for the crown, she would not have been on this particular path at this time.

One of the problems Miss Americas share is finding men strong and secure and mature enough to handle their celebrity and keep things in perspective in this regard. Jon was already established and quite able to do so.

Their next date cinched the deal. On Sunday morning, Jon drove more than thirty minutes to her hotel to pick her up, drove more than thirty minutes back past his home to church and another long trip to return her to the hotel.

"Going to church with him so soon after

242

Jon and Tara.

meeting him was a wonderful blessing," Tara said.

Tara had months of traveling scheduled for her and her time wouldn't be her own for the next seven months and beyond. Jon, too, was busy doing his work in Washington and traveling back and forth to Nebraska. The couple exchanged a couple of notes and telephone calls after she left.

"I'm very old-fashioned, and even later, when I was in D.C. a couple of times, I didn't take it upon myself to tell him I was there because he hadn't asked me."

But late in March, five weeks after their first meeting, Tara was scheduled to speak at the National Press Club on literacy.

"I was a little disappointed to see that Jon's name wasn't on the list of attendees. I spoke, then attended the reception afterwards. A man approached me and said, 'Congressman Christensen would like to see you.' The man had done this totally on his own! Jon didn't even know I was there."

Jon had arrived after her speech, urged to attend the reception by his staff. The man who unwittingly took it upon himself to tell Tara that Jon wanted to see him credits himself with the foresight to get them together. He didn't know they had already met—in Omaha, Nebraska.

And from that point on, the two saw each other whenever possible. Tara was traveling to a different state every eighteen to thirty-six hours and was unable to control her schedule, so Jon found a way to get to her whenever he could. "God helped us," she smiled wisely.

The night Tara gave up her crown in September 1997, Jon was in the audience. It was a hectic time. Jon had declared to run for governor for the state of Nebraska during the same week.

"I ran from one whirlwind to the next," she said. "And nearly three months later, on December 7, he asked me to marry him."

Not everyone gets proposed to at the White House, but being a U.S. Congressman and a Miss America has its perks.

Tara had already met President Bill Clinton and Hillary several times. Jon was invited to a congressional Christmas ball and asked Tara to go with him.

"He had gotten permission from the President to take me out onto the South Portico where he had planted a video camera behind a column. He was in a tuxedo and I was in an evening gown. It was perfect. We walked past the French door that led out to the balcony. A security guard asked Jon if he would like to take a stroll outside. I thought he was crazy. It was thirty-eight degrees outside!"

Without hesitating, Jon casually responded to the affirmative and led his lady outside to the Portico, which is normally off limits.

Among the beautiful things Jon said to his intended, the one that really captured her heart was from Proverbs: "A wife of noble character is a crown unto her husband."

A year later, on November 21, 1998, Jon and Tara were married in Mobile, Alabama. "I wanted to return to my roots to marry," she said.

During the year of their engagement, they were both so busy. She was honoring one speaking engagement after another and Jon was busy running for governor. Tara campaigned with him whenever she could. "We were trying to see each other but we never lived in the same town until we got married," she said.

In the summer of 1998, she began to use her extensive scholarship money and returned to graduate school for two months before starting up her speaking schedule once again. Simultaneously, she was preparing for the wedding.

Perhaps one of her speaking topics might have seemed a bit unusual for the general population, but not for this Miss America. The issues she focused on and continues to address are: Confidence, Pro-Life, Literacy and Abstinence.

"I was a twenty-six-year-old virgin when we married," she said. "My story and the Miss America title have given me a great opportunity to encourage others to make a stand for sexual purity."

Thankfully, Jon, being a devout Christian, was in full agreement with her decision. Tara said, "This is something I had stood for in my personal life. I made a commitment to God when I was twelve or so. Between my parents' influence and the church, I believed I needed to make that conscious choice. My mom was there every night when I got home from a date and I had to look her in the eye. I never wanted to let her down. In my choice for sexual purity, the primary reason was my faith but the motivator was my mom."

No matter what platform Miss Americas choose, the media always seems to stir the pot. Rather than hold her up as an exemplary role model, the media created a firestorm around her topic of abstinence. "They were extremely negative about it," Tara said, "and that created a lot of controversy."

But from adversity came the message Tara was trying to share and God opened a door. "I was invited to do an interview on *Focus on Family* with the host, Dr. James Dobson. He had heard about the criticism I had received about my stand on virginity and invited me to speak on abstinence. It was a wonderful opportunity to be allowed to reach even more people because of the media's negativity."

Tara still takes her messages to schools—public and private, to church groups and civic events. She never hedges away from controversy simply because it's not the most popular choice, even in the area of abortion.

She explained. "God doesn't make mistakes. Even though we may make a mistake and an unintended or unwanted pregnancy may result, the scripture says that God knew about that baby before it was born. Every child deserves life. The baby isn't the one at fault, and whether a young woman wants to keep that baby or not, there are thousands of couples who are desperately searching for a baby to love and who can't have children. God created life and life itself is a miracle."

In December of 2002, Tara graduated summa cum laude with a master's in Music Education from the University of Missouri—Kansas City Conservatory of Music. It wasn't easy, but she tackled it with the same determination that she tackled the Miss America competition. Normally, it takes a year to complete a thesis. Tara accomplished that feat in ten weeks.

And the time has sped by. Tara and Jon have been married nearly six years. And she is hopelessly in love.

"He is such a blessing to me. We're a complete team and we do everything together. I'm in the process of calling our youth pastor to discuss the possibility of even teaching Sunday School together.

"God has opened so many doors for me to be able to use the title of Miss America to promote a positive message. And if I needed to go through seven years in the pageant system so I could encourage even one teenage girl, it was worth it. That's why I wanted to become Miss America and I believe that's why God allowed me to earn the title."

Tara Dawn Christensen may be booked for speaking engagements through her Website: www.taradawn.net. Her CD is also available through that site.

Miss America 1998

Kate Shindle

Student Northwestern University
State - Illinois
Age - 20   Height 5'11''

Talent: Kate belted out the Barbra Streisand hit
Don't Rain on My Parade from *"Funny Girl."*

Photo courtesy of the Miss America Organization.

When asked about the controversy that surrounded her AIDS platform, she replied with candor and commitment, "There's nothing controversial about photocopying information packets or stuffing envelopes or taking an AIDS patient to the grocery store to help him shop for food. You do what it takes."
—Kate Shindle

Kate Shindle

When Kate Shindle was three, her family moved from Ohio, the state of her birth, to New Jersey. Baby brother Mickey was two years younger. For several years, they lived on the lovely island of Brigantine, off the Jersey shore. After first grade, Kate's family relocated to Moorestown, about an hour from Atlantic City. Could they have possibly envisioned that fifteen years later, their little girl would grow up to stand atop a tall float, a statuesque brunette in a fiery red gown, saying farewell to an incredible year as she waved to the thousands of fans who lined the famous boardwalk?

Kate had always dreamed of becoming Miss America. More than two hundred thousand Miss America aficionados came to enjoy the weeklong festivities culminating in the passing of the torch—the crystal scepter.

Kate was brought up in a loving family. Gordon and Maggie Shindle were responsible for teaching Kate a solid value system that included service to her community, a value system that served her well and one that caused her to make her mark as a global spokesperson at the tender age of twenty.

She graduated from Bishop Eustace Preparatory School in Pennsauken, New Jersey. High school wasn't a perfect social environment for Kate, to say the least. She rarely dated. What adolescent boy is secure enough to take out a girl he has

to stand on a step stool to kiss goodnight? And Kate, who would eventually grow into an incredibly elegant beauty, never had any airs about her—then or now.

At nearly six feet tall, as a self-professed awkward teenager, she would have laughed had she been told that a few short years later, she would stand poised and confident on stage, commanding the attention of twenty-thousand screaming fans as she became our country's representative of grace, beauty and achievement.

"Everything's got a positive and negative," she said matter-of-factly, "but it's difficult in middle school when you don't have it all together yet."

Kate Shindle was given enough loving confidence by her parents in knowing who she was to risk competing for the Junior Miss title in her senior year of high school.

"There is no swimsuit competition in that pageant, and SAT scores and grades are counted," Kate said. It proved to be a positive experience. She walked away as first runner-up in the state of New Jersey.

High school behind her, Kate was looking forward to college and had already chosen to major in Theatre. Upon researching schools, she found one that was quite well known for its theatre program. "Plus, I just had a gut feeling that it was the right school for me."

Kate in the 8th grade

Kate and her brother
Mickey at graduation.

The school was Northwestern University in Evanston, Illinois. The main campus is located twenty minutes north of Chicago, "unless there's construction en route..." she laughed. Although far from home, Kate was ready to try her wings and it didn't matter to her that she had to fly halfway across the country to do it.

She still remembers filling out her college application. "I was at home writing my college essays. The Phillies were playing in the World Series. As I was filling out the forms on the computer, the screen kept flipping back and forth to the Series." But she evidently got it right because she was later accepted and started school in the fall, at the age of seventeen.

The young woman, who would soon adopt a heady social platform of HIV-AIDS in a tough, national competition, began grooming herself for that responsibility without even realizing it, shortly after she arrived on campus.

"I had just come to school when I noticed some fliers on the bulletin boards. A theatre professor had died and there were fliers all over campus about his memorial. I had never met him. He died of AIDS. It really affected me."

Suddenly this disease had a *face*. "Going about our daily lives," Kate said, "unless we know someone who has it, we're usually just not aware of it. It's not so much that people are apathetic, they're just not educated!"

Her awareness was made even more poignant later that year. Her mother called her at the dorm one evening to tell her a close family friend was ill. He, too, had contracted HIV. Kate was devastated. Now the disease had a *name*...a face and a name. And she began to realize how differently this disease was accepted socially.

"When someone tells you they have cancer," she explained, "you say -Oh, that's too bad. How can I help? But when someone says they have AIDS, everyone's first concern seems to be how they got it, not how they are or how they can be helped."

The impact of this realization would eventually manifest itself into an international platform for which she would receive worldwide attention.

During one spring weekend in 1995, Kate had nothing special to do, so she did what scores of other young women do each year. She decided to compete in the Miss Chicago Pageant. She had no car, she certainly had no star-struck agenda. She simply had talent, a little curiosity, a lot of spunk and a free weekend. So she took the train into Chicago and competed in the local pageant. She didn't win and it didn't affect her one way or the other. The next year, the preliminary pageant came around again and she tried again. Once again she came home on the train without the title.

But in 1997, as a junior, with the added maturity that two years of academics and theatre performances had given her, she began to take it all a little more seriously. There were very large scholarships looming over the heads of the winners and that looked good to Kate. She suddenly realized that rather than enter the pageant just to fill up a free weekend, she needed to think it through.

She began to research further a social platform, now required even on the local level of the Miss America Pageant. She had already begun volunteering in her community. That was part of her makeup. Now she would work to shape her talent. She would take the competition seriously as if she were preparing for a performance. This time, Kate competed seriously and the results reflected her efforts. She was named first runner-up for Miss Chicago.

With her talent finely tuned and her community service in place, she competed two days later for another local pageant, Miss Lake-Cook (Lake County and Cook County, the first pageant the counties had co-sponsored). She won! This gave her the local title, allowing her to compete for the Miss Illinois title—and in short order, she walked away with that title as well.

In September 1997, she stood on the stage at The Convention Center and belted out "Don't Rain on My Parade" —and they didn't! She won the title and the crown—of Miss America.

This tall, gangly, sometimes awkward young woman was able even then to keep everything in perspective. Tuesday night's incident had helped. She had won the preliminary competition in talent and as she was

Kate is crowned by Tara Dawn Holland.
Photo courtesy of the Miss America Organization.

gold.

During her reign, she visited nearly two hundred schools. Some classrooms held twenty-five students while for other events, she would stand alone on stage in an auditorium with fifteen hundred students watching her warily, waiting cynically to hear *the AIDS lecture.* Students can be a tough crowd, but Kate never flinched.

Kate was asked frequently by school administrators as she spoke about HIV-AIDS to not mention the two 'dirty' words— sex or condoms. She agreed to keep those words out of her prepared talks, but negotiated with the authorities for freedom of speech

stepping down from the top riser, she slipped, tripped and nearly fell all the way down. Then after she was handed the talent winner's trophy, she promptly dropped it. The lovely trophy broke in half.

"Here I was, all dressed up, but somehow, I had broken off two nails, snagged a hole in my gown, tripped, then dropped the trophy!" Some Miss America! She knew then and she knows now *exactly* who she is and what she has to offer. As a result of her introspection and her ability to not take herself so seriously, her inner beauty seems to radiate more now because of her year of service than it did during the pageant.

"I've never been known to be the most coordinated girl," she laughed. No matter—Kate Shindle has scores of other gifts and a heart of

in the question-answer segment. The agreement was that if students asked questions, neither their questions nor her responses were to be restricted. They agreed, and once the initial communication barrier was torn down, students relaxed and she was able to get her message across.

The world will never know her potential impact of that year. What if she saved *even one life* because she had the courage to go out on a limb with a topic normally not discussed in polite social circles?

"The worst possible scenario," she said adamantly, "would have been for them to spend the whole Q & A session asking superficial questions about my boyfriends or my hair or something." She had chosen the HIV/AIDS platform to enlighten students as well as adults, and had no qualms about facing the issues, regardless of the age or makeup of her audiences.

During her tour, she had hundreds of special moments as she traveled the globe, but one seems to separate itself from the wash of faces and places, and that was a young man with AIDS.

"I met him in Tennessee. He was thirty-four," she explained. "When he was seventeen, he had his first sexual encounter and it happened to be with a male friend. The other boy eventually died of AIDS and when his parents told this young man, he was tested and found out he, too, was HIV positive. His parents threw him out of the house. He was homeless for nine months then joined the service so he would have a place to live. Here he was now, at thirty-four, and had learned that both his parents had recently died without ever speaking to him again. It was devastating to him."

The stigma of HIV is just one element of Kate's issue. What those parents missed by not knowing their son as an adult, and what he missed in losing loving support from his parents—these are things that once lost can never be regained. The disease destroys more than the person with AIDS; but rather whole families and friendships. The psychosocial impact on the community at large is enormous.

Kate lectures to students about prevention but some of her talks have added unnecessary controversy to her platform. "Of course, I agree abstinence is most effective," she said, "but many high school kids are already sexually active, so if they must have sex, I advocate protected sex." But more than that, she has had hands-on experience with the program at large.

Miss America visits her former elementary school for a national reading day.

In college, because of her family friend who had contracted HIV, she took a course entitled, "Rhetoric of Social Movements." She chose the AIDS prevention issue.

"There's nothing controversial about photocopying information packets or stuffing envelopes or taking an AIDS patient to the grocery store to help him shop for food," she said candidly. Her class was to be completed in two months, but Kate kept her "buddy program" going for over a year. And when she receives praise for her kindness and her efforts, she dismisses it lightly, saying, "It had to be done. He needed it."

During her tour, she visited the Centers for Disease Control in Atlanta and became the first Miss America to appear as a speaker at the 12th World AIDS Conference in Geneva. She spoke eloquently before the National Press Club. Kate has helped to raise between seventy-five to a hundred million dollars on behalf of the fight against AIDS.

And in September 1998, she relinquished her title to another young lady, just as worthy, just as dedicated to community service. Asked if she had been ready to give up the crown, Kate paraphrased what so many others have said. "I didn't have the endurance to go on. It's a long, intense year."

Her nearly sixty thousand dollars in scholarship money paid for her senior year at Northwestern and she had enough left to continue her studies in acting and voice. She was ready to focus on her upcoming move to New York so she could pursue a career in musical theatre.

During the summer of 1999, Kate took her final exams for her bachelor's degree, rehearsed for her senior recital—a two-woman, one-hour cabaret performance she did with her best friend. And she graduated from a prestigious university with a Bachelor of Science in Theatre and a minor in Music Theatre. Right after graduation, she went to summer stock—two groups— and was acting in those as well as rehearsing and recording in a studio in preparation for a benefit Christmas CD for a fundraiser. As if all that weren't enough, shortly after her tour ended, Kate was invited to become a member of the board for the National AIDS Fund.

In the fall of 1999, Kate moved to the Big Apple and celebrated her first New Year's in New York City as part of the cast of *Jekyll and Hyde* on Broadway. Although an understudy, she was able to play the role of Lucy several times. She followed up that thrilling experience with a tour of Cabaret all over the country. That show took her to January 2001. And her preparation paid off. In the summer of 2001, Kate got to play the role of Sally Bowles in Cabaret on Broadway

She has worked in regional theatre from Salt Lake City to Portland to Los Angeles, but she loves New York. She even returned to Atlantic City for a show at Caesar's.

In June 2004, a remake of the movie, *The Stepford Wives* hit theatres with Kate Shindle playing a prominent role. "I like stage work and film, but I'd like to do more film in the near future," she said.

Her theatrical work is much like the Miss America title: "It all may sound quite glamorous, but it's hard work. With theatre or film, you never know if you'll get a job on Monday or six months from now, but I focus and continue to work as hard as I can, and it works out. I've been very fortunate, but I audition all the time."

Kate does a lot of benefits. Especially with HIV/AIDS so prevalent in the theatrical community, she frequently is asked to share her tal-

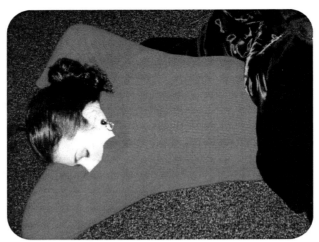

One tired diva. Not all glamour. Grabbing a nap at the airport at O'Hare.

ents to benefit others. "I don't think about it, I just do it," she said. "I've done too many to count."

Last December, Kate and a friend produced and performed in a large production of *Children of Eden*. The is the story of the first nine chapters of *Genesis*, which takes the audience from the creation through Noah's Ark. It was a concert version of the Stephen Schwartz musical. Schwartz has won several Oscars for his work. "It was a large event; using fifteen or more actors and a one hundred-member choir. We held it at Riverside Church in Manhattan and the money raised went to the National Aids Fund."

Kate's first solo CD, a collection of Broadway and cabaret songs called "Till Today" was released in 2003. She is currently working on another album and will hopefully release it in 2005.

Kate Shindle continues to use her efforts, her commitment and her voice to further the cause of AIDS prevention. "Thousands of infections occur worldwide every day," she said. "In 2003 alone, three million people died of AIDS, according to UNAIDS. Latest studies show that approximately fifty percent of all fifteen-year-olds in Africa will die of AIDS. South Africa has the largest number of people infected with HIV in the world."

This incredible woman has a social conscience that is so prevalent in her life. We have just begun to hear about the philanthropic works of Kate Shindle. She's just beginning. Just another Miss America—a "tall, sometimes gangly," tell-it-like-it-is woman of incredible honor, integrity and conviction.

To book Kate for speaking engagements and to acquire Kate's CDs, see: www.kateshindle.com

Miss America 1999
Nicole Johnson

Master's Degree: Regent University - Virginia Beach, Virginia
Graduate - University of South Florida
State - Virginia
Age - 24   Height - 5' 9"
Talent: Jazz Vocal

Photo courtesy of the Miss America Organization.

"I took my eyes off myself and I began looking toward others.
Suddenly I began to regain that sense of self I had momentarily allowed to slip away.
And I learned that diabetes doesn't have to control you. You can control it!"
—Nicole Johnson

Nicole Johnson

Nicole Johnson grew up in St. Petersburg, Florida, where George Johnson, her father, still enjoys the teaching profession. Her mother Emily is the manager of a medical office. Nicole has a brother, Scott, who is two years her junior.

To look at this striking, vivacious brunette, one would think she is the perfect picture of health. But she is the first Miss America to have a serious, life-threatening disease often referred to as "the hidden killer."

When she was nineteen, Nicole was diagnosed with Juvenile Onset Diabetes- Type 2, and today wears an insulin pump, which delivers controlled amounts of insulin to her body twenty-four hours

What a sweetheart!

a day. But this wasn't her first challenge and certainly won't be her last. Nicole Johnson made her first social impact on the world when she was in the eighth grade. This moment changed the course of her life.

Nicole in 1976.

"If I had any social life as a teenager, it existed in church rather than from my high school or school friends," she said. "My value system was established at home and reinforced in church, and it molded me into who I am today."

Nicole attended a Christian school until the eighth grade. And although she was only thirteen when she had her first taste of the difficult decisions that come with maturity, she faced her first challenge well. It was an incident that seemed small and insignificant on the outside, but one that affected her entire high school experience.

"I was new to public school," she explains. "I was invited to what was supposed to be a birthday party and I went, hoping to make new friends. I really was eager for them to accept me."

When Nicole arrived, she soon discovered that the host's older brothers and sisters had brought alcohol and drugs. There is a split second when life-changing events occur, when the mind tries to comprehend reality and you need to make a decision on how to handle that reality. She knew that what she was seeing was true, and once deciding that, called her parents immediately to come after her to take her home.

Her decision caused her a great deal of pain. "Thirteen is a tough age to go out on a limb- alone," she said. Her actions also cost her what should have been the happiest years a teenager enjoys–high school. "That's a painful time to be ostracized.

"There wasn't any question. I knew what I believed, what I had been taught. The pain was there, of course, because I wanted my new friends to like me; but I couldn't have survived through high school in that environment anyway, not if I had to use drugs and alcohol just to be liked."

She knew she had done the right thing by walking away. She knew she had a solid family support system. She was still surrounded by a loving church family as well. And whether her new schoolmates liked her or not, they could not help but respect her.

Nicole and Skip

"I went back to school Monday morning, and knew then that my entire high school experience would be quite different from what I had hoped." And it was. But Nicole had found a strength of character within her that was built on strong Christian principle, a strength she would have to rely on once again, six years later. Unknown to Nicole, with that isolated incident, that one seemingly innocuous experience, she had already begun to prepare for what was to come.

The stigma of being a goody two-shoes didn't wear off for a long time. Her first real date was to a football game, but not until her senior year. This beautiful, future Miss America was never taken to the homecoming dance, nor to her prom. She was active in sports, however, and played on the Powder Puff Football team. And her grades were exceptional. Still, the social part of high school totally passed her by. One would think she would be forever scarred. But Nicole's feet were planted solidly on the ground and her experiences at such a young age only served to develop her internal strength.

As a young woman, Nicole has already achieved a great deal. But she has achieved some of her goals amidst some rather formidable obstacles. As a sophomore at the University of South Florida, she became ill. Diagnosed with flu at the college health clinic, she thought nothing of it. Later, when she didn't respond to treatment in a timely manner, she was diagnosed with anemia. As her condition worsened, she was told she most probably had a vitamin deficiency-or was it Beijing flu? The doctors simply didn't know.

After taking massive doses of antibiotics, Nicole was still sick when she returned home for Thanksgiving. But the family holiday wasn't very special that year, for she suddenly became violently ill.

Her parents rushed her to the hospital where preliminary tests in the Emergency Room suggested that she might be diabetic. The doctors needed time for more conclusive lab results, so they sent her home. Nicole recovered enough to go back to school but soon received a call from her mother. The diagnosis was in and it wasn't good news. Nicole, while still feeling sick, was too high-spirited to let even a life-threatening illness get in the way of a personal commitment. Feeling a little better, she begged her mother to let her stay at school three more days because she was to sing in a choir concert and she didn't want to miss it.

After the concert, Nicole went home where she was admitted into the hospital. She stayed for a week while her condition was monitored and her medication was adjusted. The medical staff needed to watch her insulin regimen and to make sure she was getting the required dosage without adverse side effects. She also needed to learn her proper dietary program; all complicated but required.

Nicole's new husband gets apple crisp at the reception.

Being an excellent student, she was distraught at having to leave school for a semester, but she had to face the challenge. Her regimen consisted of pricking her finger five times a day to test her glucose levels. She had to give herself insulin injections four or five times every single day.

"My health care became a tremendous community effort by my friends and family. They showed incredible commitment," she said. "I had to move back home to learn how to live a new life. Honestly, it affected the entire family."

From a family who loved their southern fried foods to one that had to count portion sizes, bulk up on fresh vegetables and salads, it was quite a dramatic change. "We had gone from comfort foods to what we called safe foods," she explains. "We taped menus to the refrigerator door, and mom committed to do everything I did. We had a boys' cupboard and a girls' cupboard. Being diagnosed with a serous illness creates much the same response as the loss of a life. There is a definite grief response that people go through. And this illness was severe. Complications from diabetes can be fatal if the disease is left untreated.

The first stage, according to Nicole, is denial. "It's difficult for people to believe that this isn't just going to go away. Some form of depression usually sets in. Your lifestyle totally changes. The medication must be administered properly and at precise times during each day. Your condition has to be monitored several times a day by painful finger pricks. You need to rest a lot and eat small meals at specific times, take in certain foods and use small portions. And that's a lifetime of commitment."

She continued, "When people realize this isn't just a ten-day cold or flu they're dealing with, that it's something that requires incredible strength and daily discipline, the whole situation can become overwhelming. Often it leads to depression."

Nicole's mental attitude was colored by the memory of a high school friend who had died as a result of complications from diabetes. "It's difficult at any time in life to be faced with the diagnosis of a life-threatening illness, but to be so young and have a life sentence of severe illness staring you in the face makes you realize how mortal you are. At the time, this seemed almost too much to absorb.

"I was looking at it all wrong for a while," said Nicole. "I kept asking myself: 'What did we do wrong?' It took me a while to realize that this is what I'm faced with and it's permanent. Now, how do I move forward from here? We *all* had to realize and consider that."

Once her decision was made and Nicole's frame of reference changed from negative to positive, she began to commit herself to wellness and prevention. But there was still a shadow lurking over her shoulder. She had decided there might be a stigma attached to having diabetes and she decided not to tell people.

Being a giving person by nature, that philosophy didn't last much longer than her initial depression. She soon realized that if *she* could handle her situation, medically and emotionally,

254

she would be in a better position to help others if they knew about her problem and how she was facing it. She wanted others to know that they didn't have to think of diabetes as a death sentence, and she knew she could help.

"Thinking of it that way truly helped me heal emotionally. I took my eyes off myself and began looking toward others. Suddenly I began to regain that sense of self I had momentarily allowed to slip away. And I learned that diabetes doesn't have to control *you*. *You* can control *it*!" Now she was determined to take a stand once more. Not just for herself, but for what she could offer others.

"At first when I was diagnosed, I thought everything was being stolen from me. It was so difficult to totally change my busy lifestyle. I was so involved in school, in church, in music. I didn't see how I could possibly fit this into my life and come out a positive person."

But as Nicole learned how to manage her disease, she became more positive and the demands on her became less of a struggle and more of a lifestyle. Offering your body the exact fuel it needs *when* it needs it is probably one of the health rules we neglect most in caring for our bodies. It's difficult to *always* eat right, especially when you're a busy college student.

Thanks to the miracle of modern medicine, Nicole found an avenue of treatment that allowed her more freedom. Once her medication dosage was found to be compatible with her insulin needs, Nicole decided to convert to the insulin pump. This offered her the ability to travel, to be freer to eat when she wanted to and to sleep in occasionally without missing a timely injection.

Nicole wears the pump twenty-four hours a day. It automatically delivers insulin to her body without her having to stop what she's doing to find privacy so she can self-administer an injection. For a young woman who, as Miss America, traveled twenty-thousand miles a month, this medication delivery system offered Nicole incredible freedom.

The night she was crowned, Nicole stood out from all the others in a long, black, halter-top dress. It was modern, elegant and a far cry from the *antebellumesque*, flowing, white debutante gowns with yards and yards of material in the skirts that Miss America contestants wore on stage for so many years. The effect was dramatic, yet simple and understated. Asked why she chose that particular style, Nicole responded, "I wanted people to see me as me, to see who I really am, not just a beautiful gown. I wore that dress when I became Miss Virginia. It felt right for me."

The judges obviously agreed. She was stunning and her personality indeed showed through as she graciously accepted the scepter and became Miss America 1999.

In July of that year, as Nicole's first interview for this book was taking place, Nicole was the reigning Miss America. With just two months to go, she had already traveled nearly a quarter of a million miles around the country on her speaking tour, *Diabetes in America: Unmasking the Hidden Killer.*

Calling on her experience from the eighth grade party, she still uses the impact from that incident to discern good from bad. During her reign, Nicole made contact with General Barry McAfree, President Bill Clinton's appointed drug czar. She offered to help wherever needed,

once her reign was over.

As she was ending her tour, news on the homefront offered her an emotional challenge. Her parents decided to end their marriage. And as painful as that was for Nicole, her private grief never let her skip a beat in continuing to learn more about diabetes in order to help others.

She has collected a treasure chest of special moments, moments that will continue to provide a springboard for her professional career and personal life. The Miss America opportunity greatly enhanced her ability to reach out toward her professional goals.

One of the highlights of her year was the impact of meeting several of the former Miss Americas—Donna Axum, Phyllis George and Debbye Turner. It is still hard for her to believe she has taken her place in that special Hall of Fame.

During her reign, she was named an Honorary Diabetes Educator by the American Association of Diabetes Educators. She lobbied Congress and was thrilled that more than two hundred members pledged their support of her and her platform on diabetes education. She helped to pass an increase in NIH funding which contributed to a doubling of the NIH budget from 1999-2003, and during the year she was most pleased to interact with other survivors as she continued to learn about strength of character "from those who are in the trenches of living with chronic disease on a daily basis."

For two years after her reign ended, Nicole spent a great deal of time overseas. "I visited more than a dozen countries on a diabetes education tour," she said. "I visited several countries multiple times—Japan, Australia and Germany, for example. It was such an education for me, and I hope I brought something to people of other cultures, especially to all who were suffering with the common ailment of diabetes."

Personally challenged to become more active in public policy, she has used her Miss America experiences to learn how to work within the system to make things happen.

In 2004, in her final interview prior to this book's publication, she said, "I learned so much about corporate business, about politics and legislation, about the political arena and healthcare. I am eager to continue my education, my professional career, and will be forever grateful for that opportunity."

With two degrees already hanging on her wall, she is currently pursuing a third. Nicole is enrolled as a graduate student at the University of Pittsburgh and is in the process of earning a second master's degree, this one in Public Health with a focus on Behavioral and Community Science.

As a part-time consultant for the American Diabetes Association Government Relations Department, Nicole also travels across the country speaking on diabetes, teaching and motivating our country's youth to take care of their bodies.

In 2003, Nicole began to focus more on women's health and child development and is also presently working on pregnancy legislation and school legislation for the 2004 cycle in Congress.

She hasn't sat idly by since the pageant, that's obvious—but in addition to her speaking engagements, her monthly article on diabetes for Georgetown Medical Center, she has also written three books: *Autobiography: Living with Diabetes; Mr. Food's Quick and Easy Diabetic Cooking - with Nicole Johnson; and Mr. Food's Every Day's a Holiday - with Nicole Johnson.*

Her upcoming projects include two more books: *Everyday Advocacy* and *The Diabetes Workout.*

As if her life weren't busy enough, in August 2003, Nicole Johnson walked down the aisle to become the wife of Scott Baker. Scott is an ABC News Anchor in Pittsburgh and together, they are raising Scott's three adorable children, Alex, Aaron and Emma.

(Go to Nicole's Website to order her books: www.nicolejohnson.com)

Miss America 2001
Angela Perez Baraquio

Profession - Teacher and Athletic Director
Graduate - University of Hawaii at Manoa
State - Hawaii
Age - 24   Height - 5' 4"

Talent: Angela performed a hula to "I am Hawaii"
- the theme song from *Mutiny on the Bounty*

Photo courtesy of the Miss America Organization

"The strength of grace is realizing that you have God to know, to love and to
serve. When you know that, you are richer than you could possibly be."
—Angela Perez Baraquio Grey

Angela Perez Baraquio

How is it possible for a Filipina girl of immigrant parents to reach the heights of being crowned Miss America on the stage at Convention Hall in Atlantic City? This is a Miss America who, upon completion of her reign, pulled from a lifetime of faith to find the courage to begin to heal a nation after an American tragedy. This is the story of an impossible dream come true. Our young woman is Angela Perez Baraquio, devout Christian, dedicated teacher and promising humanitarian.

It was June 1976. On the beautiful island of Oahu in Honolulu, Hawaii, a baby girl was born to Philippine immigrants Claudio and Rigolette Baraquio. Teachers both, they had come to the Islands of Hawaii six years earlier with their first three children. The couple was determined to provide a better, more stable life for their family and they were committed to all the hard work it would take to achieve their goal. This couple undertook various jobs until Claudio was finally able to start his own business. The Lord continued to bless them with babies and life was becoming more and more financially taxing.

After the arrival of twins, the doctor advised Rigolette to consider surgery to prevent future pregnancies. A devout Catholic, the woman refused. A decision for which we are grateful, for number eight came along, one very special girl who would later become Miss America—Angela Perez Baraquio. The count stopped at ten and the family remained at an even dozen.

When Angela speaks of her childhood, she cannot keep from smiling. If they were lacking

for anything due to their large family, the children certainly didn't know it.

"We understood that we were rich in things that mattered, and it's true. I have such rich memories," she said.

"I sang in the church choir since the age of five and still sing for two masses a week. My husband and I are youth choir directors. The youth range from the age of eight to college age. That's just for Sunday service," she said. Angela's family sings in the choir for Saturday evening masses. Her parents always made it clear that it was never enough to simply attend church, that participating fully by sharing our God-given gifts was very important for spiritual growth. On Saturday nights after family mass, the whole family still gets together for dinner. Most of them continue to reside in

Hawaii; two siblings live in California, and one lives in Seattle.

"Family is an intrinsic part of me and always will be," she said.

When Angela was a child, her family would pile into the van "much like the Partridge family," and drive to the beach twenty minutes away with quick, chaotic stops for snacks and drinks. It was a Sunday ritual.

As Angela shares these memories, she simply radiates. "On Sunday mornings, we'd wake up and go to church. After mass, the whole family would eat breakfast together. Then we'd clean the house, take our naps, wake up and get ready to go to Ala Moana Beach Park with enough time to swim, eat, play and watch the sunset," she said.

After a game of family-invented "Baraquio Ball," they would all pile back into the van and go home, yelling on the way, "First in the shower! Second in the shower!" She added, "You rarely got a hot shower when you were the youngest. Sometimes, the girls would jump in the shower three at a time, taking quick turns under the hot water, then switch positions, yelling: 'Red Light, Green Light!'" she laughed. "Thankfully, we had three bathrooms." Their rides to school were an hour long and along the way, the family would sing songs and pray the rosary.

Angela honors her parents' expertise in raising ten children. "Mom was the disciplinarian. Getting an A in school wasn't good enough. She would insist on A++." Angela credits her dad for being the strong silent type, the provider. Whatever the roles, the balance worked well because nine children are college graduates and number ten is in the process of completing her last semester.

"I went to the University of Hawaii, but others went to Catholic universities," she said, proudly singling out a sister who attended

Notre Dame. As valedictorian of her high school class, Angela's sister received a full ride to Notre Dame and was interested in majoring in Architecture. Angela had wanted to go there as well, but by the time Angela was of college age, student loans were so hefty among the family, that she decided to be more practical and enroll at the University of Hawaii.

"My parents made sure we were all well-rounded, too," she said warmly. "Mom insisted we take music lessons and dance. I took hula and ukulele. We had several different bands. My sisters and I even had a rock band called *High Tide*." Her parents made sure the children had the quality time required to practice their instruments by limiting TV. "We weren't allowed to watch television except for Sesame Street and the news."

Church was always vitally important. Angela learned early on to count on her faith to help her work through obstacles. "When I do come across struggles, I realize I may not understand why things may be happening a certain way, but I trust God and I know I'll understand eventually." Angela paused for a moment and then continued reflectively, "The strength of grace is realizing that you have God to know, to love and to serve. When you know that, you are richer than you could possibly be, even with all the material wealth in the world."

Standing at a petite five feet four, Angela has literally looked up to her husband since he was an altar boy at church, along with her brother. Today he's six feet four, but even then, he was six feet tall. She noticed him while singing in her family choir.

"I've known Tini (Tinifuloa Grey) since we were fifteen. He's part Samoan, French,

Chinese, English and Tahitian. He's just beautiful, inside and out. I call him a gentle giant," she said. Angela didn't notice him at first. He was so shy, so quiet, he would never even say hello. She learned later on that he had admired her for three years.

As seniors in high school, the beautiful couple ended up going to several dances together and during the summer after graduation, they developed a solid friendship.

Things changed in the romance department at the end of summer when they said good-bye at the airport. Tini was leaving for Woodbury University in Burbank, California where he was to major in Architecture. Angela had earned scholarship money in Hawaii by competing in pageants, so she remained behind to attend the University of Hawaii. As the petite brunette reached up to hug Tini, he leaned down to kiss her and the rest-as they say-is history. Thus began their five-year, long-distance relationship. Circumstances would find them living an ocean apart until Tini graduated and moved back to Hawaii.

Angela resumed her studies and during the spring of 1999 was devastated, along with the

rest of the world, as the horror of the Columbine shooting in Littleton, Colorado unfolded. She was a student teacher at the time.

"I re-evaluated why I wanted to go into the teaching profession. I almost dropped out of teaching because of that incident," she said. Then she realized she had a choice. She could drop out and perhaps later regret her decision or stick to it and try to make a difference. Thus was born an ideal that would later become her platform as Miss America and later help change legislation—and even after that provide the catalyst for the development of a charitable foundation for character education. All this from a tragedy that occurred an ocean away.

"I knew I had to do something to advocate character," she said. Angela has always been inspired by the words of Theodore Roosevelt: "To educate a man in mind and not in morals is to educate a menace to society."

Angela continued, "Those words drove me and fueled my passion throughout my year of service as Miss America. Educating children isn't just about academic achievement; it's about moral development. Students will not be contributing citizens when they get out into the real world unless they build their character as well." Angela graduated in May of 1999 with a bachelor's degree in Elementary Education and a fire in her heart to change the world of education.

After graduation, she became a teacher at Holy Family Catholic Academy. She was named Athletic Director, taught physical education and was head coach for three sports.

And then the universe opened one very special door and Angela's life changed forever. Two students, girls whom she had coached in volleyball, expressed their interest in playing on the basketball team, but lacked the confidence to try out. She strongly encouraged them. They asked if she had ever challenged herself and she replied, "Sure. I ran for Miss Hawaii in 1995 and 1996 when I was eighteen and nineteen."

The students were suddenly more interested in her than their own agenda and asked, "Why don't you run again? What about the scholarship money? Don't you want to get your master's degree?"

They went on and on, completely diverted from their original conversation. Angela kept explaining that she was now a teacher and no longer felt the need to run for the pageant. But the students knew they had caught Angela in a trap and they used every bit of psychology they could to make her change her mind. She promised to think about it. How could she encourage them to reach out for their dreams if she stopped just short of hers? And her dream was a big one.

"I wanted to make a difference," she said. "Maybe as Miss America, I could address an educational issue I'd been thinking about for a long time."

Enter Tini, by this time, her closest and dearest friend. Tini made her examine her conscience. "He wanted to be sure I would be doing it for all the right reasons," she said.

Angela began to explain to him the reasons she might consider competing. She told him she wanted to testify before Congress on behalf of character education. She wanted to make a lasting impact for students and teachers. She truly wanted to make a difference.

"By the time I got off my soapbox, I was crying," she confessed. She had suddenly realized this was bigger than her dreams of being a teacher. And more than anything else, she needed to set an example for those who looked up to her. She needed to be a role model of courage and commitment.

"I returned to school and told the girls that if they tried out for the team, I would run."

After listening to her talk about her goals and dreams, Tini was also convinced that it was the right thing for Angela to do.

Angela's life changed at the very moment she made that commitment. She wasted no time. She competed in January of 2000 for Miss Oahu, a local preliminary. This year's pageant would be Angela's last chance to compete. For one thing, she was due to turn twenty-four in June and was rapidly approaching the age limit. For another, the Miss Hawaii competition allows girls to compete only in two preliminaries a year.

The Miss Oahu pageant was well attended by students from the school. "The girls came to the pageant and were so supportive," she said. "When they called my name as First Runner-up, I was excited because I had won a four hundred dollar cash grant for school, even though I didn't win the overall pageant. So in March, with the students still encouraging me, I competed for the very last time in the Miss America preliminaries."

Angela won the title of Miss Leeward and received an eight thousand dollar in-kind scholarship (free tuition waiver) at Hawaii Pacific University. Unfortunately, she was already accepted into the College of Education at the University of Hawaii and chose not to use that waiver.

Angela went on to the Miss Hawaii competition. "My school had so much faith in me that they supported me even though, if I won, I might not be coming back to teach the next year," she said. It was her third time competing for the title of Miss Hawaii and she couldn't believe she was doing this again. "All I wanted to do was to place with grace," she said.

The Miss Hawaii Pageant was an unbelievable dream to this young woman. As part of a musical group called *Reign*, Tini performed at the event. Dressed in tuxedos, the group serenaded the women during the evening gown competition and Tini got to escort Angela down the runway. Her talent was poignant, her poise phenomenal. She sang a Spanish song written by Gloria Estefan - *Con los años que me quedán—With the years that I have left.*

"When they were ready to announce, I was standing with a rose in my hand. I hadn't won any preliminary awards and I couldn't figure out who won. Then they announced my name and suddenly total strangers were mouthing 'I love you' and 'You're beautiful' and I thought at that moment—*I am Hawaii.*"

"Miss Hawaii 2000" was suddenly overcome with tears. All she could think of was how much she really wanted to represent Hawaii onstage in Atlantic City. She felt so committed to her state that she decided she would dance hula to *I am Hawaii* for the Miss America competition.

"I was ecstatic! I couldn't believe that I had finally earned something this huge, something I had worked so hard for," she said. Angela received a five thousand dollar cash grant, a five thousand dollar scholarship to the University of Hawaii, and other prizes that totaled approximately fifty thousand dollars. And nationals were yet to come.

And now it was September 2000 and Angela Perez Baraquio was preparing to leave her homeland to travel across an ocean and clear across the continent to compete for the coveted title of Miss America.

"I was having breakfast with Tini and I was crying. I had never been away from Hawaii that long and I kept saying, 'You don't understand. This thing could change my life—I may not come back!'"

On the day she left, teachers, students and their parents, scores of family and friends crowded around the gate at the airport. Angela's pastor had called the media and they were there as well. Even several of the former Miss Hawaiis had come to see her off. "It was a total surprise. I looked out from the gate and saw the school band, hula dancers, even the school's cheerleaders, all there to wish me well. My traveling companion said it was the biggest sendoff in Miss Hawaii history," she said.

By the time her plane landed in Texas, Angela was focused and mentally prepared for the challenges ahead. "I got to Texas at one o'clock in the morning, Hawaii time, and was so excited, I called my mom. I'd never been away from Hawaii for more than ten days. Suddenly I knew I belonged right where I was and soon I was off to Disney World in Florida with the contestants."

Every day during pageant week, Angela received cards from students. "This helped me remember why I was there in the first place. I wanted to prove to them that dreams can come true. It wasn't important to win; it was important to reach for your goals. I just wanted to do my best and prove that anything you put your mind to, you can do if you honor your dreams with hard work and perseverance."

Angela held her focus. She listened to Tini's CD whenever she needed to calm her nerves. There was a very special cut on the CD, a Christian song called *Draw Me Nearer.* That song helped her get through pageant week, focused on the task at hand.

In the preliminary competition, she won a thousand dollars in the swimsuit competition. And with the crown and the coveted Miss America title came a cash grant of fifty thousand dollars. "I couldn't believe I had actually won," she said. Her master's degree had suddenly become closer to her reach, but the more important goal was that she had honored her commitment to her students. She remembers walking the runway and asking herself, *Who am I to become Miss America? I'm a little girl from Hawaii from a family of twelve. This is an incredible miracle!*

Prior to each year's crowning, there are certainly a plethora of prayers from all over the country going skyward, but Angela clearly recalls her special prayer. "I just wanted to be sure that if I were called, I would be worthy of this responsibility," she said. "I asked God to only let me win if He thought I was capable of doing all that is necessary to be Miss America for the entire year. I told Him that if He didn't think I was deserving, to please not let me win." When Angela's name was announced, moments later, her hands were raised to the Heavens and she laughed at what she believed to be the response.

Joan Lunden was hosting a show called *Behind Closed Doors* for Arts & Entertainment, and she had been following Angela around for two days. The celebrated television personality was backstage when Angela won and announced to her audience that she was going to take them on a tour with Miss America, that she was just crowned.

Immediately following the pageant, Angela's parents began to profusely thank—by name—all the churches who had been praying for Angela. During her press conference, Angela found herself in a surreal experience—*Not only am I representing my state of Hawaii and my own students, I entered this pageant out of principle, trying to encourage my students to reach out for something they wanted. It was vitally important for me to reach for this goal.*

When the media started asking her how it felt to be the first Asian Miss America, Angela responded with such sincerity, such grace.

"In Hawaii," she said, "People are color blind. It doesn't matter what you look like on the outside, it matters who you are on the inside."

Angela is extremely proud of her heritage as the first Filipina and first Asian in this select group of accomplished women. She is also the first teacher to be crowned. And it was this, particularly, that meant so much to her. It was because of her students that she was here, both to prove a point and to encourage them. And now she could work toward her larger goal, to make a difference in the often under-appreciated profession of education.

In the meantime, Joan Lunden followed Angela from one interview to another. In the midst of all this, which is the custom, Angela's belongings were quickly transferred from a guest room at Caesar's Palace to the Presidential Suite.

"I had all my stuff packed and was ready to go home after the pageant," she laughed. "I had prepared for a twelve-hour flight home. The next thing you know, I'm sitting in a huge Presidential Suite being briefed and told I would have to go to sleep so I could get up in three hours. I just started laughing."

Angela jumped into her hot tub in her room that night and simply couldn't stop laughing. "I woke up after three hours of sleep and started laughing again. I just couldn't believe it all," she said.

The next morning, Angela did the required traditional Miss America romp in the surf by the famous Boardwalk for the benefit of the media. Joan Lunden's photographer was still filming her. Then someone from the Miss America Organization leaned over to her and said, "You have an hour's break. What do you want to do?"

"At first I hesitated, then I asked, 'Can I go to church?'"

Someone glibly replied, "You're Miss America, you can do whatever you want."

They were a little surprised by her request.

She kindly asked the cameras not to follow and was pleased when three of her security guards opened up to her. They happened to be Catholic and one was studying to be a Deacon, the others used to be altar boys and were still quite involved in the church. "It made it so much easier for me that they understood," she said. "It was such a blessing."

As if she were with her family, Angela had nine people accompany her to church on the first morning of her reign as Miss America. And from that morning on, Angela made it a practice throughout the year to go to church every Sunday, regardless of where she was. Her traveling companions were quite supportive and thanked her for providing that opportunity for them as well.

On this, the first morning, reporters honored her request and cameras did not follow her into the church. Angela asked the priest not to announce her visit and he kept her confidence, although it was fairly obvious everyone knew, especially at the end of mass when the organist broke into the Miss America theme song.

"It was so nice to be in God's presence and be quiet during the mass. When the organist played the song, I just laughed to myself—*they did not just do that!*"

Angela said, "It had been two and a half weeks since I'd gone to church because I had been rehearsing and all the contestants had to stay together in a group." Angela still remem-

bers the reading that day: *prophets prefer wisdom over scepter and throne.* Angela took those words to heart as she prepared herself spiritually for the journey that was about to begin.

"The year started by honoring God in September 2000 and finished with honoring God on September 11, 2001," she said.

But this first mass was a preamble to what was to come. A preamble to Angela's constantly reaching for courage through faith. Angela had walked into church that morning to see Mother Mary wearing a crown and holding the baby Jesus.

"I thought to myself—that was *her* coronation as she was crowned queen of the world—and I knew I had to keep things in perspective. I needed to remember that I had been given a crown and it was a great honor that carried with it a huge responsibility."

There are two special books Angela reads every day - *God Calling* and *Angel Wisdom*, a book Tini had given her. During her tour, this was no exception. "There's a passage in *God Calling* that says 'the one who is first shall be the servant of all' and that's when I realized this was truly to be a year of service—not about me, but about what I can give to others for His glory," she said.

And she needed all the help those little books would give her. There were days during her tour that Angela was so tired she could hardly get out of bed. People would say to her, "How did you do it?"

"I would answer, 'It's not about me. It's all about Him.'" But I never forgot that my students had encouraged me to be there and they were representative of all the students I met throughout the country."

The tour was a whirlwind. "Sometimes we would visit three or four cities in a day. There were days when I could hardly remember which city I was in," she said.

Angela's heart and soul went into her platform on education. Throughout her tour and since, this gifted professional has spoken on: "Character in the Classroom: Teaching Values, Valuing Teachers." She is an exemplary advocate, not only of students but of educators as well.

"Teaching is such a selfless profession. Teachers often have to pay for their own continuing education. I think we should put a greater value on rewarding our educators," she said.

For decades, the public at large has complained about the lack of respect and financial support given to our teachers and our school systems. This dilemma has not been lost on Angela, but this young woman has decided to take on the challenge and legitimately try to do something about it.

Coming from teaching parents and holding a bachelor's degree in Elementary Education, her desire has always been to challenge educators, parents and students to make character education an integral part of each school's everyday culture and curriculum.

As Miss America, doors do open. And Angela walked through her open door to meet with President Bush to discuss issues regarding education. She actively supported his amendment to H.R. 1, an education bill written by Congressmen Wamp and Etheridge, urging the President and Congress to support an increase in funding for character education initiatives from eight million dollars to fifty million dollars per year. During her tour, she was a featured speaker at the National Press Club in Washington, D.C. and at multiple high-level educational conferences. The crown had helped her gain access to the people who needed to hear her message. It had never been enough for her to identify the problem. Hundreds before her had done just that. Angela was committed to becoming an integral part of the solution.

The year went by so quickly—and then it was June 2001, time to return to Hawaii as the reigning Miss America for the Miss Hawaii competition. She had been asked to perform as a special guest for the Miss Hawaii pageant. The event was to be broadcast statewide on live television. During her travels, Angela had asked Tini to give her a tape of her hula number so she could practice on the road.

He didn't get the music to her until the night before the event and here she was, exhausted, having flown in from New Jersey. "I practiced all day to the tape I finally got," she said. Miss America was a little miffed at her boyfriend.

The evening came and she found herself on stage. She was a little further miffed when Tini failed to acknowledge her presence as she went onstage to dance. Tini was performing live and accompanying her as she danced hula to Blue Hawaii.

"I couldn't believe what happened next!" she said laughing. "Suddenly, in the middle of the song, he switched to a Stevie Wonder song with lyrics I had never heard."

Now she was really miffed! Angela stopped, trying desperately to maintain her composure; she went up to him with as much grace as she could muster, her smile frozen. Through clenched teeth she muttered, *"What-are-you-doing?"*

She explained that in the lyrics, somehow through a fog of confusion and as if in slow

265

motion, she heard the words, "that you would be my bride..." and she stood frozen in her tracks—in shock, as Tini knelt down on one knee and held out a ring. "Suddenly both of us were crying."

No one knew what was happening except for the producer and the Miss Hawaii organizers.

"The producer suddenly told his crew to put us on camera and suddenly the viewers saw the proposal live. The TV audience was surprised. The public wasn't aware we were together until then," she said.

Tini whispered, "Honey, finish the song. We're still on the air. We're going to cut to commercial."

Still crying, Angela finished the dance, then somehow regained her composure. At the end, she held up her hand to show the ring and the host came on, totally surprised. He said, "This wasn't in the script! By the way, she said Yes!"

Just a brief three months later came the end of the world as we knew it. Angela was due to return to Philadelphia to meet the new Miss America contestants. They were to drive to Atlantic City together. She had flown into Los Angeles from Hawaii, arriving with her sister Tess at midnight. They were to stay overnight at their sister's house in Irvine.

"It was weird because all year I had been traveling with my companion from the Miss America Organization and on this night, September 10, I was with family. We went to bed exhausted. Suddenly I woke up. I'd slept only four hours. Tess came running in and said, 'Angie, I think we're going to war! America's been attacked by terrorists! A plane hit the World Trade Center.'"

I couldn't believe what I was hearing. We ran downstairs to watch it on TV. We were all watching Katie Couric. We were sitting there crying when we suddenly saw the plane hit the second building, and later learned the Pentagon had been hit. We were in shock.

"A thousand things ran through my mind. I was worried about the people in New York. I was worried about my family. I had a million

Angela with President Bush.

things going on in my head at one time. I really took it personally. I think most Americans did. I felt as if I were being stabbed in the heart. I can't even describe the kind of pain I felt that day. I couldn't even fathom that dimension of evil, that depth of hatred."

Angela experienced an emotion that survivors of disasters often feel. She felt a certain element of guilt for being alive—called survivor's syndrome.

"I felt that I was a representative for every American citizen. The pageant was close at hand and I knew this time, it was bigger than just an event because it was a patriotic celebration at a time when our whole country had been threatened by terrorists."

But Angela wasn't permitted to think about herself for long. Suddenly she received a call from Bob Renneisen, at the time chief executive officer of the Miss America Organization. Completely sympathetic, he was forced to ask her the question: "Are you coming to Atlantic City? The girls need your leadership."

Angela's thoughts were muddled. "Initially, I thought it all seemed so inconsequential, the pageant—then realized we had to be very sensitive to whatever was going on with this event. This night represents an annual tribute to our country. Especially at a time like this, we had to be sensitive to all that it meant."

Angela was torn. The only thing she wanted to do was to get on a plane and go home to Hawaii, at least before turning around to go back to the pageant. She wanted to feel safe, surrounded by her loving family.

"I certainly didn't want to go to the east coast, and I had no qualms about their possibly postponing the pageant. While I knew it was natural to have those fears, I felt like a coward. On the other hand, I knew I needed to gather my courage."

Bob explained to Angela that the contestants had arrived in Atlantic City, that the decision had been left up to them and the majority had voted to go on with the pageant.

"I really had to question my motives," she

said. "I had to reach from deep within myself and examine my faith to find out where I could get the strength to do this. Terrorists were highjacking planes, crashing them into the Pentagon—I couldn't even breathe that day. I think the thing that hit me so hard is that I had toured so much of

America that year, flying twenty-thousand miles a month, and this event was to be the wrap-up for me and the promising beginning for someone else. These places were real to me—the Pentagon, the World Trade Center. And we had flown in and out of all the major airports so often."

With all airplanes grounded, Angela had enough time to get her head straight and on September 14, she finally boarded a plane to fly to Philadelphia.

"Everyone on board nearly collapsed with relief as we landed," she said. "I know I was holding my breath. It was the first time I had ever heard people applaud a landing." A traveling Miss America would have been a prime target for a terrorist, and that fact was not lost on Angela.

Again she turned inward to be steadied by her faith. "I was so afraid. I found myself remembering what Jesus said. I prayed, 'Please God, take this cup from me.' Then suddenly I became calm and my prayer changed. I recommitted myself to His will. 'God, I'll do whatever I'm supposed to do. I'm going to put my life in Your hands. I won't live in fear. I don't know why I'm here and why I'm the Miss America right now, but I know You've been preparing me for this all my life. I know I must be there to provide leadership.'"

Angela felt the weight of the world on her shoulders and yet she knew the Lord was going to get her through this task. "All my life I had tried to find ways to trust in God and simply do what I had to do to the best of my ability. This would be a true test of all I had been taught, a test of my faith in Him. I really believe that," she said.

Several months prior to the pageant, she had been told she would crown the new Miss America and that's all she would need to do. But with changing circumstances, the intended script, no longer appropriate, had been tossed out and pageant officials were scurrying to rewrite it. Angela was asked to co-host the event. Due to the tragedy, they explained, they really needed her to play a more prominent role. She was given the task of welcoming people, keeping contestants calm and allaying their fears.

"I had to be strong and courageous regardless of what I was feeling," she said. And yet another first: Angela Perez Baraquio was the first Miss America to host the pageant on the same night she relinquished her crown.

Without mishap and before a television audience of millions, Angela crowned a petite blonde Oregonian, Katie Harman, on that incredible night in Atlantic City in September 2001. Tini was in the audience to offer his support as he had been a year ago to see his special lady crowned. And afterwards, it was home to Hawaii for them both.

Angela returned to Hawaii to inaugurate her fledgling non-profit organization, the Angela Perez Baraquio Education Foundation. She visited three east coast states in order to honor appearance requests, logging eleven thousand miles in one week. The foundation promotes character education and provides grants and scholarships to teachers and students. She formed this enterprise with her husband Tini, her sister Tess and friend Billie Takaki who was Miss Hawaii 2000. Having no idea how to undertake such an ambitious venture, the foursome worked hard to make it happen. And in May 2003, they received approval from the Internal Revenue Service to become a tax-exempt charitable foundation. Six months later, they held a fundraiser and with their silent auction, made thirteen thousand dollars. "It's a start," Angela said.

The whole premise is that we need to build

character in our students so they can grow to be contributing members of our society. Sometimes we all forget to be respectful, we forget about integrity. We all need to be accountable and help each other grow."

In January, she allowed herself to slow down to plan a very special event. And in June 2002, nine months after surrendering her crown in Atlantic City, this accomplished young woman became Angela Perez Baraquio Grey.

Angela and Tini were married in Hawaii, surrounded by their families and scores of friends. The wedding party was huge, a reminder of all that is Angela.

"All six sisters were in my wedding," she said. Angela's friends, her Hawaii-based hair stylist and make-up artist both offered to do the hair and faces of the wedding party as a wedding gift and everyone was dressed alike and made up to look similar. "We've all fought for our own individuality, but on this one day, we were all unified in our appearance." Even our families couldn't tell all the girls apart."

After a brief honeymoon, Angela returned to school to complete her master's. She expects to graduate in December 2004. This full-time graduate student is a woman who was born to help change the world.

In May 2003, Angela and her husband Tini were invited to attend a State Dinner at the White House honoring Philippine President Gloria Macapagal-Arroyo and her husband Jose Miguel Arroyo.

"This is the third time I had met both Presidents and the second time I met Mrs. Bush. The First Lady asked me, 'Are you still teaching?' It was as if we were like old friends by this time," Angela joked.

"It was a very exciting time. Colin Powell attended with his lovely wife Alma. I had met them before as well. Alma had presented me with an award at the Kennedy Center during my tour and Secretary Powell had presented me with a token of appreciation when I visited the America's Promise Headquarters."

Angela was delighted to discover that she was sitting across from Tom Brokaw at the dinner. She later learned from her sister that Brokaw had reported on the event, mentioning that he was sitting across from Miss America.

"It was surreal," she said. "I even met Donald Rumsfeld and Condoleezza Rice. The newscast of Mr. Rumsfeld carrying the victim from the Pentagon after the plane exploded was still fresh in my mind. I was so honored to meet him."

Angela is extremely proud of her husband who, by her own accounts, is "incredibly handsome and totally supportive."

Angela is fond of relating this incident.

"I had just taken photographs with the presidents and their spouses. I was held back a moment as someone was speaking to me and was a little late following Tini into the State Dining Room. As I entered the room after him, I heard some ladies talking about how handsome he was," she said, pleased.

The next day, they discovered that Washington society had noticed them both, as the striking couple's names appeared in the Washington Times, the Post and later in People magazine. She laughed. "I couldn't believe it! The next morning, we picked up the Times and we were in it! It was such fun. This was probably the most magical time in my life because this time, my husband was able to share that unique experience with me."

Angela is so grounded that in listening to her, in realizing who she is inside, rather than being sidetracked by her celebrity, it becomes instantly obvious that the world will be hearing great things about her through the years. There is a spirit that comes from within this young woman, a certain grace that exudes from her, and a purpose that drives her.

For appearance requests, contact Tess Baraquio at harmonyproductions@msn.com. Angela's Websites are: www.angelaperezbaraquio.com and The Angela Perez Baraquio Education Foundation at: www.apbef.org.

Miss America 2002

Katie Harman

Student - Portland State University
State - Oregon
Age - 21   Height - 5' 3''

Talent: Katie sang the aria: *O Mio Babbino Caro* by Puccini

Photo courtesy of the Miss America Organization

"I have never felt so blessed, so humbled, to stand in the presence of those women.
I learned a life lesson not just that week, but during the year of my tour—about hope,
about grace. It reaffirmed my thoughts on quality of life."
—Katie Harman

Kate Harman

Katie Harman's story is an inspiration to all young hopefuls who are told they can never dream of becoming Miss America because they're not tall enough. And watching her perform today, no one could guess that this diminutive and accomplished Miss America had stage fright so badly as a child that she once ran off stage rather than sing.

Katie Harman holds the distinction of being the first Oregonian and first Pacific Northwest woman to wear the Miss America crown. She was born in Portland, Oregon into a warm, loving Christian family. Her baby sister Stacey came sixteen months later. Her dad, Glen, was a truck designer and her mom, Darla, a homemaker. "My parents have always been an inspiration for me."

Hearing Katie talk about growing up, one learns that love of family and faith in God can provide all the riches needed for a happy and fulfilling childhood.

"We were encouraged to dream. We were not well off by any means. We had more fun playing the drum with pots and pans than we could possibly have had with the most expensive toys. Mom taught us to be creative. Dad would find recycled computer paper that had been tossed out, and we'd cut out dolls and make different things. I remember being so fascinated with the mechanics of television, I got computer paper and tape and tried for hours and hours to build a TV out of it. It was certainly no hardship. It was fun!"

When Katie was three, her dad was transferred to Charlotte, North Carolina. Her memories of those eight years in Charlotte were very special as well.

"I recall thunderstorms in the summer evenings. There would be a warm rain. After the storms would die down, Stacey and I would get our swimming suits on and go outside and shake the limbs on the big trees and pretend we were taking a shower under the leaves. It doesn't take a lot of money to make children happy. Our parents gave us everything we could possibly need in the form of a good, solid education, encouraging us to build on our talents. They always gave us lots of love and their strong support."

Oh, What a Beautiful Baby!

270

Katie and Stacey—Easter - 1989.

Katie loved school. "I was so antsy to learn that Mom encouraged me to release my gifts and to challenge myself. Early on, my teachers could see that I needed to be challenged, and I had wonderful teachers all through school."

From participating in science fairs to dancing ballet, Katie pursued both academics and the arts with tremendous diligence.

"After her initial training at the Charlotte Ballet Academy, her parents enrolled her in the Royal Academy of Dance program in Charlotte, but in 1991, at the age of eleven, the family moved back to Oregon. Katie performed ballet through her sophomore year in high school."

The adjustment in moving back to the Pacific Northwest as a pre-teen was a difficult one for Katie. "Now, it was a different culture for us," she explained. "I returned to Oregon in the fifth grade and that year, although it was hard for me, became a turning point as well."

Inspired by her sister Stacey, who had been gifted with a beautiful voice, Katie decided to try out for a solo part in a play called, *Readin', Writin, and Rockin'* —the song was "The Forgetful Blues."

"To my amazement I got the part, and what an experience! Even with all my preparation, when dress rehearsal came, I stood in front of everyone, opened my mouth and thought—*Oh, no! I cannot do this!*—then ran off the stage. I hadn't realized how terribly shy I was."

But Gerutha Favorel, Katie's teacher, knew better. She held the petrified child firmly and said, "Katie, you will get up on that stage and you will sing and I know you will come back to me in a few years and thank me for it."

"So I returned to the stage and stood there and sang the song. I remember feeling in my childlike way, very thankful for her. It was a perfect time when a child needed to be challenged and the teacher needed to push."

As fortune would have it, a local voice instructor was sitting in the audience that night. She wasted no time in calling Katie's parents. She believed there was potential there and said she would like to teach Katie.

"Mom learned that there was, of course, a fee involved. She didn't know I needed lessons to sing. But she and Dad discussed the possibilities and once again made a sacrifice for my benefit. Somehow they pulled it all together and I was given voice lessons. I loved them even more for that."

And Katie took the next giant step toward developing self-esteem. The process became therapy for her. "Lessons were challenging, yet there was a goal involved. It was like entering a whole new world every time I entered my teacher's office. I loved it."

The pretty young girl quickly gravitated toward anything that was remotely classical or operatic. "My parents thought I was nuts when

Katie in 7th grade—beautiful in braces.

271

I'd open my mouth and out would come this operatic soprano voice—usually in a foreign language," she said, laughing. "My dad used to look at me as if I were an alien!"

"What's happening with our daughter?" they'd ask, surprised at this mature strong lyrical voice that was coming out of their child. Katie would have played the Nutcracker twenty-four hours a day during Christmas season, if they had let her. Her grandparents got into the spirit of helping her to develop her talent by fueling her interest with tapes and CDs of classical artists and composers.

Eventually it became too difficult for Katie's parents to support both dance and voice lessons. It was equally challenging for her, as well, adding academic commitments to the mix. Something had to give. Katie, in her ado-

Katie and sister Stacey as candy stripers.

lescent wisdom, was already well grounded.

"My parents certainly didn't want to stifle me from those things I loved so much, but they finally said, 'We need you to learn to focus your energy and manage your time. If you put only part of yourself into everything, you're not going to excel in anything.'

"They were right," Katie said. "Teens have so much energy and enthusiasm, and they think they can do it all. But I knew I had to make a choice—dance or voice."

Katie knew she might be limited with dance due to her petite stature. Topping the charts at a whopping five feet three inches, Katie realized she would never be able to create a ballerina-type presence on stage.

"I also wasn't seeing the kind of progress that my colleagues were, and although I loved the dance, I decided it was not going to take me into a professional future."

Katie continued with voice lessons, competitions, performing, musical theatre—anything she could find where she could sing. "Music was an outlet. It was incredibly challenging and fulfilling," she said. "I remember clearly that during so much of my youth, it brought me so much joy."

This young woman with the operatic voice was equally interested in science. "A gifted teacher realized my love for medicine early on."

This insightful teacher, Bruce Tolonen, saw great potential in Katie and introduced her to an apprenticeship program entitled *Saturday Academy.* This program offered high school students the opportunity to be mentored by professionals in their respective fields. Students went through a rigorous application and interview process in the fields of science, medicine and engineering. Katie applied with a trauma surgeon, Donald Trunkey, MD, at Oregon Health and Sciences University.

Katie's high school science project.

"This is one of the state's premier medical universities and teaching hospitals," she said. "I had gone through the applications process and found that there were 800 applicants to fill 120 positions. It was extremely competitive. Somehow, I was accepted and I was absolutely thrilled!"

She credits the visionary Dr. Trunkey for believing there needed to be more women entering the trauma field. "I worked in his General Surgery Lab during the summer following my junior year. I followed him in trauma surgery and ER and worked in the lab studying the effects of aluminum on normal cells and on cells affected by colon cancer. It was fascinating to be placed into that environment.

"They didn't care what I knew, only that I wanted to learn. I saw strength in action embodied. I saw compassion. I was so impressed with how he treated his patients. And whenever I met with other medical professionals, I was in awe of the healthcare field in general. That's where my passion of pursuing the medical field was ignited."

At the end of her internship, Katie presented her findings to the group of students who had participated in the program as well as to the teachers, mentors and parents. "It all absolutely fueled the fire to want to become a trauma surgeon—and singer," she said. "So during my senior year in high school, I began searching for colleges."

Katie found herself drawn to the University of Puget Sound in Washington because the prestigious school is known for their Biology program. The downside was that the university would cost approximately thirty thousand dollars a year and Katie knew she would have to figure out a way to pay her own tuition. She applied for more than thirty scholarships from community-based grants to national ones.

"Through God's grace, about twenty-four thousand dollars of the entire fee was paid for by scholarships of every kind," she said. It still wasn't enough. After a great deal of discussion, Katie's parents decided to take out a six thousand dollar loan to make up the difference.

Living in a dorm was a rude awakening for Katie. "I hadn't been sheltered, per se, but I had never been exposed to a lot of negative influences. Realizing that the world around me

Katie as an intern.

was bigger than what I had seen growing up was a bit overwhelming.

"My parents quickly took the cue to discuss this with me. I learned that it was going to be all about choices. They truly wanted me to understand the world I live in but to be able to see it in a positive light without compromising my own principles."

The family prayed about it and Katie realized then that healthy choices were important to continuing her spiritual growth and that sometime choices are made that can have a poor impact on your future. It was important to her to stay grounded.

"I knew I needed from the onset to learn to manage my choices and apply what I was seeing around me to my personal experiences and goals and my own philosophy of life and what I wanted for myself."

During her freshman year, Katie returned home for Christmas vacation and as the family sat around the dinner table, they discussed year number two. "I knew that most of my scholarships weren't renewable. And I couldn't keep

Katie with her family.

and I volunteer at an early age, so we became candy stripers at Portland Adventist Hospital and enjoyed that commitment for the next four years. That experience related well to the entire pageant premise."

Katie's strongest objection, however, was that she would have to appear onstage in a swimming suit. "I had always been extremely self-conscious and had never even worn a bikini," she said. "Plus," she laughed, "I was so short and every Miss America candidate I had ever seen seemed to be tall and gorgeous—nothing like me!

struggling like that. Moreover, that my parents simply couldn't continue to fund this level of tuition."

Katie's love and gratitude for her parents is enormous. "Without their love, and tremendous sense of humor—we all laughed a lot—and their continuing support, I never could have gotten through anything." Katie refers to her mom as 'the Energizer Bunny' and knew that her mom was actively thinking about how Katie could make this happen, but Katie realized she alone had to take final responsibility for her tuition.

Then up popped the Miss America scholarship program!

Luckily, Katie ran into Janet Mouser, her former high school drama program director. She had, in her youth, placed as a runner-up in the Miss Oregon competition. She suggested that the local pageant might be a means through which Katie could acquire additional scholarship funds, plus it would give her an opportunity to display her talent. And Katie learned that even at the local level, the pageant concentrates on academics and requires the young women to become involved in social services. She was prepared for that as well.

"My parents had always insisted that Stacey

"I told my mom about it, especially the scholarship part. Her eyes became big as saucers and she said she would think about it, too. But she understood my concerns about modesty."

Darla began suggesting, encouraging, continuing on and on until one day the two were in the car together and Katie said, "Mom, I don't want to hear the "*P*" word one more time."

Katie returned to school and about a month into the semester, she was sitting at the computer. Suddenly she felt the urging of the Holy Spirit instructing her to go to the Miss America Website. "I did, and Heather French's story was on the site. I read her story and read all about the extensive scholarship program. I read bios of some contestants, and learned a lot more about the organization. I was very impressed."

Then Katie was spiritually *nudged* to call her mom.

"Mom and I always talked a lot. It should have been just another normal conversation, but I called her and said, 'I think I'm supposed to call you about the "*P*" word now.'"

Strangely, Darla wasn't surprised. She told her daughter that she had asked God to *show* Katie when the time was right if she was sup-

Photo courtesy of the Miss America Organization

posed to do this. Darla said she would review the Website. Later that day, she called her daughter back.

Katie laughed. "Mom already had me on a three-way phone call with her *and* the director, Judy Hardy, of the Miss Portland Regional Scholarship Program!"

Through the course of the ensuing conversation, she heard all about the program. Her timing couldn't have been better. The woman informed her that rehearsals were scheduled for the following week in her dance studio in Portland, two and a half hours away from Katie's school in Tacoma. It was there the young women were to prepare for the local pageant, which was to take place in April.

Katie's parents picked her up at school every weekend, drove her to Portland for rehearsals, and returned her to school.

"I remember everyone laughed at me at first because due to my ballet training, I walked like a duck—in first position. I couldn't blame them. I was laughing at myself. I was also completely ignorant of the traditional elements relating to beauty: hair, waxing, makeup. But surprisingly, I won Miss Multnomah County. I truly was stunned. For the talent portion, Katie sang *Ah! Je Veux Vivre*, Gounod's operatic aria of Juliet's waltz from *Romeo and Juliet*. "Best of all, I won a five hundred dollar scholarship, enough to pay for books!"

She was in training all summer for the Miss Oregon pageant and when she walked away as first runner-up, she also walked away with three thousand dollars,

Photo courtesy of the Miss America Organization

enough to pay for her tuition as she transferred to the less expensive Portland State University.

Realizing the importance and the impact on her life of the pageant system as it related to scholarships, Katie, now a sophomore, decided to participate for one more year. "Ultimately, the most important thing to me at that age was just trying to find out who I was. The first year, as I competed, I had really challenged my self-image. Now I began to think there was more of a purpose here and I needed to challenge my reason for doing this, a reason even aside from scholarships."

Katie wanted to use the required platform to grow, to bring something valuable to those who needed it. "I wanted to be a conduit for a certain issue; and the message that had become important to me was the issue of people who are struggling with metastatic breast cancer."

Earlier, Katie had been involved as a model for a program entitled: Making Memories Breast Cancer Foundation. Their fund-raising effort was highly creative. "They received donated wedding gowns from all over the world and resold them. The proceeds were used to help make wishes of patients with metastatic breast cancer come true," Katie explained.

She came to love the people and the purpose of the organization and asked if she could do more. Katie was sent into the homes of wish recipients and began to ask them how others could meet their needs.

ieharman.com

KATIE HARMAN
Miss America 2002

A year after her reign on the speaking circuit.

"It helped me define quality of life. Kristy was one very special woman with breast cancer. She really had a huge impact on me. She helped me value each and every day. This woman changed the way I looked at the disease and at life in general. And I wanted to take her message to the world."

So for her next pageant competition, and as a result of working with Making Memories, Katie decided she would be a conduit for women with breast cancer. I wanted to offer a message of hope, of quality of life, of support," she said.

During the year as she became more involved in community service, she continued to hone other skills: talent, public speaking and interview abilities. "I wanted to present myself in a way that would show respect for the Miss America Organization as well as the platform I'd chosen," she said.

In the spring of 2001, Katie became Miss Portland and in July walked the state runway as Miss Oregon. She now had less than two months to prepare for the Miss America competition in Atlantic City. And at the core of all this activity was school. Katie continued to make the Dean's List.

How could she have known in July 2001 that all her preparations in learning how to "bring a vital message to the people" would translate into her being the spokesperson for the Miss America Pageant at a time when a nation was grieving and needed her unwavering strength of courage and indomitable spirit?

The Miss America contestants began their sojourn to the Atlantic City runway in Philadelphia, the City of Brotherly Love, two weeks prior to the pageant.

The group arrived in Atlantic City on the morning of September 10. The first day, they were busy getting oriented, posing for photographs, introducing themselves to the Miss America staff and each other. The next day they would begin rehearsals early in the morning. Split into groups, some Miss America hopefuls were still in their rooms and others were at their dressing room tables, waiting for the ABC staff to orient them to staging, lighting, pageant logistics.

"I was sitting at my little table journaling about the previous day when a female security guard came into the dressing room to tell us that a plane had just hit the World Trade Center. We thought a plane had hit the Tower by accident."

Personal radios and TVs had been banned from the dressing room, but one of the contestants had brought in a boom box so she could rehearse to a CD. The boom box was equipped with a radio. Now able to hear the news, the girls sat stunned while they listened to Peter Jennings offering a subdued commentary on the incident. Suddenly, they heard—live—the second Tower being hit and for a few moments confusion reigned. The pageant officials allowed the girls to call home and when Katie called her parents, they explained everything. They had seen it all unfold on television from three thousand miles away while their daughter was just within a few air miles of the disaster.

The girls quickly resumed their group and the terror magnified as the Pentagon was hit. Suddenly isolated from family and friends, they became as of one mind and spirit. Someone suggested that they pray and together they did.

Suddenly they realized that here they were, close to the disaster, a representation of a traditional American icon and a potential target, each of them—as well as the entire group as a whole.

The staff promptly gathered all the contestants together and ushered them into a secure location inside Convention Hall. Chief Executive Officer Bob Renneissen entered the room, told them exactly what he knew, and advised them that the fate of the pageant was undecided. ABC was involved as well, and decisions had to be made by so many about so many things. Airports were shutting down. If the girls were released, how would they get home? Parents were traveling to the pageant— how could they be stopped, or should they be stopped? Was this the end of the tragedy or would strikes continue? Would the girls be safer here for the moment? Should the pageant go on? What did the nation need at this defining moment?

All the girls were trying to talk it out, to figure out how they could help individually or as a group. One of the contestants was already in the Air Force studying dentistry. Not one girl was talking about the crown.

Suddenly, through a small hallway next to the room where they were cloistered, the girls heard a plaintive wail rise up from a staff member. "Oh, God—no!" The woman had just learned that her cousin was the pilot of the airplane that was flown into the second tower. He was Victor Saracini, Captain of United Air Lines Flight 175.

Now there was panic. The only way to wrap their minds around this disaster was to face it head on, and the staff took the girls into the ballroom area where they had set up two television sets so everyone could sit and watch what was being reported. No one was allowed to leave; they were kept secure, together, until four that afternoon when they were escorted back to their rooms.

After watching several hours of news reporting, Katie was finally beginning to get a handle on the enormity of the crisis. She called her state executive directors, Steve and Dana Phillips, and her parents and talked everything through. It was good for her to connect with people who loved her. Both conversations centered around purpose.

The moment she hung up, she began asking, "Lord, use me. What is it that you want me to do? This is completely out of all our hands." In an instant, she felt as if God were giving her a message. She needed desperately to write. She grabbed a pad of paper from her bedside stand and began to write. These are the words given to her:

"Miss America will be a comfort to a hurting nation, a healing presence in the sense that she represents all the values that sets America apart and all the liberties that we hold dear. She will be a conduit through which encouragement and strength will flow. She will reach out to every person as an ambassador. She will be a symbol of triumph over destruction and terrorism, a symbol of God's gift of life to all of us. She will demonstrate mercy in the acceptance of all nationalities.

She will be a light, the crown's reflection, a symbol of the extent of her influence and the power of its illumination. She will not be afraid and she will step forth as a leader of the people."

Katie wrote these words in support of the young woman who would wear the crown. "I didn't write them for myself. I knew whoever would be crowned would need these words," she said. "And I intended to offer her my full support."

And then Katie's thoughts turned back to herself. "I needed to know what God wanted from me this week, and I turned to the Word and looked for strength from Jesus and His ministry, and then thought of Mother Theresa who influenced my previous work with breast cancer survivors. She was so humble and so blind to color, to poverty, to disease. She was never in judgment and she found her purpose. I needed desperately to find, now, God's purpose for me in the week and the months to come."

After kneeling at the foot of her bed and asking the Lord to use her however He needed, she asked Him to be her source of strength and power. And Katie Harman went to bed on the night of September 11, 2001, feeling quieted, safe and sound, protected by the grace of God.

The next morning, the girls were gathered together once again in the ballroom at Convention Hall. The ABC national staff was present as well. Bob Renneissen once again discussed with them the fate of the pageant.

"We as staff and ABC as a network cannot make this decision," he said. "It's not ours to make. Emmys and other national shows have already been cancelled. But among you is the one who will be traveling the country all year as Miss America. You need to be thinking about what this is going to represent to the nation."

Renneissen left them to talk it through for an hour and a half. "There's something about going through a tragedy together that shows people's true colors," Katie said. "There were no pageant personas there, no divas. Everyone wanted to help. These were amazing women and I was inspired."

The women decided that they would take a vote and at the core would be the interests of the nation. How could they represent America best in whatever they chose to do? They decided that whatever the majority vote, whether to continue with the pageant or return home, they would keep their votes to themselves and all side together with the majority in a show of unity.

And the vote was tallied in favor of continuing the pageant. "We all knew that we wanted this week to show strength, comfort and young leadership. And this was how we could all best serve our nation," Katie said.

Katie's interview was held on Monday morning. "I felt so deeply that Miss America needed to be a comforter and encourager, to be able to grieve with the nation, but lead them in finding hope, restoration and to provide a symbol of peace. I knew that any of those young women I stood beside was capable of being that woman. And that's what I shared with the judges during the interview portion of the competition," she said.

Later, she performed and won her preliminary talent competition. The rest of the week was a whirlwind of activity and emotion. Suddenly it was Saturday night, and Katie found herself in the top ten.

"I had decided I would focus and do my very best so I would be able to walk away—regardless of whatever happened, with no regrets. I was having the time of my life! I had such peace."

And Katie Harman was named Miss America.

"I have never felt so blessed, so humbled, to stand in the presence of those women. I learned a life lesson not just that week, but during the year of my tour—about hope, about grace. It reaffirmed my thoughts on quality of life."

Katie was taken to Ground Zero at the World Trade Center two days after being crowned and just a mere two weeks after September 11. Later she was taken to the Pentagon. She met First Lady Laura Bush on that day.

And still, Katie's greatest highlights of that entire year were the moments she spent with cancer patients, rescue workers and military personnel. It was during those moments that she was indeed a conduit for hope and grace and quality of life.

In June, toward the end of her year, Katie was helping with the Miss Wyoming pageant. Gathered together with three other women who had vied for the Miss America crown in that fateful September they all shared stories of the tragedy and its aftermath.

"After the last young woman spoke, Kara Svennungsen, Miss Montana said, 'We should put this all in a book.'"

And that insightful comment sparked a commitment from Katie to organize the book entitled: *Under the Crown: 51 Stories of Courage, Determination and the American Spirit.* It is a compilation of thoughts and essays from all fifty-one competitors. And within three months, the book was published, in time for the next pageant.

On July 4, Katie was thrilled to perform with the Boston Pops.

She might have been a touch sidetracked, however—just a touch. For in May, she was introduced to a certain pilot and something was already definitely in the works. A seemingly inconsequential meeting would later turn into marriage and Lt. Tim Ebner would become her husband.

"During the course of the year, I made several appearances on bases on behalf of the military, and in May I was asked to appear at my hometown base in Portland.

"Tim was my host. He was an F-15 pilot with the Oregon Air National Guard. The guys had chosen him to accompany me on the base because he was single and because he's just about the most relaxed person you'd ever want to meet. They thought they'd be able to razz him later," she laughed. "His call sign was COMA because he was so laid back." Katie literally glows when she talks about this country boy from Klamath Falls. "He knew little about pageants—he's solid as a rock and wonderfully nice," she said.

Katie got to go inside the F-15. She and Tim spoke casually and she never gave it a thought that he would be a potential *anything* to her. "I wasn't interested in dating. I was so busy with my job," she said.

But Katie's, traveling companion, Joann Silver, saw a greater potential there and began to take every opportunity she could to get these two together. In June, Katie returned to deliver her university's commencement address.

Through several well-meaning event coordinators and friends, who thought the two would be perfect for each other, Tim discovered Katie was available that night after her appearance. Tim was given Katie's number and he called to invite her to dinner. "I could hardly remember who he was. But how could I say no?" As she got ready for her date, she complained the entire time.

"Why do I have do go out with this guy? I'll waste my evening. I don't even know him." And on and on.

Bonnie Sirgany, her current traveling companion just smiled and let her blow off steam. Then Katie suddenly realized that none of them remembered his first name.

So Bonnie went down to the lobby. Lt. Ebner stood there with flowers in his hand as she approached him. "Are you here for Katie?" she asked.

When he said he was, she said innocently, "And you are...?"

She ran back upstairs to tell Katie his name was Tim.

And then it happened. "As I rounded the bank of elevators into the lobby, I saw him. There was something so different about his

Katie and Tim in their first dance as husband and wife.

countenance, something I'd never seen in a man—he was so peaceful, so comfortable in his own skin. He was smiling from ear to ear."

Katie recalls the evening as so very special. "He was just so polite and genuine, so easy to talk to, I couldn't help but enjoy myself the rest of the evening. He made me feel so incredible."

The couple spent their precious evening at the waterfront in Portland. The setting was beautiful and the two didn't lack for conversation. "Although he was brought up in the country and I in the city, our values and morals and standards were all similar and I was so comfortable. At the outset, he was interested in getting to know me—Katie—and not just Miss America. It was refreshing."

The two began to bond as he shared with his new friend the experience of losing his mother to cancer. With Katie's work with cancer patients, she could understand his grief. And he had worked as a medic before becoming a pilot, so he was no stranger to the world of medicine and its challenges. "He was simply amazing, an admirable man," she said proudly.

As they walked on the waterfront, he shared with her his love for fishing. "I told him I'd gone fishing once in my whole life," she laughed. "And then later when he escorted me back to the hotel to drop me off, I said the dumbest thing." As she was disappearing through the bank of elevators, he asked if he could call her again and she said, "I'd love it, but remember—I don't gut fish!"

And that was his last impression of the evening of Katie Harman, Miss America and hometown girl. She was mortified.

For the next several months, as he continued his work and Katie continued her tour, they became fast friends over the telephone. They talked for hours at a time whenever they could. And he made a couple of special trips to see her when she was close by.

Eventually, they talked about their future and decided that they both wanted to be together. "There was a special moment where we sat on a little rock wall after walking on the beach. I felt impressed to tell him that I wanted him to be in my future. I looked at him and there were tears in his eyes. I knew this was very big. And from that moment, it was easier for us. Together we had a goal and there was no indecision."

Katie returned to the pageant to fulfill her Miss America duties, and two months after her official year of service concluded, the young pilot asked her to marry him. Katie and Captain Tim Ebner were married seven months later on June 14, 2003. "And I fall more and more in love with him every day," she whispered.

Katie has never stopped the whirlwind although one part of her life is settling down. She will graduate in June 2005 with a bachelor's degree in Communications and a minor in Vocal Performance.

"I recently made my professional operatic aria debut in Ft. Lauderdale in November of 2003. She sang with the Gold Coast Opera as Kathie in the Student Prince. In addition, she continues to speak throughout the country on breast cancer.

And the guy in the sky? "He's great with my traveling, with my schoolwork, with my singing—with being a husband; he's just great with everything," she said.

Katie with Susan Powell(lt) and Kylene Barker at the pageant in 2003.

And now? "From the moment I crowned Erikka Harold, I've been drawing on my Miss America experience to see what I can now do as Katie Harman, professionally and Katie Ebner, from a personal perspective. All of us know that it's not our primary identity, being Miss America. We're all complex, made up of various talents and purposes; but it is something that helps us understand our purpose even more.

Through that experience, God showed me so much about life. It was truly life education. It made me more cognizant of those things in my life that I need to value. I'm grateful for the fact that the Miss America experience continues to help me to define myself."

She was quiet for a moment, this beautiful, diminutive young woman who carried our nation through the yearlong grief period after 9/11. Then she spoke softly: "There is so much more to each of the young women who wear the crown. I want to be worthy to have worn it."

For more information on Katie Harman, her appearances, CDs, books, etc., see www.katieharman.com.

Miss America 2004
Ericka Dunlap
Student - University of Central Florida
State - Florida
Age - 21   Height - 5' 7''
Talent: Ericka sang - *If I Could*

Photos courtesy of the Miss America Organization

Quote: "When you find peace within yourself, you become the kind
of person who can live at peace with others."

—— Ericka Dunlap

281

Ericka Dunlap

As this book was being prepared for publication, Ericka Dunlap was the reigning Miss America. She was interviewed during her twenty thousand miles a month travels from her hotel in Wisconsin, then her hotel in Florida and she somehow, along with the tremendous, unfailing cooperation of the staff of the Miss America Organization, generously found the time to cap off this inaugural edition of "The Strength of Grace." How befitting the title!

Born in 1981, just a few days after Christmas, Ericka Dunlap made her debut as the baby of the family. Her four siblings, Mickel, Terri-Ann, Debbie and Cathy ranged from fourteen to twenty years older than their newborn sister. Perhaps that's why this Miss America grew up so quickly with such focus and determination. Five years later, she would inform her kindergarten teacher that she intended someday to become a "Christian lawyer." At the age of twenty-one, and now holding the title of the current Miss America, Ericka Dunlap still has her eyes on that goal.

Mrs. Richardson, an astute, progressive and creative teacher had an enormous impact on Ericka. And what a promising student! Ericka remembers the moment she defined her life in this manner and with this unique career choice.

"At kindergarten graduation, we were asked to do a paper drawing of ourselves. We each lay on the floor on a large sheet of paper and classmates outlined each of us in crayon. Then we colored in our future occupations. When I told the teacher I wanted to be a Christian lawyer, she showed me what the scales of justice looked like," Ericka laughed. "I drew a *baaaad* interpretation of the scales!"

Asked what possessed her to decide on that particular career, she explained. "Our family is Christian before anything else, so from that frame of reference came the adjective. And I loved watching The Cosby Show. Phylicia Rashad's character is a lawyer. I used to ask mom and dad and my teachers what a lawyer does and they'd tell me that lawyers help people solve their problems. I was so directed, even at a young age, that I decided that's exactly what I wanted to do."

Ericka has never thought seriously of being anything else. "I'm a firm believer in a backup plan. Brains beyond talent will help you to go so much further in life," she said wisely. Ericka had a wonderfully busy childhood, accomplishing a great deal, even as a youth. She came from hard-working parents—her dad is a roofing contractor and her mother a registered nurse. "When I was growing up, my brother and sisters had already left the house, because they were so much older," she said. "And I was always active. I did ballet, tap, jazz, clogging—being basically the only child left in the home, my mom kept me very busy."

Although Ericka soon learned to become quite independent, she enjoyed the emotional stability her siblings always offered. "They became very protective of me, very nurturing. They always wanted to be sure I had answers to all my questions—even those Mom and Dad might be a little hesitant to answer."

Ericka attended a private Christian school and the family, a non-denominational Christian church. Their spiritual foundation was strong and that background helped Ericka develop her strength of character.

Pageant life began for Ericka at the age of six. "Mom introduced me to my first pageant when she showed me a flyer for the American Co-Ed Princess Pageant in Tampa, Florida. I entered the competition, and although I was a little disappointed that I didn't win, it actually encouraged me to do more! I sang a song that was pretty bad," she laughed, "but it was my first solo." Ericka still remembers it: *Shower Me with Your Love.* "I don't know *why* in the world I sang that song, but I practiced singing it in the kitchen every single day."

Ericka decided she was better at dancing and that talent might be put to better use. She began performing in recitals and various competitions. "Pageants were great and I liked them, but sometimes they interfered with my first love, which at the time was dancing. Clogging was actually my favorite and I kept up with that more than the rest. I didn't stop clogging until I was fifteen and by then, tap, jazz and ballet had fallen by the wayside."

Always a great student, Ericka carried straight As through to high school when her volunteer work and extracurricular activities interfered a bit with academics. Still, with all that activity, she continued to be primarily an A student. The Drama Program definitely caught her attention in high school. She did a lot of auditioning as a youth for community theatre,

for Nickelodeon and Disney, who produced commercials in the area.

In 2000, she entered college. As a student at the University of Central Florida in Orlando, she was tenacious about pursuing her goals, academic and otherwise. And Ericka was soon recognized for her efforts. She was chosen for the prestigious President's Leadership Council.

She was finishing her freshman year when pageant preliminaries drew her attention and she entered the Miss Orlando competition. She sang *Golden Rainbow* and her performance took her to the top. For the Miss Florida pageant, she sang *Some of These Days.* Although she didn't win, she placed in the top ten and earned enough scholarship money to help her with her sophomore year.

The next spring, she became Miss Heart of Florida, and upon competing in Miss Florida for the second time around, she placed in the top ten again. "This time, I was very disappointed. I believed that I was ready for the top five, so this disappointment made me re-evaluate things. I thought about how much effort I had put into the competition and asked myself what did I *need* to do to make it to the top?"

Ericka studied the problem as thoroughly as if she were an entrepreneur developing a business plan. And she came up with a solution. "I decided I needed to come up with a new program and attitude about how I was going to achieve this goal. In the state of Florida, there had never been a black winner. I believed strongly that there had certainly been other black women, before my time, who had deserved to win."

At first, Ericka found herself thinking it would never happen. She asked, "Why should I keep fooling myself?" Then she redirected her thought process and created a turning point. "I had been seriously considering transferring to a state school outside of Florida. And then I told myself: *Don't run away! There are little girls who need to see you persevere!*"

As Mistress of Ceremonies at the 2004
Coca-Cola Scholarships Banquet.
Photo courtesy of the Miss America Organization

So Ericka gathered up her mom and her courage and off they went to Atlantic City to watch the Miss America pageant first-hand. "We went to as many events as we could. We simply got prepared for everything we needed to know." Treating this as perhaps one of the most important homework assignments she had ever undertaken, Ericka was inspired. "I took notes about everything."

She returned to school to finish the semester. "In December, I really got to it. During the first preliminary competition in January, I focused on changing my motivation. I was determined to make it all the way."

Ericka had already earned almost fifteen thousand dollars in scholarships. "That had really helped my parents," she said. "They had already put all four of my siblings through school. Each of my siblings had a Florida pre-paid tuition plan, but I did not. So I decided to apply for all kinds of college scholarships. This fifteen thousand, acquired solely from the Miss America program, (not including other numerous scholarships awarded in the areas of academic achievement and community service), I knew, would help me continue my education and get into law school."

Ericka maintained her focus on the national pageant, but still kept up her grades. "I wanted every single area of the competition to be different from what everyone in Florida had seen before. I knew I had to let go of a lot of things, including some personal issues that I had allowed to become part of who I was."

Ericka, admittedly a people person, often finds herself caring for others more than herself, and therein lay the problem. "I decided that in order to reach this goal, I really needed to pay attention to myself, my own needs. I had gotten to a point where I didn't even know what I liked to do anymore—I didn't know my own hobbies. I needed to take some time to get to know myself and prepare my mind for this opportunity. One must definitely be in touch with oneself, especially when you're away from family for such a long period. I realized that to be Miss America would be a prestigious job, but also a challenging one."

And yet even a further goal was still on the horizon: the scholarship on the national level would allow Ericka to obtain a law degree and specialize in entertainment and sports law. This statuesque beauty had a long way to go.

The first pageant she entered on this road to Atlantic City was Miss City Beautiful, which is Orlando's city motto. She won. The Miss Florida competition loomed before her. That one seemingly insurmountable challenge stood before her like a brick wall: Out of sixty-eight years of holding that competition, no black woman had ever won.

She knew that preparation and determination were the keys to the title. Ericka had made it a point to do things she had never done before. "I *really* went to the gym; I was *always* there. And it actually became a love of mine! I would feel guilty if I missed a day of working out, because my body just didn't feel complete without walking through the fitness center doors."

Along with her new fitness focus, Ericka began to consume the daily paper to keep up on current events and to formulate her opinions. And she found that she soon was reading for enjoyment. "I had stopped reading newspapers and news magazines because I was so active. I had only been reading my schoolbooks, but suddenly I was becoming enlightened. I stopped watching entertainment shows and started focusing on headline news and news shows. In the mornings, I'd listen to talk radio instead of music. I was learning about different world issues and finding that I wanted to figure out what I really thought about things so I could express my own opinion in an articulate and knowledgeable manner. I wrote in journals. I took notes on questions I had.

Singing to the troops in Kuwait.

*Photo courtesy of the
Miss America Organization*

And I had tons of mock interviews in preparation for the Miss Florida competition, thanks to my amazing Miss City Beautiful Board of Directors. Not only were we a team of friends, but they all showed me the utmost respect and support in helping me to achieve this goal. I had never before been enveloped by a group of people outside of my family, who cared so much about my goals."

Ericka quickly learned to delegate, a skill that was fairly foreign to her. She put together a team of people who could be of creative assistance with her wardrobe. "It was a great collaborative effort. I was always looking for new ideas. I surrounded myself with people who I knew were willing to stand by me and be my support team to help me through this process—where before, I had always been the one going out of my way to help others."

Her intense preparation solidly behind her, Ericka stepped onto the stage that night and it became hers. Ericka Dunlap became the first black woman to be awarded the title of Miss Florida.

She had to have won: by the end of the competition, Ericka had won talent, evening gown and interview. "This was the first year I had ever won any preliminary award," she said.

Ericka didn't sit on her laurels for a second. The national title now closer than ever, she continued all her preparations and maintained her focus. And on a Saturday night in September 2003, on the stage in Atlantic City before a convention full of pageant aficionados, Ericka sang her heart out. The song *If I Could* became her mantra and Ericka walked the runway fifty-five thousand dollars richer in scholarship money. Her law school aspirations were becoming closer than ever before.

"I was not prepared for the immediate aftermath. I was so in awe that I actually was Miss America." But in half-a heartbeat, in typical goal-oriented fashion, she found herself thinking, "All right—so what's next?"

Ericka's entire family was in the audience—all except for one sister. "Poor thing, she had to stay home to baby sit all the kids," Ericka laughed. "She couldn't come."

This Miss America's platform had been

Signing the flag—Thanksgiving in Kuwait.

Photo courtesy of the Miss America Organization

solidified in 2001, several years prior to her becoming Miss America. It is: "United We Stand, Divided We Fall Behind: Celebrating Diversity and Inclusion." Through her platform, she is determined to help develop and implement a Cultural Education Program into our nation's schools. She insists that she did not choose her platform—rather, it chose her. "I became sensitive to cultural confusion at a very early age. I was the only African-American girl in my classes for many years.

One such example is that Ericka absolutely loves country music. She was given a great opportunity to sing at the Grand Ole Opry's Opryland. People couldn't understand a black girl wanting to pursue that. "I was out of sync with their vision of what it means to be black in America. But my great inspiration is Charlie Pride, and I wouldn't be stopped."

For three summers, Ericka and her mom packed up and moved to Nashville where Ericka performed at the Opryland Themepark. "In Nashville, we tried to find venues where I would be seen by music executives, but no one took us seriously," she said. "Eventually, I was given an initial offer by a record label, but my mom and I decided I needed to at least complete my high school education."

Ericka has a vision of recording a country music album. Knowing her, it will happen.

Ericka's devotion to the topic of diversity is not just related to ethnic origin, although she has spent her young lifetime trying to correct people's stereotypical assumptions in this regard. Through her platform, Ericka talks about all facets of diversity, whether it stems from socio-economical conditions, ethnicity, gender, religion—even weight issues and sexual orientation. This broad topic covers issues ranging from the workplace to our children's classrooms.

"Our world is a culmination of various life experiences and viewpoints," she said. And it's already a better place today for having this Miss America who is determined to concentrate on breaking down barriers that create obstacles for productive communication and cooperation.

"The matter of choosing a platform, for me, needed to be something that reflected and affected who I was. I needed something I could talk about from the heart. I didn't want an

Ericka as a keynote speaker.
Photo courtesy of the Miss America Organization

issue where I would be spitting off memorized statistics. I really needed the platform to relate to who I was intrinsically. I have always believed that we are all different for a specific reason. In fact, our nation's first inhabitants were individuals fleeing religious and personal persecution. Therefore, it is only right to honor ourselves and our foundation by working together to alleviate our current state of social intolerance and oppression. There are those who need someone to tell their stories and share their voice with others. It's my privilege to be able to do that."

At this writing, Ericka is only halfway through her tour. Is she exhausted? "No, actually, it seems as if it's getting better all the time," she smiled.

One particularly incredible highlight for Ericka was her trip to Kuwait. "It was truly an inspirational time," she said. "A reservist and volunteer who works with Miss Philadelphia thought it would be great to have Miss America visit the troops. The Miss America Organization made it happen. I was in Kuwait for five days, during Thanksgiving 2003. It was so wonderful. It was extremely motivational for me. There were so many young women over there who had given up so much of their lives to serve their country. And to see them serve in that capacity was really inspiring to me."

One thing that Ericka hadn't thought to prepare for was obtaining a passport. "It was on express track," she laughed. "We had to get it *really fast*! In fact, it only took forty-five minutes! That was pretty impressive!"

Another important appearance was her guest shot on the Oprah Show. And she was also Grand Marshall for the NASCAR race in Alabama and featured performer for the Grandaddy of them all! "I got to perform during the pre-race at Daytona 500, which was really special. My brother lives there and I knew a lot of other people who were NASCAR fans, so I felt right at home."

The schedule of a reigning Miss America is grueling. "Even though the title is prestigious and certainly has its perks, it can be quite wearing. It's difficult if you're a people person, like myself, because even attending so many public events, you miss the closeness that comes with being around true friends. It can be lonely. Thankfully I'm protected, but also a bit isolated. As Miss America, you can no longer do normal things that you used to take for granted." Ericka keeps her cell phone handy so she can talk to her family even briefly, often in the car en route to appearances.

But the scholarship money and the doors this title will open for Ericka for the rest of her life are not lost on her. When she relinquishes the crown in September 2004, she will return to her university as a senior.

In the meantime, Ericka's faith continues to keep her strong and focused. "I've been very blessed, very fortunate in my life," she said. "Often, when I'm speaking to young people, I say—there is always someone who has had harder times than you. And things that happened in your past that you've triumphed over, you need to let go. What does it matter? And I truly believe that. People often times put themselves at the feet of personal imbalance when they hold on to past negative experiences. Everything happens for a reason. My advice is to learn the purpose of that occurrence and move on. Your success is waiting for *you* to claim it!"

For speaking engagements, please see www.erickadunlap.net.

287

How this book came to be

The Strength of Grace, a Tribute to Those Who Wear the Miss America Crown, was released in Atlantic City during pageant week in the fall of 2004. Initially inspired by the story of Jacquelyn Mayer, Miss America 1963, *The Strength of Grace* honors thirty-eight Miss Americas, beginning with the late Marilyn Meseke, Miss America 1938, who interviewed shortly before her death and includes Ericka Dunlap, Miss America 2004. It was written by Kate Kitchen, free-lance writer and inspirational speaker.

Author crashes a Miss America Photo-op at the pageant in Sept. 2003. Left to right: Maria Beale Fletcher, Traveling Companion Peggy O'Neill Lloyd, BeBe Shopp, Lee Meriwether, Jackie Mayer and Kate Kitchen.

"Jackie and I met in March 1990. I was director of public relations at a six-hospital system in the Denver area and Jackie was slated to speak to the neuroscientists. I was trying to figure out, while looking over my assignment sheet, what a Miss America could possibly have to say that would be of interest to neurosurgeons. Then I read in her bio that Jackie had suffered a near-fatal stroke at the age of twenty-eight. Wife and mother of two little ones, she had to learn to walk and talk all over again. I was stunned."

A fellow Ohioan, Kitchen remembered clearly Jackie's crowning and after suddenly realizing Miss Americas obviously didn't all live a fairy tale, happily-ever-after life, she wrote Jackie's inspirational story for the hospital newsletter. A tribute to her new friend, as yet sight unseen, Kitchen ended the article: "Jackie, you're my John Wayne." Jackie was given the story and when the two met in the lobby of Swedish Medical Center, they wept as they hugged, and a lifelong friendship was born.

As Kitchen accompanied Jackie during her hospital visits with stroke patients, she realized that this woman who has devoted her life to helping other stroke survivors and has won multiple awards for her work, had a very special gift. Because of Jackie's life-threatening experience and how she has since used her gifts to help others, Kitchen became enlightened about the depth of these women who wear the crown. And as Jackie introduced her to other Miss Americas during pageant week 1998, it became clear that these wonderful ladies deserved to have their stories told. The project was a seven-year collaboration.

Kitchen said, "Each of these women has a strength of character that not only helped them win the crown but helped direct their paths ever since. I have to praise their generosity of spirit and humility in letting me tell their stories. They share their blemishes and bruises, hopes and dreams along the way. The stories are real-life stories of tragedy and triumph. I was especially inspired by the fact that they seem to share a strong foundation of faith. Their stories are truly inspirational. And they're such *ladies*! I'm such an in-your-face person and I've always admired a gentle spirit. It was the Lord who gave me the title, *The Strength of Grace*! Maybe it'll rub off!" she laughed.

The Strength of Grace is available at *www.thestrengthofgrace.com.*

288